Working Effectively with Legacy Code

Robert C. Martin Series

The mission of this series is to improve the state of the art of software craftsmanship. The books in this series are technical, pragmatic, and substantial. The authors are highly experienced craftsmen and professionals dedicated to writing about what actually works in practice, as opposed to what might work in theory. You will read about what the author has done, not what he thinks you should do. If the book is about programming, there will be lots of code. If the book is about managing, there will be lots of case studies from real projects.

These are the books that all serious practitioners will have on their bookshelves. These are the books that will be remembered for making a difference and for guiding professionals to become true craftsman.

Managing Agile Projects
Sanjiv Augustine

Agile Estimating and Planning
Mike Cohn

Working Effectively with Legacy Code
Michael C. Feathers

Agile Java™: Crafting Code with Test-Driven Development
Jeff Langr

Agile Principles, Patterns, and Practices in C#
Robert C. Martin and Micah Martin

Agile Software Development: Principles, Patterns, and Practices
Robert C. Martin

UML For Java™ Programmers
Robert C. Martin

Fit for Developing Software: Framework for Integrated Tests
Rick Mugridge and Ward Cunningham

Agile Software Development with SCRUM
Ken Schwaber and Mike Beedle

Extreme Software Engineering: A Hands on Approach
Daniel H. Steinberg and Daniel W. Palmer

For more information, visit http://www.prenhallpofessional.com/martinseries

Working Effectively with Legacy Code

Michael C. Feathers

Addison-Wesley

Boston • Columbus • New York • San Francisco • Amsterdam • Cape Town
Dubai • London • Madrid • Milan • Munich • Paris • Montreal • Toronto • Delhi
Mexico City • São Paulo • Sydney • Hong Kong • Seoul • Singapore • Taipei • Tokyo

The authors and publisher have taken care in the preparation of this book, but make no expressed or implied warranty of any kind and assume no responsibility for errors or omissions. No liability is assumed for incidental or consequential damages in connection with or arising out of the use of the information or programs contained herein.

Publisher: John Wait
Editor in Chief: Don O'Hagan
Acquisitions Editor: Paul Petralia
Editorial Assistant: Michelle Vincenti
Marketing Manager: Chris Guzikowski
Publicist: Kerry Guiliano
Cover Designer: Sandra Schroeder
Managing Editor: Gina Kanouse
Senior Project Editor: Lori Lyons
Copy Editor: Krista Hansing
Indexer: Lisa Stumpf
Compositor: Karen Kennedy
Proofreader: Debbie Williams
Manufacturing Buyer: Dan Uhrig

For information about buying this title in bulk quantities, or for special sales opportunities (which may include electronic versions; custom cover designs; and content particular to your business, training goals, marketing focus, or branding interests), please contact our corporate sales department at corpsales@pearsoned.com or (800) 382-3419.

For government sales inquiries, please contact governmentsales@pearsoned.com.

For questions about sales outside the United States, please contact intlcs@pearson.com.

Visit us on the web: www.informit.com

Library of Congress Cataloging-in-Publication Data: 2004108115

ISBN 0-13-117705-2

283 2023

For Ann, Deborah, and Ryan,
the bright centers of my life.

— Michael

Contents

Foreword

"...then it began..."

In his introduction to this book, Michael Feathers uses that phrase to describe the start of his passion for software.

"...then it began..."

Do you know that feeling? Can you point to a single moment in your life and say: "...then it began..."? Was there a single event that changed the course of your life and eventually led you to pick up this book and start reading this foreword?

I was in sixth grade when it happened to me. I was interested in science and space and all things technical. My mother found a plastic computer in a catalog and ordered it for me. It was called *Digi-Comp I*. Forty years later that little plastic computer holds a place of honor on my bookshelf. It was the catalyst that sparked my enduring passion for software. It gave me my first inkling of how joyful it is to write programs that solve problems for people. It was just three plastic S-R flip-flops and six plastic and-gates, but it was enough—it served. Then... for me... it began...

But the joy I felt soon became tempered by the realization that software systems almost always degrade into a mess. What starts as a clean crystalline design in the minds of the programmers rots, over time, like a piece of bad meat. The nice little system we built last year turns into a horrible morass of tangled functions and variables next year.

Why does this happen? Why do systems rot? Why can't they stay clean?

Sometimes we blame our customers. Sometimes we accuse them of changing the requirements. We comfort ourselves with the belief that if the customers had just been happy with what they said they needed, the design would have been fine. It's the customer's fault for changing the requirements on us.

Well, here's a news flash: *Requirements change.* Designs that cannot tolerate changing requirements are poor designs to begin with. It is the goal of every competent software developer to create designs that tolerate change.

This seems to be an intractably hard problem to solve. So hard, in fact, that nearly every system ever produced suffers from slow, debilitating rot. The rot is so pervasive that we've come up with a special name for rotten programs. We call them: **Legacy Code.**

Legacy code. The phrase strikes disgust in the hearts of programmers. It conjures images of slogging through a murky swamp of tangled undergrowth with leeches beneath and stinging flies above. It conjures odors of murk, slime, stagnancy, and offal. Although our first joy of programming may have been intense, the misery of dealing with legacy code is often sufficient to extinguish that flame.

Many of us have tried to discover ways to *prevent* code from becoming legacy. We've written books on principles, patterns, and practices that can help programmers keep their systems clean. But Michael Feathers had an insight that many of the rest of us missed. Prevention is imperfect. Even the most disciplined development team, knowing the best principles, using the best patterns, and following the best practices will create messes from time to time. The rot still accumulates. It's not enough to try to prevent the rot—you have to be able to *reverse* it.

That's what this book is about. It's about reversing the rot. It's about taking a tangled, opaque, convoluted system and slowly, gradually, piece by piece, step by step, turning it into a simple, nicely structured, well-designed system. It's about reversing entropy.

Before you get too excited, I warn you; reversing rot is not easy, and it's not quick. The techniques, patterns, and tools that Michael presents in this book are effective, but they take work, time, endurance, and *care*. This book is not a magic bullet. It won't tell you how to eliminate all the accumulated rot in your systems overnight. Rather, this book describes a set of disciplines, concepts, and attitudes that you will carry with you for the rest of your career and that *will help you to turn systems that gradually degrade into systems that gradually improve.*

Robert C. Martin
29 June, 2004

Preface

Do you remember the first program you wrote? I remember mine. It was a little graphics program I wrote on an early PC. I started programming later than most of my friends. Sure, I'd seen computers when I was a kid. I remember being really impressed by a minicomputer I once saw in an office, but for years I never had a chance to even sit at a computer. Later, when I was a teenager, some friends of mine bought a couple of the first TRS-80s. I was interested, but I was actually a bit apprehensive, too. I knew that if I started to play with computers, I'd get sucked into it. It just looked too cool. I don't know why I knew myself so well, but I held back. Later, in college, a roommate of mine had a computer, and I bought a C compiler so that I could teach myself programming. Then it began. I stayed up night after night trying things out, poring through the source code of the emacs editor that came with the compiler. It was addictive, it was challenging, and I loved it.

I hope you've had experiences like this—just the raw joy of making things work on a computer. Nearly every programmer I ask has. That joy is part of what got us into this work, but where is it day to day?

A few years ago, I gave my friend Erik Meade a call after I'd finished work one night. I knew that Erik had just started a consulting gig with a new team, so I asked him, "How are they doing?" He said, "They're writing legacy code, man." That was one of the few times in my life when I was sucker-punched by a coworker's statement. I felt it right in my gut. Erik had given words to the precise feeling that I often get when I visit teams for the first time. They are trying very hard, but at the end of the day, because of schedule pressure, the weight of history, or a lack of any better code to compare their efforts to, many people are writing legacy code.

What is legacy code? I've used the term without defining it. Let's look at the strict definition: Legacy code is code that we've gotten from someone else. Maybe our company acquired code from another company; maybe people on the original team moved on to other projects. Legacy code is somebody else's code. But in programmer-speak, the term means much more than that. The term *legacy code* has taken on more shades of meaning and more weight over time.

What do you think about when you hear the term *legacy code*? If you are at all like me, you think of tangled, unintelligible structure, code that you have to change but don't really understand. You think of sleepless nights trying to add in features that should be easy to add, and you think of demoralization, the sense that everyone on the team is so sick of a code base that it seems beyond care, the sort of code that you just wish would die. Part of you feels bad for even thinking about making it better. It seems unworthy of your efforts. That definition of legacy code has nothing to do with who wrote it. Code can degrade in many ways, and many of them have nothing to do with whether the code came from another team.

In the industry, *legacy code* is often used as a slang term for difficult-to-change code that we don't understand. But over years of working with teams, helping them get past serious code problems, I've arrived at a different definition.

To me, *legacy code* is simply code without tests. I've gotten some grief for this definition. What do tests have to do with whether code is bad? To me, the answer is straightforward, and it is a point that I elaborate throughout the book:

> Code without tests is bad code. It doesn't matter how well written it is; it doesn't matter how pretty or object-oriented or well-encapsulated it is. With tests, we can change the behavior of our code quickly and verifiably. Without them, we really don't know if our code is getting better or worse.

You might think that this is severe. What about clean code? If a code base is very clean and well structured, isn't that enough? Well, make no mistake. I love clean code. I love it more than most people I know, but while clean code is good, it's not enough. Teams take serious chances when they try to make large changes without tests. It is like doing aerial gymnastics without a net. It requires incredible skill and a clear understanding of what can happen at every step. Knowing precisely what will happen if you change a couple of variables is often like knowing whether another gymnast is going to catch your arms after you come out of a somersault. If you are on a team with code that clear, you are in a better position than most programmers. In my work, I've noticed that teams with that degree of clarity in all of their code are rare. They seem like a statistical anomaly. And, you know what? If they don't have supporting tests, their code changes still appear to be slower than those of teams that do.

Yes, teams do get better and start to write clearer code, but it takes a long time for older code to get clearer. In many cases, it will never happen completely. Because of this, I have no problem defining legacy code as code without tests. It is a good working definition, and it points to a solution.

I've been talking about tests quite a bit so far, but this book is not about testing. This book is about being able to confidently make changes in any code base. In the following chapters, I describe techniques that you can use to understand code, get it under test, refactor it, and add features.

One thing that you will notice as you read this book is that it is not a book about pretty code. The examples that I use in the book are fabricated because I work under nondisclosure agreements with clients. But in many of the examples, I've tried to preserve the spirit of code that I've seen in the field. I won't say that the examples are always representative. There certainly are oases of great code out there, but, frankly, there are also pieces of code that are far worse than anything I can use as an example in this book. Aside from client confidentiality, I simply couldn't put code like that in this book without boring you to tears and burying important points in a morass of detail. As a result, many of the examples are relatively brief. If you look at one of them and think "No, he doesn't understand—my methods are much larger than that and much worse," please look at the advice that I am giving at face value and see if it applies, even if the example seems simpler.

The techniques here have been tested on substantially large pieces of code. It is just a limitation of the book format that makes examples smaller. In particular, when you see ellipses (...) in a code fragment like this, you can read them as "insert 500 lines of ugly code here":

```
m_pDispatcher->register(listener);
...
m_nMargins++;
```

If this book is not about pretty code, it is even less about pretty design. Good design should be a goal for all of us, but in legacy code, it is something that we arrive at in discrete steps. In some of the chapters, I describe ways of adding new code to existing code bases and show how to add it with good design principles in mind. You can start to grow areas of very good high-quality code in legacy code bases, but don't be surprised if some of the steps you take to make changes involve making some code slightly uglier. This work is like surgery. We have to make incisions, and we have to move through the guts and suspend some aesthetic judgment. Could this patient's major organs and viscera be better than they are? Yes. So do we just forget about his immediate problem, sew him up again, and tell him to eat right and train for a marathon? We could, but what we really need to do is take the patient as he is, fix what's wrong, and move him to a healthier state. He might never become an Olympic athlete, but we can't let "best" be the enemy of "better." Code bases can become healthier and easier to work in. When a patient feels a little better, often that is the time when you can help him make commitments to a healthier life style. That is what we are shooting for with legacy code. We are trying to get to the point at which we are used to ease; we expect it and actively attempt to make code change easier. When we can sustain that sense on a team, design gets better.

The techniques I describe are ones that I've discovered and learned with coworkers over the course of years working with clients to try to establish control over unruly code bases. I got into this legacy code emphasis accidentally. When I first started working with Object Mentor, the bulk of my work involved helping teams with serious problems develop their skills and interactions to the point that they could regularly deliver quality code. We often used Extreme Programming practices to help teams take control of their work, collaborate intensively, and deliver. I often feel that Extreme Programming is less a way to develop software than it is a way to make a well-jelled work team that just happens to deliver great software every two weeks.

From the beginning, though, there was a problem. Many of the first XP projects were "greenfield" projects. The clients I was seeing had significantly large code bases, and they were in trouble. They needed some way to get control of their work and start to deliver. Over time, I found that I was doing the same things over and over again with clients. This sense culminated in some work I was doing with a team in the financial industry. Before I'd arrived, they'd realized that unit testing was a great thing, but the tests that they were executing were full scenario tests that made multiple trips to a database and exercised large chunks of code. The tests were hard to write, and the team didn't run them very often because they took so long to run. As I sat down with them to break dependencies and get smaller chunks of code under test, I had a terrible sense of déjà vu. It seemed that I was doing this sort of work with every team I met, and it was the sort of thing that no one really wanted to think about. It was just the grunge work that you do when you want to start working with your code in a controlled way, if you know how to do it. I decided then that it was worth really reflecting on how we were solving these problems and writing them down so that teams could get a leg up and start to make their code bases easier to live in.

A note about the examples: I've used examples in several different programming languages. The bulk of the examples are written in Java, C++, and C. I picked Java because it is a very common language, and I included C++ because it presents some special challenges in a legacy environment. I picked C because it highlights many of the problems that come up in procedural legacy code. Among them, these languages cover much of the spectrum of concerns that arise in legacy code. However, if the languages you use are not covered in the examples, take a look at them anyway. Many of the techniques that I cover can be used in other languages, such as Delphi, Visual Basic, COBOL, and FORTRAN.

I hope that you find the techniques in this book helpful and that they allow you to get back to what is fun about programming. Programming can be very rewarding and enjoyable work. If you don't feel that in your day-to-day work, I hope that the techniques I offer you in this book help you find that feeling and grow it on your team.

Acknowledgments

First of all, I owe a serious debt to my wife, Ann, and my children, Deborah and Ryan. Their love and support made this book and all of the learning that preceded it possible. I'd also like to thank "Uncle Bob" Martin, president and founder of Object Mentor. His rigorous pragmatic approach to development and design, separating the critical from the inconsequential, gave me something to latch upon about 10 years ago, back when it seemed that I was about to drown in a wave of unrealistic advice. And thanks, Bob, for giving me the opportunity to see more code and work with more people over the past five years than I ever imagined possible.

I also have to thank Kent Beck, Martin Fowler, Ron Jeffries, and Ward Cunningham for offering me advice at times and teaching me a great deal about team work, design, and programming. Special thanks to all of the people who reviewed the drafts. The official reviewers were Sven Gorts, Robert C. Martin, Erik Meade, and Bill Wake; the unofficial reviewers were Dr. Robert Koss, James Grenning, Lowell Lindstrom, Micah Martin, Russ Rufer and the Silicon Valley Patterns Group, and James Newkirk.

Thanks also to reviewers of the very early drafts I placed on the Internet. Their feedback significantly affected the direction of the book after I reorganized its format. I apologize in advance to any of you I may have left out. The early reviewers were: Darren Hobbs, Martin Lippert, Keith Nicholas, Phlip Plumlee, C. Keith Ray, Robert Blum, Bill Burris, William Caputo, Brian Marick, Steve Freeman, David Putman, Emily Bache, Dave Astels, Russel Hill, Christian Sepulveda, and Brian Christopher Robinson.

Thanks also to Joshua Kerievsky who gave a key early review and Jeff Langr who helped with advice and spot reviews all through the process.

The reviewers helped me polish the draft considerably, but if there are errors remaining, they are solely mine.

Thanks to Martin Fowler, Ralph Johnson, Bill Opdyke, Don Roberts, and John Brant for their work in the area of refactoring. It has been inspirational.

I also owe a special debt to Jay Packlick, Jacques Morel, and Kelly Mower of Sabre Holdings, and Graham Wright of Workshare Technology for their support and feedback.

Special thanks also to Paul Petralia, Michelle Vincenti, Lori Lyons, Krista Hansing, and the rest of the team at Prentice-Hall. Thank you, Paul, for all of the help and encouragement that this first-time author needed.

Special thanks also to Gary and Joan Feathers, April Roberts, Dr. Raimund Ege, David Lopez de Quintana, Carlos Perez, Carlos M. Rodriguez, and the late Dr. John C. Comfort for help and encouragement over the years. I also have to thank Brian Button for the example in Chapter 21, *I'm Changing the Same Code All Over the Place*. He wrote that code in about an hour when we were developing a refactoring course together, and it's become my favorite piece of teaching code.

Also, special thanks to Janik Top, whose instrumental *De Futura* served as the soundtrack for my last few weeks of work on this book.

Finally, I'd like to thank everyone whom I've worked with over the past few years whose insights and challenges strengthened the material in this book.

Michael Feathers
mfeathers@objectmentor.com
www.objectmentor.com
www.michaelfeathers.com

Introduction

How to Use This Book

I tried several different formats before settling on the current one for this book. Many of the different techniques and practices that are useful when working with legacy code are hard to explain in isolation. The simplest changes often go easier if you can find seams, make fake objects, and break dependencies using a couple of dependency-breaking techniques. I decided that the easiest way to make the book approachable and handy would be to organize the bulk of it (*Part II, Changing Software*) in FAQ (frequently asked questions) format. Because specific techniques often require the use of other techniques, the FAQ chapters are heavily interlinked. In nearly every chapter, you'll find references, along with page numbers, for other chapters and sections that describe particular techniques and refactorings. I apologize if this causes you to flip wildly through the book as you attempt to find answers to your questions, but I assumed that you'd rather do that than read the book cover to cover, trying to understand how all the techniques operate.

In *Changing Software*, I've tried to address very common questions that come up in legacy code work. Each of the chapters is named after a specific problem. This does make the chapter titles rather long, but hopefully, they will allow you to quickly find a section that helps you with the particular problems you are having.

Changing Software is bookended by a set of introductory chapters (*Part I, The Mechanics of Change*) and a catalog of refactorings, which are very useful in legacy code work (*Part III, Dependency-Breaking Techniques*). Please read the introductory chapters, particularly Chapter 4, *The Seam Model.* These chapters provide the context and nomenclature for all the techniques that follow. In addition, if you find a term that isn't described in context, look for it in the Glossary.

The refactorings in *Dependency-Breaking Techniques* are special in that they are meant to be done without tests, in the service of putting tests in place. I encourage you to read each of them so that you can see more possibilities as you start to tame your legacy code.

Part I

The Mechanics of Change

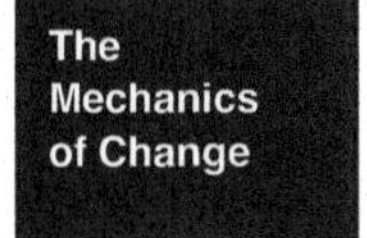

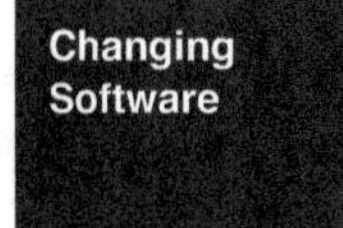

Chapter 1

Changing Software

Changing code is great. It's what we do for a living. But there are ways of changing code that make life difficult, and there are ways that make it much easier. In the industry, we haven't spoken about that much. The closest we've gotten is the literature on refactoring. I think we can broaden the discussion a bit and talk about how to deal with code in the thorniest of situations. To do that, we have to dig deeper into the mechanics of change.

Four Reasons to Change Software

For simplicity's sake, let's look at four primary reasons to change software.

1. Adding a feature
2. Fixing a bug
3. Improving the design
4. Optimizing resource usage

Adding Features and Fixing Bugs

Adding a feature seems like the most straightforward type of change to make. The software behaves one way, and users say that the system needs to do something else also.

Suppose that we are working on a web-based application, and a manager tells us that she wants the company logo moved from the left side of a page to the right side. We talk to her about it and discover it isn't quite so simple. She wants to move the logo, but she wants other changes, too. She'd like to make it animated for the next release. Is this fixing a bug or adding a new feature? It depends on your point of view. From the point of view of the customer, she is definitely asking us to fix a problem. Maybe she saw the site and attended a meeting with people in her department, and they decided to change the logo placement and ask for a bit more functionality. From a developer's point of view, the change could be seen as a completely new feature. "If they just stopped changing their minds, we'd be done by now." But in some organizations the logo move is seen as just a bug fix, regardless of the fact that the team is going to have to do a lot of fresh work.

It is tempting to say that all of this is just subjective. You see it as a bug fix, and I see it as a feature, and that's the end of it. Sadly, though, in many organizations, bug fixes and features have to be tracked and accounted for separately because of contracts or quality initiatives. At the people level, we can go back and forth endlessly about whether we are adding features or fixing bugs, but it is all just changing code and other artifacts. Unfortunately, this talk about bug-fixing and feature addition masks something that is much more important to us technically: behavioral change. There is a big difference between adding new behavior and changing old behavior.

> Behavior is the most important thing about software. It is what users depend on. Users like it when we add behavior (provided it is what they really wanted), but if we change or remove behavior they depend on (introduce bugs), they stop trusting us.

In the company logo example, are we adding behavior? Yes. After the change, the system will display a logo on the right side of the page. Are we getting rid of any behavior? Yes, there won't be a logo on the left side.

Let's look at a harder case. Suppose that a customer wants to add a logo to the right side of a page, but there wasn't one on the left side to start with. Yes, we are adding behavior, but are we removing any? Was anything rendered in the place where the logo is about to be rendered?

Are we changing behavior, adding it, or both?

We can draw a distinction that is more useful to us as programmers. If we have to modify code (and HTML kind of counts as code), we could be changing behavior. If we are only adding code and calling it, we are often adding behavior. Let's look at another example. Here is a method on a Java class:

```
public class CDPlayer
{
    public void addTrackListing(Track track) {
        ...
    }
    ...
}
```

The class has a method that lets us add track listings. Let's add another method that lets us replace track listings.

```
public class CDPlayer
{
    public void addTrackListing(Track track) {
        ...
    }

    public void replaceTrackListing(String name, Track track) {
        ...
    }
    ...
}
```

When we added that method, did we add new behavior to our application or change behavior? The answer is: neither. Adding a method doesn't change behavior unless the method is called somehow.

Let's make another code change. Let's put a new button on the user interface for the CD player and tie it to the `replaceTrackListing` method. With that move, we're adding the behavior we specified in `replaceTrackListing` method, but we're also subtly changing behavior. The UI will render differently with that new button. Chances are, the UI will take about a microsecond longer to display. It seems nearly impossible to add behavior without changing it to some degree.

Improving Design

Design improvement is a different kind of software change. When we want to alter software's structure to make it more maintainable, generally we want to keep its behavior intact also. When we drop behavior in that process, we often call that a bug. One of the main reasons why many programmers don't attempt to improve design often is because it is relatively easy to lose behavior or create bad behavior in the process of doing it.

The act of improving design without changing its behavior is called *refactoring*. The idea behind refactoring is that we can make software more maintainable without changing behavior if we write tests to make sure that existing behavior doesn't change and take small steps to verify that all along the process. People have been cleaning up code in systems for years, but only in the last few years has refactoring taken off. Refactoring differs from general cleanup in that we aren't just doing low-risk things such as reformatting source code, or invasive and risky things such as rewriting chunks of it. Instead, we are making a series of small structural modifications, supported by tests to make the code easier to change. The key thing about refactoring from a change point of view is that there aren't supposed to be any functional changes when you refactor

Optimization

Optimization is like refactoring, but when we do it, we have a different goal. With both refactoring and optimization, we say, "We're going to keep functionality exactly the same when we make changes, but we are going to change something else." In refactoring, the "something else" is program structure; we want to make it easier to maintain. In optimization, the "something else" is some resource used by the program, usually time or memory.

Putting It All Together

It might seem strange that refactoring and optimization are kind of similar. They seem much closer to each other than adding features or fixing bugs. But is this really true? The thing that is common between refactoring and optimization is that we hold functionality invariant while we let something else change.

In general, three different things can change when we do work in a system: structure, functionality, and resource usage.

Let's look at what usually changes and what stays more or less the same when we make four different kinds of changes (yes, often all three change, but let's look at what is typical):

	Adding a Feature	**Fixing a Bug**	**Refactoring**	**Optimizing**
Structure	Changes	Changes	Changes	—
Functionality	Changes	Changes	—	—
Resource Usage	—	—	—	Changes

Superficially, refactoring and optimization do look very similar. They hold functionality invariant. But what happens when we account for new functionality separately? When we add a feature often we are adding new functionality, but without changing existing functionality.

	Adding a Feature	**Fixing a Bug**	**Refactoring**	**Optimizing**
Structure	Changes	Changes	Changes	—
New Functionality	Changes	—	—	—
Functionality	—	Changes	—	—
Resource Usage	—	—	—	Changes

	Adding a Feature	Fixing a Bug	Refactoring	Optimizing
Structure	Changes	Changes	Changes	—
New Functionality	Changes	—	—	—
Functionality	—	Changes	—	—
Resource Usage	—	—	—	Changes

Adding features, refactoring, and optimizing all hold existing functionality invariant. In fact, if we scrutinize bug fixing, yes, it does change functionality, but the changes are often very small compared to the amount of existing functionality that is not altered.

Feature addition and bug fixing are very much like refactoring and optimization. In all four cases, we want to change some functionality, some behavior, but we want to preserve much more (see Figure 1.1).

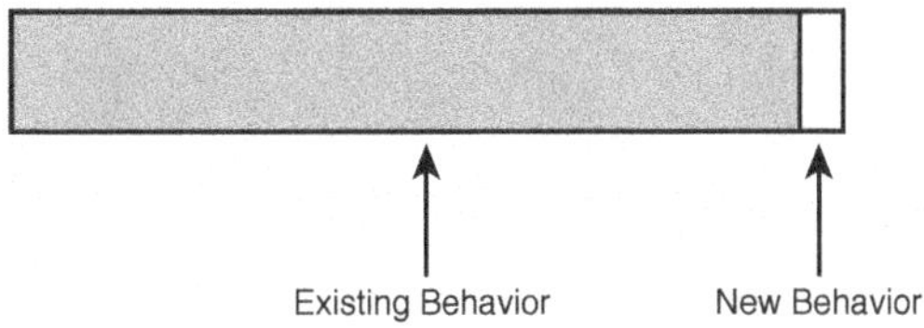

Figure 1.1 *Preserving behavior.*

That's a nice view of what is supposed to happen when we make changes, but what does it mean for us practically? On the positive side, it seems to tell us what we have to concentrate on. We have to make sure that the small number of things that we change are changed correctly. On the negative side, well, that isn't the only thing we have to concentrate on. We have to figure out how to preserve the rest of the behavior. Unfortunately, preserving it involves more than just leaving the code alone. We have to know that the behavior isn't changing, and that can be tough. The amount of behavior that we have to preserve is usually very large, but that isn't the big deal. The big deal is that we often don't know how much of that behavior is at risk when we make our changes. If we knew, we could concentrate on that behavior and not care about the rest.

To mitigate risk, we have to ask three questions:

1. What changes do we have to make?
2. How will we know that we've done them correctly?
3. How will we know that we haven't broken anything?

How much change can you afford if changes are risky?

Most teams that I've worked with have tried to manage risk in a very conservative way. They minimize the number of changes that they make to the code base. Sometimes this is a team policy: "If it's not broke, don't fix it." At other times, it isn't anything that anyone articulates. The developers are just very cautious when they make changes. "What? Create another method for that? No, I'll just put the lines of code right here in the method, where I can see them and the rest of the code. It involves less editing, and it's safer."

It's tempting to think that we can minimize software problems by avoiding them, but, unfortunately, it always catches up with us. When we avoid creating new classes and methods, the existing ones grow larger and harder to understand. When you make changes in any large system, you can expect to take a little time to get familiar with the area you are working with. The difference between good systems and bad ones is that, in the good ones, you feel pretty calm after you've done that learning, and you are confident in the change you are about to make. In poorly structured code, the move from figuring things out to making changes feels like jumping off a cliff to avoid a tiger. You hesitate and hesitate. "Am I ready to do it? Well, I guess I have to."

Avoiding change has other bad consequences. When people don't make changes often they get rusty at it. Breaking down a big class into pieces can be pretty involved work unless you do it a couple of times a week. When you do, it becomes routine. You get better at figuring out what can break and what can't, and it is much easier to do.

The last consequence of avoiding change is fear. Unfortunately, many teams live with incredible fear of change and it gets worse every day. Often they aren't aware of how much fear they have until they learn better techniques and the fear starts to fade away.

We've talked about how avoiding change is a bad thing, but what is our alternative? One alternative is to just try harder. Maybe we can hire more people so that there is enough time for everyone to sit and analyze, to scrutinize all of the code and make changes the "right" way. Surely more time and scrutiny will make change safer. Or will it? After all of that scrutiny, will anyone know that they've gotten it right?

Chapter 2

Working with Feedback

Changes in a system can be made in two primary ways. I like to call them *Edit and Pray* and *Cover and Modify*. Unfortunately, *Edit and Pray* is pretty much the industry standard. When you use *Edit and Pray*, you carefully plan the changes you are going to make, you make sure that you understand the code you are going to modify, and then you start to make the changes. When you're done, you run the system to see if the change was enabled, and then you poke around further to make sure that you didn't break anything. The poking around is essential. When you make your changes, you are hoping and praying that you'll get them right, and you take extra time when you are done to make sure that you did.

Superficially, *Edit and Pray* seems like "working with care," a very professional thing to do. The "care" that you take is right there at the forefront, and you expend extra care when the changes are very invasive because much more can go wrong. But safety isn't solely a function of care. I don't think any of us would choose a surgeon who operated with a butter knife just because he worked with care. Effective software change, like effective surgery, really involves deeper skills. Working with care doesn't do much for you if you don't use the right tools and techniques.

Cover and Modify is a different way of making changes. The idea behind it is that it is possible to work with a *safety net* when we change software. The safety net we use isn't something that we put underneath our tables to catch us if we fall out of our chairs. Instead, it's kind of like a cloak that we put over code we are working on to make sure that bad changes don't leak out and infect the rest of our software. Covering software means covering it with tests. When we have a good set of tests around a piece of code, we can make changes and find out very quickly whether the effects were good or bad. We still apply the same care, but with the feedback we get, we are able to make changes more carefully.

If you are not familiar with this use of tests, all of this is bound to sound a little bit odd. Traditionally, tests are written and executed after development. A group of programmers writes code and a team of testers runs tests against the code afterward to see if it meets some specification. In some very traditional development shops, this is just the way that software is developed. The team can get feedback, but the feedback loop is large. Work for a few weeks or months, and then people in another group will tell you whether you've gotten it right.

Testing done this way is really "testing to attempt to show correctness." Although that is a good goal, tests can also be used in a very different way. We can do "testing to detect change."

In traditional terms, this is called regression testing. We periodically run tests that check for known good behavior to find out whether our software still works the way that it did in the past.

When you have tests around the areas in which you are going to make changes, they act as a software vise. You can keep most of the behavior fixed and know that you are changing only what you intend to.

Software Vise

vise (n.). A clamping device, usually consisting of two jaws closed or opened by a screw or lever, used in carpentry or metalworking to hold a piece in position. *The American Heritage Dictionary of the English Language, Fourth Edition*

When we have tests that detect change, it is like having a vise around our code. The behavior of the code is fixed in place. When we make changes, we can know that we are changing only one piece of behavior at a time. In short, we're in control of our work.

Regression testing is a great idea. Why don't people do it more often? There is this little problem with regression testing. Often when people practice it, they do it at the application interface. It doesn't matter whether it is a web application, a command-line application, or a GUI-based application; regression testing has traditionally been seen as an application-level testing style. But this is unfortunate. The feedback we can get from it is very useful. It pays to do it at a finer-grained level.

Let's do a little thought experiment. We are stepping into a large function that contains a large amount of complicated logic. We analyze, we think, we talk to people who know more about that piece of code than we do, and then we make a change. We want to make sure that the change hasn't broken anything, but how can we do it? Luckily, we have a quality group that has a set of regression tests that it can run overnight. We call and ask them to schedule a run, and they say that, yes, they can run the tests overnight, but it is a good thing that we called early. Other groups usually try to schedule regression runs in the middle of the week, and if we'd waited any longer, there might not be a timeslot and a machine available for us. We breathe a sigh of relief and then go back to work. We have about five more changes to make like the last one. All of them are in equally complicated areas. And we're not alone. We know that several other people are making changes, too.

The next morning, we get a phone call. Daiva over in testing tells us that tests AE1021 and AE1029 failed overnight. She's not sure whether it was our changes, but she is calling us because she knows we'll take care of it for her. We'll debug and see if the failures were because of one of our changes or someone else's.

Does this sound real? Unfortunately, it is very real.

Let's look at another scenario.

We need to make a change to a rather long, complicated function. Luckily, we find a set of unit tests in place for it. The last people who touched the code wrote a set of about 20 unit tests that thoroughly exercised it. We run them and discover that they all pass. Next we look through the tests to get a sense of what the code's actual behavior is.

We get ready to make our change, but we realize that it is pretty hard to figure out how to change it. The code is unclear, and we'd really like to understand it better before making our change. The tests won't catch everything, so we want to make the code very clear so that we can have more confidence in our change. Aside from that, we don't want ourselves or anyone else to have to go through the work we are doing to try to understand it. What a waste of time!

We start to refactor the code a bit. We extract some methods and move some conditional logic. After every little change that we make, we run that little suite of unit tests. They pass almost every time that we run them. A few minutes ago, we made a mistake and inverted the logic on a condition, but a test failed and we recovered in about a minute. When we are done refactoring, the code is much clearer. We make the change we set out to make, and we are confident that it is right. We add some tests to verify the new behavior. The next programmers who work on this piece of code will have an easier time and they will have tests that cover its functionality.

Do you want your feedback in a minute or overnight? Which scenario is more efficient?

Unit testing is one of the most important components in legacy code work. System-level regression tests are great, but small, localized tests are invaluable. They can give you feedback as you develop and allow you to refactor with much more safety.

What Is Unit Testing?

The term *unit test* has a long history in software development. Common to most conceptions of unit tests is the idea that they are tests in isolation of individual components of software. What are components? The definition varies, but in unit testing, we are usually concerned with the most atomic behavioral units of a system. In procedural code, the units are often functions. In object-oriented code, the units are classes.

Test Harnesses

In this book, I use the term *test harness* as a generic term for the testing code that we write to exercise some piece of software and the code that is needed to run it. We can use many different kinds of test harnesses to work with our code. In Chapter 5, *Tools*, I discuss the xUnit testing framework and the FIT framework. Both of them can be used to do the testing I describe in this book.

Can we ever test only one function or one class? In procedural systems, it is often hard to test functions in isolation. Top-level functions call other functions, which call other functions, all the way down to the machine level. In object-oriented systems, it is a little easier to test classes in isolation, but the fact is, classes don't generally live in isolation. Think about all of the classes you've ever written that don't use other classes. They are pretty rare, aren't they? Usually they are little data classes or data structure classes such as stacks and queues (and even these might use other classes).

Testing in isolation is an important part of the definition of a unit test, but why is it important? After all, many errors are possible when pieces of software are integrated. Shouldn't large tests that cover broad functional areas of code be more important? Well, they are important, I won't deny that, but there are a few problems with large tests:

- **Error localization**—As tests get further from what they test, it is harder to determine what a test failure means. Often it takes considerable work to pinpoint the source of a test failure. You have to look at the test inputs, look at the failure, and determine where along the path from inputs to outputs the failure occurred. Yes, we have to do that for unit tests also, but often the work is trivial because the tests are so small.

- **Execution time**—Larger tests tend to take longer to execute. This tends to make test runs rather frustrating. Tests that take too long to run end up not being run.

- **Coverage**—It can be hard to see the connection between a piece of code and the values that exercise it. We can usually find out whether a piece of code is exercised by a test using coverage tools, but when we add new code, we might have to do considerable work to create high-level tests that exercise the new code.

One of the most frustrating things about larger tests is that it seems that we can have error localization if we run out tests more often, but it is an illusion. If we run our tests and they pass, and then we make a small change and they fail, we know precisely where the problem was triggered. It was something we did in that last small change. We can roll back the change and try again. But if our tests are large, execution time can be too long; our tendency will be to avoid running the tests often enough to really localize errors.

Unit tests fill in gaps that larger tests can't. We can test pieces of code independently; we can group tests so that we can run some under some conditions and others under other conditions. With them we can localize errors quickly. If we think there is an error in some particular piece of code and we can use it in a test harness, we can usually code up a test quickly to see if the error really is there.

Here are qualities of good unit tests:

1. They run fast.
2. They help us localize problems.

In the industry, people often go back and forth about whether particular tests are unit tests. Is a test really a unit test if it uses more than one production class? I go back to the two qualities: Does the test run fast? Can it help us localize errors quickly? Naturally, there is a continuum. Some tests are larger, and they use several classes together. In fact, they may seem to be little integration tests. By themselves, they might seem to run fast, but what happens when you run them all together? When you have a test that exercises a class along with several of its collaborators, it tends to grow. If you haven't taken the time to make a class separately instantiable in a test harness, how easy will it be when you add more code? It never gets easier. People put it off. Over time, the test might end up taking as long as 1/10th of a second to execute.

A unit test that takes 1/10th of a second to run is a slow unit test.

Yes, I'm serious. At the time that I'm writing this, 1/10th of a second is an eon for a unit test. Let's do the math. If you have a project with 3,000 classes and there are about 10 tests apiece, that is 30,000 tests. How long will it take to run all of the tests for that project if they take 1/10th of a second apiece? Close to an hour. That is a long time to wait for feedback. You don't have 3,000 classes? Cut it in half. That is still a half an hour. On the other hand, what if the tests take 1/100th of a second apiece? Now we are talking about 5 to 10 minutes. When they take that long, I make sure that I use a subset to work with, but I don't mind running them all every couple of hours.

With Moore's Law's help, I hope to see nearly instantaneous test feedback for even the largest systems in my lifetime. I suspect that working in those systems will be like working in code that can bite back. It will be capable of letting us know when it is being changed in a bad way.

> Unit tests run fast. If they don't run fast, they aren't unit tests.
>
> Other kinds of tests often masquerade as unit tests. A test is not a unit test if:
>
> 1. It talks to a database.
> 2. It communicates across a network.
> 3. It touches the file system.
> 4. You have to do special things to your environment (such as editing configuration files) to run it.
>
> Tests that do these things aren't bad. Often they are worth writing, and you generally will write them in unit test harnesses. However, it is important to be able to separate them from true unit tests so that you can keep a set of tests that you can run *fast* whenever you make changes.

Higher-Level Testing

Unit tests are great, but there is a place for higher-level tests, tests that cover scenarios and interactions in an application. Higher-level tests can be used to pin down behavior for a set of classes at a time. When you are able to do that, often you can write tests for the individual classes more easily.

Test Coverings

So how do we start making changes in a legacy project? The first thing to notice is that, given a choice, it is always safer to have tests around the changes that we make. When we change code, we can introduce errors; after all, we're all human. But when we cover our code with tests before we change it, we're more likely to catch any mistakes that we make.

Figure 2.1 shows us a little set of classes. We want to make changes to the `getResponseText` method of `InvoiceUpdateResponder` and the `getValue` method of `Invoice`. Those methods are our change points. We can cover them by writing tests for the classes they reside in.

To write and run tests we have to be able to create instances of `InvoiceUpdateResponder` and `Invoice` in a testing harness. Can we do that? Well, it looks like it should be easy enough to create an `Invoice`; it has a constructor that doesn't accept any arguments. `InvoiceUpdateResponder` might be tricky, though. It accepts a `DBConnection`, a real connection to a live database. How are we going to handle that in a test? Do we have to set up a database with data for our tests? That's a lot of work. Won't testing through the database be slow? We don't particularly care about the database right now anyway; we just want to cover our changes in `InvoiceUpdateResponder` and `Invoice`. We also have a bigger problem. The constructor for `InvoiceUpdateResponder` needs an `InvoiceUpdateServlet` as an argument. How easy will it be to create one of those? We could change the code so that it

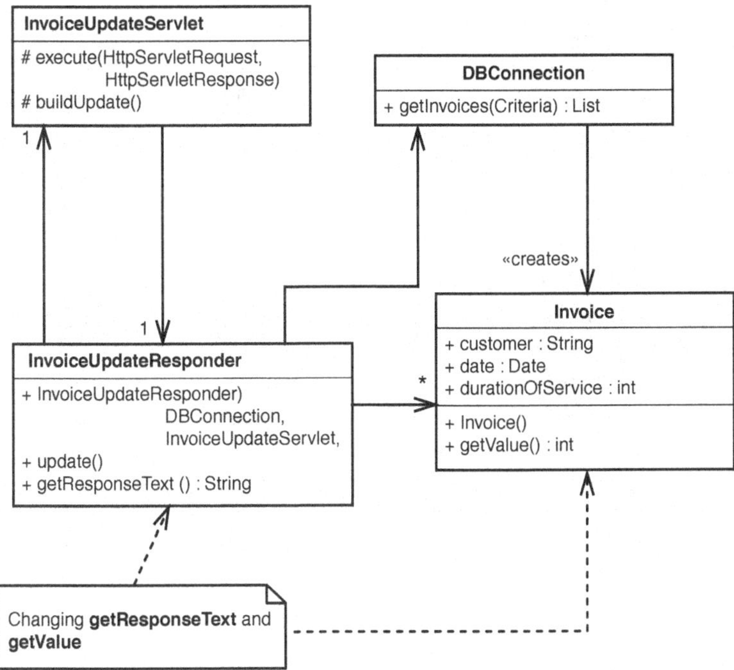

Figure 2.1 *Invoice update classes.*

doesn't take that servlet anymore. If the InvoiceUpdateResponder just needs a little bit of information from InvoiceUpdateServlet, we can pass it along instead of passing the whole servlet in, but shouldn't we have a test in place to make sure that we've made that change correctly?

All of these problems are dependency problems. When classes depend directly on things that are hard to use in a test, they are hard to modify and hard to work with.

> Dependency is one of the most critical problems in software development. Much legacy code work involves breaking dependencies so that change can be easier.

So, how do we do it? How do we get tests in place without changing code? The sad fact is that, in many cases, it isn't very practical. In some cases, it might even be impossible. In the example we just saw, we could attempt to get past the DBConnection issue by using a real database, but what about the servlet issue? Do we have to create a full servlet and pass it to the constructor of InvoiceUpdateResponder? Can we get it into the right state? It might be possible. What would we do if we were working in a GUI desktop application? We might not have any programmatic interface. The logic could be tied right into the GUI classes. What do we do then?

> **The Legacy Code Dilemma**
>
> When we change code, we should have tests in place. To put tests in place, we often have to change code.

In the Invoice example we can try to test at a higher level. If it is hard to write tests without changing a particular class, sometimes testing a class that uses it is easier; regardless, we usually have to break dependencies between classes someplace. In this case, we can break the dependency on InvoiceUpdateServlet by passing the one thing that InvoiceUpdateResponder really needs. It needs a collection of invoice IDs that the InvoiceUpdateServlet holds. We can also break the dependency that InvoiceUpdateResponder has on DBConnection by introducing an interface (IDBConnection) and changing the InvoiceUpdateResponder so that it uses the interface instead. Figure 2.2 shows the state of these classes after the changes.

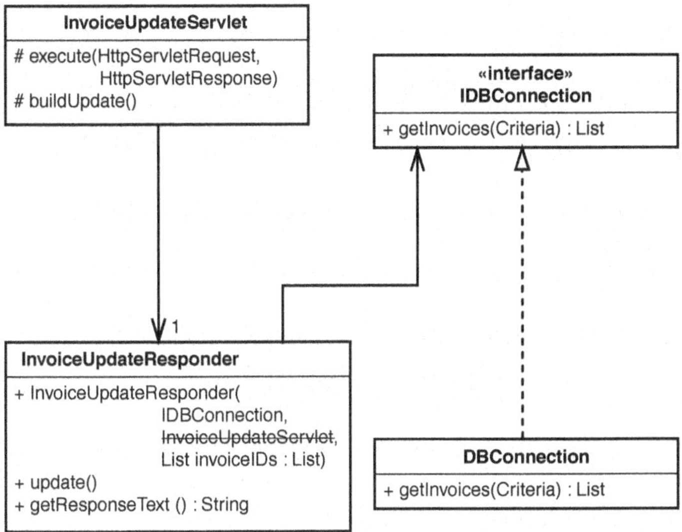

Figure 2.2 *Invoice update classes with dependencies broken.*

Is this safe to do these refactorings without tests? It can be. These refactorings are named *Primitivize Parameter (385)* and *Extract Interface (362)*, respectively. They are described in the dependency breaking techniques catalog at the end of the book. When we break dependencies, we can often write tests that make more invasive changes safer. The trick is to do these initial refactorings very conservatively.

Being conservative is the right thing to do when we can possibly introduce errors, but sometimes when we break dependencies to cover code, it doesn't turn out as nicely as what we did in the previous example. We might introduce parameters to methods that aren't strictly needed in production code, or we might break apart classes in odd ways just to be able to get tests in place. When we do that, we might end up making the code look a little poorer in that area. If we were being less conservative, we'd just fix it immediately. We can do that, but it depends upon how much risk is involved. When errors are a big deal, and they usually are, it pays to be conservative.

> When you break dependencies in legacy code, you often have to suspend your sense of aesthetics a bit. Some dependencies break cleanly; others end up looking less than ideal from a design point of view. They are like the incision points in surgery: There might be a scar left in your code after your work, but everything beneath it can get better.
>
> If you can cover code around the point where you broke dependencies later, you can heal that scar, too.

The Legacy Code Change Algorithm

When you have to make a change in a legacy code base, here is an algorithm you can use.

1. Identify change points.
2. Find test points.
3. Break dependencies.
4. Write tests.
5. Make changes and refactor.

The day-to-day goal in legacy code is to make changes, but not just any changes. We want to make functional changes that deliver value while bringing more of the system under test. At the end of each programming episode, we should be able to point not only to code that provides some new feature, but also its tests. Over time, tested areas of the code base surface like islands rising out of the ocean. Work in these islands becomes much easier. Over time, the islands become large landmasses. Eventually, you'll be able to work in continents of test-covered code.

Let's look at each of these steps and how his book will help you with them.

Identify Change Points

The places where you need to make your changes depend sensitively on your architecture. If you don't know your design well enough to feel that you are making changes in the right place, take a look at Chapter 16, *I Don't Understand the Code Well Enough to Change It*, and Chapter 17, *My Application Has No Structure.*

Find Test Points

In some cases, finding places to write tests is easy, but in legacy code it can often be hard. Take a look at Chapter 11, *I Need to Make a Change. What Methods Should I Test?*, and Chapter 12, *I Need to Make Many Changes in One Area. Do I Have to Break Dependencies for All the Classes Involved?* These chapters offer techniques that you can use to determine where you need to write your tests for particular changes.

Break Dependencies

Dependencies are often the most obvious impediment to testing. The two ways this problem manifests itself are difficulty instantiating objects in test harnesses and difficulty running methods in test harnesses. Often in legacy code, you have to break dependencies to get tests in place. Ideally, we would have tests that tell us whether the things we do to break dependencies cause problems, but often we don't. Take a look at Chapter 23, *How Do I Know That I'm Not Breaking Anything?*, to see some practices that can be used to make the first incisions in a system safer as you start to bring it under test. When you have done this, take a look at Chapter 9, *I Can't Get This Class into a Test Harness*, and Chapter 10, *I Can't Run This Method in a Test Harness*, for scenarios that show how to get past common dependency problems. These sections heavily reference the dependency breaking techniques catalog at the back of the book, but they don't cover all of the techniques. Take some time to look through the catalog for more ideas on how to break dependencies.

Dependency problems also show up when we have an idea for a test but we can't write it easily. If you find that you can't write tests because of dependencies in large methods, see Chapter 22, *I Need to Change a Monster Method and I Can't Write Tests for It*. If you find that you can break dependencies, but it takes too long to build your tests, take a look at Chapter 7, *It Takes Forever to Make a Change*. That chapter describes additional dependency-breaking work that you can do to make your average build time faster.

Write Tests

I find that the tests I write in legacy code are somewhat different from the tests I write for new code. Take a look at Chapter 13, *I Need to Make a Change but I Don't Know What Tests to Write*, to learn more about the role of tests in legacy code work.

Make Changes and Refactor

I advocate using test-driven development (TDD) to add features in legacy code. There is a description of TDD and some other feature addition techniques in Chapter 8, *How Do I Add a Feature?* After making changes in legacy code, we often are better versed with its problems, and the tests we've written to add features often give us some cover to do some refactoring. Chapter 20, *This Class Is Too Big and I Don't Want It to Get Any Bigger*; Chapter 22, *I Need to Change a Monster Method and I Can't Write Tests for It*; and Chapter 21, *I'm Changing the Same Code All Over the Place* cover many of the techniques you can use to start to move your legacy code toward better structure. Remember that the things I describe in these chapters are "baby steps." They don't show you how to make your design ideal, clean, or pattern-enriched. Plenty of books show how to do those things, and when you have the opportunity to use those techniques, I encourage you to do so. These chapters show you how to make design better, where "better" is context dependent and often simply a few steps more maintainable than the design was before. But don't discount this work. Often the simplest things, such as breaking down a large class just to make it easier to work with, can make a significant difference in applications, despite being somewhat mechanical.

The Rest of This Book

The rest of this book shows you how to make changes in legacy code. The next two chapters contain some background material about three critical concepts in legacy work: sensing, separation, and seams.

Chapter 3

Sensing and Separation

Ideally, we wouldn't have to do anything special to a class to start working with it. In an ideal system, we'd be able to create objects of any class in a test harness and start working. We'd be able to create objects, write tests for them, and then move on to other things. If it were that easy, there wouldn't be a need to write about any of this, but unfortunately, it is often hard. Dependencies among classes can make it very difficult to get particular clusters of objects under test. We might want to create an object of one class and ask it questions, but to create it, we need objects of another class, and those objects need objects of another class, and so on. Eventually, we end up with nearly the whole system in a harness. In some languages, this isn't a very big deal. In others, most notably C++, link time alone can make rapid turnaround nearly impossible if we don't break dependencies.

In systems that weren't developed concurrently with unit tests, we often have to break dependencies to get classes into a test harness, but that isn't the only reason to break dependencies. Sometimes the class we want to test has effects on other classes, and our tests need to know about them. Sometimes we can sense those effects through the interface of the other class. At other times, we can't. The only choice we have is to impersonate the other class so that we can sense the effects directly.

Generally, when we want to get tests in place, there are two reasons to break dependencies: *sensing* and *separation.*

1. **Sensing**—We break dependencies to *sense* when we can't access values our code computes.

2. **Separation**—We break dependencies to *separate* when we can't even get a piece of code into a test harness to run.

Here is an example. We have a class named NetworkBridge in a network management application:

```
public class NetworkBridge
{
    public NetworkBridge(EndPoint [] endpoints) {
        ...
    }

    public void formRouting(String sourceID, String destID) {
        ...
    }
    ...
}
```


NetworkBridge accepts an array of EndPoints and manages their configuration using some local hardware. Users of NetworkBridge can use its methods to route traffic from one endpoint to another. NetworkBridge does this work by changing settings on the EndPoint class. Each instance of the EndPoint class opens a socket and communicates across the network to a particular device.

That was just a short description of what NetworkBridge does. We could go into more detail, but from a testing perspective, there are already some evident problems. If we want to write tests for NetworkBridge, how do we do it? The class could very well make some calls to real hardware when it is constructed. Do we need to have the hardware available to create an instance of the class? Worse than that, how in the world do we know what the bridge is doing to that hardware or the endpoints? From our point of view, the class is a closed box.

It might not be too bad. Maybe we can write some code to sniff packets across the network. Maybe we can get some hardware for NetworkBridge to talk to so that at the very least it doesn't freeze when we try to make an instance of it. Maybe we can set up the wiring so that we can have a local cluster of endpoints and use them under test. Those solutions could work, but they are an awful lot of work. The logic that we want to change in NetworkBridge might not need any of those things; it's just that we can't get a hold of it. We can't run an object of that class and try it directly to see how it works.

This example illustrates both the sensing and separation problems. We can't sense the effect of our calls to methods on this class, and we can't run it separately from the rest of the application.

Which problem is tougher? Sensing or separation? There is no clear answer. Typically, we need them both, and they are both reasons why we break dependencies. One thing is clear, though: There are many ways to separate software. In fact, there is an entire catalog of those techniques in the back of this book on that topic, but there is one primary tool for sensing: fake collaborators..

Faking Collaborators

One of the big problems that we confront in legacy code work is dependency. If we want to execute a piece of code by itself and see what it does, often we have to break dependencies on other code. But it's hardly ever that simple. Often that other code is the only place we can easily sense the effects of our actions. If we can put some other code in its place and test through it, we can write our tests. In object orientation, these other pieces of code are often called *fake objects*.

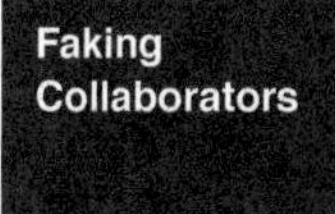

Fake Objects

A *fake object* is an object that impersonates some collaborator of your class when it is being tested. Here is an example. In a point-of-sale system, we have a class called `Sale` (see Figure 3.1). It has a method called `scan()` that accepts a bar code for some item that a customer wants to buy. Whenever `scan()` is called, the `Sale` object needs to display the name of the item that was scanned, along with its price on a cash register display.

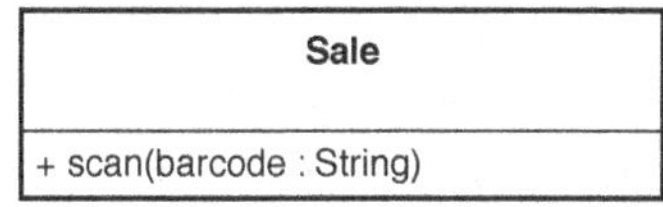

Figure 3.1 *Sale.*

How can we test this to see if the right text shows up on the display? Well, if the calls to the cash register's display API are buried deep in the `Sale` class, it's going to be hard. It might not be easy to sense the effect on the display. But if we can find the place in the code where the display is updated, we can move to the design shown in Figure 3.2.

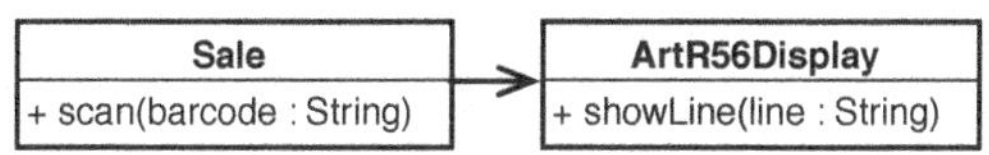

Figure 3.2 *Sale communicating with a display class.*

Here we've introduced a new class, `ArtR56Display`. That class contains all of the code needed to talk to the particular display device we're using. All we have to do is supply it with a line of text that contains what we want to display. We can move all of the display code in `Sale` over to `ArtR56Display` and have a system that does exactly the same thing that it did before. Does that get us anything? Well, once we've done that, we can move to the design shown in Figure 3.3.

The Sale class can now hold on to either an ArtR56Display or something else, a FakeDisplay. The nice thing about having a fake display is that we can write tests against it to find out what the Sale does.

How does this work? Well, Sale accepts a display, and a display is an object of any class that implements the Display interface.

```
public interface Display
{
    void showLine(String line);
}
```


Both ArtR56Display and FakeDisplay implement Display.

A Sale object can accept a display through the constructor and hold on to it internally:

```
public class Sale
{
    private Display display;

    public Sale(Display display) {
        this.display = display;
    }

    public void scan(String barcode) {
        ...
        String itemLine = item.name()
                + " " + item.price().asDisplayText();
        display.showLine(itemLine);
        ...
    }
}
```

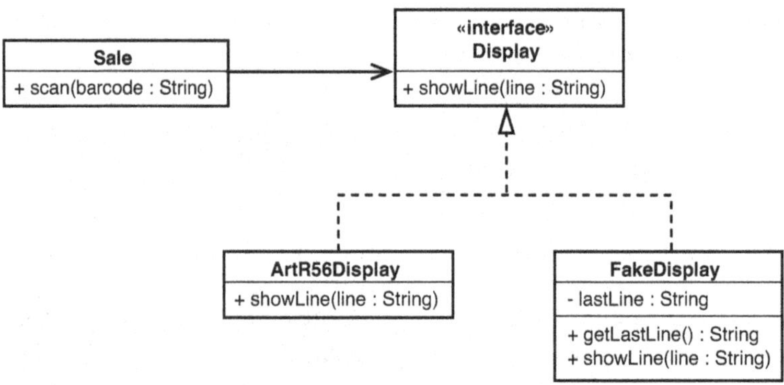

Figure 3.3 *Sale with the display hierarchy.*

In the scan method, the code calls the showLine method on the display object. But what happens depends upon what kind of a display we gave the Sale object when we created it. If we gave it an ArtR56Display, it attempts to display on the real cash register hardware. If we gave it a FakeDisplay, it won't, but we will be able to see what would've been displayed. Here is a test we can use to see that:

```
import junit.framework.*;

public class SaleTest extends TestCase
{
    public void testDisplayAnItem() {
        FakeDisplay display = new FakeDisplay();
        Sale sale = new Sale(display);

        sale.scan("1");
        assertEquals("Milk $3.99", display.getLastLine());
    }
}
```

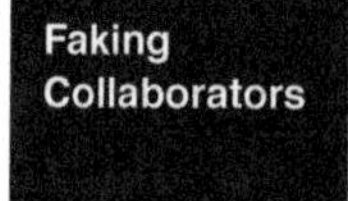

The FakeDisplay class is a little peculiar. Let's look at it:

```
public class FakeDisplay implements Display
{
    private String lastLine = "";

    public void showLine(String line) {
        lastLine = line;
    }

    public String getLastLine() {
        return lastLine;
    }
}
```

The showLine method accepts a line of text and assigns it to the lastLine variable. The getLastLine method returns that line of text whenever it is called. This is pretty slim behavior, but it helps us a lot. With the test we've written, we can find out whether the right text will be sent to the display when the Sale class is used.

Fake Objects Support Real Tests

Sometimes when people see the use of fake objects, they say, "That's not really testing." After all, this test doesn't show us what really gets displayed on the real screen. Suppose that some part of the cash register display software isn't working properly; this test would never show it. Well, that's true, but that doesn't mean that this isn't a real test. Even if we could devise a test that really showed us exactly which pixels were set on a real cash register display, does that mean that the software would work with all hardware? No, it doesn't—but that doesn't mean that that isn't a test, either. When we write tests, we have to divide and conquer. This test tells us how `Sale` objects affect displays, that's all. But that isn't trivial. If we discover a bug, running this test might help us see that the problem isn't in `Sale`. If we can use information like that to help us localize errors, we can save an incredible amount of time.

When we write tests for individual units, we end up with small, well-understood pieces. This can make it easier to reason about our code.

The Two Sides of a Fake Object

Fake objects can be confusing when you first see them. One of the oddest things about them is that they have two "sides," in a way. Let's take a look at the `FakeDisplay` class again, in Figure 3.4.

The `showLine` method is needed on `FakeDisplay` because `FakeDisplay` implements `Display`. It is the only method on `Display` and the only one that `Sale` will see. The other method, `getLastLine`, is for the use of the test. That is why we declare `display` as a `FakeDisplay`, not a `Display`:

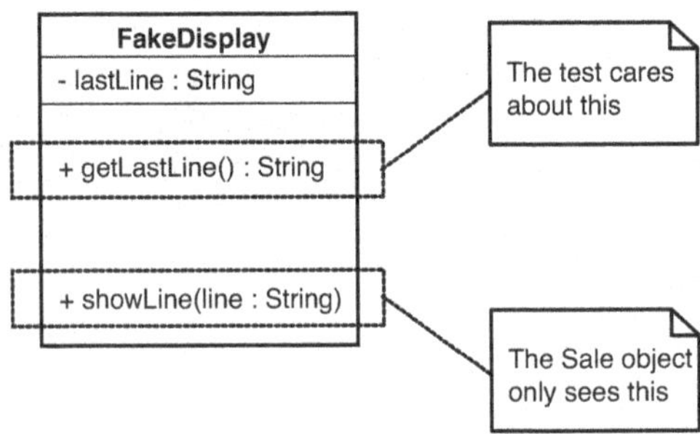

Figure 3.4 *Two sides to a fake object.*

```
import junit.framework.*;

public class SaleTest extends TestCase
{
    public void testDisplayAnItem() {
        FakeDisplay display = new FakeDisplay();
        Sale sale = new Sale(display);

        sale.scan("1");
        assertEquals("Milk $3.99", display.getLastLine());
    }
}
```

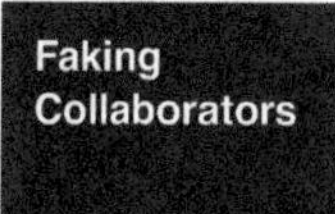

The Sale class will see the fake display as Display, but in the test, we need to hold on to the object as FakeDisplay. If we don't, we won't be able to call getLastLine() to find out what the sale displays.

Fakes Distilled

The example I've shown in this section is very simple, but it shows the central idea behind fakes. They can be implemented in a wide variety of ways. In OO languages, they are often implemented as simple classes like the FakeDisplay class in the previous example. In non-OO languages, we can implement a fake by defining an alternative function, one which records values in some global data structure that we can access in tests. See Chapter 19, *My Project is Not Object-Oriented. How Do I Make Safe Changes?*, for details.

Mock Objects

Fakes are easy to write and are a very valuable tool for sensing. If you have to write a lot of them, you might want to consider a more advanced type of fake called a *mock object*. Mock objects are fakes that perform assertions internally. Here is an example of a test using a mock object:

```
import junit.framework.*;

public class SaleTest extends TestCase
{
    public void testDisplayAnItem() {
        MockDisplay display = new MockDisplay();
        display.setExpectation("showLine", "Milk $3.99");
        Sale sale = new Sale(display);
        sale.scan("1");
        display.verify();
    }
}
```

In this test, we create a mock display object. The nice thing about mocks is that we can tell them what calls to expect, and then we tell them to check and see if they received those calls. That is precisely what happens in this test case. We tell the display to expect its `showLine` method to be called with an argument of `"Milk $3.99"`. After the expectation has been set, we just go ahead and use the object inside the test. In this case, we call the method `scan()`. Afterward, we call the `verify()` method, which checks to see if all of the expectations have been met. If they haven't, it makes the test fail.

Mocks are a powerful tool, and a wide variety of mock object frameworks are available. However, mock object frameworks are not available in all languages, and simple fake objects suffice in most situations.

Chapter 4

The Seam Model

One of the things that nearly everyone notices when they try to write tests for existing code is just how poorly suited code is to testing. It isn't just particular programs or languages. In general, programming languages just don't seem to support testing very well. It seems that the only ways to end up with an easily testable program are to write tests as you develop it or spend a bit of time trying to "design for testability." There is a lot of hope for the former approach, but if much of the code in the field is evidence, the latter hasn't been very successful.

One thing that I've noticed is that, in trying to get code under test, I've started to think about code in a rather different way. I could just consider this some private quirk, but I've found that this different way of looking at code helps me when I work in new and unfamiliar programming languages. Because I won't be able to cover every programming language in this book, I've decided to outline this view here in the hope that it helps you as well as it helps me.

A Huge Sheet of Text

When I first started programming, I was lucky that I started late enough to have a machine of my own and a compiler to run on that machine; many of my friends starting programming in the punch-card days. When I decided to study programming in school, I started working on a terminal in a lab. We could compile our code remotely on a DEC VAX machine. There was a little accounting system in place. Each compile cost us money out of our account, and we had a fixed amount of machine time each term.

At that point in my life, a program was just a listing. Every couple of hours, I'd walk from the lab to the printer room, get a printout of my program and scrutinize it, trying to figure out what was right or wrong. I didn't know enough to care much about modularity. We had to write modular code to show that we could do it, but at that point I really cared more about whether the code was going to produce the right answers. When I got around to writing object-oriented code, the modularity was rather academic. I wasn't going to be swapping in one class for another in the course of a school assignment. When I got out in the industry, I started to care a lot about those things, but in school, a program was just a listing to me, a long set of functions that I had to write and understand one by one.

This view of a program as a listing seems accurate, at least if we look at how people behave in relation to programs that they write. If we knew nothing about what programming was and we saw a room full of programmers working, we might think that they were scholars inspecting and editing large important documents. A program can seem like a large sheet of text. Changing a little text can cause the meaning of the whole document to change, so people make those changes carefully to avoid mistakes.

Superficially, that is all true, but what about modularity? We are often told it is better to write programs that are made of small reusable pieces, but how often are small pieces reused independently? Not very often. Reuse is tough. Even when pieces of software look independent, they often depend upon each other in subtle ways.

Seams

When you start to try to pull out individual classes for unit testing, often you have to break a lot of dependencies. Interestingly enough, you often have a lot of work to do, regardless of how "good" the design is. Pulling classes out of existing projects for testing really changes your idea of what "good" is with regard to design. It also leads you to think of software in a completely different way. The idea of a program as a sheet of text just doesn't cut it anymore. How should we look at it? Let's take a look at an example, a function in C++.

```
bool CAsyncSslRec::Init()
{
    if (m_bSslInitialized) {
        return true;
    }
    m_smutex.Unlock();
    m_nSslRefCount++;

    m_bSslInitialized = true;

    FreeLibrary(m_hSslDll1);
    m_hSslDll1=0;
    FreeLibrary(m_hSslDll2);
```

```
    m_hSslDll2=0;

    if (!m_bFailureSent) {
        m_bFailureSent=TRUE;
        PostReceiveError(SOCKETCALLBACK, SSL_FAILURE);
    }

    CreateLibrary(m_hSslDll1,"syncesel1.dll");
    CreateLibrary(m_hSslDll2,"syncesel2.dll");

    m_hSslDll1->Init();
    m_hSslDll2->Init();

    return true;
}
```


It sure looks like just a sheet of text, doesn't it? Suppose that we want to run all of that method except for this line:

```
        PostReceiveError(SOCKETCALLBACK, SSL_FAILURE);
```

How would we do that?

It's easy, right? All we have to do is go into the code and delete that line.

Okay, let's constrain the problem a little more. We want to avoid executing that line of code because `PostReceiveError` is a global function that communicates with another subsystem, and that subsystem is a pain to work with under test. So the problem becomes, how do we execute the method without calling `PostReceiveError` under test? How do we do that and still allow the call to `PostReceiveError` in production?

To me, that is a question with many possible answers, and it leads to the idea of a seam.

Here's the definition of a seam. Let's take a look at it and then some examples.

> **Seam**
>
> A seam is a place where you can alter behavior in your program without editing in that place.

Is there a seam at the call to `PostReceiveError`? Yes. We can get rid of the behavior there in a couple of ways. Here is one of the most straightforward ones. `PostReceiveError` is a global function, it isn't part of the `CAsynchSslRec` class. What happens if we add a method with the exact same signature to the `CAsynchSslRec` class?

```
class CAsyncSslRec
{
    ...
    virtual void PostReceiveError(UINT type, UINT errorcode);
    ...
};
```

In the implementation file, we can add a body for it like this:

```
void CAsyncSslRec::PostReceiveError(UINT type, UINT errorcode)
{
    ::PostReceiveError(type, errorcode);
}
```

That change should preserve behavior. We are using this new method to delegate to the global PostReceiveError function using C++'s scoping operator (::). We have a little indirection there, but we end up calling the same global function.

Okay, now what if we subclass the CAsyncSslRec class and override the PostReceiveError method?


```
class TestingAsyncSslRec : public CAsyncSslRec
{
    virtual void PostReceiveError(UINT type, UINT errorcode)
    {
    }
};
```

If we do that and go back to where we are creating our CAsyncSslRec and create a TestingAsyncSslRec instead, we've effectively nulled out the behavior of the call to PostReceiveError in this code:

```
bool CAsyncSslRec::Init()
{
    if (m_bSslInitialized) {
        return true;
    }
    m_smutex.Unlock();
    m_nSslRefCount++;

    m_bSslInitialized = true;

    FreeLibrary(m_hSslDll1);
    m_hSslDll1=0;
    FreeLibrary(m_hSslDll2);
    m_hSslDll2=0;

    if (!m_bFailureSent) {
        m_bFailureSent=TRUE;
        PostReceiveError(SOCKETCALLBACK, SSL_FAILURE);
    }

    CreateLibrary(m_hSslDll1,"syncesel1.dll");
    CreateLibrary(m_hSslDll2,"syncesel2.dll");

    m_hSslDll1->Init();
    m_hSslDll2->Init();

    return true;
}
```

Now we can write tests for that code without the nasty side effect.

This seam is what I call an *object seam*. We were able to change the method that is called without changing the method that calls it. *Object seams* are available in object-oriented languages, and they are only one of many different kinds of seams.

Why seams? What is this concept good for?

One of the biggest challenges in getting legacy code under test is breaking dependencies. When we are lucky, the dependencies that we have are small and localized; but in pathological cases, they are numerous and spread out throughout a code base. The seam view of software helps us see the opportunities that are already in the code base. If we can replace behavior at seams, we can selectively exclude dependencies in our tests. We can also run other code where those dependencies were if we want to sense conditions in the code and write tests against those conditions. Often this work can help us get just enough tests in place to support more aggressive work.

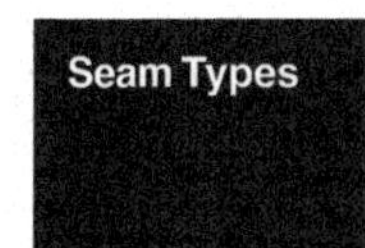

Seam Types

The types of seams available to us vary among programming languages. The best way to explore them is to look at all of the steps involved in turning the text of a program into running code on a machine. Each identifiable step exposes different kinds of seams.

Preprocessing Seams

In most programming environments, program text is read by a compiler. The compiler then emits object code or bytecode instructions. Depending on the language, there can be later processing steps, but what about earlier steps?

Only a couple of languages have a build stage before compilation. C and C++ are the most common of them.

In C and C++, a macro preprocessor runs before the compiler. Over the years, the macro preprocessor has been cursed and derided incessantly. With it, we can take lines of text as innocuous looking as this:

```
TEST(getBalance,Account)
{
    Account account;
    LONGS_EQUAL(0, account.getBalance());
}
```

and have them appear like this to the compiler.

```
class AccountgetBalanceTest : public Test
    { public: AccountgetBalanceTest () : Test ("getBalance" "Test") {}
          void run (TestResult& result_); }
  AccountgetBalanceInstance;
    void AccountgetBalanceTest::run (TestResult& result_)
{
    Account account;
{ result_.countCheck();
  long actualTemp = (account.getBalance());
  long expectedTemp = (0);
  if ((expectedTemp) != (actualTemp))
{ result_.addFailure (Failure (name_, "c:\\seamexample.cpp", 24,
StringFrom(expectedTemp),
StringFrom(actualTemp))); return; } }

}
```


We can also nest code in conditional compilation statements like this to support debugging and different platforms (aarrrgh!):

```
...
m_pRtg->Adj(2.0);

#ifdef DEBUG
#ifndef WINDOWS
    { FILE *fp = fopen(TGLOGNAME,"w");
    if (fp) { fprintf(fp,"%s", m_pRtg->pszState); fclose(fp); }}
#endif

m_pTSRTable->p_nFlush |= GF_FLOT;
#endif

...
```

It's not a good idea to use excessive preprocessing in production code because it tends to decrease code clarity. The conditional compilation directives (`#ifdef`, `#ifndef`, `#if`, and so on) pretty much force you to maintain several different programs in the same source code. Macros (defined with `#define`) can be used to do some very good things, but they just do simple text replacement. It is easy to create macros that hide terribly obscure bugs.

These considerations aside, I'm actually glad that C and C++ have a preprocessor because the preprocessor gives us more seams. Here is an example. In a C program, we have dependencies on a library routine named `db_update`. The `db_update` function talks directly to a database. Unless we can substitute in another implementation of the routine, we can't sense the behavior of the function.

```
#include <DFHLItem.h>
#include <DHLSRecord.h>
```

```
extern int db_update(int, struct DFHLItem *);

void account_update(
    int account_no, struct DHLSRecord *record, int activated)
{
    if (activated) {
        if (record->dateStamped && record->quantity > MAX_ITEMS) {
            db_update(account_no, record->item);
        } else {
            db_update(account_no, record->backup_item);
        }
    }
    db_update(MASTER_ACCOUNT, record->item);
}
```


We can use preprocessing seams to replace the calls to `db_update`. To do this, we can introduce a header file called `localdefs.h`.

```
#include <DFHLItem.h>
#include <DHLSRecord.h>

extern int db_update(int, struct DFHLItem *);

#include "localdefs.h"

void account_update(
    int account_no, struct DHLSRecord *record, int activated)
{
    if (activated) {
        if (record->dateStamped && record->quantity > MAX_ITEMS) {
            db_update(account_no, record->item);
        } else {
            db_update(account_no, record->backup_item);
        }
    }
    db_update(MASTER_ACCOUNT, record->item);
}
```

Within it, we can provide a definition for `db_update` and some variables that will be helpful for us:

```
#ifdef TESTING
...
struct DFHLItem *last_item = NULL;
int last_account_no = -1;

#define db_update(account_no,item)\
    {last_item = (item); last_account_no = (account_no);}
...
#endif
```

With this replacement of db_update in place, we can write tests to verify that db_update was called with the right parameters. We can do it because the #include directive of the C preprocessor gives us a seam that we can use to replace text before it is compiled.

Preprocessing seams are pretty powerful. I don't think I'd really want a preprocessor for Java and other more modern languages, but it is nice to have this tool in C and C++ as compensation for some of the other testing obstacles they present.

I didn't mention it earlier, but there is something else that is important to understand about seams: Every seam has an *enabling point*. Let's look at the definition of a seam again:

Seam Types

Seam

A seam is a place where you can alter behavior in your program without editing in that place.

When you have a seam, you have a place where behavior can change. We can't really go to that place and change the code just to test it. The source code should be the same in both production and test. In the previous example, we wanted to change the behavior at the text of the db_update call. To exploit that seam, you have to make a change someplace else. In this case, the enabling point is a preprocessor define named TESTING. When TESTING is defined, the localdefs.h file defines macros that replace calls to db_update in the source file.

Enabling Point

Every seam has an enabling point, a place where you can make the decision to use one behavior or another.

Link Seams

In many language systems, compilation isn't the last step of the build process. The compiler produces an intermediate representation of the code, and that representation contains calls to code in other files. Linkers combine these representations. They resolve each of the calls so that you can have a complete program at runtime.

In languages such as C and C++, there really is a separate linker that does the operation I just described. In Java and similar languages, the compiler does the linking process behind the scenes. When a source file contains an import statement, the compiler checks to see if the imported class really has been compiled. If the class hasn't been compiled, it compiles it, if necessary, and then checks to see if all of its calls will really resolve correctly at runtime.

Regardless of which scheme your language uses to resolve references, you can usually exploit it to substitute pieces of a program. Let's look at the Java case. Here is a little class called `FitFilter`:

```
package fitnesse;

import fit.Parse;
import fit.Fixture;

import java.io.*;
import java.util.Date;


import java.io.*;
import java.util.*;

public class FitFilter {

    public String input;
    public Parse tables;
    public Fixture fixture = new Fixture();
    public PrintWriter output;

    public static void main (String argv[]) {
        new FitFilter().run(argv);
    }

    public void run (String argv[]) {
        args(argv);
        process();
        exit();
    }

    public void process() {
        try {
            tables = new Parse(input);
            fixture.doTables(tables);
        } catch (Exception e) {
            exception(e);
        }
        tables.print(output);
    }
    ...
}
```

In this file, we import `fit.Parse` and `fit.Fixture`. How do the compiler and the JVM find those classes? In Java, you can use a classpath environment variable to determine where the Java system looks to find those classes. You can actually create classes with the same names, put them into a different directory, and alter the classpath to link to a different fit.Parse and fit.Fixture. Although it would be confusing to use this trick in production code, when you are testing, it can be a pretty handy way of breaking dependencies.

Suppose we wanted to supply a different version of the Parse class for testing. Where would the seam be?

The seam is the new Parse *call in the* process *method.*

Where is the enabling point?

The enabling point is the classpath.

Seam Types

This sort of dynamic linking can be done in many languages. In most, there is some way to exploit link seams. But not all linking is dynamic. In many older languages, nearly all linking is static; it happens once after compilation.

Many C and C++ build systems perform static linking to create executables. Often the easiest way to use the link seam is to create a separate library for any classes or functions you want to replace. When you do that, you can alter your build scripts to link to those rather than the production ones when you are testing. This can be a bit of work, but it can pay off if you have a code base that is littered with calls to a third-party library. For instance, imagine a CAD application that contains a lot of embedded calls to a graphics library. Here is an example of some typical code:

```
void CrossPlaneFigure::rerender()
{
    // draw the label
    drawText(m_nX, m_nY, m_pchLabel, getClipLen());
    drawLine(m_nX, m_nY, m_nX + getClipLen(), m_nY);
    drawLine(m_nX, m_nY, m_nX, m_nY + getDropLen());
    if (!m_bShadowBox) {
        drawLine(m_nX + getClipLen(), m_nY,
                 m_nX + getClipLen(), m_nY + getDropLen());
        drawLine(m_nX, m_nY + getDropLen(),
                 m_nX + getClipLen(), m_nY + getDropLen());
    }

    // draw the figure
    for (int n = 0; n < edges.size(); n++) {
        ...
    }

    ...
}
```

This code makes many direct calls to a graphics library. Unfortunately, the only way to really verify that this code is doing what you want it to do is to look at the computer screen when figures are redrawn. In complicated code, that is pretty error prone, not to mention tedious. An alternative is to use link seams. If all of the drawing functions are part of a particular library, you can create stub versions that link to the rest of the application. If you are interested in only separating out the dependency, they can be just empty functions:

```
void drawText(int x, int y, char *text, int textLength)
{
}

void drawLine(int firstX, int firstY, int secondX, int secondY)
{
}
```


If the functions return values, you have to return something. Often a code that indicates success or the default value of a type is a good choice:

```
int getStatus()
{
    return FLAG_OKAY;
}
```

The case of a graphics library is a little atypical. One reason that it is a good candidate for this technique is that it is almost a pure "tell" interface. You issue calls to functions to tell them to do something, and you aren't asking for much information back. Asking for information is difficult because the defaults often aren't the right thing to return when you are trying to exercise your code.

Separation is often a reason to use a link seam. You can do sensing also; it just requires a little more work. In the case of the graphics library we just faked, we could introduce some additional data structures to record calls:

```
std::queue<GraphicsAction>  actions;

void drawLine(int firstX, int firstY, int secondX, int secondY)
{
    actions.push_back(GraphicsAction(LINE_DRAW,
            firstX, firstY, secondX, secondY);
}
```

With these data structures, we can sense the effects of a function in a test:

```
TEST(simpleRender,Figure)
{
    std::string text = "simple";
    Figure figure(text, 0, 0);

    figure.rerender();
    LONGS_EQUAL(5, actions.size());
```

```
    GraphicsAction action;
    action  = actions.pop_front();
    LONGS_EQUAL(LABEL_DRAW, action.type);

    action  = actions.pop_front();
    LONGS_EQUAL(0, action.firstX);
    LONGS_EQUAL(0, action.firstY);
    LONGS_EQUAL(text.size(), action.secondX);
}
```

The schemes that we can use to sense effects can grow rather complicated, but it is best to start with a very simple scheme and allow it to get only as complicated as it needs to be to solve the current sensing needs.

The enabling point for a link seam is always outside the program text. Sometimes it is in a build or a deployment script. This makes the use of link seams somewhat hard to notice.

Usage Tip

If you use link seams, make sure that the difference between test and production environments is obvious.

Object Seams

Object seams are pretty much the most useful seams available in object-oriented programming languages. The fundamental thing to recognize is that when we look at a call in an object-oriented program, it does not define which method will actually be executed. Let's look at a Java example:

```
cell.Recalculate();
```

When we look at this code, it seems that there has to be a method named `Recalculate` that will execute when we make that call. If the program is going to run, there has to be a method with that name; but the fact is, there can be more than one:

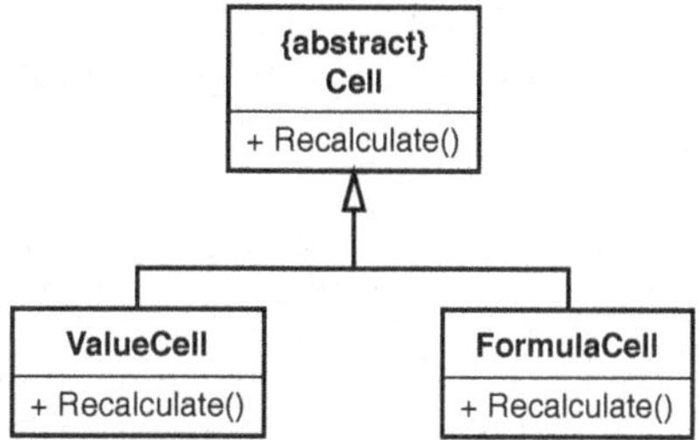

Figure 4.1 *Cell hierarchy.*

Which method will be called in this line of code?

```
cell.Recalculate();
```

Without knowing what object `cell` points to, we just don't know. It could be the `Recalculate` method of `ValueCell` or the `Recalculate` method of `FormulaCell`. It could even be the `Recalculate` method of some other class that doesn't inherit from `Cell` (if that's the case, `cell` was a particularly cruel name to use for that variable!). If we can change which `Recalculate` is called in that line of code without changing the code around it, that call is a seam.

In object-oriented languages, not all method calls are seams. Here is an example of a call that isn't a seam:

```
public class CustomSpreadsheet extends Spreadsheet
{
    public Spreadsheet buildMartSheet() {
        ...
        Cell cell = new FormulaCell(this, "A1", "=A2+A3");
        ...
        cell.Recalculate();
        ...
    }
    ...
}
```

In this code, we're creating a cell and then using it in the same method. Is the call to `Recalculate` an object seam? No. There is no enabling point. We can't change which `Recalculate` method is called because the choice depends on the class of the cell. The class of the cell is decided when the object is created, and we can't change it without modifying the method.

What if the code looked like this?

```
public class CustomSpreadsheet extends Spreadsheet
{
    public Spreadsheet buildMartSheet(Cell cell) {
        ...
        cell.Recalculate();
        ...
    }
    ...
}
```

Is the call to cell.Recalculate in buildMartSheet a seam now? Yes. We can create a CustomSpreadsheet in a test and call buildMartSheet with whatever kind of Cell we want to use. We'll have ended up varying what the call to cell.Recalculate does without changing the method that calls it.

Where is the enabling point?

In this example, the enabling point is the argument list of buildMartSheet. We can decide what kind of an object to pass and change the behavior of Recalculate any way that we want to for testing.

Okay, most object seams are pretty straightforward. Here is a tricky one. Is there an object seam at the call to Recalculate in this version of buildMartSheet?

```
public class CustomSpreadsheet extends Spreadsheet
{
    public Spreadsheet buildMartSheet(Cell cell) {
        ...
        Recalculate(cell);
        ...
    }

    private static void Recalculate(Cell cell) {
        ...
    }

    ...
}
```

The Recalculate method is a static method. Is the call to Recalculate in buildMartSheet a seam? Yes. We don't have to edit buildMartSheet to change behavior at that call. If we delete the keyword static on Recalculate and make it a protected method instead of a private method, we can subclass and override it during test:

```
public class CustomSpreadsheet extends Spreadsheet
{
    public Spreadsheet buildMartSheet(Cell cell) {
        ...
        Recalculate(cell);
        ...
    }
```

```
    protected void Recalculate(Cell cell) {
        ...
    }

    ...
}

public class TestingCustomSpreadsheet extends CustomSpreadsheet {
    protected void Recalculate(Cell cell) {
        ...
    }
}
```

Isn't this all rather indirect? If we don't like a dependency, why don't we just go into the code and change it? Sometimes that works, but in particularly nasty legacy code, often the best approach is to do what you can to modify the code as little as possible when you are getting tests in place. If you know the seams that your language offers and how to use them, you can often get tests in place more safely than you could otherwise.

The seams types I've shown are the major ones. You can find them in many programming languages. Let's take a look at the example that led off this chapter again and see what seams we can see:

```
bool CAsyncSslRec::Init()
{
    if (m_bSslInitialized) {
        return true;
    }
    m_smutex.Unlock();
    m_nSslRefCount++;

    m_bSslInitialized = true;

    FreeLibrary(m_hSslDll1);
    m_hSslDll1=0;
    FreeLibrary(m_hSslDll2);
    m_hSslDll2=0;

    if (!m_bFailureSent) {
        m_bFailureSent=TRUE;
        PostReceiveError(SOCKETCALLBACK, SSL_FAILURE);
    }

    CreateLibrary(m_hSslDll1,"syncesel1.dll");
    CreateLibrary(m_hSslDll2,"syncesel2.dll");

    m_hSslDll1->Init();
    m_hSslDll2->Init();
    return true;
}
```

What seams are available at the `PostReceiveError` call? Let's list them.

1. `PostReceiveError` is a global function, so we can easily use the *link seam* there. We can create a library with a stub function and link to it to get rid of the behavior. The enabling point would be our makefile or some setting in our IDE. We'd have to alter our build so that we would link to a testing library when we are testing and a production library when we want to build the real system.
2. We could add a `#include` statement to the code and use the preprocessor to define a macro named `PostReceiveError` when we are testing. So, we have a *preprocessing seam* there. Where is the *enabling point*? We can use a preprocessor define to turn the macro definition on or off.
3. We could also declare a virtual function for `PostRecieveError` like we did at the beginning of this chapter, so we have an *object seam* there also. Where is the enabling point? In this case, the enabling point is the place where we decide to create an object. We can create either an `CAsyncSslRec` object or an object of some testing subclass that overrides `PostRecieveError`.

It is actually kind of amazing that there are so many ways to replace the behavior at this call without editing the method:

```
bool CAsyncSslRec::Init()
{
    ...
    if (!m_bFailureSent) {
        m_bFailureSent=TRUE;
        PostReceiveError(SOCKETCALLBACK, SSL_FAILURE);
    }
    ...

    return true;
}
```

It is important to choose the right type of seam when you want to get pieces of code under test. In general, *object seams* are the best choice in object-oriented languages. *Preprocessing seams* and *link seams* can be useful at times but they are not as explicit as *object seams*. In addition, tests that depend upon them can be hard to maintain. I like to reserve *preprocessing seams* and *link seams* for cases where dependencies are pervasive and there are no better alternatives.

When you get used to seeing code in terms of seams, it is easier to see how to test things and how to structure new code to make testing easier.

Chapter 5

Tools

What tools do you need when you work with legacy code? You need an editor (or an IDE) and your build system, but you also need a testing framework. If there are refactoring tools for your language, they can be very helpful as well.

In this chapter, I describe some of the tools that are currently available and the role that they can play in your legacy code work.

Automated Refactoring Tools

Refactoring by hand is fine, but when you have a tool that does some refactoring for you, you have a real time saver. In the 1990s, Bill Opdyke started work on a C++ refactoring tool as part of his thesis work on refactoring. Although it never became commercially available, to my knowledge, his work inspired many other efforts in other languages. One of the most significant was the Smalltalk refactoring browser developed by John Brant and Don Roberts at the University of Illinois. The Smalltalk refactoring browser supported a very large number of refactorings and has served as a state-of-the-art example of automated refactoring technology for a long while. Since then, there have been many attempts to add refactoring support to various languages in wider use. At the time of this writing, many Java refactoring tools are available; most are integrated into IDEs, but a few are not. There are also refactoring tools for Delphi and some relatively new ones for C++. Tools for C# refactoring are under active development at the time of this writing.

With all of these, tools it seems that refactoring should be much easier. It is, in some environments. Unfortunately, the refactoring support in many of these tools varies. Let's remember what refactoring is again. Here is Martin Fowler's definition from *Refactoring: Improving the Design of Existing Code* (Addison-Wesley 1999):

> **refactoring** (n.). A change made to the internal structure of software to make it easier to understand and cheaper to modify without changing its existing behavior.

A change is a refactoring only if it doesn't change behavior. Refactoring tools should verify that a change does not change behavior, and many of them do. This was a cardinal rule in the Smalltalk refactoring browser, Bill Opdyke's work, and many of the early Java refactoring tools. At the fringes, however, some tools don't really check—and if they don't check, you could be introducing subtle bugs when you refactor.

It pays to choose your refactoring tools with care. Find out what the tool developers say about the safety of their tool. Run your own tests. When I encounter a new refactoring tool, I often run little sanity checks. When you attempt to extract a method and give it the name of a method that already exists in that class, does it flag that as an error? What if it is the name of a method in a base class—does the tool detect that? If it doesn't, you could mistakenly override a method and break code.

In this book, I discuss work with and without automated refactoring support. In the examples, I mention whether I am assuming the availability of a refactoring tool.

In all cases, I assume that the refactorings supplied by the tool preserve behavior. If you discover that the ones supplied by your tool don't preserve behavior, don't use the automated refactorings. Follow the advice for cases in which you don't have a refactoring tool—it will be safer.

Tests and Automated Refactoring

When you have a tool that does refactorings for you, it's tempting to believe that you don't have to write tests for the code you are about to refactor. In some cases, this is true. If your tool performs safe refactorings and you go from one automated refactoring to another without doing any other editing, you can assume that your edits haven't changed behavior. However, this isn't always the case.

Here is an example:

```
public class A {
    private int alpha = 0;
    private int getValue() {
        alpha++;
        return 12;
    }
    public void doSomething() {
        int v = getValue();
        int total = 0;
        for (int n = 0; n < 10; n++) {
            total += v;
        }
    }
}
```

In at least two Java refactoring tools, we can use a refactoring to remove the v variable from doSomething. After the refactoring, the code looks like this:

```
public class A {
    private int alpha = 0;
    private int getValue() {
        alpha++;
        return 12;
    }
    public void doSomething() {
      int total = 0;
      for (int n = 0; n < 10; n++) {
          total += getValue();
      }
    }
}
```

See the problem? The variable was removed, but now the value of alpha is incremented 10 times rather than 1. This change clearly didn't preserve behavior.

It is a good idea to have tests around your code before you start to use automated refactorings. You can do some automated refactoring without tests, but you have to know what the tool is checking and what it isn't. When I start to use a new tool, the first thing that I do is put its support for extracting methods through its paces. If I can trust it well enough to use it without tests, I can get the code into a much more testable state.

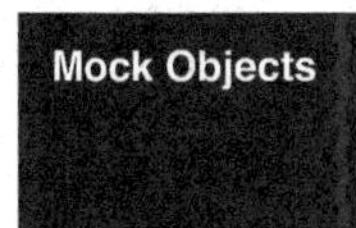

Mock Objects

One of the big problems that we confront in legacy code work is dependency. If we want to execute a piece of code by itself and see what it does, often we have to break dependencies on other code. But it's hardly ever that simple. If we remove the other code, we need to have something in its place that supplies the right values when we are testing so that we can exercise our piece of code thoroughly. In object-oriented code, these are often called mock objects.

Several mock object libraries are freely available. The web site www.mockobjects.com is a good place to find references for most of them.

Unit-Testing Harnesses

Testing tools have a long and varied history. Not a year goes by that I don't run into four or five teams that have bought some expensive license-per-seat testing tool that ends up not living up to its price. In fairness to tool vendors, testing is a tough problem, and people are often seduced by the idea that they can test through a GUI or web interface without having to do anything special to their application. It can be done, but it is usually more work than anyone on a team is prepared to admit. In addition, a user interface often isn't the best place to write tests. UIs are often volatile and too far from the functionality being tested. When UI-based tests fail, it can be hard to figure out why. Regardless, people often spend considerable money trying to do all of their testing with those sorts of tools.

The most effective testing tools I've run across have been free. The first one is the xUnit testing framework. Originally written in Smalltalk by Kent Beck and then ported to Java by Kent Beck and Erich Gamma, xUnit is a small, powerful design for a unit-testing framework. Here are its key features:

- It lets programmers write tests in the language they are developing in.
- All tests run in isolation.
- Tests can be grouped into suites so that they can be run and rerun on demand.

The xUnit framework has been ported to most major languages and quite a few small, quirky ones.

The most revolutionary thing about xUnit's design is its simplicity and focus. It allows us to write tests with little muss and fuss. Although it was originally designed for unit testing, you can use it to write larger tests because xUnit really doesn't care how large or small a test is. If the test can be written in the language you are using, xUnit can run it.

In this book, most of the examples are in Java and C++. In Java, JUnit is the preferred xUnit harness, and it looks very much like most of the other xUnits. In C++, I often use a testing harness I wrote named CppUnitLite. It looks quite a bit different, and I describe it in this chapter also. By the way, I'm not slighting the original author of CppUnit by using CppUnitLite. I was that guy a long time ago, and I discovered only after I released CppUnit that it could be quite a bit smaller, easier to use, and far more portable if it used some C idioms and only a bare subset of the C++ language.

JUnit

In JUnit, you write tests by subclassing a class named TestCase.

```
import junit.framework.*;

public class FormulaTest extends TestCase {
    public void testEmpty() {
        assertEquals(0, new Formula("").value());
    }

    public void testDigit() {
        assertEquals(1, new Formula("1").value());
    }
}
```

Each method in a test class defines a test if it has a signature of this form: `void testXXX()`, where XXX is the name you want to give the test. Each test method can contain code and assertions. In the `testEmpty` method shown above, there is code to create a new `Formula` object and call its `value` method. There is also assertion code that checks to see if that value is equal to `0`. If it is, the test passes. If it isn't, the test fails.

In a nutshell, here is what happens when you run JUnit tests. The JUnit test runner loads a test class like the one shown previously, and then it uses reflection to find all of its test methods. What it does next is kind of sneaky. It creates a completely separate object for each one of those test methods. From the previous code, it creates two of them: an object whose only job is to run the `testEmpty` method, and an object whose only job is to run the `testDigit` object. If you are wondering what the classes of the objects are, in both cases, it is the same: `FormulaTest`. Each object is configured to run exactly one of the test methods on `FormulaTest`. The key thing is that we have a completely separate object for each method. There is no way that they can affect each other. Here is an example.

```
public class EmployeeTest extends TestCase {
    private Employee employee;

    protected void setUp() {
        employee = new Employee("Fred", 0, 10);
        TDate cardDate = new TDate(10, 10, 2000);
        employee.addTimeCard(new TimeCard(cardDate,40));
    }

    public void testOvertime() {
        TDate newCardDate = new TDate(11, 10, 2000);
        employee.addTimeCard(new TimeCard(newCardDate, 50));
        assertTrue(employee.hasOvertimeFor(newCardDate));
    }
```

```
    public void testNormalPay() {
        assertEquals(400, employee.getPay());
    }
}
```

In the EmployeeTest class, we have a special method named setUp. The setUp method is defined in TestCase and is run in each test object before the test method is run. The setUp method allows us to create a set of objects that we'll use in a test. That set of objects is created the same way before each test's execution. In the object that runs testNormalPay, an employee created in setUp is checked to see if it calculates pay correctly for one timecard, the one added in setUp. In the object that runs testOvertime, an employee created in setUp for that object gets an additional timecard, and there is a check to verify that the second timecard triggers an overtime condition. The setUp method is called for each object of the class EmployeeTest, and each of those objects gets its own set of objects created via setUp. If you need to do anything special after a test finishes executing, you can override another method named tearDown, defined in TestCase. It runs after the test method for each object.

When you first see an xUnit harness, it is bound to look a little strange. Why do test case classes have setUp and tearDown at all? Why can't we just create the objects we need in the constructor? Well, we could, but remember what the test runner does with test case classes. It goes to each test case class and creates a set of objects, one for each test method. That is a large set of objects, but it isn't so bad if those objects haven't allocated what they need yet. By placing code in setUp to create what we need just when we need it, we save quite a bit on resources. In addition, by delaying setUp, we can also run it at a time when we can detect and report any problems that might happen during setup.

CppUnitLite

When I did the initial port of CppUnit, I tried to keep it as close as I could to JUnit. I figured it would be easier for people who'd seen the xUnit architecture before, so it seemed to be the better thing to do. Almost immediately, I ran into a series of things that were hard or impossible to implement cleanly in C++ because of differences in C++ and Java's features. The primary issue was C++'s lack of reflection. In Java, you can hold on to a reference to a derived class's methods, find methods at runtime, and so on. In C++, you have to write code to register the method you want to access at runtime. As a result, CppUnit became a little bit harder to use and understand. You had to write your own suite function on a test class so that the test runner could run objects for individual methods.

```
Test *EmployeeTest::suite()
{
    TestSuite *suite = new TestSuite;
    suite.addTest(new TestCaller<EmployeeTest>("testNormalPay",
            testNormalPay));
    suite.addTest(new TestCaller<EmployeeTest>("testOvertime",
            testOvertime));
    return suite;
}
```

Needless to say, this gets pretty tedious. It is hard to maintain momentum writing tests when you have to declare test methods in a class header, define them in a source file, and register them in a suite method. A variety of macro schemes can be used to get past these issues, but I choose to start over. I ended up with a scheme in which someone could write a test just by writing this source file:


```
#include "testharness.h"
#include "employee.h"
#include <memory>

using namespace std;

TEST(testNormalPay,Employee)
{
    auto_ptr<Employee>  employee(new Employee("Fred", 0, 10));
    LONGS_EQUALS(400, employee->getPay());
}
```

This test uses a macro named LONGS_EQUAL that compares two long integers for equality. It behaves the same way that assertEquals does in JUnit, but it's tailored for longs.

The TEST macro does some nasty things behind the scenes. It creates a subclass of a testing class and names it by pasting the two arguments together (the name of the test and the name of the class being tested). Then it creates an instance of that subclass that is configured to run the code in braces. The instance is static; when the program loads, it adds itself to a static list of test objects. Later a test runner can rip through the list and run each of the tests.

After I wrote this little framework, I decided not to release it because the code in the macro wasn't terribly clear, and I spend a lot of time convincing people to write clearer code. A friend of mine, Mike Hill, ran into some of the same issues before we met and created a Microsoft-specific testing framework called TestKit that handled registration the same way. Emboldened by Mike, I started to reduce the number of late C++ features used in my little framework, and then I released it. (Those issues had been a big issue in CppUnit. Nearly every day I received e-mail from people who couldn't use templates, exceptions, or the standard library with their C++ compiler.)

Both CppUnit and CppUnitLite are adequate as testing harnesses. Tests written using CppUnitLite are a little briefer, so I use it for the C++ examples in this book.

NUnit

NUnit is a testing framework for the .NET languages. You can write tests for C# code, VB.NET code, or any other language that runs on the .NET platform. NUnit is very close in operation to JUnit. The one significant difference is that it uses attributes to mark test methods and test classes. The syntax of attributes depends upon the .NET language the tests are written in.

Here is an NUnit test written in VB.NET:


```
Imports NUnit.Framework

<TestFixture()> Public Class LogOnTest
    Inherits Assertion

    <Test()> Public Sub TestRunValid()
        Dim display As New MockDisplay()
        Dim reader As New MockATMReader()
        Dim logon As New LogOn(display, reader)
        logon.Run()
        AssertEquals("Please Enter Card", display.LastDisplayedText)
        AssertEquals("MainMenu",logon.GetNextTransaction().GetType.Name)
    End Sub

End Class
```

`<TestFixture()>` and `<Test()>` are attributes that mark `LogonTest` as a test class and `TestRunValid` as a test method, respectively.

Other xUnit Frameworks

There are many ports of xUnit to many different languages and platforms. In general, they support the specification, grouping, and running of unit tests. If you need to find an xUnit port for your platform or language, go to www.xprogramming.com and look in the Downloads section. This site is run by Ron Jeffries, and it is the de facto repository for all of the xUnit ports.

General Test Harnesses

The xUnit frameworks I described in the preceding section were designed to be used for unit testing. They can be used to test several classes at a time, but that sort of work is more properly the domain of FIT and Fitnesse.

Framework for Integrated Tests (FIT)

FIT is a concise and elegant testing framework that was developed by Ward Cunningham. The idea behind FIT is simple and powerful. If you can write documents about your system and embed tables within them that describe inputs and outputs for your system, and if those documents can be saved as HTML, the FIT framework can run them as tests.

FIT accepts HTML, runs tests defined in HTML tables in it, and produces HTML output. The output looks the same as the input, and all text and tables are preserved. However, the cells in the tables are colored green to indicate values that made a test pass and red to indicate values that caused a test to fail. You also can use options to have test summary information placed in the resulting HTML.

The only thing you have to do to make this work is to customize some table-handling code so that it knows how to run chunks of your code and retrieve results from them. Generally, this is rather easy because the framework provides code to support a number of different table types.

One of the very powerful things about FIT is its capability to foster communication between people who write software and people who need to specify what it should do. The people who specify can write documents and embed actual tests within them. The tests will run, but they won't pass. Later developers can add in the features, and the tests will pass. Both users and developers can have a common and up-to-date view of the capabilities of the system.

There is far more to FIT than I can describe here. There is more information about FIT at http://fit.c2.com.

Fitnesse

Fitnesse is essentially FIT hosted in a wiki. Most of it was developed by Robert Martin and Micah Martin. I worked on a little bit of it, but I dropped out to concentrate on this book. I'm looking forward to getting back to work on it soon.

Fitnesse supports hierarchical web pages that define FIT tests. Pages of test tables can be run individually or in suites, and a multitude of different options make collaboration easy across a team. Fitnesse is available at http://www.fitnesse.org. Like all of the other testing tools described in this chapter, it is free and supported by a community of developers.

Part II

Changing Software

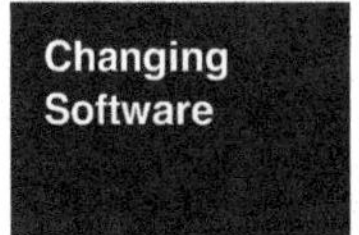

Chapter 6

I Don't Have Much Time and I Have to Change It

Let's face facts: The book you are reading right now describes additional work—work that you probably aren't doing now and work that could make it take longer to finish some change you are about to make in your code. You might be wondering whether it's worth doing these things right now.

The truth is, the work that you do to break dependencies and write tests for your changes is going to take some time, but in most cases, you are going to end up saving time—and a lot of frustration. When? Well, it depends on the project. In some cases, you might write tests for some code that you need to change, and it takes you two hours to do that. The change that you make afterward might take 15 minutes. When you look back on the experience, you might say, "I just wasted two hours—was it worth it?" It depends. You don't know how long that work might have taken you if you hadn't written the tests. You also don't know how much time it would've taken you to debug if you made a mistake, time you could have saved if you had tests in place. I'm not only talking about the amount of time you would save if the tests caught the error, but also the amount of time tests save you when you are trying to find an error. With tests around the code, nailing down functional problems is often easier.

Let's look at the costs. Suppose, we make a simple change and we write tests to support ourselves; we make all of our changes correctly. Were the tests worth it? We don't know when we'll get back to that area of the code and make another change. In the best case, you go back into the code the next iteration, and you start to recoup your investment quickly. In the worst case, it's years before anyone goes back and modifies that code. But, chances are, we'll read it periodically, if only to find out whether we need to make a change there or someplace else. Would it be easier to understand if the classes were smaller and there were unit tests? Chances are, it would. But this is just the worst case. How often does it happen? Typically, changes cluster in systems. If you are changing it today, chances are, you'll have a change close by pretty soon.

When I work with teams, I often start by asking them to take part in an experiment. For an iteration, we try to make no change to the code without having tests that cover the change. If anyone thinks that they can't write a test, they have to call a quick meeting in which they ask the group whether it is possible to write the test. The beginnings of those iterations are terrible. People feel that they aren't getting all the work done that they need to. But slowly, they start to discover that they are revisiting better code. Their changes are getting easier, and they know in their gut that this is what it takes to move forward in a better way. It takes time for a team to get over that hump, but if there is one thing that I could instantaneously do for every team in the world, it would be to give them that shared experience, that experience that you can see in their faces: "Boy, we aren't going back to that again."

If you haven't had that experience yet, you need to.

Ultimately, this is going to make your work go faster, and that's important in nearly every development organization. But frankly, as a programmer, I'm just happy that it makes work much less frustrating.

When you get over the hump, life isn't completely rosy, but it is better. When you know the value of testing and you've felt the difference, the only thing that you have to deal with is the cold, mercenary decision of what to do in each particular case.

It Happens Someplace Every Day

You boss comes in. He says, "Clients are clamoring for this feature. Can we get it done today?"

"I don't know."

You look around. Are there tests in place? No.

You ask, "How bad do you need it?"

You know that you can make the changes inline in all 10 places where you need to change things, and it will be done by 5:00. This is an emergency right? We're going to fix this tomorrow, aren't we?

Remember, code is your house, and you have to live in it.

The hardest thing about trying to decide whether to write tests when you are under pressure is the fact that you just might not know how long it is going to take to add the feature. In legacy code, it is particularly hard to come up with estimates that are meaningful. There are some techniques that can help. Take a look at Chapter 16, *I Don't Understand the Code Well Enough to Change It*, for details. When you don't really know how long it is going to take to add a feature and you suspect that it will be longer than the amount of time you have, it is tempting to just hack the feature in the quickest way that you can. Then if you have enough time, you can go back and do some testing and refactoring. The hard part is actually going back and doing that testing and refactoring. Before people get over the hump, they often avoid that work. It can be a morale problem. Take a look at Chapter 24, *We Feel Overwhelmed. It Isn't Going to Get Any Better*, for some constructive ways to move forward.

So far, what I've described sounds like a real dilemma: Pay now or pay more later. Either write tests as you make your changes or live with the fact that it is going to get tougher over time. It can be that tough, but sometimes it isn't.

If you have to make a change to a class right now, try instantiating the class in a test harness. If you can't, take a look at Chapter 9, *I Can't Get This Class into a Test Harness*, or Chapter 10, *I Can't Run This Method in a Test Harness*, first. Getting the code you are changing into a test harness might be easier than you think. If you look at those sections and you decide that you really can't afford to break dependencies and get tests in place now, scrutinize the changes that you need to make. Can you make them by writing fresh code? In many cases, you can. The rest of this chapter contains descriptions of several techniques we can use to do this.

Read about these techniques and consider them, but remember that these techniques have to be used carefully. When you use them, you are adding tested code into your system, but unless you cover the code that calls it, you aren't testing its use. Use caution.

Sprout Method

When you need to add a feature to a system and it can be formulated completely as new code, write the code in a new method. Call it from the places where the new functionality needs to be. You might not be able to get those call points under test easily, but at the very least, you can write tests for the new code. Here is an example.

```
public class TransactionGate
{
    public void postEntries(List entries) {
        for (Iterator it = entries.iterator(); it.hasNext(); ) {
            Entry entry = (Entry)it.next();
            entry.postDate();
```

```
        }
        transactionBundle.getListManager().add(entries);
    }
    ...
}
```

We need to add code to verify that none of the new entries are already in `transactionBundle` before we post their dates and add them. Looking at the code, it seems that this has to happen at the beginning of the method, before the loop. But, actually, it could happen inside the loop. We could change the code to this:

```
public class TransactionGate
{
    public void postEntries(List entries) {
        List entriesToAdd = new LinkedList();
        for (Iterator it = entries.iterator(); it.hasNext(); ) {
            Entry entry = (Entry)it.next();
            if (!transactionBundle.getListManager().hasEntry(entry) {
                 entry.postDate();
                 entriesToAdd.add(entry);
            }
        }
        transactionBundle.getListManager().add(entriesToAdd);
    }
    ...
}
```

Sprout Method

This seems like a simple change, but it was pretty invasive. How do we know we got it right? There isn't any separation between the new code we've added and the old code. Worse, we're making the code a little muddier. We're mingling two operations here: date posting and duplicate entry detection. This method is rather small, but already it is a little less clear, and we've also introduced a temporary variable. Temporaries aren't necessarily bad, but sometimes they attract new code. If the next change that we have to make involves work with all non-duplicated entries before they are added, well, there is only one place in the code that a variable like that exists: right in this method. It will be tempting to just put that code in the method also. Could we have done this in a different way?

Yes. We can treat duplicate entry removal as a completely separate operation. We can use *test-driven development (88)* to create a new method named `uniqueEntries`:

```
public class TransactionGate
{
    ...
    List uniqueEntries(List entries) {
        List result = new ArrayList();
```

```
        for (Iterator it = entries.iterator(); it.hasNext(); ) {
            Entry entry = (Entry)it.next();
            if (!transactionBundle.getListManager().hasEntry(entry) {
                result.add(entry);
            }
        }
        return result;
    }
    ...
}
```

It would be easy to write tests that would drive us toward code like that for this method. When we have the method, we can go back to the original code and add the call.

```
public class TransactionGate
{
    ...
    public void postEntries(List entries) {
        List entriesToAdd = uniqueEntries(entries);
        for (Iterator it = entriesToAdd.iterator(); it.hasNext(); ) {
            Entry entry = (Entry)it.next();
            entry.postDate();
        }
        transactionBundle.getListManager().add(entriesToAdd);
    }
    ...
}
```


We still have a new temporary variable here, but the code is much less cluttered. If we need to add more code that works with the nonduplicated entries, we can make a method for that code also and call it from here. If we end up with yet more code that needs to work with them, we can introduce a class and shift all of those new methods over to it. The net effect is that we end up keeping this method small and we end up with shorter, easier-to-understand methods overall.

That was an example of *Sprout Method*. Here are the steps that you actually take:

1. Identify where you need to make your code change.
2. If the change can be formulated as a single sequence of statements in one place in a method, write down a call for a new method that will do the work involved and then comment it out. (I like to do this before I even write the method so that I can get a sense of what the method call will look like in context.)

3. Determine what local variables you need from the source method, and make them arguments to the call.
4. Determine whether the sprouted method will need to return values to source method. If so, change the call so that its return value is assigned to a variable.
5. Develop the sprout method using *test-driven development (88)*.
6. Remove the comment in the source method to enable the call.

I recommend using *Sprout Method* whenever you can see the code that you are adding as a distinct piece of work or you can't get tests around a method yet. It is far preferable to adding code inline.

Sometimes when you want to use *Sprout Method*, the dependencies in your class are so bad that you can't create an instance of it without faking a lot of constructor arguments. One alternative is to use *Pass Null (111)*. When that won't work, consider making the sprout a public static method. You might have to pass in instance variables of the source class as arguments, but it will allow you to make your change. It might seem weird to make a static for this purpose, but it can be useful in legacy code. I tend to look at static methods on classes as a staging area. Often after you have several statics and you notice that they share some of the same variables, you are able to see that you can make a new class and move the statics over to the new class as instance methods. When they really deserve to be instance methods on the current class, they can be moved back into the class when you finally get it under test.

Advantages and Disadvantages

Sprout Method has some advantages and disadvantages. Let's look at the disadvantages first. What are the downsides of *Sprout Method*? For one thing, when you use it, in effect you essentially are saying that you are giving up on the source method and its class for the moment. You aren't going to get it under test, and you aren't going to make it better—you are just going to add some new functionality in a new method. Giving up on a method or a class is the practical choice sometimes, but it still is kind of sad. It leaves your code in limbo. The source method might contain a lot of complicated code and a single sprout of a new method. Sometimes it isn't clear why only that work is happening someplace else, and it leaves the source method in an odd state. But at least that points to some additional work that you can do when you get the source class under test later.

Although there are some disadvantages, there are a couple of key advantages. When you use *Sprout Method*, you are clearly separating new code from old code. Even if you can't get the old code under test immediately, you can at least see your changes separately and have a clean interface between the new code and the old code. You see all of the variables affected, and this can make it easier to determine whether the code is right in context.

Sprout Class

Sprout Method is a powerful technique, but in some tangled dependency situations, it isn't powerful enough.

Consider the case in which you have to make changes to a class, but there is just no way that you are going to be able to create objects of that class in a test harness in a reasonable amount of time, so there is no way to sprout a method and write tests for it on that class. Maybe you have a large set of creational dependencies, things that make it hard to instantiate your class. Or you could have many hidden dependencies. To get rid of them, you'd need to do a lot of invasive refactoring to separate them out well enough to compile the class in a test harness.

Sprout Class

In these cases, you can create another class to hold your changes and use it from the source class. Let's look at a simplified example.

Here is an ancient method on a C++ class called `QuarterlyReportGenerator`:

```
std::string QuarterlyReportGenerator::generate()
{
    std::vector<Result> results = database.queryResults(
                                        beginDate, endDate);
    std::string pageText;

    pageText += "<html><head><title>"
            "Quarterly Report"
            "</title></head><body><table>";
    if (results.size() != 0) {
        for (std::vector<Result>::iterator it = results.begin();
                it != results.end();
                ++it) {
            pageText += "<tr>";
            pageText += "<td>" + it->department + "</td>";
            pageText += "<td>" + it->manager + "</td>";
            char buffer [128];
            sprintf(buffer, "<td>$%d</td>", it->netProfit / 100);
            pageText += std::string(buffer);
            sprintf(buffer, "<td>$%d</td>", it->operatingExpense / 100);
            pageText += std::string(buffer);
            pageText += "</tr>";
        }
```

```
    } else {
        pageText += "No results for this period";
    }
    pageText += "</table>";
    pageText += "</body>";
    pageText += "</html>";

    return pageText;
}
```

Let's suppose that the change that we need to make to the code is to add a header row for the HTML table it's producing. The header row should look something like this:

```
"<tr><td>Department</td><td>Manager</td><td>Profit</td><td>Expenses</td></tr>"
```

Furthermore, let's suppose that this is a huge class and that it would take about a day to get the class in a test harness, and this is time that we just can't afford right now.

We could formulate the change as a little class called `QuarterlyReportTableHeaderProducer` and develop it using *test-driven development (88)*.

Sprout Class

```
using namespace std;

class QuarterlyReportTableHeaderProducer
{
public:
    string makeHeader();
};

string QuarterlyReportTableProducer::makeHeader()
{
    return "<tr><td>Department</td><td>Manager</td>"
        "<td>Profit</td><td>Expenses</td>";
}
```

When we have it, we can create an instance and call it directly in `QuarterlyReportGenerator::generate()`:

```
...
QuarterlyReportTableHeaderProducer producer;
pageText += producer.makeHeader();
...
```

I'm sure that at this point you're looking at this and saying, "He can't be serious. It's ridiculous to create a class for this change! It's just a tiny little class that doesn't give you any benefit in the design. It introduces a completely new concept that just clutters the code." Well, at this point, that is true. The only reason we're doing it is to get out of a bad dependency situation, but let's take a closer look.

What if we'd named the class QuarterlyReportTableHeaderGenerator and gave it this sort of an interface?

```
class QuarterlyReportTableHeaderGenerator
{
public:
    string generate();
};
```

Now the class is part of a concept that we're familiar with. QuarterlyReportTableHeaderGenerator is a generator, just like QuarterlyReportGenerator. They both have generate() methods that return strings. We can document that commonality in the code by creating an interface class and having them both inherit from it:

```
class HTMLGenerator
{
public:
    virtual ~HTMLGenerator() = 0;
    virtual string generate() = 0;
};

class QuarterlyReportTableHeaderGenerator : public HTMLGenerator
{
public:
    ...
    virtual string generate();
    ...
};

class QuarterlyReportGenerator : public HTMLGenerator
{
public:
    ...
    virtual string generate();
    ...
};
```


As we do more work, we might be able to get QuarterlyReportGenerator under test and change its implementation so that it does most of its work using generator classes.

In this case, we were able to quickly fold the class into the set of concepts that we already had in the application. In many other cases, we can't, but that doesn't mean that we should hold back. Some sprouted classes never fold back into the main concepts in the application. Instead, they become new ones. You might sprout a class and think that it is rather insignificant to your design until you do something similar someplace else and see the similarity. Sometimes you are able to factor out duplicated code in the new classes, and often you have to rename them, but don't expect it all to happen at once.

The way that you look at a sprouted class when you first create it and the way that you look at it after a few months are often significantly different. The fact that you have this odd new class in your system gives you plenty to think about. When you need to make a change close to it, you might start to think about whether the change is part of the new concept or whether the concept needs to change a little. This is all part of the ongoing process of design.

Essentially two cases lead us to *Sprout Class*. In one case, your changes lead you toward adding an entirely new responsibility to one of your classes. For instance, in tax-preparation software, certain deductions might not be possible at certain times of the year. You can see how to add a date check to the `TaxCalculator` class, but isn't checking that off to the side of `TaxCalculator`'s main responsibility: calculating tax? Maybe it should be a new class. The other case is the one we led off this chapter with. We have a small bit of functionality that we could place into an existing class, but we can't get the class into a test harness. If we could get it to at least compile into a harness, we could attempt to use *Sprout Method*, but sometimes we're not even that lucky.

The thing to recognize about these two cases is that even though the motivation is different, when you look at the results, there isn't really a hard line between them. Whether a piece of functionality is strong enough to be a new responsibility is a judgment call. Moreover, because the code changes over time, the decision to sprout a class often looks better in retrospect.

Here are the steps for *Sprout Class*:

1. Identify where you need to make your code change.

2. If the change can be formulated as a single sequence of statements in one place in a method, think of a good name for a class that could do that work. Afterward, write code that would create an object of that class in that place, and call a method in it that will do the work that you need to do; then comment those lines out.

3. Determine what local variables you need from the source method, and make them arguments to the classes' constructor.

4. Determine whether the sprouted class will need to return values to the source method. If so, provide a method in the class that will supply those values, and add a call in the source method to receive those values.

5. Develop the sprout class test first (see *test-driven development (88)*).

6. Remove the comment in the source method to enable the object creation and calls.

Advantages and Disadvantages

The key advantage of *Sprout Class* is that it allows you to move forward with your work with more confidence than you could have if you were making invasive changes. In C++, *Sprout Class* has the added advantage that you don't have to modify any existing header files to get your change in place. You can include the header for the new class in the implementation file for the source class. In addition, the fact that you are adding a new header file to your project is a good thing. Over time, you'll put declarations into the new header file that could have ended up in the header of the source class. This decreases the compilation load on the source class. At least you'll know that you aren't making a bad situation worse. At some time later, you might be able to revisit the source class and put it under test.

The key disadvantage of *Sprout Class* is conceptual complexity. As programmers learn new code bases, they develop a sense of how the key classes work together. When you use *Sprout Class*, you start to gut the abstractions and do the bulk of the work in other classes. At times, this is entirely the right thing to do. At other times, you move toward it only because your back is against the wall. Things that ideally would have stayed in that one class end up in sprouts just to make safe change possible.

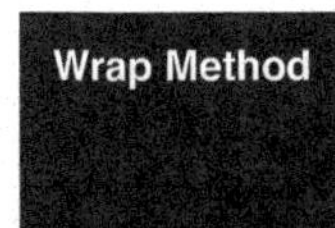

Wrap Method

Adding behavior to existing methods is easy to do, but often it isn't the right thing to do. When you first create a method, it usually does just one thing for a client. Any additional code that you add later is sort of suspicious. Chances are, you're adding it just because it has to execute at the same time as the code you're adding it to. Back in the early days of programming, this was named *temporal coupling*, and it is a pretty nasty thing when you do it excessively. When you group things together just because they have to happen at the same time, the relationship between them isn't very strong. Later you might find that you have to do one of those things without the other, but at that point they might have grown together. Without a seam, separating them can be hard work.

When you need to add behavior, you can do it in a not-so-tangled way. One of the techniques that you can use is *Sprout Method*, but there is another that is very useful at times. I call it *Wrap Method*. Here is a simple example.

```
public class Employee
{
    ...
    public void pay() {
        Money amount = new Money();
        for (Iterator it = timecards.iterator(); it.hasNext(); ) {
            Timecard card = (Timecard)it.next();
            if (payPeriod.contains(date)) {
                amount.add(card.getHours() * payRate);
            }
        }
        payDispatcher.pay(this, date, amount);
    }
}
```

In this method, we are adding up daily timecards for an employee and then sending his payment information to a PayDispatcher. Let's suppose that a new requirement comes along. Every time that we pay an employee, we have to update a file with the employee's name so that it can be sent off to some reporting software. The easiest place to put the code is in the pay method. After all, it has to happen at the same time, right? What if we do this instead?

Wrap Method

```
public class Employee
{
    private void dispatchPayment() {
        Money amount = new Money();
        for (Iterator it = timecards.iterator(); it.hasNext(); ) {
            Timecard card = (Timecard)it.next();
            if (payPeriod.contains(date)) {
                amount.add(card.getHours() * payRate);
            }
        }
        payDispatcher.pay(this, date, amount);
    }

    public void pay() {
        logPayment();
        dispatchPayment();
    }


    private void logPayment() {
    ...
    }
}
```

In the code, I've renamed pay() as dispatchPayment() and made it private. Next, I created a new pay method that calls it. Our new pay() method logs a payment and then dispatches payment. Clients who used to call pay() don't have to know or care about the change. They just make their call, and everything works out okay.

to add behavior to existing calls of the original method. If every time a client calls pay() we want logging to occur, this technique can be very useful.

There is another form of *Wrap Method* that we can use when we just want to add a new method, a method that no one calls yet. In the previous example, if we wanted logging to be explicit, we could add a makeLoggedPayment method to Employee like this:

```
public class Employee
{
    public void makeLoggedPayment() {
        logPayment();
        pay();
    }

    public void pay() {
        ...
    }

    private void logPayment() {
        ...
    }

}
```


Now users have the option of paying in either way.

Wrap Method is a great way to introduce seams while adding new features. There are only a couple of downsides. The first is that the new feature that you add can't be intertwined with the logic of the old feature. It has to be something that you do either before or after the old feature. Wait, did I say that is bad? Actually, it isn't. Do it when you can. The second (and more real) downside is that you have to make up a new name for the old code that you had in the method. In this case, I named the code in the pay() method dispatchPayment(). That is a bit of a stretch, and, frankly, I don't like the way the code ended up in this example. The dispatchPayment() method is really doing more than dispatching; it calculates pay also. If I had tests in place, chances are, I'd extract the first part of dispatchPayment() into its own method named calculatePay() and make the pay() method read like this:

```
public void pay() {
    logPayment();
```

```
public void pay() {
    logPayment();
    Money amount = calculatePay();
    dispatchPayment(amount);
}
```

That seems to separate all of the responsibilities well.

Here are the steps for the first version of the *Wrap Method*:

1. Identify a method you need to change.
2. If the change can be formulated as a single sequence of statements in one place, rename the method and then create a new method with the same name and signature as the old method. Remember to *Preserve Signatures (312)* as you do this.
3. Place a call to the old method in the new method
4. Develop a method for the new feature, test first (see *test-driven development (88)*), and call it from the new method

In the second version, when we don't care to use the same name as the old method, the steps look like this:

1. Identify a method you need to change.
2. If the change can be formulated as a single sequence of statements in one place, develop a new method for it using *test-driven development (88)*.
3. Create another method that calls the new method and the old method.

Advantages and Disadvantages

Wrap Method is a good way of getting new, tested functionality into an application when we can't easily write tests for the calling code. *Sprout Method* and *Sprout Class* add code to existing methods and make them longer by at least one line, but *Wrap Method* does not increase the size of existing methods.

Another advantage of *Wrap Method* is that it explicitly makes the new functionality independent of existing functionality. When you wrap, you are not intertwining code for one purpose with code for another.

The primary disadvantage of *Wrap Method* is that it can lead to poor names. In the previous example, we renamed the `pay` method `dispatchPay()` just because we needed a different name for code in the original method. If our code isn't terribly brittle or complex, or if we have a refactoring tool that does *Extract Method (415)* safely, we can do some further extractions and end up with better names. However, in many cases, we are wrapping because we don't have any tests, the code is brittle and those tools aren't available.

Wrap Class

The class-level companion to *Wrap Method* is *Wrap Class*. *Wrap Class* uses pretty much the same concept. If we need to add behavior in a system, we can add it to an existing method, but we can also add it to something else that uses that method. In *Wrap Class*, that something else is another class.

Let's take a look at the code from the Employee class again.

```
class Employee
{
    public void pay() {
        Money amount = new Money();
        for (Iterator it = timecards.iterator(); it.hasNext(); ) {
            Timecard card = (Timecard)it.next();
            if (payPeriod.contains(date)) {
                amount.add(card.getHours() * payRate);
            }
        }
        payDispatcher.pay(this, date, amount);
    }
    ...
}
```


We want to log the fact that we are paying a particular employee. One thing that we can do is make another class that has a pay method. Objects of that class can hold on to an employee, do the logging work in the pay() method, and then delegate to the employee so that it can perform payment. Often the easiest way to do this, if you can't instantiate the original class in a test harness, is to use *Extract Implementer (356)* or *Extract Interface (362)* on it and have the wrapper implement that interface.

In the following code we've used *Extract Implementer* to turn the Employee class into an interface. Now a new class, LoggingEmployee, implements that class. We can pass any Employee to a LoggingEmployee so that it will log as well as pay.

```
class LoggingEmployee implements Employee
{
    public LoggingEmployee(Employee e) {
        employee = e;
    }

    public void pay() {
        logPayment();
        employee.pay();
    }

    private void logPayment() {
```

```
        ...
    }
    ...
}
```

This technique is called the *decorator pattern*. We create objects of a class that wraps another class and pass them around. The class that wraps should have the same interface as the class it is wrapping so that clients don't know that they are working with a wrapper. In the example, LoggingEmployee is a decorator for Employee. It needs to have a pay() method and any other methods on Employee that are used by the client.

Wrap Class

The Decorator Pattern

Decorator allows you to build up complex behaviors by composing objects at runtime. For example, in an industrial process-control system, we might have a class called ToolController with methods such as raise(), lower(), step(), on(), and off(). If we need to have additional things happen whenever we raise() or lower() (things such as audible alarms to tell people to get out of the way), we could put that functionality right in those methods in the ToolController class. Chances are, though, that wouldn't be the end to the enhancements. Eventually, we might need to log the number of times we turn the controller on and off. We might also need to notify other controllers that are close by when we step so that they can avoid stepping at the same time. The list of things that we can do along with our five simple operations (raise, lower, step, on and off) is endless, and it won't do to just create subclasses for each combination of things. The number of combinations of those behaviors could be endless.

The decorator pattern is an ideal fit for this sort of problem. When you use decorator, you create an abstract class that defines the set of operations you need to support. Then you create a subclass that inherits from that abstract class, accepts an instance of the class in its constructor, and provides a body for each of those methods. Here is that class for the ToolController problem:

```
abstract class ToolControllerDecorator extends ToolController
{
protected ToolController controller;
    public ToolControllerDecorator(ToolController controller) {
        this.controller = controller;
    }
    public void raise() { controller.raise(); }
    public void lower() { controller.lower(); }
    public void step() { controller.step(); }
    public void on() { controller.on(); }
    public void off() { controller.off(); }
}
```

This class might not look very useful, but it is. You can subclass it and override any or all of the methods to add additional behavior. For example, if we need to notify other controllers when we step, we could have a StepNotifyingController that looks like this:

```
public class StepNotifyingController extends ToolControllerDecorator
{
    private List notifyees;
    public StepNotifyingController(ToolController controller,
            List notifyees) {
        super(controller);
        this.notifyees = notifyees;
    }
    public void step() {
        // notify all notifyees here
            ...
        controller.step();
    }
}
```

The really neat thing is that we can nest the subclasses of ToolControllerDecorator:

```
ToolController controller = new StepNotifyingController(
                        new AlarmingController
                        (new ACMEController()), notifyees);
```

When we perform an operation such as step() on the controller, it notifies all notifyees, issues an alarm, and actually performs the stepping action. That latter part, actually performing the step action, happens in ACMEController, which is a concrete subclass of ToolController, not ToolControllerDecorator. It doesn't pass the buck to anyone else; it just does each of the tool controller actions. When you are using the decorator pattern, you need to have at least one of these "basic" classes that you wrap around.

Decorator is a nice pattern, but it is good to use it sparingly. Navigating through code that contains decorators that decorate other decorators is a lot like peeling away the layers of an onion. It is necessary work, but it does make your eyes water.

This is a fine way of adding functionality when you have many existing callers for a method like pay(). However, there is another way of wrapping that is not so decorator-ish. Let's look at a case where we need to log calls to pay() in only one place. Instead of wrapping in the functionality as a decorator, we can put it in another class that accepts an employee, does payment, and then logs information about it.

Here is a little class that does this:

```
class LoggingPayDispatcher
{
    private Employee e;
```

```
    public LoggingPayDispatcher(Employee e) {
        this.e  = e;
    }

    public void pay() {
        employee.pay();
        logPayment();
    }

    private void logPayment() {
        ...
    }
    ...
}
```

Now we can create LogPayDispatcher in the one place where we need to log payments.

The key to *Wrap Class* is that you are able to add new behavior into a system without adding it to an existing class. When there are many calls to the code you want to wrap, it often pays to move toward a decorator-ish wrapper. When you use the *decorator pattern*, you can transparently add new behavior to a set of existing calls like pay() all at once. On the other hand, if the new behavior only has to happen in a couple of places, creating a wrapper that isn't decorator-ish can be very useful. Over time, you should pay attention to the responsibilities of the wrapper and see if the wrapper can become another high-level concept in your system.

Here are the steps for *Wrap Class*:

1. Identify a method where you need to make a change.
2. If the change can be formulated as a single sequence of statements in one place, create a class that accepts the class you are going to wrap as a constructor argument. If you have trouble creating a class that wraps the original class in a test harness, you might have to use *Extract Implementer (356)* or *Extract Interface (362)* on the wrapped class so that you can instantiate your wrapper.
3. Create a method on that class, using *test-driven development (88)*, that does the new work. Write another method that calls the new method and the old method on the wrapped class.
4. Instantiate the wrapper class in your code in the place where you need to enable the new behavior.

The difference between *Sprout Method* and *Wrap Method* is pretty trivial. You are using *Sprout Method* when you choose to write a new method and call it from an existing method. You are using *Wrap Method* when you choose to rename a method and replace it with a new one that does the new work and calls the old one. I usually use *Sprout Method* when the code I have in the existing method communicates a clear algorithm to the reader. I move toward *Wrap Method* when I think that the new feature I'm adding is as important as the work that was there before. In that case, after I've wrapped, I often end up with a new high-level algorithm, something like this:

```
public void pay() {
    logPayment();
    Money amount = calculatePay();
    dispatchPayment(amount);
}
```

Choosing to use *Wrap Class* is a whole other issue. There is a higher threshold for this pattern. Generally two cases tip me toward using *Wrap Class*:

1. The behavior that I want to add is completely independent, and I don't want to pollute the existing class with behavior that is low level or unrelated.

2. The class has grown so large that I really can't stand to make it worse. In a case like this, I wrap just to put a stake in the ground and provide a roadmap for later changes.

The second case is pretty hard to do and get used to. If you have a very large class that has, say, 10 or 15 different responsibilities, it might seem a little odd to wrap it just to add some trivial functionality. In fact, if you can't present a compelling case to your coworkers, you might get beat up in the parking lot or, worse, ignored for the rest of your workdays, so let me help you make that case.

The biggest obstacle to improvement in large code bases is the existing code. "Duh," you might say. But I'm not talking about how hard it is to work in difficult code; I'm talking about what that code leads you to believe. If you spend most of your day wading through ugly code, it's very easy to believe that it will always be ugly and that any little thing that you do to make it better is simply not worth it. You might think, "What does it matter whether I make this little piece nicer if 90 percent of the time I'll still being working with murky slime? Sure, I can make this piece better, but what will that do for me this afternoon? Tomorrow?" Well, if you look at it that way, I'd have to agree with you. Not much. But if you consistently do these little improvements, your system will start to look significantly different over the course of a couple of months. At some point, you'll come to work in the morning expecting to sink your hands into some slime and discover, "Huh, this code looks pretty good. It looks like someone was in here refactoring recently." At that point, when you feel the difference between good code and bad code in your gut, you are a changed person. You might even find yourself wanting to refactor far in excess of what you need to get the job done, just to make your life easier. It probably sounds silly to you if you haven't experienced it, but I've seen it happen to teams over and over again. The hard part is the initial set of steps because sometimes they look silly. "What? Wrap a class just to add this little feature? It looks worse than it did before. It's more complicated." Yes, it is, for now. But when you really start to break out those 10 or 15 responsibilities in that wrapped class, it will look far more appropriate.

Summary

In this chapter, I outlined a set of techniques you can use to make changes without getting existing classes under test. From a design point of view, it is hard to know what to think about them. In many cases, they allow us to put some distance between distinct new responsibilities and old ones. In other words, we start to move toward better design. But in other cases, we know that the only reason we've created a class is because we wanted to write new code with tests and we weren't prepared to take the time to get the existing class under test. This is a very real situation. When people do this in projects, you start to see new classes and methods sprouting around the carcasses of the old big classes. But then an interesting thing happens. After a while, people get tired of sidestepping the old carcasses, and they start to get them under test. Part of this is familiarity. If you have to look at this big, untested class repeatedly to figure out where to sprout from it, you get to know it better. It gets less scary. The other part of it is sheer tiredness. You get tired of looking at the trash in your living room, and you want to take it out. Chapter 9, *I Can't Get This Class into a Test Harness,* and Chapter 20, *This Class Is Too Big and I Don't Want It to Get Any Bigger,* are good places to start.

Chapter 7

It Takes Forever to Make a Change

How long does it take to make changes? The answer varies widely. On projects with terribly unclear code, many changes take a long time. We have to hunt through the code, understand all of the ramifications of a change, and then make the change. In clearer areas of the code, this can be very quick, but in really tangled areas, it can take a very long time. Some teams have it far worse than others. For them, even the simplest code changes take a long time to implement. People on those teams can find out what feature they need to add, visualize exactly where to make the change, go into the code and make the change in five minutes, and still not be able to release their change for several hours.

Let's look at the reasons and some of the possible solutions.

Understanding

As the amount of code in a project grows, it gradually surpasses understanding. The amount of time it takes to figure out what to change just keeps increasing.

Part of this is unavoidable. When we add code to a system, we can add it to existing classes, methods, or functions, or we can add new ones. In either case, it is going to take a while to figure out how to make a change if we are unfamiliar with the context.

However, there is one key difference between a well-maintained system and a legacy system. In a well-maintained system, it might take a while to figure out how to make a change, but once you do, the change is usually easy and you feel much more comfortable with the system. In a legacy system, it can take a long time to figure out what to do, and the change is difficult also. You might also feel like you haven't learned much beyond the narrow understanding you had to acquire to make the change. In the worst cases, it seems like no amount of time will be enough to understand everything you need to do to make a change, and you have to walk blindly into the code and start, hoping that you'll be able to tackle all the problems that you encounter.

Systems that are broken up into small, well-named, understandable pieces enable faster work. If understanding is a big issue on your project, take a look at Chapter 16, *I Don't Understand the Code Well Enough to Change It*, and Chapter 17, *My Application Has No Structure*, to get some ideas about how to proceed.

Lag Time

Changes often take a long time for another very common reason: lag time. Lag time is the amount of time that passes between a change that you make and the moment that you get real feedback about the change. At the time of this writing, the Mars rover Spirit is crawling across the surface of Mars taking pictures. It takes about seven minutes for signals to get from Earth to Mars. Luckily, Spirit has some onboard guidance software that helps it move around on its own. Imagine what it would be like to drive it manually from Earth. You operate the controls and find out 14 minutes later how far the rover moved. Then you decide what you want to do next, do it, and wait another 14 minutes to find out what happened. It seems ridiculously inefficient, right? Yet, when you think about it, that is exactly the way most of us work right now when we develop software. We make some changes, start a build, and then find out what happened later. Unfortunately, we don't have software that knows how to navigate around obstacles in the build, things such as test failures. What we try to do instead is bundle a bunch of changes and make them all at once so that we don't have to build too often. If our changes are good, we move along, albeit as slow as the Mars rover. If we hit an obstacle, we go even slower.

The sad thing about this way of working is that, in most languages, it is completely unnecessary. It's a complete waste of time. In most mainstream languages, you can always break dependencies in a way that lets you recompile and run tests against whatever code you are working on in less than 10 seconds. If a team is really motivated, its members can get it down to less than five seconds, in most cases. What it comes down to is this: You should be able to compile every class or module in your system separately from the others and in its own test harness. When you have that, you can get very rapid feedback, and that just helps development go faster.

The human mind has some interesting qualities. If we have to perform a short task (5-10 seconds long) and we can only take a step once every minute, we usually do it and then pause. If we have to do some work to figure out what to do at the next step, we start to plan. After we plan, our minds wander until we can do the next step. If we compress the time between steps down from a minute to a few seconds, the quality of the mental work becomes different. We can use feedback to try out approaches quickly. Our work becomes more like driving than like waiting at a bus stop. Our concentration is more intense because we aren't constantly waiting for the next chance to do something. Most important, the amount of time that it takes us to notice and correct mistakes is much smaller.

What keeps us from being able to work this way all the time? Some people can. People who program in interpreted languages can often get near-instantaneous feedback when they work. For the rest of us, who work in compiled languages, the main impediment is dependency, the need to compile something that we don't care about just because we want to compile something else.

Breaking Dependencies

Dependencies can be problematic, but, fortunately, we can break them. In object-oriented code, often the first step is to attempt to instantiate the classes that we need in a test harness. In the easiest cases, we can do this just by importing or including the declaration of the classes we depend upon. In harder cases, try the techniques in Chapter 9, *I Can't Get This Class into a Test Harness*. When you are able to create an object of a class in a test harness, you might have other dependencies to break if you want to test individual methods. In those cases, see Chapter 10, *I Can't Run This Method in a Test Harness*.

When you have a class that you need to change in a test harness, generally, you can take advantage of very fast edit-compile-link-test times. Usually, the execution cost for most methods is relatively low compared to the costs of the methods that they call, particularly if the calls are calls to external resources such as the database, hardware, or the communications infrastructure. The times when this doesn't happen are usually cases in which the methods are very calculation-intensive. The techniques I've outlined in Chapter 22, *I Need to Change a Monster Method and I Can't Write a Test for It*, can help.

In many cases, change can be this straightforward, but often people working in legacy code are stopped dead in their tracks by the first step: attempting to get a class into a test harness. This can be a very large effort in some systems. Some classes are very huge; others have so many dependencies that they seem to overwhelm the functionality that you want to work on entirely. In cases like these, it pays to see if you can cut out a larger chunk of the code and put it under test. See Chapter 12, *I Need to Make Many Changes in One Area. Do I Have to Break Dependencies for All the Classes Involved?* That chapter contains a set of techniques that you can use to find *pinch points (180)*, places where test writing is easier.

In the rest of this chapter, I describe how you can go about changing the way that your code is organized to make builds easier.

Build Dependencies

In an object-oriented system, if you have a cluster of classes that you want to build more quickly, the first thing that you have to figure out is which dependencies will get in the way. Generally, that is rather easy: You just attempt to use the classes in a test harness. Nearly every problem that you run into will be the result of some dependency that you should break. After the classes run in a test harness, there are still some dependencies that can affect compile time. It pays to look at everything that depends upon what you've been able to instantiate. Those things will have to recompile when you rebuild the system. How can you minimize this?

The way to handle this is to extract interfaces for the classes in your cluster that are used by classes outside the cluster. In many IDEs, you can extract an interface by selecting a class and making a menu selection that shows you a list of all of the methods in the class and allows you to choose which ones you want to be part of the new interface. Afterward, the tools allow you to provide the name of the new interface. They also give you the option of letting it replace references to the class with references to the interface everywhere it can in the code base. It's an incredibly useful feature. In C++, *Extract Implementer (356)* is a little easier than *Extract Interface (362)*. You don't have to change the names of references all over the place, but you do have to change the places that create instances of the old class (see *Extract Implementer (356)* for details).

When we have these clusters of classes under test, we have the option of changing the physical structure of our project to make builds easier. We do this by moving the clusters off to a new package or library. Builds do become more complex when we do this, but here is the key: As we break dependencies and section off classes into new packages or libraries, the overall cost of a rebuild of the entire system grows slightly, but the average time for a build can decrease dramatically.

Let's look at an example. Figure 7.1 shows a small set of collaborating classes, all in the same package.

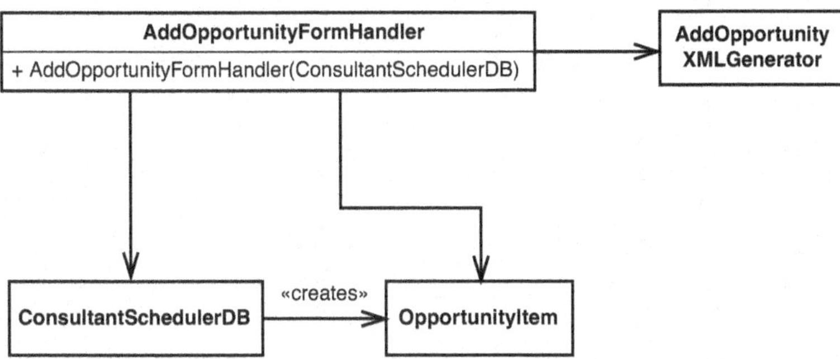

Figure 7.1 *Opportunity handling classes.*

We want to make some changes to the `AddOpportunityFormHandler` class, but it would be nice if we could make our build faster, too. The first step is to try to instantiate an `AddOpportunityFormHandler`. Unfortunately, all of the classes it depends upon are concrete. `AddOpportunityFormHandler` needs a `ConsultantSchedulerDB` and an `AddOpportunityXMLGenerator`. It could very well be the case that both of those classes depend on other classes that aren't in the diagram.

If we attempt to instantiate an `AddOpportunityFormHandler`, who knows how many classes we'll end up using? We can get past this by starting to break dependencies. The first dependency we encounter is `ConsultantSchedulerDB`. We need to create one to pass to the `AddOpportunityFormHandler` constructor. It would be awkward to use that class because it connects to the database, and we don't want to do that during testing. However, we could use *Extract Implementer (356)* and break the dependency as shown in Figure 7.2.

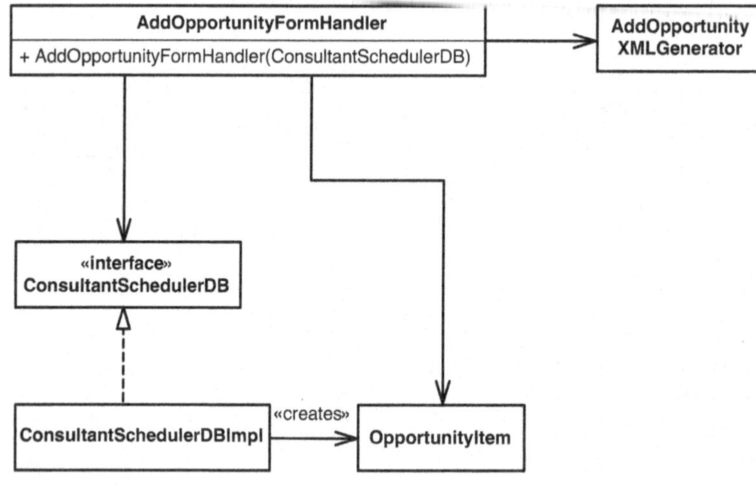

Figure 7.2 *Extracting an implementer on* `ConsultantSchedulerDB`.

Now that `ConsultantSchedulerDB` is an interface, we can create an `AddOpportunityFormHandler` using a fake object that implements the `ConsultantSchedulerDB` interface. Interestingly, by breaking that dependency, we've made our build faster under some conditions. The next time that we make a modification to `ConsultantSchedulerDBImpl`, `AddOpportunityFormHandler` doesn't have to recompile. Why? Well, it doesn't directly depend on the code in `ConsultantSchedulerDBImpl` anymore. We can make as many changes as we want to the `ConsultantSchedulerDBImpl` file, but unless we do something that forces us to change the `ConsultantSchedulerDB` interface, we won't have to rebuild the `AddOpportunityFormHandler` class.

If we want, we can isolate ourselves from forced recompilation even further, as shown in Figure 7.3. Here is another design for the system that we arrive at by using *Extract Implementer (356)* on the `OpportunityItem` class.

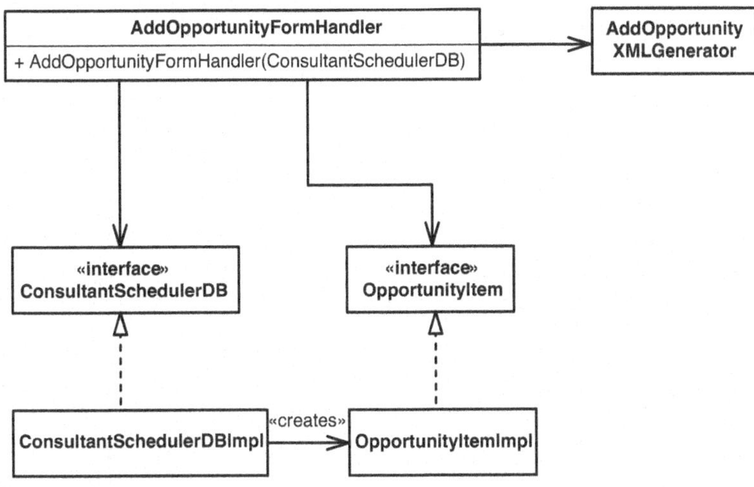

Figure 7.3 *Extracting an implementer on* `OpportunityItem`.

Now `AddOpportunityFormHandler` doesn't depend on the original code in `OpportunityItem` at all. In a way, we've put a "compilation firewall" in the code. We can make as many changes as we want to `ConsultantSchedulerDBImpl` and `OpportunityItemImpl`, but that won't force `AddOpportunityFormHandler` to recompile, and it won't force any users of `AddOpportunityFormHandler` to recompile. If we wanted to make this very explicit in the package structure of the application, we could break up our design into the separate packages shown in Figure 7.4.

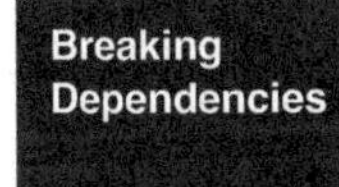

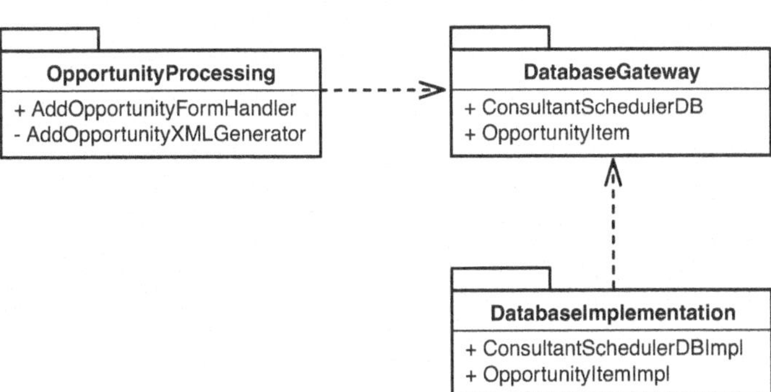

Figure 7.4 *Refactored package structure.*

Now we have a package, `OpportunityProcessing`, that really has no dependencies on the database implementation. Whatever tests we write and place in the package should compile quickly, and the package itself doesn't have to recompile when we change code in the database implementation classes.

The Dependency Inversion Principle

When your code depends on an interface, that dependency is usually very minor and unobtrusive. Your code doesn't have to change unless the interface changes, and interfaces typically change far less often than the code behind them. When you have an interface, you can edit classes that implement that interface or add new classes that implement the interface, all without impacting code that uses the interface.

For this reason, it is better to depend on interfaces or abstract classes than it is to depend on concrete classes. When you depend on less volatile things, you minimize the chance that particular changes will trigger massive recompilation.

So far, we've done a few things to prevent `AddOpportunityFormHandler` from being recompiled when we modify classes it depends upon. That does make builds faster, but it is only half of the issue. We can also make builds faster for code that depends on `AddOpportunityFormHandler`. Let's look at the package design again, in Figure 7.5.

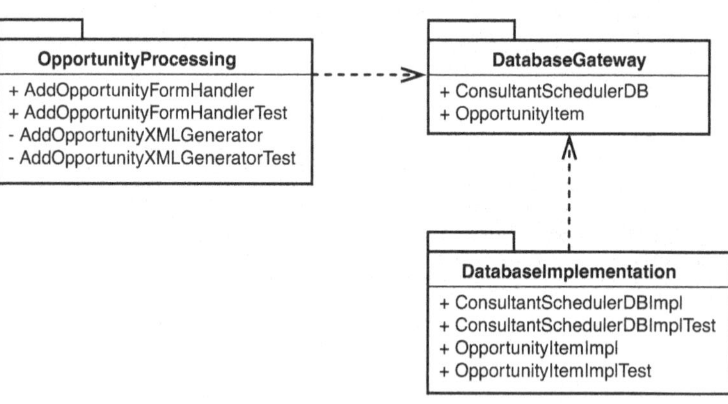

Figure 7.5 *Package structure.*

`AddOpportunityFormHandler` is the only public production (non-test) class in `OpportunityProcessing`. Any classes in other packages that depend on it have to recompile when we change it. We can break that dependency also by using *Extract Interface (362)* or *Extract Implementer (356)* on `AddOpportunityFormHandler`. Then, classes in other packages can depend on the interfaces. When we do that, we've effectively shielded all of the users of this package from recompilation when we make most changes.

We can break dependencies and allocate classes across different packages to make build time faster, and doing it is very worthwhile. When you can rebuild and run your tests very quickly, you can get greater feedback as you develop. In most cases, that means fewer errors and less aggravation. But it isn't free. There is some conceptual overhead in having more interfaces and packages. Is that a fair price to pay compared to the alternative? Yes. At times, it can take a little longer to find things when you have more packages and interfaces, but when you do, you can work with them very easily.

> When you introduce more interfaces and packages into your design to break dependencies, the amount of time it takes to rebuild the entire system goes up slightly. There are more files to compile. But the average time for a make, a build based on what *needs* to be recompiled, can go down dramatically.

When you start to optimize your average build time, you end up with areas of code that are very easy to work with. It might be a bit of a pain to get a small set of classes compiling separately and under test, but the important thing to remember is that you have to do it only once for that set of classes; afterward, you get to reap the benefits forever.

Summary

The techniques I've shown in this chapter can be used to speed up build time for small clusters of classes, but this is only a small portion of what you can do using interfaces and packages to manage dependencies. Robert C. Martin's book *Agile Software Development: Principles, Patterns, and Practices* (Pearson Education, 2002) presents more techniques along these lines that every software developer should know.

Chapter 8

How Do I Add a Feature?

This has to be the most abstract and problem-domain-specific question in the book. I almost didn't add it because of that. But the fact is, regardless of our design approach or the particular constraints we face, there are some techniques that we can use to make the job easier.

Let's talk about context. In legacy code, one of the most important considerations is that we don't have tests around much of our code. Worse, getting them in place can be difficult. People on many teams are tempted to fall back on the techniques in Chapter 6, *I Don't Have Much Time and I Have to Change It*, because of this. We can use the techniques described there (sprouting and wrapping) to add to code without tests, but there are some hazards aside from the obvious ones. For one thing, when we sprout or wrap, we don't significantly modify the existing code, so it isn't going to get any better for a while. Duplication is another hazard. If the code that we add duplicates code that exists in the untested areas, it might just lie there and fester. Worse, we might not realize that we are going to have duplication until we get far along making our changes. The last hazards are fear and resignation: fear that we can't change a particular piece of code and make it easier to work with, and resignation because whole areas of the code just aren't getting any better. Fear gets in the way of good decision making. The sprouts and wraps left in the code are little reminders of it.

In general, it's better to confront the beast than hide from it. If we can get code under test, we can use the techniques in this chapter to move forward in a good way. If you need to find ways to get tests in place, look at Chapter 13, *I Need to Make a Change, but I Don't Know What Tests to Write*. If dependencies are getting in your way, look at Chapter 9, *I Can't Get This Class into a Test Harness*, and Chapter 10, *I Can't Run This Method in a Test Harness*.

Once we have tests in place, we are in a better position to add new features. We have a solid foundation.

Test-Driven Development (TDD)

The most powerful feature-addition technique I know of is test-driven development (TDD). In a nutshell, it works like this: We imagine a method that will help us solve some part of a problem, and then we write a failing test case for it. The method doesn't exist yet, but if we can write a test for it, we've solidified our understanding of what the code we are about to write should do.

Test-driven development uses a little algorithm that goes like this:

1. Write a failing test case.
2. Get it to compile.
3. Make it pass.
4. Remove duplication.
5. Repeat.

Here is an example. We're working on a financial application, and we need a class that is going to use some high-powered mathematics to verify whether certain commodities should be traded. We need a Java class that calculates something called the first statistical moment about a point. We don't have a method that does that yet, but we do know that we can write a test case for the method. We know the math, so we know that the answer should be `-0.5` for the data we code in the test.

Write a Failing Test Case

Here is a test case for the functionality we need.

```
public void testFirstMoment() {
    InstrumentCalculator calculator = new InstrumentCalculator();
    calculator.addElement(1.0);
    calculator.addElement(2.0);

    assertEquals(-0.5, calculator.firstMomentAbout(2.0), TOLERANCE);
}
```

Get It to Compile

The test we just wrote is nice, but it doesn't compile. We don't have a method named `firstMomentAbout` on `InstrumentCalculator`. But we add it as an empty method. We want the test to fail, so we have it return the double value `NaN` (which definitely is not the expected value of `-0.5`).

```
public class InstrumentCalculator
{
    double firstMomentAbout(double point) {
        return Double.NaN;
    }
    ...
}
```

Make It Pass

With that test in place, we write the code that makes it pass.

```
public double firstMomentAbout(double point) {
    double numerator = 0.0;
    for (Iterator it = elements.iterator(); it.hasNext(); ) {
        double element = ((Double)(it.next())).doubleValue();
        numerator += element - point;
    }
    return numerator / elements.size();
}
```

This is an abnormally large amount of code to write in response to a test in TDD. Typically, steps are much smaller, although they can be this large if you are certain of the algorithm you need to use.

Remove Duplication

Do we have any duplication here? Not really. We can go on to the next case.

Write a Failing Test Case

The code we just wrote makes the test pass, but it definitely won't be good for all cases. In the return statement, we could accidentally divide by 0. What should we do in that case? What do we return when we have no elements? In this case, we want to throw an exception. The results will be meaningless for us unless we have data in our elements list.

This next test is special. It fails if an `InvalidBasisException` isn't thrown, and it passes if no exceptions are thrown or any other exception is thrown. When we run it, it fails because an `ArithmeticException` is thrown when we divide by 0 in `firstMomentAbout`.

```
public void testFirstMoment() {
    try {
        new InstrumentCalculator().firstMomentAbout(0.0);
        fail("expected InvalidBasisException");
    }
```

```
    catch (InvalidBasisException e) {
    }
}
```

Get It to Compile

To do this, we have to alter the declaration of `firstMomentAbout` so that it throws an `InvalidBasisException`.

```
public double firstMomentAbout(double point)
        throws InvalidBasisException {

    double numerator = 0.0;
    for (Iterator it = elements.iterator(); it.hasNext(); ) {
        double element = ((Double)(it.next())).doubleValue();
        numerator += element - point;
    }
    return numerator / elements.size();
}
```

But that doesn't compile. The compiler errors tell us that we have to actually throw the exception if it is listed in the declaration, so we go ahead and write the code.

```
public double firstMomentAbout(double point)
            throws InvalidBasisException  {

    if (elements.size() == 0)
        throw new InvalidBasisException("no elements");

    double numerator = 0.0;
    for (Iterator it = elements.iterator(); it.hasNext(); ) {
        double element = ((Double)(it.next())).doubleValue();
        numerator += element - point;
    }
    return numerator / elements.size();
}
```


Make It Pass

Now our tests pass.

Remove Duplication

There isn't any duplication in this case.

Write a Failing Test Case

The next piece of code that we have to write is a method that calculates the second statistical moment about a point. Actually, it is just a variation of the first. Here is a test that moves us toward writing that code. In this case, the expected value is `0.5` rather than `-0.5`. We write a new test for a method that doesn't exist yet: `secondMomentAbout`.

```
public void testSecondMoment() throws Exception {
    InstrumentCalculator calculator = new InstrumentCalculator();
    calculator.addElement(1.0);
    calculator.addElement(2.0);

    assertEquals(0.5, calculator.secondMomentAbout(2.0), TOLERANCE);
}
```

Get It to Compile

To get it to compile, we have to add a definition for `secondMomentAbout`. We can use the same trick we used for the `firstMomentAbout` method, but it turns out that the code for the second moment is only a slight variation of the code for the first moment.

This line in `firstMoment`:

```
numerator += element - point;
```

has to become this in the case of the second moment:

```
numerator += Math.pow(element - point, 2.0);
```

And there is a general pattern for this sort of thing. The *n*th statistic moment is calculated using this expression:

```
numerator += Math.pow(element - point, N);
```

The code in `firstMomentAbout` works because `element - point` is the same as `Math.pow(element - point, 1.0)`.

At this point, we have a couple of choices. We can notice the generality and write a general method that accepts an "about" point and a value for `N`. Then we can replace every use of `firstMomentAbout(double)` with a call to that general method. We can do that, but it would burden the callers with the need to supply an `N` value, and we don't want to allow clients to supply an arbitrary value for `N`. It seems like we are getting lost in thought here. We should put this on hold and finish what we've started so far. Our only job right now is to make it compile. We can generalize later if we find that we still want to.

To make it compile, we can make a copy of the `firstMomentAbout` method and rename it so that it is now called `secondMomentAbout`:

```
public double secondMomentAbout(double point)
        throws InvalidBasisException {

    if (elements.size() == 0)
        throw new InvalidBasisException("no elements");

    double numerator = 0.0;
    for (Iterator it = elements.iterator(); it.hasNext(); ) {
        double element = ((Double)(it.next())).doubleValue();
        numerator += element - point;
    }
    return numerator / elements.size();
}
```

Make It Pass

This code fails the test. When it fails, we can go back and make it pass by changing the code to this:

```
public double secondMomentAbout(double point)
        throws InvalidBasisException {

    if (elements.size() == 0)
        throw new InvalidBasisException("no elements");

    double numerator = 0.0;
    for (Iterator it = elements.iterator(); it.hasNext(); ) {
        double element = ((Double)(it.next())).doubleValue();
        numerator += Math.pow(element - point, 2.0);
    }
    return numerator / elements.size();
}
```

Test-Driven Development (TDD)

You might be shocked by the cut/copy/paste we just did, but we're going to remove duplication in a second. This code that we are writing is fresh code. But the trick of just copying the code that we need and modifying it in a new method is pretty powerful in the context of legacy code. Often when we want to add features to particularly awful code, it's easier to understand our modifications if we put them in some new place and can see them side by side with the old code. We can remove duplication later to fold the new code into the class in a nicer way, or we can just get rid of the modification and try it in a different way, knowing that we still have the old code to look at and learn from.

Remove Duplication

Now that we have both tests passing, we have to do the next step: remove duplication. How do we do it?

One way to do it is to extract the entire body of secondMomentAbout, call it nthMomentAbout and give it a parameter, N:

```
public double secondMomentAbout(double point)
        throws InvalidBasisException {
    return nthMomentAbout(point, 2.0);
}

private double nthMomentAbout(double point, double n)
        throws InvalidBasisException {

    if (elements.size() == 0)
        throw new InvalidBasisException("no elements");

    double numerator = 0.0;
    for (Iterator it = elements.iterator(); it.hasNext(); ) {
        double element = ((Double)(it.next())).doubleValue();
        numerator += Math.pow(element - point, n);
    }
    return numerator / elements.size();
}
```

If we run our tests now, we'll see that they pass. We can go back to firstMomentAbout and replace its body with a call to nthMomentAbout:

```
public double firstMomentAbout(double point)
        throws InvalidBasisException {
    return nthMomentAbout(point, 1.0);
}
```


This final step, removing duplication, is very important. We can quickly and brutally add features to code by copying whole blocks of code, but if we don't remove the duplication afterward, we are just causing trouble and making a maintenance burden. On the other hand, if we have tests in place, we are able to remove duplication easily. We definitely saw this here, but the only reason we had tests is because we used TDD from the start. In legacy code, the tests that we write around existing code when we use TDD are very important. When we have them in place, we have a free hand to write what-

whatever code we need to add a feature, and we know that we'll be able to fold it into the rest of the code without making things worse.

TDD and Legacy Code

One of the most valuable things about TDD is that it lets us concentrate on one thing at a time. We are either writing code or refactoring; we are never doing both at once.

That separation is particularly valuable in legacy code because it lets us write new code independently of new code.

After we have written some new code, we can refactor to remove any duplication between it and the old code.

For legacy code, we can extend the TDD algorithm this way:

0. *Get the class you want to change under test.*
1. Write a failing test case.
2. Get it to compile.
3. Make it pass. (*Try not to change existing code as you do this.*)
4. Remove duplication.
5. Repeat.

Programming by Difference

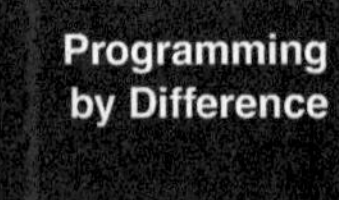

Test-driven development isn't tied to object orientation. In fact, the example in the previous section is really just a piece of procedural code wrapped up in a class. In OO, we have another option. We can use inheritance to introduce features without modifying a class directly. After we've added the feature, we can figure out exactly how we really want the feature integrated.

The key technique for doing this is something called *programming by difference*. It is a rather old technique that was discussed and used quite a bit in the 1980s, but it fell out of favor in the 1990s when many people in the OO community noticed that inheritance can be rather problematic if it is overused. But just because we use inheritance initially doesn't mean that we have to keep it in place. With the help of the tests, we can move easily to other structures if the inheritance becomes problematic.

Here's an example that shows how it works. We have a tested Java class called `MailForwarder` that is part of a Java program that manages mailing lists. It has a method named `getFromAddress`. This is what it looks like:

```
private InternetAddress getFromAddress(Message message)
        throws MessagingException {

    Address [] from = message.getFrom ();
    if (from != null && from.length > 0)
        return new InternetAddress (from [0].toString ());
    return new InternetAddress (getDefaultFrom());
}
```

The purpose of this method is to strip out the "from" address of a received mail message and return it so that it can be used as the "from" address of the message that is forwarded to list recipients.

It's used in only one place, these lines in a method named forwardMessage:

```
MimeMessage forward = new MimeMessage (session);
forward.setFrom (getFromAddress (message));
```

Now, what do we need to do if we have a new requirement? What if we need to support mailing lists that are anonymous? Members of these lists can post, but the "from" address of their messages should be set to a particular e-mail address based upon the value of domain (an instance variable of the MessageFowarder class). Here is a failing test case for that change (when the test executes, the expectedMessage variable is set to the message that the MessageFowarder forwards):

```
public void testAnonymous () throws Exception  {
    MessageForwarder forwarder = new MessageForwarder();
    forwarder.forwardMessage (makeFakeMessage());
    assertEquals ("anon-members@" + forwarder.getDomain(),
        expectedMessage.getFrom ()[0].toString());
}
```

Do we have to modify MessageForwarder to add this functionality? Not really—we could just subclass MessageForwarder and make a class called AnonymousMessageForwarder. We can use it in the test instead.

Programming by Difference

```
public void testAnonymous () throws Exception  {
    MessageForwarder forwarder = new AnonymousMessageForwarder();
    forwarder.forwardMessage (makeFakeMessage());
    assertEquals ("anon-members@" + forwarder.getDomain(),
        expectedMessage.getFrom ()[0].toString());
}
```

Then we subclass (see Figure 8.1).

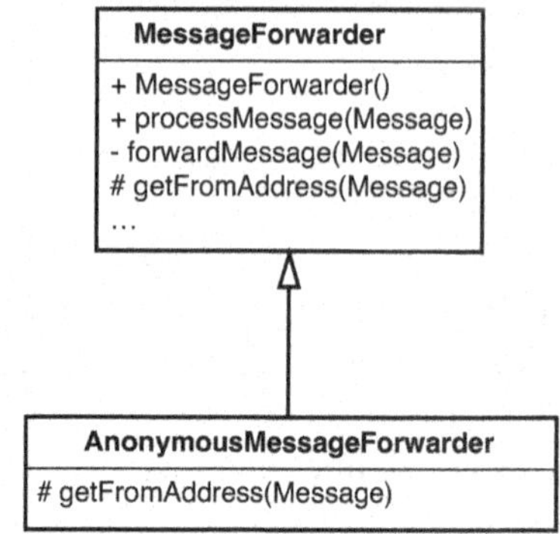

Figure 8.1 *Subclassing* `MessageForwarder`.

Here we've made the `getFromAddress` method protected in `MessageForwarder` rather than private. Then we overrode it in `AnonymousMessageForwarder`. In that class, it looks like this:

```
protected InternetAddress getFromAddress(Message message)
        throws MessagingException {
    String anonymousAddress = "anon-" + listAddress;
    return new InternetAddress(anonymousAddress);
}
```

Programming by Difference

What does that get us? Well, we've solved the problem, but we've added a new class to our system for some very simple behavior. Does it make sense to subclass a whole message-forwarding class just to change its "from" address? Not in the long term, but the thing that is nice is that it allows us to pass our test quickly. And when we have that test passing, we can use it to make sure that we preserve this new behavior when we decide that we want to change the design.

```
public void testAnonymous () throws Exception  {
    MessageForwarder forwarder = new AnonymousMessageForwarder();
    forwarder.forwardMessage (makeFakeMessage());
    assertEquals ("anon-members@" + forwarder.getDomain(),
        expectedMessage.getFrom ()[0].toString());
}
```

That almost seemed too easy. What's the catch? Well, here it is: If we use this technique repeatedly and we don't pay attention to some key aspects of our design, it starts to degrade rapidly. To see what can happen, let's consider another change. We want to forward messages to the mailing list recipients, but we also want to send them via blind carbon copy (bcc) to some other people who can't be on the official mailing list. We can call them off-list recipients.

It looks easy enough; we could subclass `MessageForwarder` again and override its process method so that it sends messages to that destination, as in Figure 8.2.

That could work fine except for one thing. What if we need a `MessageForwarder` that does both things: send all messages to off-list recipients and do all forwarding anonymously?

This is one of the big problems with using inheritance extensively. If we put features into distinct subclasses, we can only have one of those features at a time.

How can we get out of this bind? One way is to stop before adding the off-list recipients feature and refactor so that it can go in cleanly. Luckily, we have that test in place that we wrote earlier. We can use it to verify that we preserve behavior as we move to another scheme.

For the anonymous forwarding feature, there is a way that we could've implemented it without subclassing. We could have chosen to make anonymous forwarding a configuration option. One way of doing this is to change the constructor of the class so that it accepts a collection of properties:

```
Properties configuration = new Properties();
configuration.setProperty("anonymous", "true");
MessageForwarder forwarder = new MessageForwarder(configuration);
```

Can we make our test pass when we do that? Let's look at the test again:

```
public void testAnonymous () throws Exception  {
    MessageForwarder forwarder = new AnonymousMessageForwarder();
   forwarder.forwardMessage (makeFakeMessage());
```


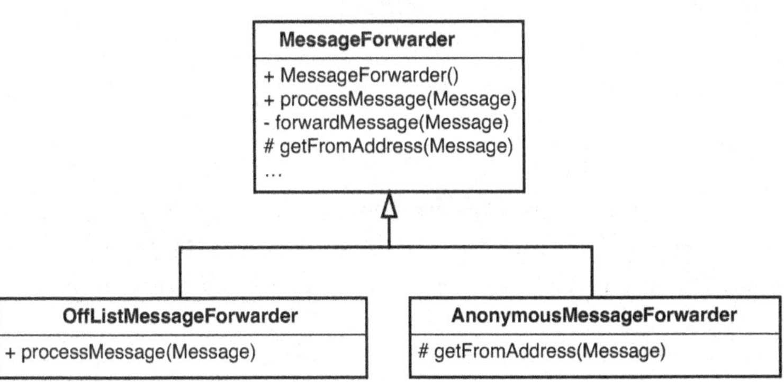

Figure 8.2 *Subclassing for two differences.*

```
    assertEquals ("anon-members@" + forwarder.getDomain(),
        expectedMessage.getFrom ()[0].toString());
}
```

Currently, this test passes. AnonymousMessageForwarder overrides the getFrom method from MessageForwarder. What if we alter the getFrom method in MessageForwarder like this?

```
private InternetAddress getFromAddress(Message message)
        throws MessagingException {

    String fromAddress = getDefaultFrom();
    if (configuration.getProperty("anonymous").equals("true")) {
        fromAddress = "anon-members@" + domain;
    }
    else {
        Address [] from = message.getFrom ();
        if (from != null && from.length > 0) {
            fromAddress = from [0].toString ();
        }
    }
    return new InternetAddress (fromAddress);
}
```

Now we have a getFrom method in MessageFowarder that should be able to handle the anonymous case and the regular case. We can verify this by commenting out the override of getFrom in AnonymousMessageForwarder and seeing if the tests pass:

```
public class AnonymousMessageForwarder extends MessageForwarder
{
/*
    protected InternetAddress getFromAddress(Message message)
            throws MessagingException {
        String anonymousAddress = "anon-" + listAddress;
        return new InternetAddress(anonymousAddress);
    }
*/
}
```

Programming by Difference

Sure enough, they do.

We don't need the AnonymousMessageForwarder class any longer, so we can delete it. Then we have to find each place that we create an AnonymousMessageForwarder and replace its constructor call with a call to the constructor that accepts a properties collection.

We can use the properties collection to add the new feature also. We can have a property that enables the off-list recipient feature.

Are we done? Not really. We've made the getFrom method on Message-Forwarder a little messy, but because we have tests, we can very quickly do an extract method to clean it up a little. Right now it looks like this:

```
private InternetAddress getFromAddress(Message message)
        throws MessagingException {

    String fromAddress  = getDefaultFrom();
    if (configuration.getProperty("anonymous").equals("true")) {
        fromAddress = "anon-members@" + domain;
    }
    else {
        Address [] from = message.getFrom ();
        if (from != null && from.length > 0)
        fromAddress = from [0].toString ();
    }
    return new InternetAddress (fromAddress);
}
```

After some refactoring, it looks like this:

```
private InternetAddress getFromAddress(Message message)
        throws MessagingException {

    String fromAddress  = getDefaultFrom();
    if (configuration.getProperty("anonymous").equals("true")) {
        from  = getAnonymousFrom();
    }
    else {
        from = getFrom(Message);
    }
    return new InternetAddress (from);
}
```


That's a little cleaner but the anonymous mailing and off-list recipient features are folded into the MessageForwarder now. Is this bad in light of the *Single Responsibility Principle (246)*? It can be. It depends on how large the code related to a responsibility gets and how tangled it is with the rest of the code. In this case, determining whether the list is anonymous isn't that big of a deal. The property approach allows us to move on in a nice way. What can we do when there are many properties and the code of the MessageForwarder starts to get littered with conditional statements? One thing we can do is start to use a class rather than a properties collection. What if we created a class called MailingConfiguration and let it hold the properties collection? (See Figure 8.3.)

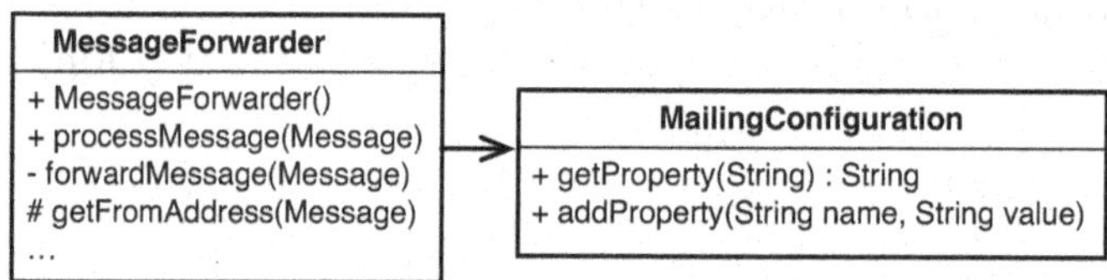

Figure 8.3 *Delegating to* `MailingConfiguration`.

Looks nice, but isn't this overkill? It looks like the `MailingConfiguration` just does the same things that a properties collection does.

What if we decided to move `getFromAddress` to the `MailingConfiguration` class? The `MailingConfiguration` class could accept a message and decide what "from" address to return. If the configuration is set up for anonymity, it would return the anonymous mailing "from" address. If it isn't, it could take the first address from the message and return it. Our design would be as it appears in Figure 8.4. Notice that we don't have to have method to get and set properties any longer. `MailingConfiguration` now supports higher-level functionality.

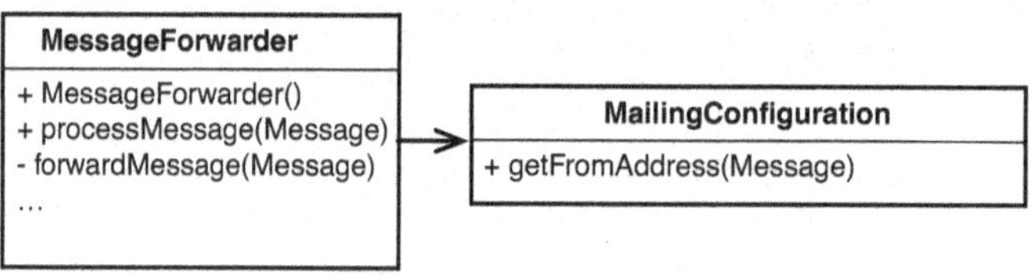

Figure 8.4 *Moving behavior to* `MailingConfiguration`.

We could also start to add other methods to `MailingConfiguration`. For instance, if we want to implement that off-list recipients feature, we can add a method named `buildRecipientList` on the `MailingConfiguration` and let the `MessageForwarder` use it, as shown in Figure 8.5.

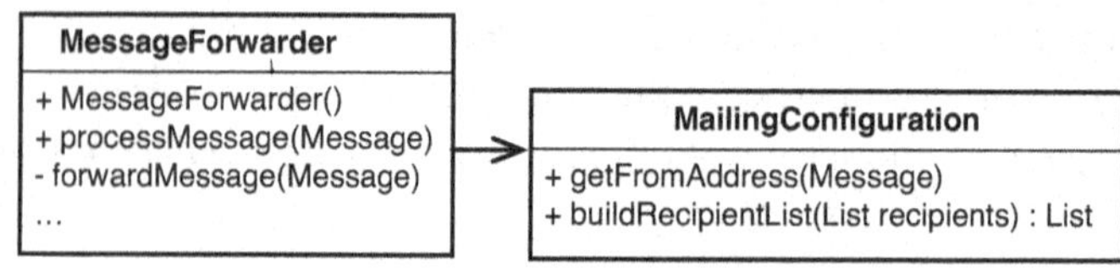

Figure 8.5 *Moving more behavior to* `MailingConfiguration`.

With these changes, the name of the class isn't as nice as it was. A configuration is usually a rather passive thing. This class actively builds and modifies data for MessageFowarders at their request. If there isn't another class with the same name in the system already, the name MailingList might be a good fit. MessageForwarders ask mailing lists to calculate from addresses and build recipient lists. We can say that it is the responsibility of a mailing list to determine how messages are altered. Figure 8.6 shows our design after the renaming.

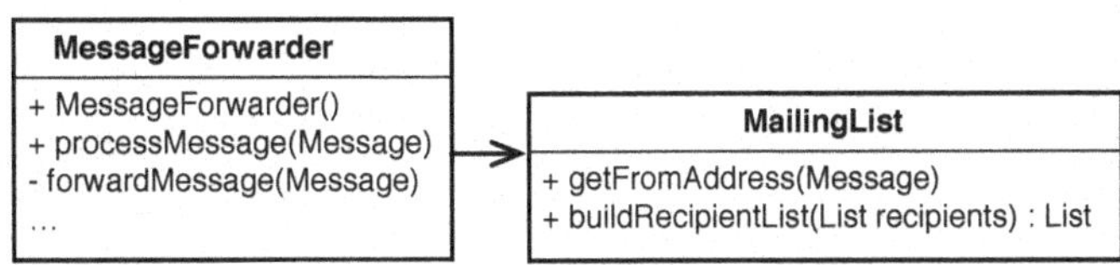

Figure 8.6 MailingConfiguration *renamed as* MailingList.

There are many powerful refactorings, but Rename Class is the most powerful. It changes the way people see code and lets them notice possibilities that they might not have considered before.

Programming by Difference is a useful technique. It allows us to make changes quickly, and we can use tests to move to a cleaner design. But to do it well, we have to look out for a couple of "gotchas." One of them is *Liskov substitution principle (LSP)* violation.

Programming by Difference

The Liskov Substitution Principle

There are some subtle errors that we can cause when we use inheritance. Consider the following code:

```
public class Rectangle
{
    ...
    public Rectangle(int x, int y, int width, int height) { ... }
    public void setWidth(int width) { ... }
    public void setHeight(int height) { ... }
    public int getArea() { ... }
}
```

We have a Rectangle class. Can we create a subclass named Square?

(continues)

```
public class Square extends Rectangle
{
    ...
    public Square(int x, int y, int width) { ... }
    ...
}
```

Square inherits the setWidth and setHeight methods of Rectangle. What should the area be when we execute this code?

```
Rectangle r = new Square();
r.setWidth(3);
r.setHeight(4);
```

If the area is 12, the Square really isn't a square is it? We could override setWidth and setHeight so that they can keep the Square "square". We could have setWidth and setHeight both modify the width variable in squares, but that could lead to some counterintuitive results. Anyone who expects that all rectangles will have an area of 12 when their width is set to 3 and their height is set to 4 is in for a surprise. They'd get 16 instead.

This is a classic example of a Liskov Substitution Principle (LSP) violation. Objects of subclasses should be substitutable for objects of their superclasses throughout our code. If they aren't we could have silent errors in our code.

The LSP implies that clients of a class should be able to use objects of a subclass without having to know that they are objects of a subclass. There aren't any mechanical ways to completely avoid LSP violations. Whether a class is LSP conformant depends upon the clients that it has and what they expect. However, some rules of thumb help:

Programming by Difference

1. Whenever possible, avoid overriding concrete methods.
2. If you do, see if you can call the method you are overriding in the overriding method.

Wait, we didn't do those things in the MessageForwarder. In fact, we did the opposite. We overrode a concrete method in a subclass (AnonymousMessageForwarder). What's the big deal?

Here's the issue: When we override concrete methods as we did when we overrode the getFromAddress of MessageForwarder in AnonymousMessageForwarder, we could be changing the behavior of some of the code that uses MessageFowarders. If there are references to MessageForwarder scattered throughout our application and we set one of them to an AnonymousMessageForwarder, people who are using it might think that it is a simple MessageFowarder and that it gets the "from" address from the message it's processing and uses it when it processes messages. Would it matter to people who use this class whether it does that or uses another special address as the "from" address? That depends on the application. In general, code gets confusing when we override concrete methods too often. Someone can notice a `MessageForwarder` reference in code, take a look at the `MessageFowarder` class, and think that the code it has for `getFromAddress` is executed. They might have no idea that the reference is pointing to an `AnonymousMessageForwarder` and that its `getFromAddress` method is the one that is used. If we really wanted to keep the inheritance around, we could have made `MessageForwarder` abstract, given it an abstract method for `getFromAddress`, and let the subclasses provide concrete bodies. Figure 8.7 shows what the design would look like after these changes.

I call this sort of hierarchy a *normalized hierarchy.* In a normalized hierarchy, no class has more than one implementation of a method. In other words, none of the classes has a method that overrides a concrete method it inherited from a superclass. When you ask the question "How does this class do X?" you can answer it by going to class X and looking. Either the method is there or it is abstract and implemented in one of the subclasses. In a normalized hierarchy you don't have to worry about subclasses overriding behavior they inherited from their superclasses.

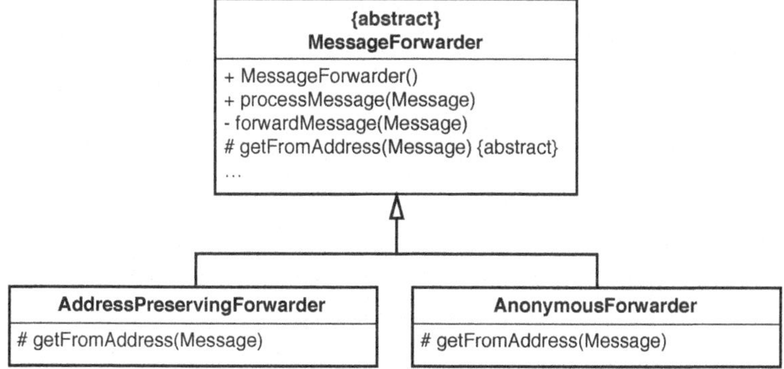

Figure 8.7 *Normalized hierarchy.*

Is it worth doing this all of the time? A few concrete overrides every once in a while don't hurt, as long as it doesn't cause a *Liskov substitution principle* violation. However, it's good to think about how far classes are from normalized form every once in a while and at times to move toward it when we prepare to separate out responsibilities.

Programming by Difference lets us introduce variations quickly in systems. When we do, we can use our tests to pin down the new behavior and move to more appropriate structures when we need to. Tests can make the move very rapid.

Summary

You can use the techniques in this chapter to add features to any code that you can get under test. The literature on *test-driven development* has grown in recent years. In particular, I recommend Kent Beck's book *Test-Driven Development by Example* (Addison-Wesley, 2002), and Dave Astel's *Test-Driven Development: A Practical Guide* (Prentice Hall Professional Technical Reference, 2003).

Chapter 9

I Can't Get This Class into a Test Harness

This is the hard one. If it were always easy to instantiate a class in a test harness, this book would be a lot shorter. Unfortunately, it's often hard to do.

Here are the four most common problems we encounter:

1. Objects of the class can't be created easily.
2. The test harness won't easily build with the class in it.
3. The constructor we need to use has bad side effects.
4. Significant work happens in the constructor, and we need to sense it.

In this chapter, we go through a series of examples that highlight these problems in different languages. There is more than one way to tackle each of these problems. However, reading through these examples is a great way of becoming familiar with the arsenal of dependency breaking techniques and learning how to trade them off and apply them in particular situations.

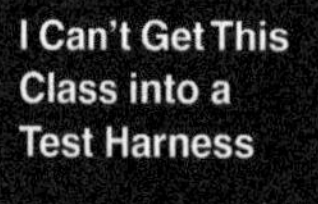

The Case of the Irritating Parameter

When I need to make a change in a legacy system, I usually start out buoyantly optimistic. I don't know why I do. I try to be a realist as much as I can, but the optimism is always there. "Hey," I say to myself (or a partner), "this sounds like it will be easy. We just have to make the `Floogle` `flumoux` a bit, and then we'll be done." It all sounds so easy in words until we get to the `Floogle` class (whatever that is) and look at it a bit. "Okay, so we need to add a method here, and change this other method, and, of course we'll need to get it in a testing harness." At this point, I start to doubt a little. "Gee, it looks like the simplest constructor on this class accepts three parameters. But," I say optimistically, "maybe it won't be too hard to construct it."

Let's take a look at an example and see whether my optimism is appropriate or just a defense mechanism.

In the code for a billing system, we have an untested Java class named `CreditValidator`.

```
public class CreditValidator
{
    public CreditValidator(RGHConnection connection,
                           CreditMaster master,
                           String validatorID) {
        ...
    }

    Certificate validateCustomer(Customer customer)
            throws InvalidCredit {
        ...
    }

    ...
}
```


One of the many responsibilities of this class is to tell us whether customers have valid credit. If they do, we get back a certificate that tells us how much credit they have. If they don't, the class throws an exception.

Our mission, should we choose to accept it, it is to add a new method to this class. The method will be named `getValidationPercent`, and its job will be to tell us the percentage of successful `validateCustomer` calls we've made over the life of the `validator`.

How do we get started?

When we need to create an object in a test harness, often the best approach is to just try to do it. We could do a lot of analysis to find out why it would or would not be easy or hard, but it is just as easy to create a JUnit test class, type this into it, and compile the code:

```
public void testCreate() {
    CreditValidator validator = new CreditValidator();
}
```

The best way to see if you will have trouble instantiating a class in a test harness is to just try to do it. Write a test case and attempt to create an object in it. The compiler will tell you what you need to make it really work.

This test is a construction test. Construction tests do look a little weird. When I write one, I usually don't put an assertion in it. I just try to create the object. Later, when I'm finally able to construct an object in the test harness, I usually get rid of the test or rename it so that I can use it to test something more substantial.

Back to our example:

We haven't added any of the arguments to the constructor yet, so the compiler complains. It tells us that there is no default constructor for `CreditValidator`. Hunting through the code, we discover that we need an `RGHConnection`, a `CreditMaster`, and a password. Each of these classes has only one constructor. This is what they look like:

```
public class RGHConnection
{
    public RGHConnection(int port, String Name, string passwd)
            throws IOException {
        ...
    }
}

public class CreditMaster
{
    public CreditMaster(String filename, boolean isLocal) {
        ...
    }
}
```


When an `RGHConnection` is constructed, it connects with a server. The connection uses that server to get all of the reports it needs to validate a customer's credit.

The other class, `CreditMaster`, gives us some policy information that we use in our credit decisions. On construction, a `CreditMaster` loads the information from a file and holds it in memory for us.

So, it does seem pretty easy to get this class in a testing harness, right? Not so fast. We can write the test, but can we live with it?

```
public void testCreate() throws Exception {
    RGHConnection connection = new RGHConnection(DEFAULT_PORT,
                                              "admin", "rii8ii9s");
    CreditMaster master = new CreditMaster("crm2.mas", true);
    CreditValidator validator = new CreditValidator(
                                        connection, master, "a");
}
```

It turns out that establishing RGHConnections to the server in a test is not a good idea. It takes a long time, and the server isn't always up. On the other hand, the CreditMaster is not really a problem. When we create a CreditMaster, it loads its file quickly. In addition, the file is read-only, so we don't have to worry about our tests corrupting it.

The thing that is really getting in our way when we want to create the validator is the RGHConnection. It is an *irritating parameter.* If we can create some sort of a fake RGHConnection object and make CreditValidator believe that it's talking to a real one, we can avoid all sorts of connection trouble. Let's take a look at the methods that RGHConnection provides (see Figure 9.1).

It looks like RGHConnection has a set of methods that deal with the mechanics of forming a connection: connect, disconnect, and retry, as well as more business-specific methods such as RFDIReportFor and ACTIOReportFor. When we write our new method on CreditValidator, we are going to have to call RFDIReportFor to get all of the information that we need. Normally, all of that information comes from the server, but because we want to avoid using a real connection, we'll have to supply it ourselves using a fake object.

In this case, the best way to make a fake object is to use *Extract Interface (362)* on the RGHConnection class. If you have a tool with refactoring support, chances are good that it supports *Extract Interface.* If you don't have a tool that supports *Extract Interface*, remember that it is easy enough to do by hand.

RGHConnection
+ RGHConnection(port, name, password) + connect() + disconnect() + RFDIReportFor(id : int) : RFDIReport + ACTIOReportFor(customerID : int) : ACTIOReport - retry() - formPacket() : RFPacket

Figure 9.1 RGHConnection.

After we do *Extract Interface (362)*, we end up with a structure like the one shown in Figure 9.2.

We can start to write tests by creating a little fake class that provides the reports that we need:

```
public class FakeConnection implements IRGHConnection
{
    public RFDIReport report;

    public void connect() {}
    public void disconnect() {}
    public RFDIReport RFDIReportFor(int id) { return report; }
    public ACTIOReport ACTIOReportFor(int customerID) { return null; }
}
```

With that class, we can start to write tests like this:

```
void testNoSuccess() throws Exception {
    CreditMaster master = new CreditMaster("crm2.mas", true);
    IRGHConnection connection = new FakeConnection();
    CreditValidator validator = new CreditValidator(
                                    connection, master, "a");
    connection.report  = new RFDIReport(...);

    Certificate result = validator.validateCustomer(new Customer(...));

    assertEquals(Certificate.VALID, result.getStatus());
}
```

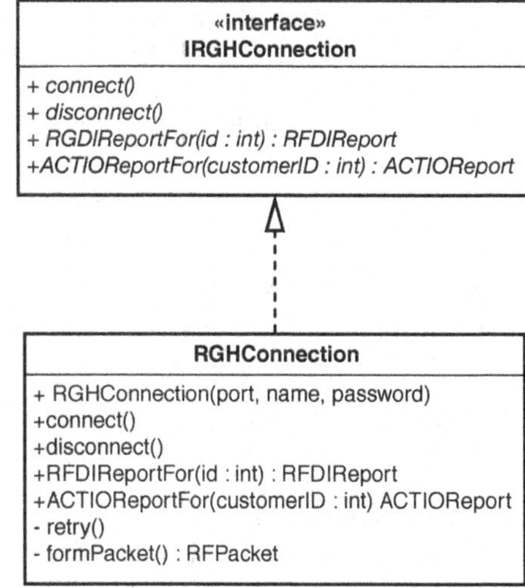

Figure 9.2 `RGHConnection` *after extracting an interface*

The FakeConnection class is a little weird. How often do we ever write methods that don't have any bodies or that just return null to callers? Worse, it has a public variable that anyone can set whenever they want to. It seems like the class violates all of the rules. Well, it doesn't really. The rules are different for classes that we use to make testing possible. The code in FakeConnection isn't production code. It won't ever run in our full working application—just in the test harness.

Now that we can create a validator, we can write our getValidationPercent method. Here is a test for it.

```
void testAllPassed100Percent() throws Exception {
    CreditMaster master = new CreditMaster("crm2.mas", true);
    IRGHConnection connection = new FakeConnection("admin", "rii8ii9s");
    CreditValidator validator = new CreditValidator(
                                    connection, master, "a");

    connection.report  = new RFDIReport(...);
    Certificate result = validator.validateCustomer(new Customer(...));
    assertEquals(100.0, validator.getValidationPercent(), THRESHOLD);
}
```

Test Code vs. Production Code

Test code doesn't have to live up to the same standards as production code. In general, I don't mind breaking encapsulation by making variables public if it makes it easier to write tests. However, test code should be clean. It should be easy to understand and change.

Take a look at the testNoSuccess and testAllPassed100Percent tests in the example. Do they have any duplicate code? Yes. The first three lines are duplicated. They should be extracted and placed in a common place, the setUp() method for this test class.

The test checks to see if the validation percent is roughly 100.0 when we get a single valid credit certificate.

The Case of the Irritating Parameter

The test works fine, but as we write the code for getValidationPercent, we notice something interesting. It turns out that getValidationPercent isn't going to use the CreditMaster at all, so why are we making one and passing it into the CreditValidator? Maybe we don't need to. We could create the CreditValidator like this in our test:

```
CreditValidator validator = new CreditValidator(connection, null, "a");
```

Are you still there?

The way people react to lines of code like that often says a lot about the kind of system they work on. If you looked at it and said, "Oh, fine, so he's passing a null into the constructor—we do that all the time in our system," chances are, you've got a pretty nasty system on your hands. You probably have checks for null all over the place and a lot of conditional code that you use to figure out what you have and what you can do with it. On the other hand, if you looked at it and said, "What is wrong with this guy?! Passing null around in a system? Doesn't he know anything at all?", well, for those of you in the latter group (at least those who are still reading and haven't slammed the book shut in the bookstore), I just have this to say: Remember, we're only doing this in the tests. The worst that can happen is that some code will attempt to use the variable. In that case, the Java runtime will throw an exception. Because the harness catches all exceptions thrown in tests, we'll find out pretty quickly whether the parameter is being used at all.

Pass Null

When you are writing tests and an object requires a parameter that is hard to construct, consider just passing null instead. If the parameter is used in the course of your test execution, the code will throw an exception and the test harness will catch the exception. If you need behavior that really requires an object, you can construct it and pass it as a parameter at that point.

Pass Null is a very handy technique in some languages. It works well in Java and C# and in just about every language that throws an exception when null references are used at runtime. This implies that it really isn't a great idea to do this in C and C++ unless you know that the runtime will detect null pointer errors. If it doesn't, you'll just end up with tests that will crash mysteriously, if you are lucky. If you are unlucky, your tests will just be silently and hopelessly wrong. They will corrupt memory as they run, and you'll never know.

When I work in Java, I often start with a test like this in the beginning and fill in the parameters as I need them.

```
public void testCreate() {
    CreditValidator validator = new CreditValidator(null, null, "a");
}
```

The important thing to remember is this: Don't pass null in production code unless you have no other choice. I know that some libraries out there expect you to, but when you write fresh code there are better alternatives. If you are tempted to use null in production code, find the places where you are returning nulls and passing nulls, and consider a different protocol. Consider using the *Null Object Pattern* instead.

Null Object Pattern

The *Null Object Pattern* is a way of avoiding the use of null in programs. For example, if we have a method that is going to return an employee given an ID, what should we return if there is no employee with that ID?

```
for(Iterator it = idList.iterator(); it.hasNext(); ) {
        EmployeeID id = (EmployeeID)it.next();
        Employee e = finder.getEmployeeForID(id);
        e.pay();
}
```

We have a couple of choices. We could just decide to throw an exception so that we don't have to return anything, but that would force clients to deal with the error explicitly. We could also return null, but then clients would have to check for null explicitly.

There is a third alternative. Does the previous code really care whether there is an employee to pay? Does it have to? What if we had a class called `NullEmployee`? An instance of `NullEmployee` has no name and no address, and when you tell it to pay, it just does nothing.

Null objects can be useful in contexts like this; they can shield clients from explicit error checking. As nice as null objects are, you have to be cautious when you use them. For instance, here is a very bad way of counting the number of paid employees:

```
int employeesPaid = 0;
for(Iterator it = idList.iterator(); it.hasNext(); ) {
   EmployeeID id = (EmployeeID)it.next();
   Employee e = finder.getEmployeeForID(id);
   e.pay();
   employeesPaid++;          // bug!
}
```

If any of the returned employees are null employees, the count will be wrong.

Null objects are useful specifically when a client doesn't have to care whether an operation is successful. In many cases, we can finesse our design so that this is the case.

The Case of the Irritating Parameter

Pass Null and *Extract Interface (362)* are two ways of approaching irritating parameters. But another alternative can be used at times. If the problematic dependency in a parameter isn't hard-coded into its constructor, we can use *Subclass and Override Method (401)* to get rid of the dependency. That could be possible in this case. If the constructor of `RGHConnection` uses its `connect` method to form a connection, we could break the dependency by overriding `connect()` in a testing subclass. *Subclass and Override Method (401)* can be a very useful way of breaking dependencies, but we have to be sure that we aren't altering the behavior we want to test when we use it.

The Case of the Hidden Dependency

Some classes are deceptive. We look at them, we find a constructor that we want to use, and we try to call it. Then, bang! We run into an obstacle. One of the most common obstacles is *hidden dependency*; the constructor uses some resource that we just can't access nicely in our test harness. We run into this situation in this next example, a poorly designed C++ class that manages a mailing list:

```
class mailing_list_dispatcher
{
public:
                    mailing_list_dispatcher ();
    virtual         ~mailing_list_dispatcher;

    void            send_message(const std::string& message);
    void            add_recipient(const mail_txm_id id,
                            const mail_address& address);
    ...

private:
    mail_service    *service;
    int             status;
};
```

Here is part of the constructor of the class. It allocates a `mail_service` object using `new` in the constructor initializer list. That is poor style, and it gets worse. The constructor does a lot of detailed work with the `mail_service`. It also uses a magic number, 12—what does 12 mean?


```
mailing_list_dispatcher::mailing_list_dispatcher()
: service(new mail_service), status(MAIL_OKAY)
{
    const int client_type = 12;
    service->connect();
    if (service->get_status() == MS_AVAILABLE) {
        service->register(this, client_type, MARK_MESSAGES_OFF);
        service->set_param(client_type, ML_NOBOUNCE | ML_REPEATOFF);
    }
    else
        status = MAIL_OFFLINE;
    ...
}
```

We can create an instance of this class in a test, but it's probably not going to do us much good. First of all, we'll have to link to the mail libraries and configure the mail system to handle registrations. And if we use the send_message function in our tests, we'll really be sending mail to people. It will be hard to test that functionality in an automated way unless we set up a special mailbox and connect to it repeatedly, waiting for a mail message to arrive. That could be great as an overall system test, but if all we want to do now is add some new tested functionality to the class, that could be overkill. How can we create an test a simple object so that we can add some new functionality?

The fundamental problem here is that the dependency on mail_service is hidden in the mailing_list_dispatcher constructor. If there was some way to replace the mail_service object with a fake, we could sense through the fake and get some feedback as we change the class.

One of the techniques we can use is *Parameterize Constructor (379)*. With this technique, we externalize a dependency that we have in a constructor by passing it into the constructor.

This is what the constructor code looks like after *Parameterize Constructor (379)*:

```
mailing_list_dispatcher::mailing_list_dispatcher(mail_service *service)
: status(MAIL_OKAY)
{
    const int client_type = 12;
    service->connect();
    if (service->get_status() == MS_AVAILABLE) {
        service->register(this, client_type, MARK_MESSAGES_OFF);
        service->set_param(client_type, ML_NOBOUNCE | ML_REPEATOFF);
    }
    else
        status = MAIL_OFFLINE;
    ...
}
```

The Case of the Hidden Dependency

The only difference, really, is that the mail_service object is created outside the class and passed in. That might not seem like much of an improvement, but it does give us incredible leverage. We can use *Extract Interface (362)* to make an interface for mail_service. One implementer of the interface can be the production class that really sends mail. Another can be a fake class that senses the things that we do to it under test and lets us make sure that they happened.

Parameterize Constructor (379) is a very convenient way to externalize constructor dependencies, but people don't think of it very often. One of the stumbling blocks is that people often assume that all clients of the class will have to be changed to pass the new parameter, but that isn't true. We can handle it like this. First we extract the body of the constructor into a new method that we can call initialize. Unlike most method extractions, this one is pretty safe to attempt without tests because we can *Preserve Signatures (312)* as we do it.

```
void mailing_list_dispatcher::initialize(mail_service *service)
{
    status = MAIL_OKAY;
    const int client_type = 12;
    service.connect();
    if (service->get_status() == MS_AVAILABLE) {
        service->register(this, client_type, MARK_MESSAGES_OFF);
        service->set_param(client_type, ML_NOBOUNCE | ML_REPEATOFF);
    }
    else
        status = MAIL_OFFLINE;
    ...
}

mailing_list_dispatcher::mailing_list_dispatcher(mail_service *service)
{
    initialize(service);
}
```

Now we can supply a constructor that has the original signature. Tests can call the constructor parameterized by mail_service, and clients can call this one. They don't need to know that anything has changed.

```
mailing_list_dispatcher::mailing_list_dispatcher()
{
    initialize(new mail_service);
}
```

This refactoring is even easier in languages such as C# and Java because we can call constructors from other constructors in those languages.

For instance, if we were doing something similar in C#, the resultant code would look like this:


```
public class MailingListDispatcher
{
    public MailingListDispatcher()
    : this(new MailService())
    {}

    public MailingListDispatcher(MailService service) {
        ...
    }
}
```

Dependencies hidden in constructors can be tackled with many techniques. Often we can use *Extract and Override Getter (352)*, *Extract and Override*

Factory Method (350), and *Supersede Instance Variable (404)*, but I like to use *Parameterize Constructor (379)* as often as I can. When an object is created in a constructor and it doesn't have any construction dependencies itself, *Parameterize Constructor* is a very easy technique to apply.

The Case of the Construction Blob

Parameterize Constructor (379) is one of the easiest techniques that we can use to break hidden dependencies in a constructor, and it is the one that I often turn to first. Unfortunately, it isn't always the best choice. If a constructor constructs a large number of objects internally or accesses a large number of globals, we could end up with a very large parameter list. In worse situations, a constructor creates a few objects and then uses them to create other objects, like this:

```
class WatercolorPane
{
public:
    WatercolorPane(Form *border, WashBrush *brush, Pattern *backdrop)
    {
        ...
        anteriorPanel  = new Panel(border);
        anteriorPanel->setBorderColor(brush->getForeColor());
        backgroundPanel = new Panel(border, backdrop);

        cursor = new FocusWidget(brush, backgroundPanel);
        ...
    }
    ...
}
```


If we want to sense through the cursor, we are in trouble. The cursor object is embedded in a blob of object creation. We can try to move all of the code used to create the cursor outside of the class. Then a client can create the cursor and pass it as an argument. But that isn't very safe if we don't have tests in place, and it could be a big burden on clients on this class.

If we have a refactoring tool that safely extracts methods, we can use *Extract and Override Factory Method (350)* on code in a constructor, but that doesn't work in all languages. In Java and C#, we can do it, but C++ doesn't allow calls to virtual functions in constructors to resolve to virtual functions defined in derived classes. And in general, it isn't a good idea. Functions in derived classes often assume that they can use variables from their base class. Until the constructor of the base class is completely finished, there is a chance that an overridden function that it calls can access an uninitialized variable.

Another option is *Supersede Instance Variable (404)*. We write a setter on the class that allows us to swap in another instance after we construct the object.

```
class WatercolorPane
{
public:
    WatercolorPane(Form *border, WashBrush *brush, Pattern *backdrop)
    {
        ...
        anteriorPanel  = new Panel(border);
        anteriorPanel->setBorderColor(brush->getForeColor());
        backgroundPanel = new Panel(border, backdrop);

        cursor = new FocusWidget(brush, backgroundPanel);
        ...
    }

    void supersedeCursor(FocusWidget *newCursor)
    {
        delete cursor;
        cursor = newCursor;
    }
}
```

In C++, we have to be very careful with this refactoring. When we replace an object, we have to get rid of the old one. Often that means that we have to use the delete operator to call its destructor and destroy its memory. When we do that, we have to understand what the destructor does and whether it destroys anything that is passed to the object's constructor. If we are not careful about how we clean up memory, we can introduce some subtle bugs.

In most other languages, *Supersede Instance Variable (404)* is pretty straightforward. Here is the result recoded in Java. We don't have to do anything special to get rid of the object that `cursor` was referring to; the garbage collector will get rid of it eventually. But we should be very careful not to use the superseding method in production code. If the objects that we are superseding manage other resources, we can cause some serious resource problems.


```
void supersedeCursor(FocusWidget newCursor) {
    cursor = newCursor;
}
```

Now that we have a superseding method, we can attempt to create a `FocusWidget` outside the class and then pass it into the object after construction. Because we need to sense, we can use *Extract Interface (362)* or *Extract Implementer (356)* on the `FocusWidget` class and create a fake object to pass in. It will certainly be easier to create than the `FocusWidget` that is created in the constructor.

```
TEST(renderBorder, WatercolorPane)
{
    ...
    TestingFocusWidget *widget = new TestingFocusWidget;
    WatercolorPane pane(form, border, backdrop);

    pane.supersedeCursor(widget);

    LONGS_EQUAL(0, pane.getComponentCount());
}
```

I don't like to use *Supersede Instance Variable (404)* unless I can't avoid it. The potential for resource-management problems is too great. However, I do use it in C++ at times. Often I'd like to use *Extract and Override Factory Method (350)*, and we can't do that in C++ constructors. For that reason, I use *Supersede Instance Variable (404)* occasionally.

The Case of the Irritating Global Dependency

For years in the software industry, people have bemoaned the fact that there aren't more reusable components on the market. It's getting better over time; there are plenty of commercial and open-source frameworks, but in general, many of them are not really things that we use; they are things that use our code. Frameworks often manage the lifecycle of an application, and we write code to fill in the holes. We can see this in all sorts of frameworks, from ASP.NET to Java Struts. Even the xUnit frameworks behave this way. We write test classes; xUnit calls them and displays their results.

Frameworks solve many problems, and they do give us a boost when we start projects, but this isn't the kind of reuse that people really expected early on in software development. Old-style reuse happens when we find some class or set of classes that we want to use in our application and we just do it. We just add them to a project and use them. It would be nice to be able to do this routinely, but frankly, I think we are kidding ourselves even thinking about that sort of reuse if we can't pull a random class out of an average application and compile it independently in a test harness without doing a lot of work (grumble, grumble).

The Case of the Irritating Global Dependency

Many different kinds of dependency can make it hard to create and use classes in a testing framework, but one of the hardest to deal with is global variable usage. In simple cases, we can use *Parameterize Constructor (379)*, *Parameterize Method (383)*, and *Extract and Override Call (348)* to get past these dependencies, but sometimes dependencies on globals are so extensive that it is

easier to deal with the problem at the source. We run into this situation in this next example, a class in a Java application that records building permits for a governmental agency. Here is one of the primary classes:

```
public class Facility
{
    private Permit basePermit;

    public Facility(int facilityCode, String owner, PermitNotice notice)
            throws PermitViolation {

        Permit associatedPermit =
            PermitRepository.getInstance().findAssociatedPermit(notice);

        if (associatedPermit.isValid() && !notice.isValid()) {
            basePermit = associatedPermit;
        }
        else if (!notice.isValid()) {
            Permit permit = new Permit(notice);
            permit.validate();
            basePermit = permit;
        }
        else
            throw new PermitViolation(permit);
    }
    ...
}
```

We want to create a Facility in a test harness, so we start by trying to create an object in the test harness:

```
public void testCreate() {
    PermitNotice notice = new PermitNotice(0, "a");
    Facility facility = new Facility(Facility.RESIDENCE, "b", notice);
}
```

The Case of the Irritating Global Dependency

The test compiles okay, but when we start to write additional tests, we notice a problem. The constructor uses a class named PermitRepository, and it needs to be initialized with a particular set of permits to set up our tests properly. Sneaky, sneaky. Here is the offending statement in the constructor:

```
Permit associatedPermit =
            PermitRepository.getInstance().findAssociatedPermit(notice);
```

We could get past this by parameterizing the constructor, but in this application, this isn't an isolated case. There are 10 other classes that have roughly the same line of code. It sits in constructors, regular methods, and static methods. We can imagine spending a lot of time confronting this problem in the code base.

If you've studied design patterns, you probably recognize this as an example of the *Singleton Design Pattern (372)*. The `getInstance` method of `PermitRepository` is a static method whose job is to return the only instance of `PermitRepository` that can exist in our application. The field that holds that instance is static also, and it lives in the `PermitRepository` class.

In Java, the singleton pattern is one of the mechanisms people use to make global variables. In general, global variables are a bad idea for a couple of reasons. One of them is opacity. When we look at a piece of code, it is nice to be able to know what it can affect. For instance, in Java, when we want to understand how this piece of code can affect things, there are only a couple of places we have to look.

```
Account example = new Account();
example.deposit(1);
int balance = example.getBalance();
```

We know that an account object can affect things that we pass into the `Account` constructor, but we aren't passing anything in. `Account` objects can also affect objects that we pass as parameters to methods, but in this case, we aren't passing anything in that can be changed—it's just an int. Here we are assigning the return value of `getBalance` to a variable, and that is really the only value that should be affected by this set of statements.

When we use global variables, this situation is turned upside down. We can look at the use of a class such as `Account` and not have a clue whether it is accessing or modifying variables declared someplace else in the program. Needless to say, this can make it harder to understand programs.

The tough part in a testing situation is that we have to figure which globals are being used by a class and set them up with the proper state for a test. And we have to do that before each test if the setup is different. It's pretty tedious; I've done it on dozens of systems to get them under test, and it doesn't get any more enjoyable.

The Case of the Irritating Global Dependency

Back to our regularly scheduled example:

`PermitRepository` is a singleton. Because it is, it is particularly hard to fake. The whole idea of the singleton pattern is to make it impossible to create more than one instance of a singleton in an application. That might be fine in production code, but, when testing, each test in a suite of tests should be a mini-application, in a way: It should be totally isolated from the other tests. So, to run code containing singletons in a test harness, we have to relax the singleton property. Here's how we do it.

The first step is to add a new static method to the singleton class. The method allows us to replace the static instance in the singleton. We'll call it `setTestingInstance`.

```
public class PermitRepository
{
    private static PermitRepository instance = null;

    private PermitRepository() {}

    public static void setTestingInstance(PermitRepository newInstance)
    {
        instance = newInstance;
    }

    public static PermitRepository getInstance()
    {
        if (instance == null) {
            instance = new PermitRepository();
        }
        return instance;
    }

    public Permit findAssociatedPermit(PermitNotice notice) {
        ...
    }
    ...
}
```

Now that we have that setter, we can create a testing instance of a `PermitRepository` and set it. We'd like to write code like this in our test setup:

```
public void setUp() {
    PermitRepository repository = new PermitRepository();
    ...
    // add permits to the repository here
    ...
    PermitRepository.setTestingInstance(repository);
}
```

Introduce Static Setter (372) isn't the only way of handling this situation. Here is another approach. We can add a `resetForTesting()` method to the singleton that looks like this:

```
public class PermitRepository
{
    ...
    public void resetForTesting() {
        instance = null;
    }
    ...
}
```

If we call this method in our test `setUp` (and it's a good idea to call it in `tearDown` also), we can create fresh singletons for every test. The singleton will reintialize itself for every test. This scheme works well when the public methods on the singleton allow you to set up the singleton's state every way you need to during testing. If the singleton doesn't have those public methods or uses some external resources that affect its state, *Introduce Static Setter (372)* is the better choice. You can subclass the singleton, override methods to break dependencies, and add public methods to the subclass to set up state properly.

Will that work? Not yet. When people use the *Singleton Design Pattern (372)*, they often make the constructor of the singleton class private, and with good reason. That is the clearest way to make sure that no one outside the class can make another instance of the singleton.

At this point, we have a conflict between two design goals. We want to make sure that we have only one instance of a `PermitRepository` in a system, and we want a system in which the classes are testable independently. Can we have both?

Let's backtrack for a minute. Why do we want only one instance of a class in a system? The answer varies depending on the system, but here are some of the most common answers:

1. **We are modeling the real world, and there is only one of these things in the real world.** Some hardware-control systems are like this. People make a class for each circuit board they need to control; they figure that if there is just one of each, it should be a singleton. The same holds true for databases. There is only one collection of permits in our agency, so the thing that provides access to it should be a singleton.

2. **If two of these things are created, we could have a serious problem.** This often happens, again, in the hardware control domain. Imagine accidentally creating two nuclear control rod controllers and having two different parts of a program operating the same control rods without knowing about each other.

3. **If someone creates two of these things, we'll be using too many resources.** This happens often. The resources can be physical things such as disk space or memory consumption, or they can be abstract things such as the number of software licenses.

Those are the primary reasons why people want to enforce a single instance, but they aren't the primary reasons why people use singletons. Often people create singletons because they want to have a global variable. They feel that it would be too painful to pass the variable around to the places where it is needed.

If we have a singleton for the latter reason, there really isn't any reason to keep the singleton property. We can make the constructor protected, public, or package scope and still have a decent, testable system. In the other cases, it is still worth exploring that alternative. We can introduce other protection if we need to. We could add a check to our build system in which we search through all the source files to make sure that `setTestingInstance` is not called by non-testing code. We can do the same thing with runtime checks. If `setTestingInstance` is called at runtime, we can issue an alarm or suspend the system and wait for operator intervention. The truth is, it wasn't possible to enforce singleton-ness in many pre-OO languages, and people did manage to make many safe systems. In the end, it comes down to responsible design and coding.

If breaking the singleton property isn't a serious problem, we can rely on a team rule. For instance, everyone on the team should understand that we have one instance of the database in the application and that we shouldn't have another.

To relax the singleton property on `PermitRepository`, we can make the constructor public. And that will work fine for us as long as the public methods on `PermitRepository` allow us to do everything that we need to set up a repository for our tests. For example, if `PermitRepository` has a method named `addPermit` that allows us to fill it up with whatever permits we need for our tests, it might be enough to just allow ourselves to make repositories and use them in our tests. At other times, we might not have the access we need, or, worse, the singleton might be doing things that we would not want to have happen in a test harness, such as talk to a database in the background. In these cases, we can *Subclass and Override Method (401)* and make derived classes that make testing easier.

Here is an example in our permit system. In addition to the method and variables that make `PermitRepository` a singleton, we have the following method:

```
public class PermitRepository
{
    ...
    public Permit findAssociatedPermit(PermitNotice notice) {
```

```
            // open permit database
            ...

            // select using values in notice
            ...

            // verify we have only one matching permit, if not report error
            ...

            // return the matching permit
            ...
        }
}
```

If we want to avoid talking to the database, we can subclass PermitRepository like this:

```
public class TestingPermitRepository extends PermitRepository
{
    private Map permits = new HashMap();

    public void addAssociatedPermit(PermitNotice notice, permit) {
        permits.put(notice, permit);
    }

    public Permit findAssociatedPermit(PermitNotice notice) {
        return (Permit)permits.get(notice);
    }
}
```

When we do this, we can preserve part of the singleton property. Because we are using a subclass of PermitRepository, we can make the constructor of PermitRepository protected rather than public. That will prevent the creation of more than one PermitRepository, although it does allow us to create subclasses.


```
public class PermitRepository
{
    private static PermitRepository instance = null;

    protected PermitRepository() {}

    public static void setTestingInstance(PermitRepository newInstance)
    {
        instance = newInstance;
    }

    public static PermitRepository getInstance()
    {
        if (instance == null) {
            instance = new PermitRepository();
        }
```

```
        return instance;
    }

    public Permit findAssociatedPermit(PermitNotice notice)
    {
        ...
    }
    ...
}
```

In many cases, we can use *Subclass and Override Method (401)* like this to get a fake singleton in place. At other times, the dependencies are so extensive that it is easier to use *Extract Interface (362)* on the singleton and change all of the references in the application so that they use the interface name. This can be a lot of work, but we can *Lean on the Compiler (315)* to make the change. This is what the `PermitRepository` class will look like after the extraction:

```
public class PermitRepository implements IPermitRepository
{
    private static IPermitRepository instance = null;

    protected PermitRepository() {}

    public static void setTestingInstance(IPermitRepository newInstance)
    {
        instance = newInstance;
    }

    public static IPermitRepository getInstance()
    {
        if (instance == null) {
            instance = new PermitRepository();
        }
        return instance;
    }

    public Permit findAssociatedPermit(PermitNotice notice)
    {
        ...
    }
    ...
}
```

The `IPermitRepository` interface will have signatures for all of the public non-static methods on `PermitRepository`.

```
public interface IPermitRepository
{
    Permit findAssociatedPermit(PermitNotice notice);
    ...
}
```

If you are using a language that has a refactoring tool, you might be able to perform this interface extraction automatically. If you are using a language without one, it might be easier to use *Extract Implementer (356)* instead.

The name for this whole refactoring is *Introduce Static Setter (372)*. This is a technique that we can use to get tests in place despite extensive global dependencies. Unfortunately, it doesn't do much to get past the global dependencies. If you choose to tackle that problem, you can do so by using *Parameterize Method (383)* and *Parameterize Constructor (379)*. With those refactorings, you trade a global reference for either a temporary variable in a method or a field in an object. The downside to *Parameterize Method (383)* is that you can end up with many additional methods that distract people when they try to understand the classes. The downside to *Parameterize Constructor (379)* is that each object that currently uses the global ends up with an additional field. The field will have to be passed to its constructor, so the class that creates the object needs to have access to the instance also. If too many objects need this additional field, it can substantially impact the amount of memory used by the application, but often that indicates other design problems.

Let's look at the worst case. We have an application with several hundred classes that creates thousands of objects at runtime, and each of them needs access to the database. Without even looking at the application, the first question that comes to my mind is, why? If the system does anything more than access a database, it can be factored so that some classes do those other things and others store and retrieve data. When we make a concerted effort to separate responsibilities in an application, dependencies become localized; we might not need a reference to a database in every object. Some objects are populated using data retrieved from the database. Others perform calculation on data supplied through their constructors.

As an exercise, pick a global variable in a large application and search for it. In most cases, variables that are global are globally accessible, but they really aren't globally used. They are used in a relatively small number of places. Imagine how we could get that object to the objects that need it if it couldn't be a global variable. How would we refactor the application? Are there responsibilities that we can separate out of sets of classes to decrease the scope of the global?

If you find a global variable that really is being used every place, it means there isn't any layering in your code. Take a look at Chapter 15, *My Application Is All API Calls,* and Chapter 17, *My Application Has No Structure.*

The Case of the Horrible Include Dependencies

C++ was my first OO language, and I have to admit that I felt very proud of myself for learning many of its details and complexities. It became dominant in the industry because it was an utterly pragmatic solution to many vexing problems at the time. Machines are too slow? Okay, here is a language in which everything is optional. You can get all of the efficiency of raw C if you use only the C features. Can't get your team to use an OO language? Okay, here is a C++ compiler; you can write in the C subset of C++ and learn OO as you go.

Although C++ became very popular for a while, it eventually fell behind Java and some of the newer languages in popularity. There was leverage in maintaining backward compatibility with C, but there was much more leverage in making languages easier to work with. Repeatedly, C++ teams have learned that the language defaults are not ideal for maintenance, and they have to go beyond them a bit to keep a system nimble and easy to change.

One part of C++'s C legacy that is especially problematic is its way of letting one part of a program know about another part. In Java and C#, if a class in one file needs to use a class in another file, we use an `import` or `using` statement to make its definition available. The compiler looks for that class and checks to see if it has been compiled already. If it hasn't, it compiles it. If it has been compiled, the compiler reads a brief snippet of information from the compiled file, getting only as much information as it needs to make sure that all of the methods the original class needs are on that class.

C++ compilers generally don't have this optimization. In C++, if a class needs to know about another class, the declaration of the class (in another file) is textually included in the file that needs to use it. This can be a much slower process. The compiler has to reparse the declaration and build up an internal representation every time it sees that declaration. Worse, the include mechanism is prone to abuse. A file can include a file that includes a file, and so on. On projects in which people haven't avoided this, it's not uncommon to find small files that end up transitively including tens of thousands of lines of code. People wonder why their builds take so long, but because the includes are spread around the system, it is hard to point at any one particular file and understand why it is taking so long to compile.

It might seem like I'm getting down on C++, but I'm not. It is an important language, and there is an incredible amount of C++ code out there—but it does take extra care to work with it well.

In legacy code, it can be hard to instantiate a C++ class in a test harness. One of the most immediate issues we confront is header dependency. What header files do we need to create a class by itself in a test harness?

Here is part of the declaration of a huge C++ class named `Scheduler`. It has more than 200 methods, but I've shown only about 5 of them in the declaration. In addition to being large, the class has very severe and tangled dependencies on many other classes. How can we make a `Scheduler` in a test?

```
#ifndef SCHEDULER_H
#define SCHEDULER_H

#include "Meeting.h"
#include "MailDaemon.h"
...
#include "SchedulerDisplay.h"
#include "DayTime.h"

class Scheduler
{
public:
        Scheduler(const string& owner);
        ~Scheduler();

    void addEvent(Event *event);
    bool hasEvents(Date date);
    bool performConsistencyCheck(string& message);
    ...
};

#endif
```

The Case of the Horrible Include Dependencies

Among other things, the `Scheduler` class uses `Meetings`, `MailDaemons`, `Events`, `SchedulerDisplays`, and `Dates`. If we want to create a test for Schedulers, the easiest thing that we can do is try to build one in the same directory in another file named `SchedulerTests`. Why do we want the tests in the same directory? In the presence of the preprocessor, it is often just easier. If the project doesn't use paths to include files in consistent ways, we could have a lot of work to do if we try to create the tests in other directories.

```
#include "TestHarness.h"
#include "Scheduler.h"

TEST(create,Scheduler)
{
    Scheduler scheduler("fred");
}
```

If we create a file and attempt to create a scheduler in a test, we'll be confronted with the include problem. To compile a `Scheduler`, we have to make sure that the compiler and linker know about all of the things that `Scheduler` needs, and all of the things those things need, and so on. Luckily, the build system gives us a large number of error messages and tells us about these things in exhaustive detail.

In simple cases, the `Scheduler.h` file includes everything we need to be able to create a `Scheduler`, but in some cases, the header file doesn't include everything. We have to supply some additional includes to create and use an object.

We could just copy over all of the `#include` directives from the `Scheduler` class source file, but the fact is, we might not need them all. The best tack to take is to add them one at a time and decide whether we really need those particular dependencies. Often we can avoid them by adding forward declarations.

In an ideal world, the easiest thing would be to include all of the files that we need until we don't have any build errors, but that can force us into a muddle. If there is a long line of transitive dependencies, we could end up including far more than we really need. Even if the line of dependencies isn't too long, we could end up depending on things that are very hard to work with in a test harness. In this example, the `SchedulerDisplay` class is one of those dependencies. I'm not showing it here, but it is actually accessed in the constructor of `Scheduler`. We can get rid of the dependency like this:

```
#include "TestHarness.h"
#include "Scheduler.h"

void SchedulerDisplay::displayEntry(const string& entityDescription)
{
}

TEST(create,Scheduler)
{
    Scheduler scheduler("fred");
}
```


Here we've introduced an alternative definition for `SchedulerDisplay::displayEntry`. Unfortunately, when we do this, we need to have a separate build for the test cases in this file. We can have only one definition for each method in

SchedulerDisplay in a program, so we need to have a separate program for our scheduler tests.

Luckily, we can get some reuse for the fakes that we create this way. Instead of putting the definitions of classes such as SchedulerDisplay inline in the test file, we can put them in a separate include file that can be used across a set of test files:

```
#include "TestHarness.h"
#include "Scheduler.h"
#include "Fakes.h"

TEST(create,Scheduler)
{
    Scheduler scheduler("fred");
}
```

After doing it a couple of times, getting a C++ class instantiable in a harness like this is pretty easy and pretty mechanical, but there are a couple of very serious downsides. We have to create that separate program, and we really aren't breaking dependencies at the language level, so we aren't making the code cleaner as we break dependencies. Worse, those duplicate definitions that we put in the test file (SchedulerDisplay::displayEntry in this example) have to be maintained as long as we keep this set of tests in place.

I reserve this technique for cases in which I have a very huge class with very severe dependency problems. It is not a technique to use often or lightly. If that class is going to be broken up into a large number of smaller classes over time, creating a separate test program for a class can be useful. It can act as a testing point for a lot of refactoring. Over time, this separate testing program can go away as you extract more classes and get them under test.

The Case of the Onion Parameter

I like simple constructors. I really do. It is great to be able to decide to create a class and then just type in a constructor call and have a nice live, working object available to use. But in many cases, it can be hard to create objects. Every object needs to be set up in a good state, a state that makes it ready for additional work. In many cases, this means we have to supply it with objects that are set up properly themselves. Those objects might require other objects so that they can be set up also, so we end up having to create objects to create objects to create objects to create a parameter for a constructor of the class that we want to test. Objects inside of other objects—it seems like a big onion. Here is an example of this sort of problem.

We have a class that displays a SchedulingTask:

```
public class SchedulingTaskPane extends SchedulerPane
{
    public SchedulingTaskPane(SchedulingTask task) {
        ...
    }
}
```

To create it, we need to pass it a SchedulingTask, but to create a SchedulingTask, we have to use its one and only one constructor:

```
public class SchedulingTask extends SerialTask
{
    public SchedulingTask(Scheduler scheduler, MeetingResolver resolver)
    {
        ...
    }
}
```

If we discover that we need more objects to create Schedulers and MeetingResolvers, we're liable to pull our hair out. The only thing that keeps us from total despair is the fact that there has to be at least one class that doesn't require objects of another class as arguments. If there isn't, there is no way the system could ever have compiled.

The way to handle this situation is to take a close look at what we want to do. We need to write tests, but what do we really need from the parameters passed into the constructor? If we don't need anything from them in the tests, we can *Pass Null (111)*. If we just need some rudimentary behavior, we can use *Extract Interface (362)* or *Extract Implementer (356)* on the most immediate dependency and use the interface to create a fake object. In this case, the most immediate dependency of SchedulingTaskPane is SchedulingTask. If we can create a fake SchedulingTask, we can create a SchedulingTaskPane.

Unfortunately, SchedulingTask inherits from a class named SerialTask, and all it does is override some protected methods. All of the public methods are in SerialTask. Can we use *Extract Interface (362)* on SchedulingTask, or do we have to use it on SerialTask, too? In Java, we don't. We can create an interface for SchedulingTask that includes methods from SerialTask also.

Our resulting hierarchy looks like Figure 9.3.

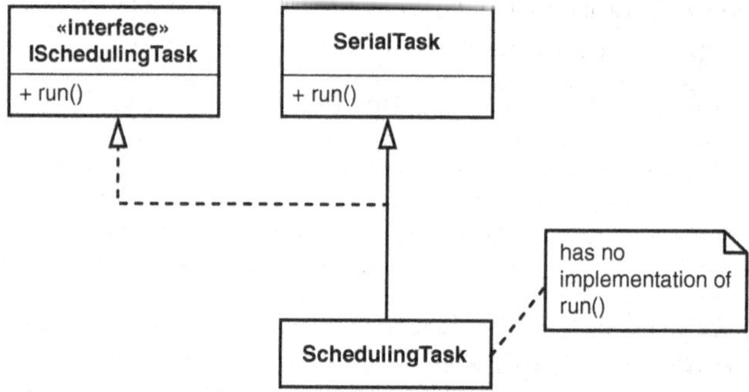

Figure 9.3 SchedulingTask.

In this case, we are lucky that we are using Java. In C++, unfortunately, we can't handle this case like this. There is no separate interface construct. Interfaces are typically implemented as classes containing only pure virtual functions. If this example was ported to C++, the SchedulingTask would become abstract because it inherits a pure virtual function from SchedulingTask. To instantiate a SchedulingTask, we'd need to provide a body for run() in SchedulingTask, which delegates to the run() from SerialTask. Fortunately, that would be easy enough to add. Here is what it looks like in code:

```
class SerialTask
{
public:
    virtual void run();
    ...
};

class ISchedulingTask
{
public:
    virtual void run() = 0;
    ...
};

class SchedulingTask : public SerialTask, public ISchedulingTask
{
public:
    virtual void run() { SerialTask::run(); }
};
```

The Case of the Onion Parameter

In any language where we can create interfaces or classes that act like interfaces, we can systematically use them to break dependencies.

The Case of the Aliased Parameter

Often when we have parameters to constructors that get in the way, we can get past the problem by using *Extract Interface (362)* or *Extract Implementer (356)*. But sometimes this isn't practical. Let's take a look at another class in that building permit system that we saw in a previous section:

```
public class IndustrialFacility extends Facility
{
    Permit basePermit;

    public IndustrialFacility(int facilityCode, String owner,
                          OriginationPermit permit) throws PermitViolation {

        Permit associatedPermit =
            PermitRepository.GetInstance()
                          .findAssociatedFromOrigination(permit);

        if (associatedPermit.isValid() && !permit.isValid()) {
            basePermit = associatedPermit;
        }
        else if (!permit.isValid()) {
            permit.validate();
            basePermit = permit;
        }
        else
            throw new PermitViolation(permit);
    }
    ...
}
```

We want to instantiate this class in a harness, but there are a couple of problems. One is that we are accessing a singleton again, `PermitRepository`. We can get past that problem by using the techniques we saw in the earlier section "The Case of the Irritating Global Dependency." But before we even get to that problem, we have another. It is hard to make the origination permit that we need to pass into the constructor. `OriginationPermits` have horrible dependencies. The immediate thought that I have is "Oh, I can use *Extract Interface* on the `OriginationPermit` class to get past this dependency," but it isn't that easy. Figure 9.4 shows the structure of the `Permit` hierarchy.

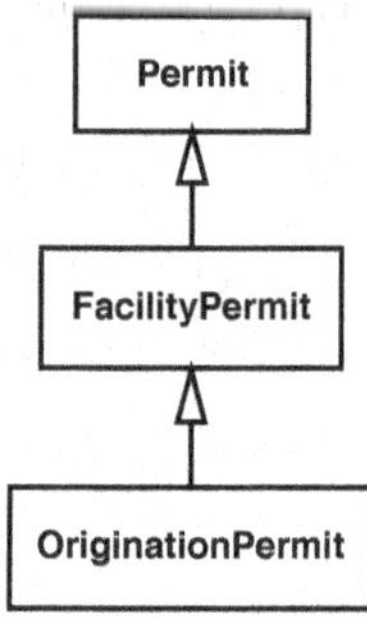

Figure 9.4 *The* `Permit` *hierarchy*

The `IndustrialFacility` constructor accepts an `OriginationPermit` and goes to the `PermitRepository` to get an associated permit; we use a method on `PermitRepository` that accepts an `OriginationPermit` and returns a `Permit`. If the repository finds the associated permit, it saves it to the `permit` field. If it doesn't, it saves the `OriginationPermit` to the `permit` field. We could create an interface for `OriginationPermit`, but that wouldn't do us any good. We would have to assign an `IOriginationPermit` to a `Permit` field, and that won't work. In Java, interfaces can't inherit from classes. The most obvious solution is to create interfaces all the way down and turn the `Permit` field into an `IPermit` field. Figure 9.5 shows what this would look like.

Yuck. That is a ridiculous amount of work, and I don't particularly like how the code ends up. Interfaces are great for breaking dependencies, but when we get to the point that we have nearly a one-to-one relationship between classes and interfaces, the design gets cluttered. Don't get me wrong: If our backs are against the wall, it would be fine to move toward this design, but if there are other possibilities, we should explore them. Fortunately, there are.

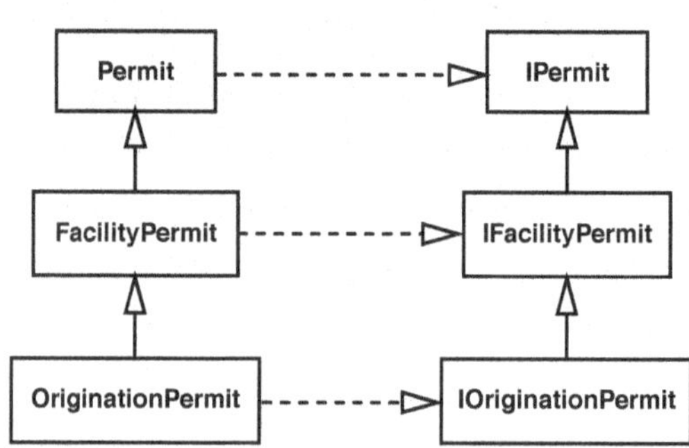

Figure 9.5 `Permit` *hierarchy with extract interfaces.*

Extract Interface (362) is just one way of breaking a dependency on a parameter. Sometimes it pays to ask why the dependency is bad. Sometimes creation is a pain. At other times, the parameter has a bad side effect. Maybe it talks to the file system or a database. At still other times, it just might take too long for its code to run. When we use *Extract Interface (362)*, we can get past all of these issues, but we do it by brutally severing the connection to a class. If only pieces of a class are problems, we can take another approach and just sever the connection to them.

Let's look closer at the `OriginationPermit` class. We don't want to use it in a test because it silently accesses a database when we tell it to validate itself:

```
public class OriginationPermit extends FacilityPermit
{
    ...
    public void validate() {
        // form connection to database
        ...
        // query for validation information
        ...
        // set the validation flag
        ...
        // close database
        ...
    }
}
```

We don't want to do this in a test: We'd have to make some fake entries in the database, and the DBA will get upset. We'd have to take him to lunch when he found out, and even then he'd still be upset. His job is hard enough as it is.

Another strategy that we can use is *Subclass and Override Method (401)*. We can make a class called `FakeOriginationPermit` that supplies methods that make it easy to change the validation flag. Then, in subclasses, we can override the `validate` method and set the validation flag any way that we need to while we are testing the `IndustrialFacility` class. Here is a good first test:


```
public void testHasPermits() {
    class AlwaysValidPermit extends FakeOriginationPermit
    {
        public void validate() {
            // set the validation flag
            becomeValid();
        }
    };

    Facility facility = new IndustrialFacility(Facility.HT_1, "b",
                                        new AlwaysValidPermit());
    assertTrue(facility.hasPermits());
}
```

In many languages, we can create classes "on the fly" like this in methods. Although I don't like to do it often in production code, it is very convenient when we are testing. We can make special cases very easily.

Subclass and Override Method (401) helps us break dependencies on parameters, but sometimes the factoring of methods in a class isn't ideal for it. We were lucky that the dependencies we didn't like were isolated in that `validate` method. In worse cases, they are intermingled with logic that we need, and we have to extract methods first. If we have a refactoring tool, that can be easy. If we don't, some of the techniques in Chapter 22, *I Need to Change a Monster Method and I Can't Write Tests for It*, might help.

Chapter 10

I Can't Run This Method in a Test Harness

Getting tests in place to make changes can be a bit of a problem. If you can instantiate your class separately in a test harness, consider yourself lucky. Many people can't. If you're having trouble, take a look at Chapter 9, *I Can't Get This Class into a Test Harness.*

Instantiating a class is often only the first part of the battle. The second part is writing tests for the methods we need to change. Sometimes we can do this without instantiating the class at all. If the method doesn't use much instance data, we can use *Expose Static Method (345)* to get access to the code. If the method is pretty long and difficult to deal with, we can use *Break Out Method Object (330)* to move the code to a class that we can instantiate more easily.

Fortunately, in most cases, the amount of work that we have to do to write tests for methods isn't as drastic. Here are some of the problems that we can run into.

- The method might not be accessible to the test. It could be private or have some other accessibility problem.
- It might be hard to call the method because it is hard to construct the parameters we need to call it.
- The method might have bad side effects (modifying a database, launching a cruise missile, and so on), so it is impossible to run in a test harness.
- We might need to sense through some object that the method uses.

The rest of this chapter contains a set of scenarios that show different ways of getting these problems and some of the trade-offs involved.

The Case of the Hidden Method

We need to make a change to a method in a class, but it's a private method. What should we do?

The first question to ask is whether we can test through a public method. If we can, it is a worthwhile thing to do. It saves us the trouble of trying to find a way of accessing the private method, and it has another benefit. If we test through public methods, we are guaranteed to be testing the method as it is used in the code. This can help us constrain our work a bit. In legacy code, there are often methods of very dubious quality lying around in classes. The amount of refactoring we'd have to do to make a private method useful for all callers might be rather large. Although it's nice to have very general methods that are useful to many callers, the fact is that each method has to be just functional enough to support the callers that use it and clear enough to understand and change easily. If we test a private method through the public methods that use it, there isn't much danger of making it too general. If the method needs to become public someday, the first user outside of the class should write test cases that explain exactly what the method does and how a caller can use it correctly.

All that is fine, but in some cases, we just want to write a test case for a private method, a method whose call is buried deep in a class. We want concrete feedback and tests that explain how it is used—or, who knows, maybe it is just a pain to test it through the public methods on the class.

So, how do we write a test for a private method? This has to be one of the most common testing-related questions. Fortunately, there is a very direct answer for this question: If we need to test a private method, we should make it public. If making it public bothers us, in most cases, it means that our class is doing too much and we ought to fix it. Let's look at the cases. Why would making a private method public bother us? Here are some reasons:

1. The method is just a utility; it isn't something clients would care about.
2. If clients use the method, they could adversely affect results from other methods on the class.

The first reason isn't very severe. An extra public method in a class's interface is forgivable, although we should try to figure out whether it would be better to put the method on another class. The second reason is a bit more serious, but fortunately there is a remedy: The private methods can be moved to a new class. They can be public on that class and our class can create an internal instance of it. That makes the methods testable and the design better.

Yes, I know this advice sounds strident, but it has some very positive effects. The fact remains: Good design is testable, and design that isn't testable is bad. The answer in cases like this is to start using the techniques in Chapter 20, *This Class Is Too Big and I Don't Want It to Get Any Bigger.* However, when there aren't many tests in place, we might have to move carefully and do some other work until we can break things down.

Let's see how to get past this problem in a realistic case. Here is part of a class declaration in C++:

```
class CCAImage
{
private:
    void setSnapRegion(int x, int y, int dx, int dy);
    ...
public:
    void snap();
    ...
};
```

The `CCAImage` class is used to take pictures in a security system. You might wonder why an image class is snapping pictures, but this is legacy code, remember? The class has a `snap()` method that uses a low-level C API to control a camera and "take" the picture, but this is a very special kind of image. A single call to `snap()` can result in a couple of different camera actions, each of which takes a picture and places it on a different part of an image buffer held in the class. The logic used to decide where to place each picture is dynamic. It depends on the motion of the subject, the thing we are taking a picture of. Depending upon how the subject moves, the `snap()` method can make several repeated calls to `setSnapRegion` to determine where the current picture will be placed on the buffer. Unfortunately, the API for the camera has changed, so we need to make a change to `setSnapRegion`. What should we do?

One thing that we could do is just make it public. Unfortunately, that could have some very negative consequences. The `CCAImage` class holds on to some variables that determine the current location of the snap region. If someone starts to call `setSnapRegion` in production code outside of the `snap()` method, it could cause serious trouble with the camera's tracking system.

Well, that is the problem. Before we look into some solutions, let's talk about how we got into this mess. The real reason we can't test the image class well is that it has too many responsibilities. Ideally, it would be great to break it down into smaller classes using the techniques described in Chapter 20, but we have to carefully consider whether we want to do that much refactoring right now. It would be great to do it, but whether we can depends on where we are in our release cycle, how much time we have, and all the associated risks.

If we can't afford to separate the responsibilities right now, can we still write tests for the method that we are changing? Fortunately, yes. Here's how we can do it.

The first step is to change setSnapRegion from private to protected.

```
class CCAImage
{
protected:
    void setSnapRegion(int x, int y, int dx, int dy);
    ...
public:
    void snap();
    ...
};
```

Next, we can subclass CCAImage to get access to that method:

```
class TestingCCAImage : public CCAImage
{
public:
    void setSnapRegion(int x, int y, int dx, int dy)
    {
        // call the setSnapRegion of the superclass
      CCAImage::setSnapRegion(x, y, dx, dy);
    }
};
```

In most modern C++ compilers, we can also use a using declaration in the testing subclass to perform the delegation automatically:

```
class TestingCCAImage : public CCAImage
{
public:
   // Expose all CCAImage implementations of setSnapRegion
   // as part of my public interface. Delegate all calls to CCAImage.
   using CCAImage::setSnapRegion;
}
```

The Case of the Hidden Method

After we've done this, we can call setSnapRegion on CCAImage in a test, albeit indirectly. But is this a good idea? Earlier, we didn't want to make the method public, but we are doing something similar. We're making it protected and making the method more accessible.

Frankly, I don't mind doing this. For me, getting the tests in place is a fair trade. Yes, this change does let us violate encapsulation. When we are reasoning about how the code works, we do have to consider that setSnapRegion can be called in subclasses now, but that is relatively minor. Maybe that little piece will be enough to trigger us to do the full refactoring the next time we touch the class. We can separate the responsibilities in CCAImage into different classes and make them testable.

Subverting Access Protection

In many OO languages newer than C++, we can use reflection and special permissions to access private variables at runtime. Although that can be handy, it is a bit of a cheat, really. It is very helpful when we want to break dependencies, but I don't like to keep tests that access private variables around in projects. That sort of subterfuge really prevents a team from noticing just how bad the code is getting. It might sound kind of sadistic, but the pain that we feel working in a legacy code base can be an incredible impetus to change. We can take the sneaky way out, but unless we deal with the root causes, overly responsible classes and tangled dependencies, we are just delaying the bill. When everyone discovers just how bad the code has gotten, the costs to make it better will have gotten too ridiculous.

The Case of the "Helpful" Language Feature

Language designers often try to make our lives easier, but they have a tough job. They have to balance ease of programming against security concerns and safety. Some features initially look like a clear "win" balancing all of these concerns well, but when we attempt to test code that uses them, we discover the cruel reality.

Here is a piece of C# code that accepts a collection of uploaded files from a web client. The code iterates through each of them and returns a list of streams associated with files that have particular characteristics.

```
public void IList getKSRStreams(HttpFileCollection files) {
    ArrayList list = new ArrayList();
    foreach(string name in files) {
        HttpPostedFile file = files[name];
        if (file.FileName.EndsWith(".ksr") ||
                (file.FileName.EndsWith(".txt")
                        && file.ContentLength > MIN_LEN)) {
            ...
            list.Add(file.InputStream);
        }
    }
    return list;
}
```


We'd like to make some changes to this piece of code and maybe refactor it a little, but writing tests is going to be difficult. We'd like to create an HttpFileCollection object and populate it with HttpPostedFile objects, but that is impossible. First of all, the HttpPostedFile class doesn't have a public constructor. Second, the class is sealed. In C#, this means that we can't create an instance of an HttpPostedFile, and we can't subclass it. HttpPostedFile is part of the .NET library. At runtime, some other class creates instances of this class, but we don't have access to it. A quick look at the HttpFileCollection class shows us that it has the same problems: no public constructors and no way to created derived classes.

Why did Bill Gates do this to us? After all, we've kept our licenses up-to-date and everything. I don't think he hates us. But if he does, well, maybe Scott McNealy does, too, because it's not just an issue with Microsoft's languages. Sun has a parallel syntax for preventing subclassing. They use the keyword final in Java to mark classes that are particularly sensitive when it comes to security. If just anyone could create a subclass of HttpPostedFile or even a class such as String, they could write some malicious code and pass it around in code that uses those classes. It's a very real danger, but sealed and final are pretty drastic tools; they leave us in a bind here.

What can we do to write tests for the getKSRStreams method? We can't use *Extract Interface (362)* or *Extract Implementer (356)*; the HttpPostedFile and HttpFileCollection classes aren't under our control, they are library classes and we can't change them. At first glance, it appears that the only technique that we can use here is *Adapt Parameter (326)*.

We're lucky, in this case, because the only thing that we do to the collection is iterate over it. Fortunately, the sealed HttpFileCollection class that our code uses has an unsealed superclass named NameObjectCollectionBase. We can subclass it and pass an object of that subclass to the getKSRStreams method. The change is safe and easy if we *Lean on the Compiler (315)*.

```
public void LList getKSRStreams(OurHttpFileCollection files) {
    ArrayList list = new ArrayList();
    foreach(string name in files) {
        HttpPostedFile file = files[name];
        if (file.FileName.EndsWith(".ksr") ||
                (file.FileName.EndsWith(".txt")
                    && file.ContentLength > MAX_LEN)) {
            ...
            list.Add(file.InputStream);
        }
    }
    return list;
}
```

The Case of the "Helpful" Language Feature

OurHttpFileCollection is a subclass of NameObjectCollectionBase and NameObjectCollectionBase is an abstract class that associates strings with objects.

That gets us past one problem. The next problem is tougher. We need HttpPostedFiles to run getKSRStreams in a test, but we can't create them. What do we need from them? It looks like we need a class that provides a couple of properties: FileName and ContentLength. We can use *Skin and Wrap the API (205)* to get some separation between us and HttpPostedFile class. To do that, we extract an interface (IHttpPostedFile) and write a wrapper (HttpPostedFileWrapper):

```
public class HttpPostedFileWrapper : IHttpPostedFile
{
    public HttpPostedFileWrapper(HttpPostedFile file) {
        this.file = file;
    }

    public int ContentLength {
        get { return file.ContentLength; }
    }
    ...
}
```

Because we have an interface, we can also create a class for testing:

```
public class FakeHttpPostedFile : IHttpPostedFile
{
    public FakeHttpPostedFile(int length, Stream stream, ...) { ... }

    public int ContentLength {
        get { return length; }
    }
}
```

Now, if we *Lean on the Compiler (315)* and change our production code, we can use HttpPostedFileWrapper objects or FakeHttpPostedFile objects through the IHttpPostedFile interface without knowing which is being used.

```
public IList getKSRStreams(OurHttpFileCollection) {
    ArrayList list = new ArrayList();
    foreach(string name in files) {
        IHttpPostedFile file = files[name];
        if (file.FileName.EndsWith(".ksr") ||
                (file.FileName.EndsWith(".txt"))
                    && file.ContentLength > MAX_LEN)) {
            ...
            list.Add(file.InputStream);
        }
    }
    return list;
}
```

The Case of the "Helpful" Language Feature

The only annoyance is that we have to iterate the original HttpFileCollection in the production code, wrap each HttpPostedFile that it contains, and then add it to a new collection that we pass to the `getKSRStreams` method. That's the price of security.

Seriously, it is easy to believe that `sealed` and `final` are a wrong-headed mistake, that they should never have been added to programming languages. But the real fault lies with us. When we depend directly on libraries that are out of our control, we are just asking for trouble.

Some day, mainstream programming languages might provide special access permissions for tests, but in the meantime, it is good to use mechanisms such as `sealed` and `final` sparingly. And when we need to use library classes that use them, it's a good idea to isolate them behind some wrapper so that we have some wiggle room when we make our changes. See Chapter 14, *Dependencies on Libraries Are Killing Me*, and Chapter 15, *My Application Is All API Calls*, for more discussion and techniques that address this problem.

The Case of the Undetectable Side Effect

In theory, writing a test for a piece of functionality shouldn't be too bad. We instantiate a class, call its methods, and check their results. What could go wrong? Well, it can be that easy if the object we create doesn't communicate with any other objects. If other objects use it and it doesn't use anything else, our tests can use it also and act just like the rest of our program would. But objects that don't use other objects are rare.

Programs build on themselves. Often we have objects with methods that don't return values. We call their methods, and they do some work, but we (the calling code) never get to know about it. The object calls methods on other objects, and we never have a clue how things turned out.

Here is a class with this problem:


```
public class AccountDetailFrame extends Frame
        implements ActionListener, WindowListener
{
    private TextField display = new TextField(10);
    ...
    public AccountDetailFrame(...) { ... }

    public void actionPerformed(ActionEvent event) {
        String source = (String)event.getActionCommand();
        if (source.equals("project activity")) {
            DetailFrame detailDisplay = new DetailFrame();
            detailDisplay.setDescription(
                    getDetailText() + " " + getProjectionText());
            detailDisplay.show();
```

```
            String accountDescription
                    = detailDisplay.getAccountSymbol();
            accountDescription += ": ";
            ...
            display.setText(accountDescription);
            ...
        }
    }
    ...
}
```

This old class in Java does it all. It creates GUI components, it receives notifications from them using its `actionPerformed` handler, and it calculates what it needs to display and displays it. It does all of this in a particularly strange way: It builds up detailed text and then creates and displays another window. When the window is done with its work, it grabs information from it directly, processes it a bit, and then sets it onto one of its own text fields.

We could try running this method in a test harness, but it would be pointless. It would create a window, show it to us, prompt us for input, and then go on to display something in another window. There is no decent place to sense what this code does.

What can we do? First, we can start to separate work that is independent of the GUI from work that is really dependent on the GUI. Because we are working in Java, we can take advantage of one of the available refactoring tools. Our first step is to perform a set of *Extract Method (415)* refactorings to divide up the work in this method.

Where should we start?

The method itself is primarily a hook for notifications from the windowing framework. The first thing it does is get the name of a command from the action event that is passed to it. If we extract the whole body of the method, we can separate ourselves from any dependency on the `ActionEvent` class.

```
public class AccountDetailFrame extends Frame
        implements ActionListener, WindowListener
{
    private TextField display = new TextField(10);
    ...
    public AccountDetailFrame(...) { ... }

    public void actionPerformed(ActionEvent event) {
        String source = (String)event.getActionCommand();
        performCommand(source);
    }

    public void performCommand(String source) {
        if (source.equals("project activity")) {
```

```
            DetailFrame detailDisplay = new DetailFrame();
            detailDisplay.setDescription(
                    getDetailText() + " " + getProjectionText());
            detailDisplay.show();
            String accountDescription
                    = detailDisplay.getAccountSymbol();
            accountDescription += ": ";
            ...
            display.setText(accountDescription);
            ...
        }
    }
    ...
}
```

But that isn't enough to make the code testable. The next step is to extract methods for the code that accesses the other frame. It will help to make the detailDisplay frame an instance variable of the class.

```
public class AccountDetailFrame extends Frame
            implements ActionListener, WindowListener
{
    private TextField display = new TextField(10);
    private DetailFrame detailDisplay;
    ...
    public AccountDetailFrame(...) { .. }

    public void actionPerformed(ActionEvent event) {
        String source = (String)event.getActionCommand();
        performCommand(source);
    }

    public void performCommand(String source) {
        if (source.equals("project activity")) {
            detailDisplay = new DetailFrame();
            detailDisplay.setDescription(
                    getDetailText() + " " + getProjectionText());
            detailDisplay.show();
            String accountDescription
                    = detailDisplay.getAccountSymbol();
            accountDescription +=  ": ";
            ...
            display.setText(accountDescription);
            ...
        }
    }
    ...
}
```

Now we can extract the code that uses that frame into a set of methods. What should we name the methods? To get ideas for names, we should take a look at what each piece of code does from the perspective of this class, or what it calculates for this class. In addition, we should not use names that mention the display components. We can use display components in the code that we extract, but the names should hide that fact. With these things in mind, we can create either a command method or a query method for each chunk of code.

Command/Query Separation

Command/Query Separation is a design principle first described by Bertrand Meyer. Simply put, it is this: A method should be a command or a query, but not both. A command is a method that can modify the state of the object but that doesn't return a value. A query is a method that returns a value but that does not modify the object.

Why is this principle important? There are a number of reasons, but the most primary is communication. If a method is a query, we shouldn't have to look at its body to discover whether we can use it several times in a row without causing some side effect.

Here's what the performCommand method looks like after a series of extractions:

```
public class AccountDetailFrame extends Frame
        implements ActionListener, WindowListener
{
    public void performCommand(String source) {
        if (source.equals("project activity")) {
            setDescription(getDetailText() + " " + getProjectionText());
            ...
            String accountDescription = getAccountSymbol();
            accountDescription +=  ": ";
            ...
            display.setText(accountDescription);
            ...
        }
    }

    void setDescription(String description) {
        detailDisplay = new DetailFrame();
        detailDisplay.setDescription(description);
        detailDisplay.show();
    }

    String getAccountSymbol() {
        return detailDisplay.getAccountSymbol();
    }
    ...
}
```

Now that we've extracted all of the code that deals with the detailDisplay frame, we can go through and extract the code that accesses components on the AccountDetailFrame.

```
public class AccountDetailFrame extends Frame
                implements ActionListener, WindowListener {
    public void performCommand(String source) {
        if (source.equals("project activity")) {
            setDescription(getDetailText() + " " + getProjectionText());
            ...
            String accountDescription
                    = detailDisplay.getAccountSymbol();
            accountDescription +=  ": ";
            ...
            setDisplayText(accountDescription);
            ...
        }
    }

    void setDescription(String description) {
        detailDisplay = new DetailFrame();
        detailDisplay.setDescription(description);
        detailDisplay.show();
    }

    String getAccountSymbol() {
        return detailDisplay.getAccountSymbol();
    }

    void setDisplayText(String description) {
        display.setText(description);
    }
    ...
}
```

After those extractions, we can *Subclass and Override Method (401)* and test whatever code is left in the performCommand method. For example, if we subclass AccountDetailFrame like this, we can verify that given the "project activity" command, the display gets the proper text:


```
public class TestingAccountDetailFrame extends AccountDetailFrame
{
    String displayText = "";
    String accountSymbol = "";

    void setDescription(String description) {
    }

    String getAccountSymbol() {
        return accountSymbol;
```

```
    }

    void setDisplayText(String text) {
        displayText = text;
    }

}
```

Here is a test that exercises the performCommand method:

```
public void testPerformCommand() {
    TestingAccountDetailFrame frame = new TestingAccountDetailFrame();
    frame.accountSymbol = "SYM";
    frame.performCommand("project activity");
    assertEquals("SYM: basic account", frame.displayText);
}
```

When we separate out dependencies this way, very conservatively, by doing automated extracting method refactorings, we might end up with code that makes us flinch a bit. For instance, a setDescription method that creates a frame and shows it is downright nasty. What happens if we call it twice? We have to deal with that issue, but doing these coarse extractions is a decent first step. Afterward, we can see if we can relocate the frame creation to a better place.

Where are we now? We started with a class that had one class with one important method on it: performAction. We ended up with what is shown in Figure 10.1.

We can't really see this in a UML diagram, but getAccountSymbol and setDescription use the detailDisplay field and nothing else. The setDisplayText method uses only the TextField named display. We could recognize these as separate responsibilities. If we do, we can eventually move to something like what is shown in Figure 10.2.

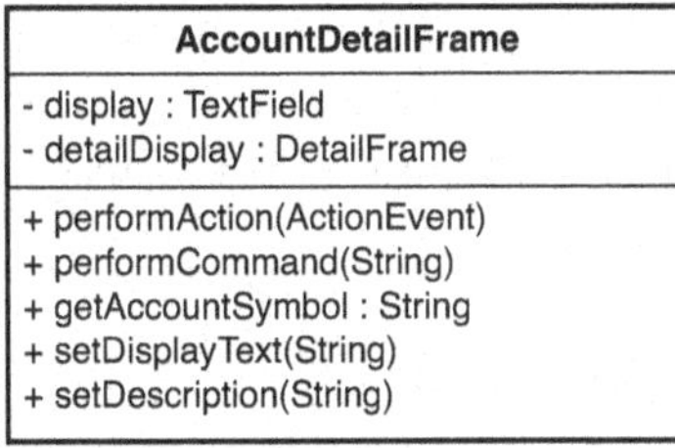

Figure 10.1 AccountDetailFrame.

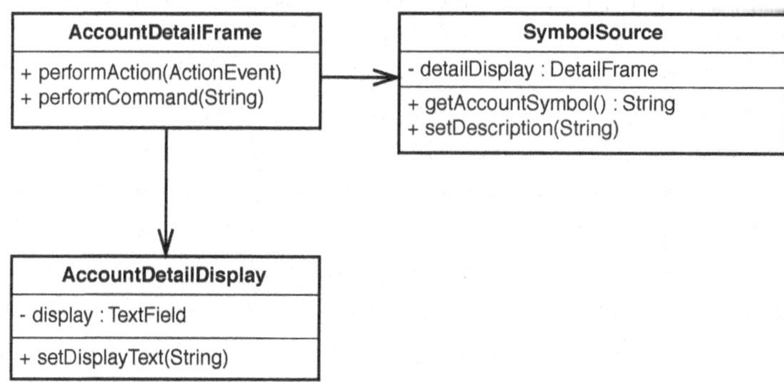

Figure 10.2 `AccountDetailFrame` *crudely refactored.*

This is an extremely crude refactoring of the original code, but at least it separates responsibilities somewhat. The `AccountDetailFrame` is tied to the GUI (it is a subclass of `Frame`) and it still contains business logic. With further refactoring, we can move beyond that, but at the very least, now we can run the method that contained business logic in a test case. It is a positive step forward.

The `SymbolSource` class is a concrete class that represents the decision to create another `Frame` and get information from it. However, we named it `SymbolSource` here because, from the point of view of the `AccountDetailFrame`, its job is to get symbol information any way it needs to. I wouldn't be surprised to see `SymbolSource` become an interface, if that decision ever changes.

The steps we took in this example are very common. When we have a refactoring tool, we can easily extract methods on a class and then start to identify groups of methods that can be moved to new classes. A good refactoring tool will only allow you to do an automated extract method refactoring when it is safe. However, that just makes the editing that we do between uses of the tool the most hazardous part of the work. Remember that it is okay to extract methods with poor names or poor structure to get tests in place. Safety first. After the tests are in place, you can make the code much cleaner.

Chapter 11

I Need to Make a Change. What Methods Should I Test?

We need to make some changes, and we need to write *characterization tests (186)* to pin down the behavior that is already there. Where should we write them? The simplest answer is to write tests for each method that we change. But is that enough? It can be if the code is simple and easy to understand, but in legacy code, often all bets are off. A change in one place can affect behavior someplace else; unless we have a test in place, we might never know about it.

When I need to make changes in particularly tangled legacy code, I often spend time trying to figure out where I should write my tests. This involves thinking about the change I am going to make, seeing what it will affect, seeing what the affected things will affect, and so on. This type of reasoning is nothing new; people have been doing it since the dawn of the computer age.

Programmers sit down and reason about their programs for many reasons. The funny thing is, we don't talk about it much. We just assume that everyone knows how to do it and that doing it is "just part of being a programmer." Unfortunately, that doesn't help us much when we are confronted with terribly tangled code that goes far beyond our ability to reason easily about it. We know that we should refactor it to make it more understandable, but then there is that issue of testing again. If we don't have tests, how do we know that we are refactoring correctly?

I wrote the techniques in this chapter to bridge the gap. Often we do have to reason about programs in non-trivial ways to find the best places to test.

Reasoning About Effects

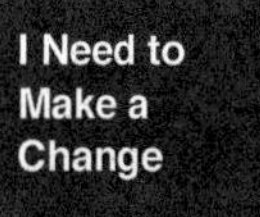

In the industry, we don't talk about this often, but for every functional change in software, there is some associated chain of effects. For instance, if I change the 3 to 4 in the following C# code, it changes the result of the method when it is called. It could also change the results of methods that call that method, and so on, all the way back to some system boundary. Despite this, many parts of the code won't have different behavior. They won't produce different results because they don't call getBalancePoint() directly or indirectly.

```
int getBalancePoint() {
    const int SCALE_FACTOR = 3;
    int result = startingLoad + (LOAD_FACTOR * residual * SCALE_FACTOR);
    foreach(Load load in loads) {
        result += load.getPointWeight() * SCALE_FACTOR;
    }
    return result;
}
```

IDE Support for Effect Analysis

Sometimes I wish that I had an IDE that would help me see effects in legacy code. I would be able to highlight a piece of code and hit a hotkey. Then the IDE would give me a list of all of the variables and methods that could be impacted when I change the selected code.

Perhaps someday someone will develop a tool like this. In the meantime, we have to reason about effects without tools. It is a very learnable skill, but it is hard to know when we've gotten it right.

The best way to get a sense of what effect reasoning is like is to look at an example. Here is a Java class that is part of an application that manipulates C++ code. It sounds pretty domain intensive, doesn't it? But domain knowledge doesn't matter when we reason about effects.

Let's try a little exercise. Make a list of all of the things that can be changed after a CppClass object is created that would affect results returned by any of its methods.

```
public class CppClass {
    private String name;
    private List declarations;

    public CppClass(String name, List declarations) {
        this.name = name;
        this.declarations = declarations;
    }

    public int getDeclarationCount() {
        return declarations.size();
    }

    public String getName() {
```

```
        return name;
    }

    public Declaration getDeclaration(int index) {
        return ((Declaration)declarations.get(index));
    }

    public String getInterface(String interfaceName, int [] indices) {
        String result = "class " + interfaceName + " {\npublic:\n";
        for (int n = 0; n < indices.length; n++) {
            Declaration virtualFunction
                    = (Declaration)(declarations.get(indices[n]));
            result += "\t" + virtualFunction.asAbstract() + "\n";
        }
        result += "};\n";
        return result;
    }
}
```

Your list should look something like this:

1. Someone could add additional elements to the declarations list after passing it to the constructor. Because the list is held by reference, changes made to it can alter the results of `getInterface`, `getDeclaration`, and `getDeclarationCount`.

2. Someone can alter one of the objects held in the declarations list or replace one of its elements, affecting the same methods.

Some people look at the `getName` method and suspect that it could return a different value if anyone changes the `name` string, but in Java, `String` objects are immutable. You can't change their value after they are created. After a `CppClass` object is created, `getName` always returns the same string value.

We can make a sketch that shows that changes in `declarations` have an effect on `getDeclarationCount()` (see Figure 11.1).

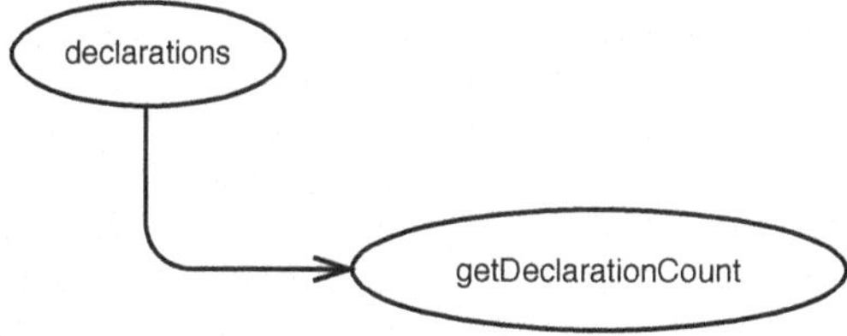

Figure 11.1 `declarations` *impacts* `getDeclarationCount`.

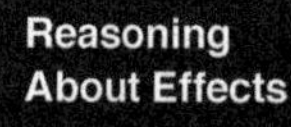

This sketch shows that if `declarations` changes in some way—for instance, if its size grows—`getDeclarationCount()` can return a different value.

We can make a sketch for `getDeclaration(int index)` also (see Figure 11.2).

The return values of calls to `getDeclaration(int index)` can change if something causes `declarations` to change or if the declarations within it change.

Figure 11.3 shows that similar things impact the `getInterface` method also.

We can bundle all of these sketches together into a larger sketch (see Figure 11.4).

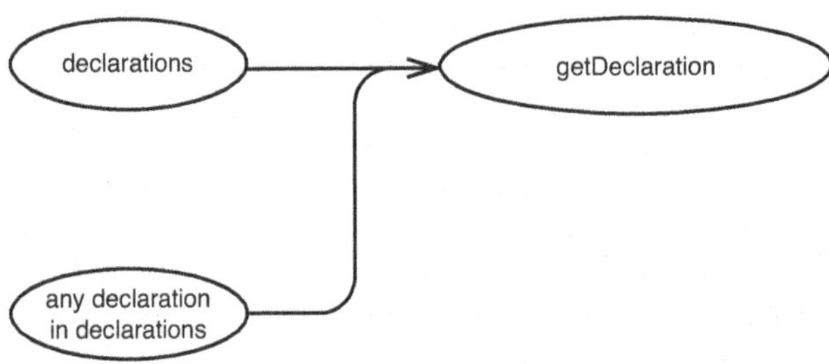

Figure 11.2 `declarations` *and the objects it holds impact* `getDeclarationCount`.

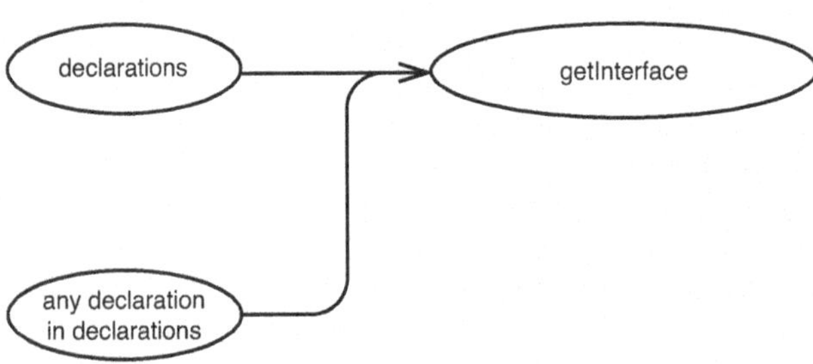

Figure 11.3 *Things that affect* `getInterface`.

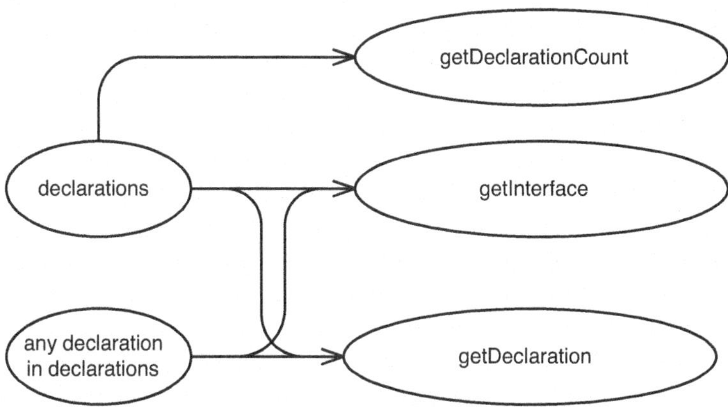

Figure 11.4 *Combined effect sketch.*

There isn't much syntax in these diagrams. I just call them *effect sketches*. The key is to have a separate bubble for each variable that can be affected and each method whose return value can change. Sometimes the variables are on the same object, and sometimes they are on different objects. It doesn't matter: We just make a bubble for the things that will change and draw an arrow to everything whose value can change at runtime because of them.

> If your code is well structured, most of the methods in your software have simple effect structures. In fact, one measure of goodness in software is that rather complicated effects on the outside world are the sum of a much simpler set of effects in the code. Almost anything that you can do to make the effect sketch simpler for a piece of code makes it more understandable and maintainable.

Let's widen our picture of the system that the previous class comes from and look at a bigger effect picture. `CppClass` objects are created in a class named `ClassReader`. In fact, we've been able to determine that they are created only in `ClassReader`.

```
public class ClassReader {
    private boolean inPublicSection = false;
    private CppClass parsedClass;
    private List declarations = new ArrayList();
    private Reader reader;

    public ClassReader(Reader reader) {
        this.reader = reader;
    }
```

```
    public void parse() throws Exception {
        TokenReader source = new TokenReader(reader);
        Token classToken = source.readToken();
        Token className = source.readToken();

        Token lbrace = source.readToken();
        matchBody(source);
        Token rbrace = source.readToken();

        Token semicolon = source.readToken();

        if (classToken.getType() == Token.CLASS
                && className.getType() == Token.IDENT
                && lbrace.getType() == Token.LBRACE
                && rbrace.getType() == Token.RBRACE
                && semicolon.getType() == Token.SEMIC) {
            parsedClass = new CppClass(className.getText(),
                                       declarations);
        }
    }
    ...
}
```

Remember what we learned about CppClass? Do we know that the list of declarations won't ever change after a CppClass is created? The view that we have of CppClass doesn't really tell us. We need to figure out how the declarations list gets populated. If we look at more of the class, we can see that declarations are added in only one place in CppClass, a method named matchVirtualDeclaration that is called by matchBody in parse.

```
private void matchVirtualDeclaration(TokenReader source)
                    throws IOException {
    if (!source.peekToken().getType() == Token.VIRTUAL)
        return;
    List declarationTokens = new ArrayList();
    declarationTokens.add(source.readToken());
    while(source.peekToken().getType() != Token.SEMIC) {
        declarationTokens.add(source.readToken());
    }
    declarationTokens.add(source.readToken());
    if (inPublicSection)
        declarations.add(new Declaration(declarationTokens));
}
```


It looks like all of the changes that happen to this list happen before the CppClass object is created. Because we add new declarations to the list and don't hold on to any references to them, the declarations aren't going to change, either.

Let's think about the things held by the declarations list. The readToken method of TokenReader returns token objects that just hold a string and an integer that never changes. I'm not showing it here, but a quick look at the Declaration class shows that nothing else can change its state after it is created, so we can feel pretty comfortable saying that when a CppClass object is created, its declaration list and the list's contents aren't going to change.

How does this knowledge help us? If we were getting unexpected values from CppClass, we would know that we have to look at only a couple things. Generally, we can start to really look back at the places where the sub-objects of CppClass are created to figure out what is going on. We can also make the code clearer by starting to mark some of the references in CppClass constant using Java's final keyword.

In programs that aren't written very well, we often find it very difficult to figure out why the results we are looking at are what they are. When we are at that point, we have a debugging problem and we have to reason backward from the problem to its source. When we are working with legacy code, we often have to ask a different question: If we make a particular change, how could it possibly affect the rest of the results of the program?

This involves reasoning forward from points of change. When you get a good handle on this sort of reasoning, you have the beginnings of a technique for finding good places to write tests.

Reasoning Forward

In the previous example, we tried to deduce the set of objects that affect values at a particular point in code. When we are writing *characterization tests (186)*, we invert this process. We look at a set of objects and try to figure out what will change downstream if they stop working. Here is an example. The following class is part of an in-memory file system. We don't have any tests for it, but we want to make some changes.

```
public class InMemoryDirectory {
    private List elements = new ArrayList();

    public void addElement(Element newElement) {
        elements.add(newElement);
    }
```

```
    public void generateIndex() {
        Element index = new Element("index");
        for (Iterator it = elements.iterator(); it.hasNext(); ) {
            Element current = (Element)it.next();
            index.addText(current.getName() + "\n");
        }
        addElement(index);
    }

    public int getElementCount() {
        return elements.size();
    }

    public Element getElement(String name) {
        for (Iterator it = elements.iterator(); it.hasNext(); ) {
            Element current = (Element)it.next();
            if (current.getName().equals(name)) {
                return current;
            }
        }
        return null;
    }
}
```

`InMemoryDirectory` is a little Java class. We can create an `InMemoryDirectory` object, add elements into it, generate an index, and then access the elements. `Elements` are objects that contain text, just like files. When we generate an index, we create an element named `index` and append the names of all of the other elements to its text.

One odd feature of `InMemoryDirectory` is that we can't call `generateIndex` twice without gumming things up. If we call `generateIndex` twice, we end up with two index elements (the second one created actually lists the first one as an element of the directory).

Fortunately, our application uses `InMemoryDirectory` in a very constrained way. It creates directories, fills them with elements, calls `generateIndex`, and then passes the directory around so that other parts of the application can access its elements. It all works fine right now, but we need to make a change. We need to modify the software to allow people to add elements at any time during the directory's lifetime.

Reasoning Forward

Ideally, we'd like to have index creation and maintenance happen as a side effect of adding elements. The first time someone adds an element, the index element should be created and it should contain the name of the element that was added. The second time, that same index element should be updated with the name of the element that is added. It'll be easy enough to write tests for the new behavior and the code that satisfies them, but we don't have any tests for the current behavior. How do we figure out where to put them?

In this example, the answer is clear enough: We need a series of tests that call `addElement` in various ways, generate an index, and then get the various elements to see if they are correct. How do we know that these are the right methods to use? In this case, the problem is simple. The tests are just a description of how we expect to use the directory. We could probably write them without even looking at the directory code because we have a good idea of what the directory is supposed to do. Unfortunately, figuring out where to test isn't always that simple. I could have used a big complicated class in this example, one that is kind of like the ones that are often lurking in legacy systems, but you would have gotten bored and closed the book. So let's pretend that this is a tough one and take a look at how we can figure out what to test by looking at the code. The same kind of reasoning applies to thornier problems.

In this example, the first thing that we need to do is figure out where we are going to make our changes. We need to remove functionality from `generateIndex` and add functionality to `addElement`. When we've identified those as the points of change, we can start to sketch effects.

Let's start with `generateIndex`. What calls it? No other methods in the class do. The method is called only by clients. Do we modify anything in `generateIndex`? We do create a new element and add it to the directory, so `generateIndex` can have an effect on the `elements` collection in the class (see Figure 11.5).

Now we can take a look at the `elements` collection and see what it can affect. Where else is it used? It looks like it is used in `getElementCount` and `getElement`. The `elements` collection is used in `addElement` also, but we don't need to count that because `addElement` behaves the same way, regardless of what we do to the `elements` collection: No user of `addElements` can be impacted by anything we do to the `elements` collection (see Figure 11.6).

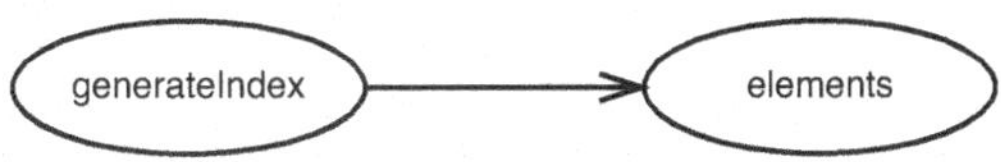

Figure 11.5 `generateIndex` *affects* `elements`.

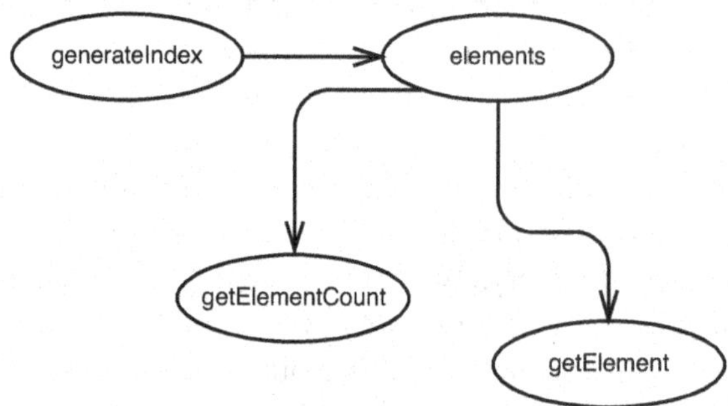

Figure 11.6 *Further effects of changes in* `generateIndex`.

Are we done? No, our change points were the `generateIndex` method and the `addElement` method, so we need to look at how `addElement` affects surrounding software also. It looks like `addElement` affects the `elements` collection (see Figure 11.7).

We can look to see what elements affects, but we've done that already because `generateIndex` affects `elements`.

The whole sketch appears in Figure 11.8.

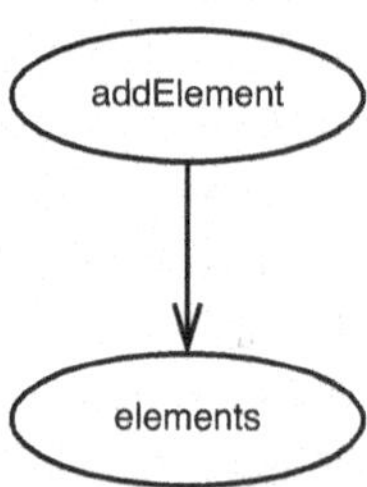

Figure 11.7 `addElement` *affects* `elements`.

The only way that users of the `InMemoryDirectory` class can sense effects is through the `getElementCount` and `getElement` methods. If we can write tests at those methods, it appears that we should be able to cover all of the effects of our change.

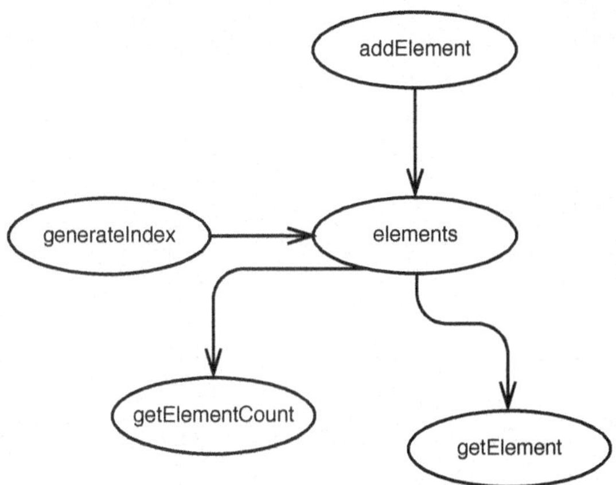

Figure 11.8 *Effect sketch of the* `InMemoryDirectory` *class.*

But is there any chance we've missed anything? What about superclasses and subclasses? If any data in `InMemoryDirectory` is public, protected, or package-scoped, a method in a subclass could use it in ways that we won't know about. In this example, the instance variables in `InMemoryDirectory` are private, so we don't have to worry about that.

> When you are sketching effects, make sure that you have found all of the clients of the class you are examining. If your class has a superclass or subclasses, there might be other clients that you haven't considered.

Are we done? Well, there is one thing that we've glossed over completely. We're using the `Element` class in the directory, but it isn't part of our effect sketch. Let's look at it more closely.

When we call `generateIndex`, we create an `Element` and repeatedly call `addText` on it. Let's look at the code for `Element`:

```
public class Element {
    private String name;
    private String text = "";

    public Element(String name) {
        this.name = name;
    }
```

```
    public String getName() {
        return name;
    }

    public void addText(String newText) {
        text += newText;
    }

    public String getText() {
        return text;
    }
}
```

Fortunately, it is very simple. Let's create a bubble for the new element that `generateIndex` creates (see Figure 11.9).

When we have a new element and it is filled with text, `generateIndex` adds it to the collection, so the new element affects the collection (see Figure 11.10).

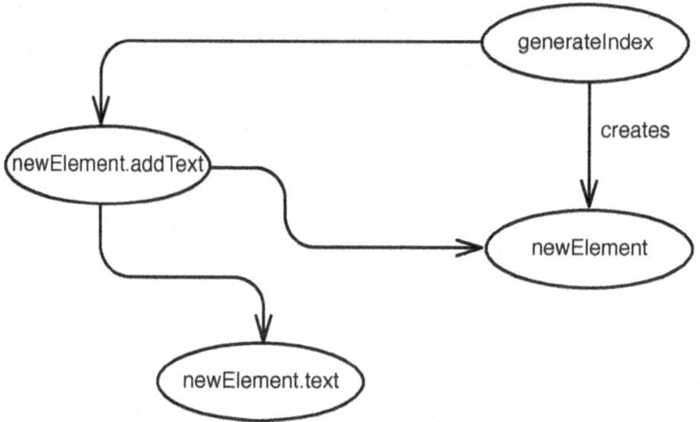

Figure 11.9 *Effects through the* `Element` *class.*

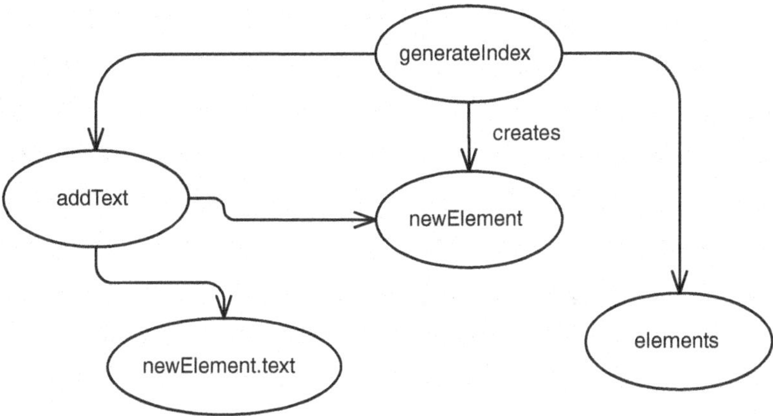

Figure 11.10 `generateIndex` *affecting the* `elements` *collection.*

We know from our previous work that the `addText` method affects the `elements` collection, which, in turn, affects the return values of `getElement` and `getElementCount`. If we want to see that the text is generated correctly, we can call `getText` on an element returned by `getElement`. Those are the only places that we have to write tests to detect the effects of our changes.

As I mentioned earlier, this is a rather small example, but it is very representative of the type of reasoning that we need to do when we assess the impact of changes in legacy code. We need to find places to test, and the first step is figuring out where change can be detected: what the effects of the change are. When we know where we can detect effects, we can pick and choose among them when we write our tests.

Effect Propagation

Some ways that effects propagate are easier to notice than others. In the `InMemoryDirectory` example in the last section, we ended up finding methods that returned values to the caller. Even though I start by tracing effects from change points, places where I am making a change, I usually notice methods with return values first. Unless their return values aren't being used, they propagate effects to code that calls them.

Effects can also propagate in silent, sneaky ways. If we have an object that accepts some object as a parameter, it can modify its state, and the change is reflected back into the rest of the application.

> Each language has rules about how parameters to methods are handled. The default in many cases is to pass references to objects by value. This is the default in Java and C#. Objects aren't passed to methods; instead, "handles" to objects are passed. As a result, any method can change the state of objects through the handle they were passed. Some of these languages have keywords that you can use to make it impossible to modify the state of an object that is passed to them. In C++, the `const` keyword does this when you use it in the declaration of a method parameter.

The sneakiest way that a piece of code can affect other code is through global or static data. Here is an example:

```
public class Element {
    private String name;
    private String text = "";

    public Element(String name) {
        this.name = name;
    }

    public String getName() {
        return name;
    }

    public void addText(String newText) {
        text += newText;
        View.getCurrentDisplay().addText(newText);
    }

    public String getText() {
        return text;
    }
}
```

This class is nearly the same as the `Element` class that we used in the `InMemoryDirectory` example. In fact, only one line of code is different: the second line in `addText`. Looking at the signatures of the methods on `Element` isn't going to help us find the effect that elements have on views. Information hiding is great, unless it is information that we need to know.

Effects propagate in code in three basic ways:

1. Return values that are used by a caller
2. Modification of objects passed as parameters that are used later
3. Modification of static or global data that is used later

Some languages provide additional mechanisms. For instance, in aspect-oriented languages, programmers can write constructs called aspects that affect the behavior of code in other areas of the system.

Here is a heuristic that I use when looking for effects:

1. Identify a method that will change.
2. If the method has a return value, look at its callers.
3. See if the method modifies any values. If it does, look at the methods that use those values, and the methods that use those methods.
4. Make sure you look for superclasses and subclasses that might be users of these instance variables and methods also.
5. Look at parameters to the methods. See if they or any objects that their methods return are used by the code that you want to change.
6. Look for global variables and static data that is modified in any of the methods you've identified.

Tools for Effect Reasoning

The most important tool that we have in our arsenal is knowledge of our programming language. In every language, there are little "firewalls," things that prevent effect propagation. If we know what they are, we know that we don't have to look past them.

Let's suppose that we are about to change the representation in the following coordinate class. We want to move toward using a vector to hold on to the x and y values because we want to generalize the `Coordinate` class so that it can represent three- and four-dimensional coordinates. In the following Java code, we don't have to look beyond the class to understand the effect of that change:


```
public class Coordinate {
    private double x = 0;
    private double y = 0;

    public Coordinate() {}
```

```
    public Coordinate(double x, double y) {
        this.x = x; this.y = y;
    }
    public double distance(Coordinate other) {
        return Math.sqrt(
            Math.pow(other.x - x, 2.0) + Math.pow(other.y - y, 2.0));
    }
}
```

Here is some code that we do have to look beyond:

```
public class Coordinate {
    double x = 0;
    double y = 0;

    public Coordinate() {}
    public Coordinate(double x, double y) {
        this.x = y; this.y = y;
    }
    public double distance(Coordinate other) {
        return Math.sqrt(
            Math.pow(other.x - x, 2.0) + Math.pow(other.y - y, 2.0));
    }
}
```

See the difference? It's subtle. In the first version of the class, the x and y variables were private. In the second, they had package scope. In the first version, if we do anything that changes the x and y variables, it impacts clients only through the `distance` function, regardless of whether clients use `Coordinate` or a subclass of `Coordinate`. In the second version, clients in the package could be accessing the variables directly. We should look for that or try making them private to make sure that they aren't. Subclasses of `Coordinate` can use the instance variables, too, so we have to look at them and see if they are being used in methods of any subclasses.

Knowing our language is important because the subtle rules can often trip us up. Let's take a look at a C++ example:

```
class PolarCoordinate : public Coordinate {
public:
            PolarCoordinate();
    double getRho() const;
    double getTheta() const;
};
```

Tools for Effect Reasoning

In C++, when the keyword `const` comes after a method declaration, the method can't modify the instance variables of the object. Or can it? Suppose that the superclass of `PolarCoordinate` looks like this:

```
class Coordinate {
protected:
    mutable double first, second;
};
```

In C++, when the keyword `mutable` is used in a declaration, it means that those variables can be modified in `const` methods. Admittedly, this use of `mutable` is particularly odd, but when it comes to figuring out what can and can't change in a program that we don't know well, we have to look for effects regardless of how odd they might be. Taking `const` to mean `const` in C++ without really checking can be dangerous. The same holds true for other language constructs that can be circumvented.

Know your language.

Learning from Effect Analysis

Try to analyze effects in code whenever you get a chance. Sometimes you will notice that as you get very familiar with a code base, you feel that you don't have to look for certain things. When you feel that way, you've found some "basic goodness" in your code base. In the best code, there aren't many "gotchas." Some "rules" embodied in the code base, whether they are explicitly stated or not, prevent you from having to be paranoid as you look for possible effects. The best way to find these rules is to think of a way that a piece of software could have an effect on another, a way that you've never seen in the code base. Then say to yourself, "But, no, that would be stupid." When your code base has a lot of rules like that, it is far easier to deal with. In bad code, people don't know what the "rules" are, or the "rules" are littered with exceptions.

The "rules" for a code base aren't necessarily grand statements of programming style, things such as "Never use protected variables." Instead, they are often contextual things. In the `CppClass` example at the beginning of chapter, we did a little exercise in which we tried to figure out what would affect users of a `CppClass` object after we created it. Here is an excerpt of that code:

```
public class CppClass {
    private String name;
    private List declarations;

    public CppClass(String name, List declarations) {
        this.name = name;
        this.declarations = declarations;
    }
    ...
}
```

We listed the fact that someone could modify the declarations list after passing it to the constructor. This is an ideal candidate for a "but that would be stupid" rule. If we know when we start to look at the CppClass that we have been given a list that won't change, our reasoning is much easier.

In general, programming gets easier as we narrow effects in a program. We need to know less to understand a piece of code. At the extreme, we end up with functional programming in languages such as Scheme and Haskell. Programs can actually be very easy to understand in those languages, but those languages aren't in widespread use. Regardless, in OO languages, restricting effects can make testing much easier, and there aren't any hurdles to doing it.

Simplifying Effect Sketches

This book is about making legacy code easier to work with, so there is a sort of "spilt milk" quality to a lot of the examples. However, I wanted to take the opportunity to show you something very useful that you can see through effect sketches. This could affect how you write code as you move forward.

Remember the effect sketch for the CppClass class? (See Figure 11.11.)

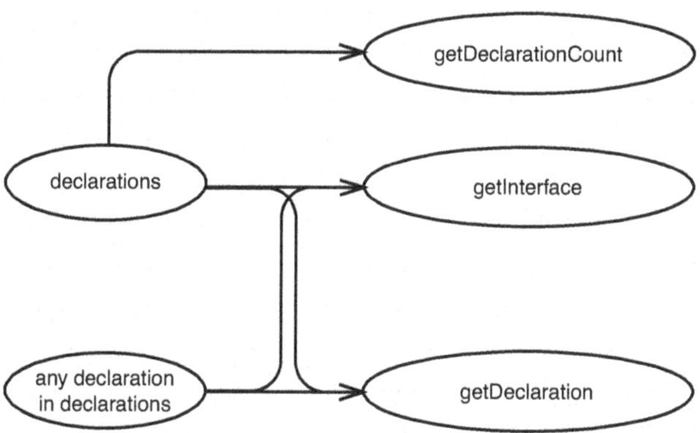

Figure 11.11 *Effect sketch for* CppClass.

It looks like there is a little fan-out. Two pieces of data, a declaration and the declarations collection, have effects on several different methods. We can pick and choose which ones we want to use for our tests. The best one to use is getInterface because it exercises declarations a bit more. Some things we can sense through the getInterface method that we can't as easily through getDeclaration and getDeclarationCount. I wouldn't mind writing only tests for getInterface if I was characterizing CppClass, but it would be a shame that getDeclaration and getDeclarationCount wouldn't be covered. But what if getInterface looked like this?

```
public String getInterface(String interfaceName, int [] indices) {
    String result = "class " + interfaceName + " {\npublic:\n";
    for (int n = 0; n < indices.length; n++) {
        Declaration virtualFunction = getDeclaration(indices[n]);
        result += "\t" + virtualFunction.asAbstract() + "\n";
    }
    result += "};\n";
    return result;
}
```

The difference here is subtle; the code now uses getDeclaration internally. So our sketch changes from Figure 11.12 to Figure 11.13.

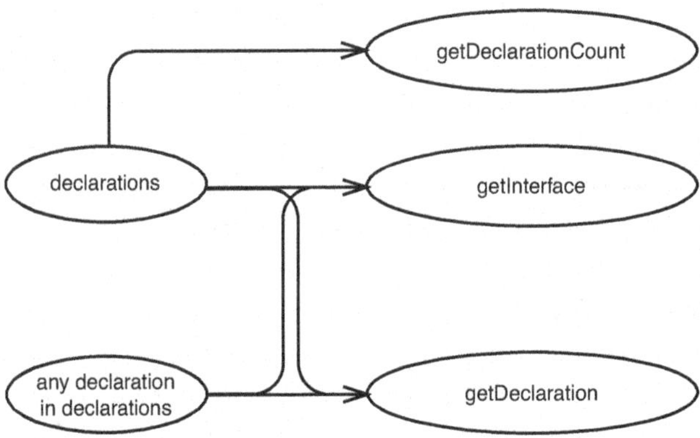

Figure 11.12 *Effect sketch for* `CppClass`.

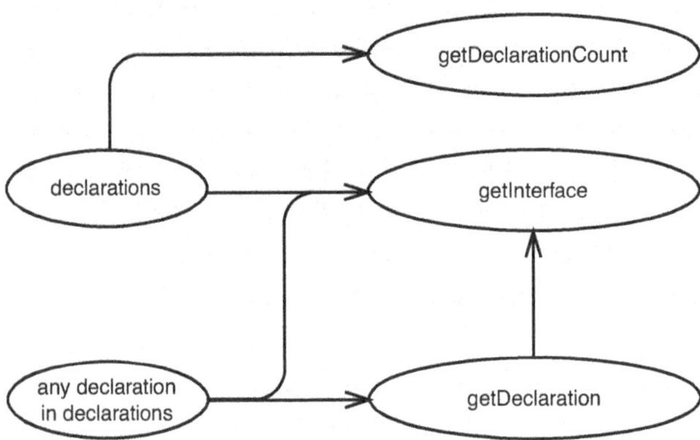

Figure 11.13 *Effect sketch for Changed* `CppClass`.

It's just a small change, but it's a pretty significant one. The `getInterface` method now uses `getDeclaration` internally. We end up exercising `getDeclaration` whenever we test `getInterface`.

When we remove tiny pieces of duplication, we often end up getting effect sketches with a smaller set of endpoints. This often translates into easier testing decisions.

Effects and Encapsulation

One of the often-mentioned benefits of object orientation is encapsulation. Many times when I show people the dependency-breaking techniques in this book, they point out that many of them break encapsulation. That's true. Many of them do.

Encapsulation is important, but the reason why it is important is *more* important. Encapsulation helps us reason about our code. In well-encapsulated code, there are fewer paths to follow as you try to understand it. For instance, if we add another parameter to a constructor to break a dependency as we do in the *Parameterize Constructor (379)* refactoring, we have one more path to follow when we are reasoning about effects. Breaking encapsulation can make reasoning about our code harder, but it can make it easier if we end up with good explanatory tests afterward. When we have test cases for a class, we can use them to reason about our code more directly. We can also write new tests for any questions that we might have about the behavior of the code.

Encapsulation and test coverage aren't always at odds, but when they are, I bias toward test coverage. Often it can help me get more encapsulation later.

Encapsulation isn't an end in itself; it is a tool for understanding.

When we need to find out where to write our tests, it's important to know what can be affected by the changes we are making. We have to reason about effects. We can do this sort of reasoning informally or in a more rigorous way with little sketches, but it pays to practice it. In particularly tangled code, it is one of the only skills we can depend upon in the process of getting tests in place.

Chapter 12

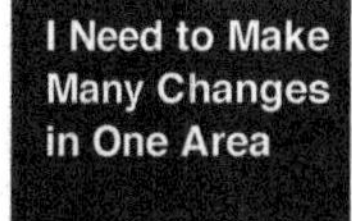

I Need to Make Many Changes in One Area. Do I Have to Break Dependencies for All the Classes Involved?

In some cases, it's easy to start writing tests for a class. But in legacy code, it's often difficult. Dependencies can be hard to break. When you've made a commitment to get classes into test harnesses to make work easier, one of the most infuriating things that you can encounter is a closely scattered change. You need to add a new feature to a system, and you find that you have to modify three or four closely related classes. Each of them would take a couple of hours to get under test. Sure, you know that the code will be better for it at the end, but do you really have to break all of those dependencies individually? Maybe not.

Often it pays to test "one level back," to find a place where we can write tests for several changes at once. We can write tests at a single public method for changes in a number of private methods, or we can write tests at the interface of one object for a collaboration of several objects that it holds. When we do this, we can test the changes we are making, but we also give ourselves some "cover" for more refactoring in the area. The structure of code below the tests can change radically as long as the tests pin down its behavior.

Higher-level tests can be useful in refactoring. Often people prefer them to finely grained tests at each class because they think that change is harder when lots of little tests are written against an interface that has to change. In fact, changes are often easier than you would expect because you can make changes to the tests and then make changes to the code, moving the structure along in small safe increments.

While higher-level tests are an important tool, they shouldn't be a substitute for unit tests. Instead, they should be a first step toward getting unit tests in place.

How do we get these "covering tests" in place? The first thing that we have to figure out is where to write them. If you haven't already, take a look at Chapter 11, *I Need to Make a Change. What Methods Should I Test?* That chapter describes *effect sketches (155)*, a powerful tool that you can use to figure out where to write tests. In this chapter, I describe the concept of an *interception point* and show how to find them. I also describe the best kind of interception points you can find in code, *pinch points*. I show you how to find them and how they can help you when you want to write tests to cover the code you are going to change.

Interception Points

An *interception point* is simply a point in your program where you can detect the effects of a particular change. In some applications, finding them is tougher than it is in others. If you have an application whose pieces are glued together without many natural seams, finding a decent *interception point* can be a big deal. Often it requires some effect reasoning and a lot of dependency breaking. How do we start?

The best way to start is to identify the places where you need to make changes and start tracing effects outward from those change points. Each place where you can detect effects is an *interception point*, but it might not be the best *interception point*. You have to make judgment calls throughout the process.

The Simple Case

Imagine that we have to modify a Java class called `Invoice`, to change the way that costs are calculated. The method that calculates all of the costs for `Invoice` is called `getValue`.

```
public class Invoice
{
    ...
    public Money getValue() {
        Money total = itemsSum();
        if (billingDate.after(Date.yearEnd(openingDate))) {
            if (originator.getState().equals("FL") ||
                    originator.getState().equals("NY"))
                total.add(getLocalShipping());
            else
                total.add(getDefaultShipping());
        }
        else
            total.add(getSpanningShipping());
        total.add(getTax());
        return total;
    }
    ...
}
```

We need to change the way that we calculate shipping costs for New York. The legislature just added a tax that affects our shipping operation there, and, unfortunately, we have to pass the cost on to the consumer. In the process, we are going to extract the shipping cost logic into a new class called `ShippingPricer`. When we're done, the code should look like this:

```
public class Invoice
{
    public Money getValue() {
        Money total = itemsSum();
        total.add(shippingPricer.getPrice());
        total.add(getTax());
        return total;
    }
}
```

All of that work that was done in `getValue` is done by a `ShippingPricer`. We'll have to alter the constructor for `Invoice` also to create a `ShippingPricer` that knows about the invoice dates.

To find our interception points, we have to start tracing effects forward from our change points. The `getValue` method will have a different result. It turns out that no methods in `Invoice` use `getValue`, but `getValue` is used in another class: The `makeStatement` method of a class named `BillingStatement` uses it. This is shown in Figure 12.1.

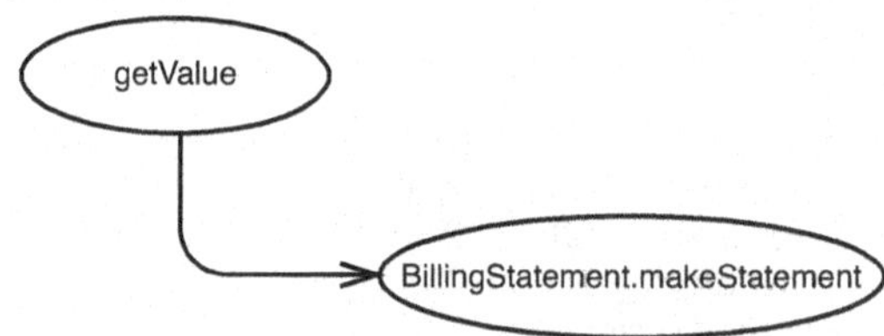

Figure 12.1 `getValue` *affects* `BillingStatement.makeStatement`.

We're also going to be modifying the constructor, so we have to look at code that depends on that. In this case, we're going to be creating a new object in the constructor, a `ShippingPricer`. The pricer won't affect anything except for the methods that use it, and the only one that will use it is the `getValue` method. Figure 12.2 shows this effect.

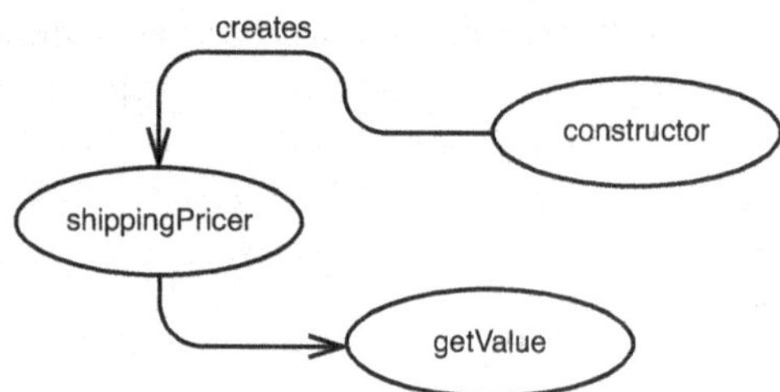

Figure 12.2 *Effects on* `getValue`.

We can piece together the sketches as in Figure 12.3.

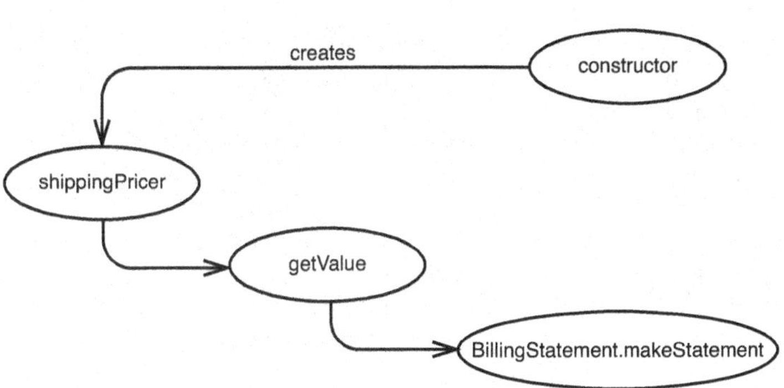

Figure 12.3 *A chain of effects.*

So, where are our interception points? Really, we can use any of the bubbles in the diagram as an *interception point* here, provided that we have access to whatever they represent. We could try to test through the `shippingPricer` variable, but it is a private variable in the `Invoice` class, so we don't have access to it. Even if it were accessible to tests, `shippingPricer` is a pretty narrow *interception point*. We can sense what we've done to the constructor (create the `shippingPricer`) and make sure that the `shippingPricer` does what it is supposed to do, but we can't use it to make sure that `getValue` doesn't change in a bad way.

We could write tests that exercise the `makeStatement` method of `BillingStatement` and check its return value to make sure that we've made our changes correctly. But better than that, we can write tests that exercise `getValue` on `Invoice` and check there. It might even be less work. Sure, it would be nice to get `BillingStatement` under test, but it just isn't necessary right now. If we have to make a change to `BillingStatement` later, we can get it under test then.

Interception Points

In general, it is a good idea to pick *interception points* that are very close to your change points, for a couple of reasons. The first reason is safety. Every step between a change point and an interception point is like a step in a logical argument. Essentially, we are saying, "We can test here because this affects this and that affects this other thing, which affects this thing that we are testing." The more steps you have in the argument, the harder it is know that you have it right. Sometimes the only way you can be sure is by writing tests at the *interception point* and then going back to the change point to alter the code a little bit and see if the test fails. Sometimes you have to fall back on that technique, but you shouldn't have to do it all the time. Another reason why more distant interception points are worse is that it is often harder to set up tests at them. This isn't always true; it depends on the code. What can make it harder is, again, the number of steps between the change and the interception point. Often you have to "play computer" in your mind to know that a test covers some distant piece of functionality.

In the example, the changes that we want to make to `Invoice` are probably best tested for there. We can create an `Invoice` in a test harness, set it up in various ways, and call `getValue` to pin down its behavior while we make our changes.

Higher-Level Interception Points

In most cases, the best *interception point* we can have for a change is a public method on the class we're changing. These interception points are easy to find and easy to use, but sometimes they aren't the best choice. We can see this if we expand the `Invoice` example a bit.

Let's suppose that, in addition to changing the way that shipping costs are calculated for `Invoices`, we have to modify a class named `Item` so that it contains a new field for holding the shipping carrier. We also need a separate per-shipper breakdown in the `BillingStatement`. Figure 12.4 shows what our current design looks like in UML.

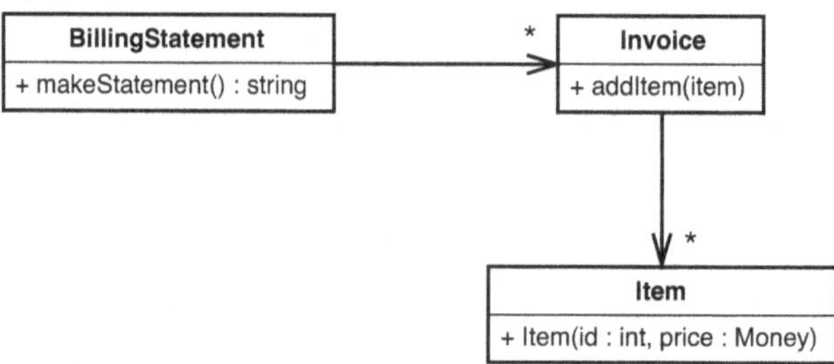

Figure 12.4 *Expanded billing system.*

If none of these classes have tests, we could start by writing tests for each class individually and making the changes that we need. That would work, but it can be more efficient to start out by trying to find a higher-level *interception point* that we can use to characterize this area of the code. The benefits of doing this are twofold: We could have less dependency breaking to do, and we're also holding a bigger chunk in the vise. With tests that characterize this group of classes, we have more cover for refactoring. We can alter the structure of `Invoice` and `Item` using the tests we have at `BillingStatement` as an invariant. Here is a good starter test for characterizing `BillingStatement`, `Invoice`, and `Item` together:

```
void testSimpleStatement() {
    Invoice invoice = new Invoice();
    invoice.addItem(new Item(0,new Money(10));
    BillingStatement statement = new BillingStatement();
    statement.addInvoice(invoice);
    assertEquals("", statement.makeStatement());
}
```

We can find out what `BillingStatement` creates for an invoice of one item and change the test to use that value. Afterward, we can add more tests to see how statement formatting happens for different combinations of invoices and items. We should be especially careful to write cases that exercise areas of the code where we'll be introducing seams.

What makes `BillingStatement` an ideal *interception point* here? It is a single point that we can use to detect effects from changes in a cluster of classes. Figure 12.5 shows the effect sketch for the changes we are going to make.

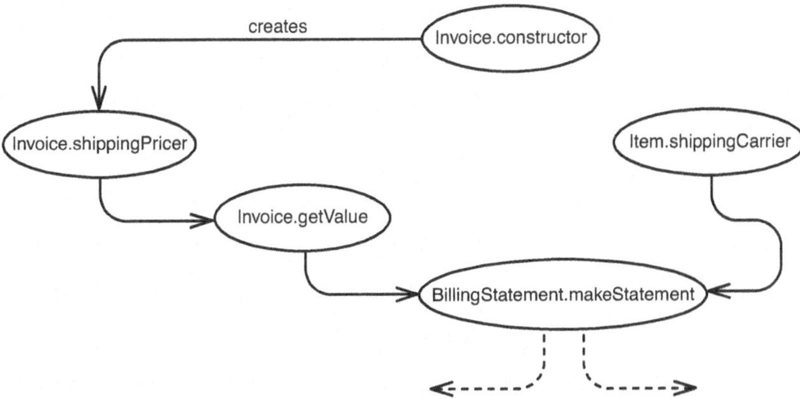

Figure 12.5 *Billing system effect sketch.*

Interception Points

Notice that all effects are detectable through makeStatement. They might not be easy to detect through makeStatement, but, at the very least, this is one place where it is possible to detect them all. The term I use for a place like this in a design is *pinch point*. A *pinch point* is a narrowing in an *effect sketch (155)*, a place where it is possible to write tests to cover a wide set of changes. If you can find a *pinch point* in a design, it can make your work a lot easier.

The key thing to remember about *pinch points*, though, is that they are determined by change points. A set of changes to a class might have a good pinch point even if the class has multiple clients. To see this, let's take a wider look at the invoicing system in Figure 12.6.

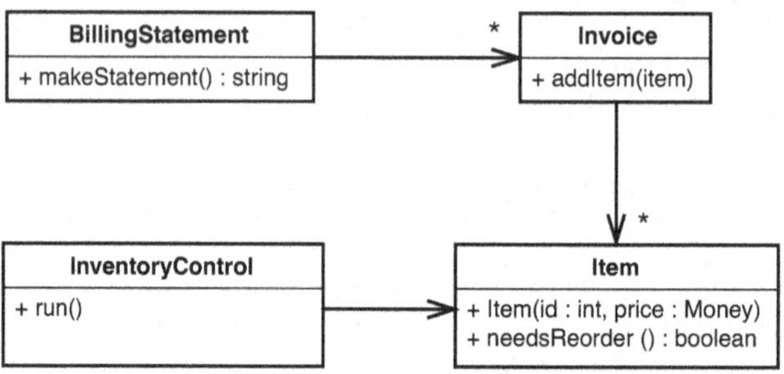

Figure 12.6 *Billing system with inventory.*

We didn't notice it earlier, but Item also has a method named needsReorder. The InventoryControl class calls it whenever it needs to figure out whether it needs to place an order. Does this change our effect sketch for the changes we need to make? Not a bit. Adding a shippingCarrier field to Item doesn't impact the needsReorder method at all, so BillingStatement is still our *pinch point*, our narrow place where we can test.

Let's vary the scenario a bit more. Suppose that we have another change that we need to make. We have to add methods to Item that allow us to get and set the supplier for an Item. The InventoryControl class and the BillingStatement will use the name of the supplier. Figure 12.7 shows what this does to our effect sketch.

Things don't look as good now. The effects of our changes can be detected through the makeStatement method of BillingStatement and through variables affected by the run method of InventoryControl, but there isn't a single *interception point* any longer. However, taken together, the run method and the makeStatement method can be seen as a *pinch point;* together they are just two

methods, and that is a narrower place to detect problems than the eight methods and variables that have to be touched to make the changes. If we get tests in place there, we will have cover for a lot of change work.

Pinch Point

A *pinch point* is a narrowing in an effect sketch, a place where tests against a couple of methods can detect changes in many methods.

In some software, it is pretty easy to find pinch points for sets of changes, but in many cases it is nearly impossible. A single class or method might have dozens of things that it can directly affect, and an effect sketch drawn from it might look like a large tangled tree. What can we do then? One thing that we can do is revisit our change points. Maybe we are trying to do too much at once. Consider finding *pinch points* for only one or two changes at a time. If you can't find a pinch point at all, just try to write tests for individual changes as close as you can.

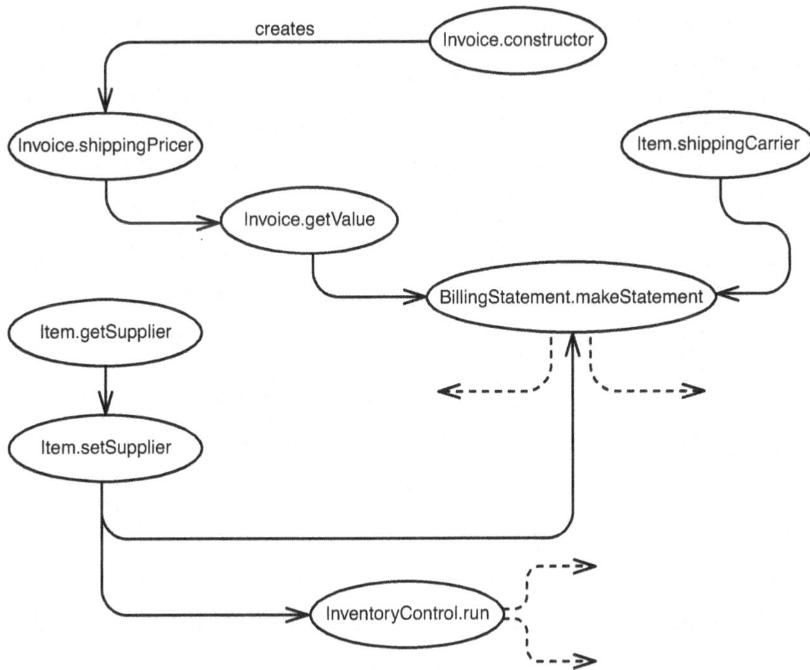

Figure 12.7 *Full billing system scenario.*

Another way of finding a pinch point is to look for common usage across an *effect sketch (155)*. A method or variable might have three users, but that doesn't mean that it is being used in three distinct ways. For example, suppose that we need to do some refactoring of the `needsReorder` method of the `Item` class in the previous example. I haven't shown you the code, but if we sketched out effects, we'd see that we can get a *pinch point* that includes the `run` method of `InventoryControl` and the `makeStatement` method of `BillingStatement`, but we can't really get any narrower than that. Would it be okay to write tests at only one of those classes and not the other? The key question to ask is, "If I break this method, will I be able to sense it in this place?" The answer depends on how the method is used. If it is used the same way on objects that have comparable values, it could be okay to test in one place and not the other. Work through the analysis with a coworker.

Judging Design with Pinch Points

In the previous section, we talked about how useful *pinch points* are in testing, but they have other uses, too. If you pay attention to where your pinch points are, they can give you hints about how to make your code better.

What is a *pinch point*, really? A pinch point is a natural encapsulation boundary. When you find a *pinch point*, you've found a narrow funnel for all of the effects of a large piece of code. If the method `BillingStatement.makeStatement` is a *pinch point* for a bunch of invoices and items, we know where to look when the statement isn't what we expect. The problem then has to be because of the `BillingStatement` class or the invoices and items. Likewise, we don't need to know about invoices and items to call `makeStatement`. This is pretty much the definition of encapsulation: We don't have to care about the internals, but when we do, we don't have to look at the externals to understand them. Often when I look for *pinch points*, I start to notice how responsibilities can be reallocated across classes to give better encapsulation.

Using Effect Sketches to Find Hidden Classes

Sometimes when you have a large class, you can use effect sketches to discover how to break the class into pieces. Here is a little example in Java. We have a class called `Parser` that has a public method named `parseExpression`.

```
public class Parser
{
    private Node root;
    private int currentPosition;
    private String stringToParse;
    public void parseExpression(String expression) { .. }
    private Token getToken() { .. }
    private boolean hasMoreTokens() { .. }
}
```

If we drew an effect sketch for this class, we'd find that `parseExpression` depends on `getToken` and `hasMoreTokens`, but it doesn't directly depend on `stringToParse` or `currentPosition`, even though `getToken` and `hasMoreTokens` do. What we have here is a natural encapsulation boundary, even though it isn't really narrow (two methods hide two pieces of information). We can extract those methods and fields to a class called `Tokenizer` and end up with a simpler `Parser` class.

This isn't the only way to figure out how to separate responsibilities in a class; sometimes the names will give you a hint, as they do in this case (we have two methods with the word `Token` in their names). This can help you see a large class in a different way, and that could lead to some good class extractions.

As an exercise, create an effect sketch for changes in a large class and forget about the names of the bubbles. Just look at how they are grouped. Are there any natural encapsulation boundaries? If there are, look at the bubbles inside a boundary. Think about the name that you would use for that cluster of methods and variables: It could become the name of a new class. Think about whether changing any of the names would help.

When you do this, do it with your teammates. The discussions that you have about naming have benefits far beyond the work that you are currently doing. They help you and your team develop a common view of what the system is and what it can become.

Writing tests at *pinch points* is an ideal way to start some invasive work in part of a program. You make an investment by carving out a set of classes and getting them to the point that you can instantiate them together in a test harness. After you write your *characterization tests (186)*, you can make changes with impunity. You've made a little oasis in your application where the work has just gotten easier. But be careful—it could be a trap.

Pinch Point Traps

We can get in trouble in a couple of ways when we write unit tests. One way is to let unit tests slowly grow into mini-integration tests. We need to test a class, so we instantiate several of its collaborators and pass them to the class. We check some values, and we can feel confident that the whole cluster of objects works well together. The downside is that, if we do this too often, we'll end up with a lot of big, bulky unit tests that take forever to run.

The trick when we are writing unit tests for new code is to test classes as independently as possible. When you start to notice that your tests are too large, you should break down the class that you are testing, to make smaller independent pieces that can be tested more easily. At times, you will have to fake out collaborators because the job of a unit test isn't to see how a cluster of objects behaves together, but rather how a single object behaves. We can test that more easily through a fake object.

When we are writing tests for existing code, the tables are turned. Sometimes it pays to carve off a piece of an application and build it up with tests. When we have those tests in place, we can more easily write narrower unit tests for each of the classes we are touching as we do our work. Eventually, the tests at the *pinch point* can go away.

Tests at *pinch points* are kind of like walking several steps into a forest and drawing a line, saying "I own all of this area." After you know that you own all of that area, you can develop it by refactoring and writing more tests. Over time, you can delete the tests at the *pinch point* and let the tests for each class support your development work.

Chapter 13

I Need to Make a Change, but I Don't Know What Tests to Write

When people talk about testing, they are usually referring to tests that they use to find bugs. Often these tests are manual tests. Writing automated tests to find bugs in legacy code often doesn't feel as efficient as just trying out the code. If you have some way of exercising legacy code manually, you can usually find bugs very quickly. The downside is that you have to do that manual work over and over again whenever you change the code. And, frankly, people just don't do that. Nearly every team I've worked with that depended on manual testing for its changes has ended far behind. The confidence levels of those teams weren't what they could've been.

No, finding bugs in legacy code usually isn't a problem. In terms of strategy, it can actually be misdirected effort. It is usually better to do something that helps your team start to write correct code consistently. The way to win is to concentrate effort on not putting bugs into code in the first place.

Automated tests are a very important tool, but not for bug finding—not directly, at least. In general, automated tests should specify a goal that we'd like to fulfill or attempt to preserve behavior that is already there. In the natural flow of development, tests that *specify* become tests that *preserve*. You will find bugs, but usually not the first time that a test is run. You find bugs in later runs when you change behavior that you didn't expect to.

Where does this leave us with legacy code? In legacy code, we might not have any tests for the changes we need to make, so there isn't any way to really verify that we're preserving behavior when we make changes. For this reason, the best approach we can take when we need to make changes is to bolster the area we want to change with tests to provide some kind of safety net. We'll find bugs along the way, and we'll have to deal with them, but in most legacy code, if we make finding and fixing all of the bugs our goal, we'll never finish.

Characterization Tests

Okay, so we need tests—how do we write them? One way of approaching this is to find out what the software is supposed to do and then write tests based on those ideas. We can try to dig up old requirements documents and project memos, and just sit down and start writing tests. Well, that's one approach, but it isn't a very good one. In nearly every legacy system, what the system does is more important than what it is supposed to do. If we write tests based on our assumption of what the system is supposed to do, we're back to bug finding again. Bug finding is important, but our goal right now is to get tests in place that help us make changes more deterministically.

The tests that we need when we want to preserve behavior are what I call *characterization tests*. A *characterization test* is a test that characterizes the actual behavior of a piece of code. There's no "Well, it should do this" or "I think it does that." The tests document the actual current behavior of the system.

Here is a little algorithm for writing characterization tests:

1. Use a piece of code in a test harness.
2. Write an assertion that you know will fail.
3. Let the failure tell you what the behavior is.
4. Change the test so that it expects the behavior that the code produces.
5. Repeat.

In the following example, I'm reasonably sure that a `PageGenerator` is not going to generate the string `"fred"`:

```
void testGenerator() {
    PageGenerator generator = new PageGenerator();
    assertEquals("fred", generator.generate());
}
```

Run your test and let it fail. When it does, you have found out what the code actually does under that condition. For instance, in the preceding code, a freshly created `PageGenerator` generates an empty string when its `generate` method is called:

```
.F
Time: 0.01
There was 1 failure:
1) testGenerator(PageGeneratorTest)
junit.framework.ComparisonFailure: expected:<fred> but was:<>
     at PageGeneratorTest.testGenerator
         (PageGeneratorTest.java:9)
     at sun.reflect.NativeMethodAccessorImpl.invoke0
         (Native Method)
     at sun.reflect.NativeMethodAccessorImpl.invoke
        (NativeMethodAccessorImpl.java:39)
     at sun.reflect.DelegatingMethodAccessorImpl.invoke
        (DelegatingMethodAccessorImpl.java:25)

FAILURES!!!
Tests run: 1,  Failures: 1,  Errors: 0
```

We can alter the test so that it passes:

```
void testGenerator() {
    PageGenerator generator = new PageGenerator();
    assertEquals("", generator.generate());
}
```

The test passes now. More than that, it documents one of the most basic facts about the `PageGenerator`: When we create one and immediately ask it to generate, it generates an empty string.

We can use the same trick to find out what its behavior would be when we feed it other data:

```
void testGenerator() {
    PageGenerator generator = new PageGenerator();
    generator.assoc(RowMappings.getRow(Page.BASE_ROW));
    assertEquals("fred", generator.generate());
}
```

In this case, the error message of the test harness tells us that the resultant string is "`<node><carry>1.1 vectrai</carry></node>`", so we can make that string the expected value in the test:

```
void testGenerator() {
    PageGenerator generator = new PageGenerator();
    generator.assoc(RowMappings.getRow(Page.BASE_ROW));
    assertEquals("<node><carry>1.1 vectrai</carry></node>",
            generator.generate());
}
```

There is something fundamentally weird about doing this if you are used to thinking about these tests as, well, tests. If we are just putting the values that the software produces into the tests, are our tests really testing anything at all?

What if the software has a bug? The expected values that we're putting in our tests could just simply be wrong.

This problem goes away if we think of our tests in a different way. They aren't really tests written as a gold standard that the software must live up to. We aren't trying to find bugs right now. We are trying to put in a mechanism to find bugs later, bugs that show up as differences from the system's current behavior. When we adopt this perspective, our view of our tests is different: They don't have any moral authority; they just sit there documenting what pieces of the system really do. When we can see what the pieces do, we can use that knowledge along with our knowledge of what the system is supposed to do to make changes. Frankly, it's very important to have that knowledge of what the system actually does someplace. We can usually figure out what behavior we need to add by talking to other people or doing some calculations, but short of the tests, there is no other way to know what a system actually does except by "playing computer" in our minds, reading code and trying to reason through what the values will be at particular times. Some people do that faster than others, but regardless of how fast we can do it, it's pretty tedious and wasteful to have to do it over and over again.

> Characterization tests record the actual behavior of a piece of code. If we find something unexpected when we write them, it pays to get some clarification. It could be a bug. That doesn't mean that we don't include the test in our test suite; instead, we should mark it as suspicious and find out what the effect would be of fixing it.

There is a lot more to writing characterization tests than what I've described so far. In the page generator example, it seemed like we were getting test values blindly by throwing values at the code and getting them back in the assertions. We can do that if we have a good sense of what the code is supposed to do. Some cases, such as not doing anything to an object and then seeing what its methods produce, are easy to think of and worth characterizing, but where do we go next? What is the total number of tests that we can apply to something like the page generator? It's infinite. We could dedicate a good portion of our lives to writing case after case for this class. When do we stop? Is there any way of knowing which cases are more important than others?

The important thing to realize is that we aren't writing black-box tests here. We are allowed to look at the code we are characterizing. The code itself can give us ideas about what it does, and if we have questions, tests are an ideal way of asking them. The first step in characterizing is to get into a state of curiosity about the code's behavior. At that point, we just write tests until we are satisfied that we understand it. Does that cover everything in the code? It might not. But then we do the next step. We think about the changes that we want to make in the code and try to figure out whether the tests that we have will sense any problems that we can cause. If they won't, we add more tests until we feel confidence that they will. If we can't feel that confidence, it's safer to consider changing the software in a different way. Maybe we can do a piece of what we were considering first.

The Method Use Rule

Before you use a method in a legacy system, check to see if there are tests for it. If there aren't, write them. When you do this consistently, you use tests as a medium of communication. People can look at them and get a sense of what they can and cannot expect from the method. The act of making a class testable in itself tends to increase code quality. People can find out what works and how; they can change it, correct bugs, and move forward.

Characterizing Classes

We have a class, and we want to figure out what to test. How do we do it? The first thing to do is to try to figure out what the class does at a high level. We can write tests for the simplest thing that we can imagine it doing and then let our curiosity guide us from there. Here are some heuristics that can help:

1. Look for tangled pieces of logic. If you don't understand an area of code, consider introducing a *sensing variable (301)* to characterize it. Use sensing variables to make sure you execute particular areas of the code.

2. As you discover the responsibilities of a class or method, stop to make a list of the things that can go wrong. See if you can formulate tests that trigger them.

3. Think about the inputs you are supplying under test. What happens at extreme values?

4. Should any conditions be true at all times during the lifetime of the class? Often these are called invariants. Attempt to write tests to verify them. Often you might have to refactor to discover these conditions. If you do, the refactorings often lead to new insight about how the code should be.

The tests that we write to characterize code are very important. They are the documentation of the system's actual behavior. Like any documentation that you write, you have to think about what will be important to the reader. Put yourself in the reader's shoes. What would you like to know about the class you are working with if you'd never seen it? In what order would you like the information? When you use the xUnit frameworks, tests are just methods in a file.

You can put them in an order that makes it easier for people to learn about the code they exercise. Start with some easy cases that show the main intent of the class, and then move into cases that highlight its idiosyncrasies. Make sure you document the important things that you discover as tests. When you get to making your changes, often you'll find that the tests you've written are very appropriate for the work you are about to do. Whether we think about it consciously or not, the change that we set out to make often guides our curiosity.

When You Find Bugs

When you characterize legacy code, you will find bugs throughout the entire process. All legacy code has bugs, usually in direct proportion to how little it is understood. What should you do when you find a bug?

The answer depends on the situation. If the system has never been deployed, the answer is simple: You should fix the bug. If the system has been deployed, you need to examine the possibility that someone is depending on that behavior, even though you see it as a bug. Often it takes a bit of analysis to figure out how to fix a bug without causing ripple effects.

My bias is toward fixing bugs as soon as they are found. When behavior is clearly in error, it should be fixed. If you suspect that some behavior is wrong, mark it in the test code as suspicious and then escalate it. Find out as quickly as you can whether it is a bug and how best to deal with it.

Targeted Testing

After we've written tests to understand a section of code, we have to look at the things that we want to change and see if our tests really cover them. Here is an example, a method on a Java class that computes the value of fuel in leased tanks:

```
public class FuelShare
{
    private long cost = 0;
    private double corpBase = 12.0;
    private ZonedHawthorneLease lease;
    ...
    public void addReading(int gallons, Date readingDate){
        if (lease.isMonthly()) {
            if (gallons < Lease.CORP_MIN)
                cost += corpBase;
            else
                cost += 1.2 * priceForGallons(gallons);
        }
        ...
```

```
        lease.postReading(readingDate, gallons);
    }
    ...
}
```

We want to make a very direct change to the FuelShare class. We've already written some tests for it, so we are ready. Here is the change: We want to extract the top-level if-statement to a new method and then move that method to the ZonedHawthorneLease class. The lease variable in the code is an instance of that class.

We can imagine what the code will look like after we refactor:

```
public class FuelShare
{
    public void addReading(int gallons, Date readingDate){
        cost += lease.computeValue(gallons,
                               priceForGallons(gallons));
        ...
        lease.postReading(readingDate, gallons);
    }
    ...
}

public class ZonedHawthorneLease extends Lease
{
    public long computeValue(int gallons, long totalPrice) {
        long cost = 0;
        if (lease.isMonthly()) {
            if (gallons < Lease.CORP_MIN)
                cost += corpBase;
            else
                cost += 1.2 * totalPrice;
        }
        return cost;
    }
    ...
}
```

What kind of tests do we need to make sure that we do these refactorings correctly? One thing is certain: We know that we aren't going to be modifying this piece of logic at all:

```
    if (gallons < Lease.CORP_MIN)
        cost += corpBase;
```

Having a test in place to see how the value is computed below the Lease.CORP_MIN limit would be nice, but it is not strictly necessary. On the other hand, this else-statement in the original code is going to change:

```
else
    cost += 1.2 * priceForGallons(gallons);
```

When that code moves over to the new method, it will become this:

```
else
    cost += 1.2 * totalPrice;
```


That's a small change, but it is a change nonetheless. If we can make sure that the else-statement executes in one of our tests, we're better off. Let's look at the original method again:

```
public class FuelShare
{
    public void addReading(int gallons, Date readingDate){
        if (lease.isMonthly()) {
            if (gallons < CORP_MIN)
                cost += corpBase;
            else
                cost += 1.2 * priceForGallons(gallons);
        }
        ...
        lease.postReading(readingDate, gallons);
    }
    ...
}
```

If we are able to make a `FuelShare` with a monthly lease and we attempt to `addReading` for a number of gallons greater than `Lease.CORP_MIN`, we'll go through that leg of the else:

```
public void testValueForGallonsMoreThanCorpMin() {
    StandardLease lease = new  StandardLease(Lease.MONTHLY);
    FuelShare share = new FuelShare(lease);

    share.addReading(FuelShare.CORP_MIN +1, new Date());
    assertEquals(12, share.getCost());
}
```

When you write a test for a branch, ask yourself whether there is any other way that the test could pass, aside from executing that branch. If you are not sure, use a *sensing variable (301)* or the debugger to find out whether the test is hitting it.

One important thing to figure out when you are characterizing branches such as this is whether the inputs that you provide have special behavior that could lead a test to succeed when it should fail. Here's an example. Suppose that the code used doubles instead of ints to represent money:

```
public class FuelShare
{
    private double cost = 0.0;
    ...
    public void addReading(int gallons, Date readingDate){
        if (lease.isMonthly()) {
            if (gallons < CORP_MIN)
                cost += corpBase;
            else
                cost += 1.2 * priceForGallons(gallons);
        }
        ...
        lease.postReading(readingDate, gallons);
    }
    ...
}
```


We could run into some serious trouble. And, no, I'm not referring to the fact that the application probably leaks fractional cents all over the place because of floating-point rounding errors. Unless we pick our inputs well, we could make a mistake when we extract a method and never know it. One possible mistake could happen if we extract a method and make one of its arguments an int rather than a double. In Java and many other languages, there is an automatic conversion from doubles to ints; the runtime just truncates the value. Unless we take care to devise inputs that will force us to see that error, we'll miss it.

Let's look at an example. What would be the effect on the previous code if the value of Lease.`CORP_MIN` is `10` and the value of `corpBase` is `12.0` when we run this test?

```
public void testValue () {
    StandardLease lease = new  StandardLease(Lease.MONTHLY);
    FuelShare share = new FuelShare(lease);

    share.addReading(1, new Date());
    assertEquals(12, share.getCost());
}
```

Because 1 is less than 10, we just add 12.0 to the initial value of `cost`, which is 0. At the end of the calculation, the value of `cost` is `12.0`. That is perfectly fine, but what if we extract the method like this and declare the value of `cost` as a long rather than a double?

```
public class ZonedHawthorneLease
{
    public long computeValue(int gallons, long totalPrice) {
        long cost = 0;
        if (lease.isMonthly()) {
```

```
            if (gallons < CORP_MIN)
                cost += corpBase;
            else
                cost += 1.2 * totalPrice;
        }
        return cost;
    }
}
```

That test that we wrote still passes, even though we are silently truncating the value of `cost` when we return it. A conversion from double to int is being executed, but it isn't really being fully exercised. It does the same thing that it would if there was no conversion, if we were just assigning an int to an int.

> When we refactor, we generally have to check for two things: Does the behavior exist after the refactoring, and is it connected correctly?
>
> Many characterization tests look like "sunny day" tests. They don't test many special conditions; they just verify that particular behaviors are present. From their presence, we can infer that refactorings that we've done to move or extract code have preserved behavior.

How can we handle this? There are a couple of general strategies. One is to manually calculate the expected values for a piece of code. At each conversion, we see whether there is a truncation issue. Another technique is to use a debugger and step through assignments so that we can see what conversions a particular set of inputs triggers. A third technique is to use *sensing variables (301)* to verify that a particular path is being covered and that the conversions are exercised.

> The most valuable characterization tests exercise a specific path and exercise each conversion along the path.

There is a fourth option also. We can just decide to characterize a smaller chunk of code. If we have a refactoring tool that helps us extract methods safely, we can extract methods smaller than `computeValue` method and write tests for its pieces. Unfortunately, not all languages have refactoring tools—and at times, even the tools that are available don't extract methods the way that you wish they would.

Refactoring Tool Quirks

A good refactoring tool is invaluable, but often people who have these tools have to resort to refactoring by hand. Here is one common case. We have a class A with some code that we'd like to extract in its b() method:

```
public class A
{
    int x = 1;
    public void b() {
        int y = 0;
        int c = x + y;
    }
};
```

If we want to extract the `x + y` expression in method `b` and make a method called `add`, at least one tool on the market will extract it as `add(y)` rather than `add(x,y)`. Why? Because `x` is an instance variable and it is available to whatever methods we extract.

A Heuristic for Writing Characterization Tests

1. Write tests for the area where you will make your changes. Write as many cases as you feel you need to understand the behavior of the code.

2. After doing this, take a look at the specific things you are going to change, and attempt to write tests for those.

3. If you are attempting to extract or move some functionality, write tests that verify the existence and connection of those behaviors on a case-by-case basis. Verify that you are exercising the code that you are going to move and that it is connected properly. Exercise conversions.

Chapter 14

Dependencies on Libraries Are Killing Me

One thing that really helps development is code reuse. If we can buy a library that solves some problem for us (and figure out how to use it), we can often cut substantial time off a project. The only problem is that it is very easy to become over-reliant on a library. If you use it promiscuously throughout your code, you are pretty much stuck with it. Some teams I've worked with have been severely burned by their over-reliance on libraries. In one case, a vendor raised royalties so high that the application couldn't make money in the marketplace. The team couldn't easily use another vendor's library because removing all of the calls to the original vendor's code would've amounted to a rewrite.

Avoid littering direct calls to library classes in your code. You might think that you'll never change them, but that can become a self-fulfilling prophecy.

At the time of this writing, much of the development world is polarized around Java and .NET. Both Microsoft and Sun have tried to make their platforms as broad as possible, creating many libraries so that people will continue to use their products. In a way, it is a win for many projects, but you can still over rely on particular libraries. Every hard-coded use of a library class is a place where you could have had a seam. Some libraries are very good about defining interfaces for all of their concrete classes. In other cases, classes are concrete and declared *final* or *sealed*, or they have key functions that are non-virtual, leaving no way to fake them out under test. In these cases, sometimes the best thing you can do is write a thin wrapper over the classes that you need to separate out. Make sure that you write your vendor and give them grief about making your development work difficult.

Library designers who use language features to enforce design constraints are often making a mistake. They forget that good code runs in production and test environments. Constraints for the former can make working in the latter nearly impossible.

A fundamental tension exists between language features that try to enforce good design and things you have to do to test code. One of the most prevalent tensions is the *once dilemma*. If library assumes that there is going to be only one instance of a class in a system, it can make the use of fake objects difficult. There might not be any way to use *Introduce Static Setter (372)* or many of the other dependency-breaking techniques that you can use to deal with singletons. Sometimes wrapping the singleton is the only choice available to you.

A related problem is the *restricted override dilemma*. In some OO languages, all methods are virtual. In others, they are virtual by default, but they can be made non-virtual. In others, you have to explicitly make them virtual. From a design perspective, there is some value in making some methods non-virtual. At times, various people in the industry have recommended making as many methods non-virtual as possible. Sometimes the reasons they give are good, but it is hard to deny that this practice makes it hard to introduce sensing and separation in code bases. It is also hard to deny that people often write very good code in Smalltalk, where that practice is impossible; in Java, where people generally don't do it; and even in C++, where plenty of code has been written without it. You can do very well just pretending that a public method is non-virtual in production code. If you do that, you can override it selectively in test and get the best of both worlds.

Sometimes using a coding convention is just as good as using a restrictive language feature. Think about what your tests need.

Chapter 15

My Application Is All API Calls

Build, buy, or borrow. It's a choice we all have to make when we develop software. Many times when we're working on an application, we suspect that we can save ourselves some time and effort by buying some vendor library, using some open source, or even just using significant chunks of code from libraries that come bundled with our platform (J2EE, .NET, and so on). There are many different things to consider when choosing to integrate code we can't change easily. We have to know how stable it is, whether it is sufficient, and how easy it is to use. And, when we do finally decide to use someone else's code, we're often left with another problem. We end up with applications that look like they are nothing but repeated calls to someone else's library. How do we make changes in code like that?

The immediate temptation is to say that we don't really need tests. After all, we aren't really doing anything significant; we're just calling a method here and there, and our code is simple. It's really simple. What can go wrong?

Many legacy projects have started from those humble beginnings. The code grows and grows, and things aren't quite as simple anymore. Over time, we might still be able to see areas of code that don't touch an API, but they are embedded in a patchwork of untestable code. We have to run the application every time we change something to make sure that it still works, and we are right back in the central dilemma of the legacy system programmer. Changes are uncertain; we didn't write all of the code, but we have to maintain it.

Systems that are littered with library calls are harder to deal with than home-grown systems, in many respects. The first reason is that it is often hard to see how to make the structure better because all you can see are the API calls. Anything that would've been a hint at a design just isn't there. The second reason that API-intensive systems are difficult is that we don't own the API. If we did, we could rename interfaces, classes, and methods to make things clearer for us, or add methods to classes to make them available to different parts of the code.

Here is an example. This is a listing of very poorly written code for a mailing list server. We're not even sure it works.

```
import java.io.IOException;
import java.util.Properties;

import javax.mail.*;
import javax.mail.internet.*;


public class MailingListServer
{
  public static final String SUBJECT_MARKER = "[list]";
  public static final String LOOP_HEADER = "X-Loop";

  public static void main (String [] args) {
    if (args.length != 8) {
      System.err.println ("Usage: java MailingList <popHost> " +
          "<smtpHost> <pop3user> <pop3password> " +
          "<smtpuser> <smtppassword> <listname> " +
          "<relayinterval>");
      return;
    }

    HostInformation host = new HostInformation (
            args [0], args [1], args [2], args [3],
            args [4], args [5]);
    String listAddress = args[6];
    int interval = new Integer (args [7]).intValue ();
    Roster roster = null;
    try {
      roster = new FileRoster("roster.txt");
    } catch (Exception e) {
      System.err.println ("unable to open roster.txt");
      return;
    }
    try {
      do {
        try {
          Properties properties = System.getProperties ();
          Session session = Session.getDefaultInstance (
              properties, null);
          Store store = session.getStore ("pop3");
          store.connect (host.pop3Host, -1,
              host.pop3User, host.pop3Password);
          Folder defaultFolder = store.getDefaultFolder();
          if (defaultFolder == null) {
            System.err.println("Unable to open default folder");
            return;
          }
          Folder folder = defaultFolder.getFolder ("INBOX");
          if (folder == null) {
```

```
          System.err.println("Unable to get: "
                  + defaultFolder);
          return;
        }
        folder.open (Folder.READ_WRITE);
        process(host, listAddress, roster, session,
            store, folder);
      } catch (Exception e) {
        System.err.println(e);
        System.err.println ("(retrying mail check)");
      }
      System.err.print (".");
      try { Thread.sleep (interval * 1000); }
      catch (InterruptedException e) {}
    } while (true);
  }
  catch (Exception e) {
    e.printStackTrace ();
  }
}

private static void process(
    HostInformation host, String listAddress, Roster roster,
    Session session,Store store, Folder folder)
        throws MessagingException {
  try {
    if (folder.getMessageCount() != 0) {
      Message[] messages = folder.getMessages ();
      doMessage(host, listAddress, roster, session,
          folder, messages);
    }
  } catch (Exception e) {
    System.err.println ("message handling error");
    e.printStackTrace (System.err);
  }
  finally {
    folder.close (true);
    store.close ();
  }
}

private static void doMessage(
        HostInformation host,
        String listAddress,
        Roster roster,
        Session session,
        Folder folder,
        Message[] messages) throws
            MessagingException, AddressException, IOException,
            NoSuchProviderException {
  FetchProfile fp = new FetchProfile ();
  fp.add (FetchProfile.Item.ENVELOPE);
```

```
    fp.add (FetchProfile.Item.FLAGS);
    fp.add ("X-Mailer");
    folder.fetch (messages, fp);
    for (int i = 0; i < messages.length; i++) {
      Message message = messages [i];
      if (message.getFlags ().contains (Flags.Flag.DELETED))
        continue;
      System.out.println("message received: "
          + message.getSubject ());
      if (!roster.containsOneOf (message.getFrom ()))
        continue;
      MimeMessage forward = new MimeMessage (session);
      InternetAddress result = null;
      Address [] fromAddress = message.getFrom ();
      if (fromAddress != null && fromAddress.length > 0)
        result =
            new InternetAddress (fromAddress [0].toString ());
      InternetAddress from = result;
      forward.setFrom (from);
      forward.setReplyTo (new Address [] {
        new InternetAddress (listAddress) });
      forward.addRecipients (Message.RecipientType.TO,
          listAddress);
      forward.addRecipients (Message.RecipientType.BCC,
        roster.getAddresses ());
      String subject = message.getSubject();
      if (-1 == message.getSubject().indexOf (SUBJECT_MARKER))
        subject = SUBJECT_MARKER + " " + message.getSubject();
      forward.setSubject (subject);
      forward.setSentDate (message.getSentDate ());
      forward.addHeader (LOOP_HEADER, listAddress);
      Object content = message.getContent ();
      if (content instanceof Multipart)
        forward.setContent ((Multipart)content);
      else
        forward.setText ((String)content);

      Properties props = new Properties ();
      props.put ("mail.smtp.host", host.smtpHost);

      Session smtpSession =
          Session.getDefaultInstance (props, null);
      Transport transport = smtpSession.getTransport ("smtp");
      transport.connect (host.smtpHost,
          host.smtpUser, host.smtpPassword);
      transport.sendMessage (forward, roster.getAddresses ());
      message.setFlag (Flags.Flag.DELETED, true);
    }
  }
}
```

It's a pretty small piece of code, but it isn't very clear. It's hard to see any lines of code that don't touch an API. Could this code be structured better? Could it be structured in a way that makes change easier?

Yes, it can.

The first step is to identify the computational core of code: What is this chunk of code really doing for us?

It might help to try to write a brief description of what it does:

> *This code reads configuration information from the command line and a list of e-mail addresses from a file. It checks for mail periodically. When it finds mail, it forwards it to each of the e-mail addresses in the file.*

It seems that this program is mainly about input and output, but there is a little bit more. We're running a thread in the code. It sleeps and then wakes up periodically to check for mail. In addition, we aren't just sending out the incoming mail messages again; we're making new messages based on the incoming one. We have to set all of the fields and then check and alter the subject line so that it shows that the message is coming from the mailing list. So, we are doing some real work.

If we try to separate the code's responsibilities, we might end up with something like this:

1. We need something that can receive each incoming message and feed it into our system.
2. We need something that can just send out a mail message.
3. We need something that can make new messages for each incoming message, based on our roster of list recipients.
4. We need something that sleeps most of the time but wakes up periodically to see if there is more mail.

Now when we look at those responsibilities, does it seem like some are more tied to the Java Mail API than others? Responsibilities 1 and 2 are definitely tied to the mail API. Responsibility 3 is a little trickier. The message classes that we need are part of the mail API, but we can probably test the responsibility independently by creating dummy incoming messages. Responsibility 4 doesn't really have anything to do with mail; it just requires a thread that is set to wake up at certain intervals.

Figure 15.1 shows a little design that separates out these responsibilities.

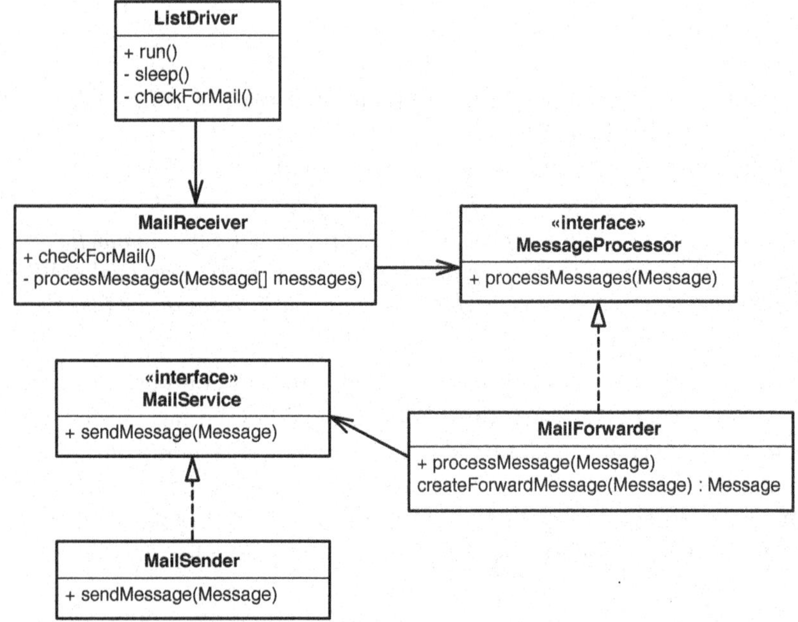

Figure 15.1 *A better mailing list server.*

`ListDriver` drives the system. It has a thread that sleeps most of the time and wakes up periodically to check for mail. `ListDriver` checks for mail by telling the `MailReceiver` to check for mail. The `MailReceiver` reads the mail and sends the messages one by one to a `MessageForwarder`. The `MessageForwarder` creates messages for each of the list recipients and mails them using the `MailSender`.

This design is pretty nice. The `MessageProcessor` and `MailService` interfaces are handy because they allow us to test the classes independently. In particular, it's great to be able to work on the `MessageFowarder` class in a test harness without actually sending mail. That's easily achievable if we make a `FakeMailSender` class that implements the `MailService` interface.

Nearly every system has some core logic that can be peeled away from API calls. Although this case is small, it is actually worse than most. `MessageForwarder` is the piece of the system whose responsibility is most independent of the mechanics of sending and receiving mail, but it still uses the message classes of the JavaMail API. It doesn't seem like there are many places for plain old Java classes. Regardless, factoring the system into four classes and two interfaces in the diagram does give us some layering. The primary logic of the mailing list is in the MessageForwarder class, and we can get it under test. In the original code, it was buried and unapproachable. It's nearly impossible to break up a system into smaller pieces without ending up with some that are "higher level" than others.

When we have a system that looks like it is nothing but API calls, it helps to imagine that it is just one big object and then apply the responsibility-separation heuristics in Chapter 20, *This Class Is Too Big and I Don't Want It to Get Any Bigger.* We might not be able to move toward a better design immediately, but just the act of identifying the responsibilities can make it easier to make better decisions as we move forward.

Okay, that was what a better design looks like. It's nice to know that it's possible, but back to reality: How do we move forward? There are essentially two approaches:

1. Skin and Wrap the API
2. Responsibility-Based Extraction

When we *Skin and Wrap the API*, we make interfaces that mirror the API as close as possible and then create wrappers around that API. To minimize our chances of making mistakes, we can *Preserve Signatures (312)* as we work. One advantage to skinning and wrapping an API is that we can end up having no dependencies on the underlying API code. Our wrappers can delegate to the real API in production code and we can use fakes during test.

Can we use this technique with the mailing list code?

This is the code in the mailing list server that actually sends the mail messages:

```
...
Session smtpSession = Session.getDefaultInstance (props, null);
Transport transport = smtpSession.getTransport ("smtp");
transport.connect (host.smtpHost, host.smtpUser,
    host.smtpPassword);
transport.sendMessage (forward, roster.getAddresses ());
...
```

If we wanted to break the dependency on the Transport class, we could make a wrapper for it, but in this code, we don't create the Transport object; we get it from the Session class. Can we create a wrapper for Session? Not really—Session is a final class. In Java, final classes can't be subclassed (grumble, grumble).

This mailing list code is really a poor candidate for skinning. The API is relatively complicated. But if we don't have any refactoring tools available, it could be the safest course.

Luckily, there are refactoring tools available for Java, so we can do something else called *Responsibility-Based Extraction.* In *Responsibility-Based Extraction*, we identify responsibilities in the code and start extracting methods for them.

What are the responsibilities in the preceding snippet of code? Well, its overall goal is to send a message. What does it need to do this? It needs an SMTP session and a connected transport. In the following code, we've extracted the responsibility of sending messages into its own method and added that method to a new class: `MailSender`.


```
import javax.mail.*;
import javax.mail.internet.InternetAddress;
import java.util.Properties;

public class MailSender
{
  private HostInformation host;
  private Roster roster;

  public MailSender (HostInformation host, Roster roster) {
    this.host = host;
    this.roster = roster;
  }

  public void sendMessage (Message message) throws Exception {
    Transport transport
        = getSMTPSession ().getTransport ("smtp");
    transport.connect (host.smtpHost,
                       host.smtpUser, host.smtpPassword);
    transport.sendMessage (message, roster.getAddresses ());
  }

  private Session getSMTPSession () {
    Properties props = new Properties ();
    props.put ("mail.smtp.host", host.smtpHost);
    return Session.getDefaultInstance (props, null);
  }
}
```

How do we choose between *Skin and Wrap the API* and *Responsibility-Based Extraction*? Here are the trade-offs:

Skin and Wrap the API is good in these circumstances:

- The API is relatively small.
- You want to completely separate out dependencies on a third-party library.

- You don't have tests, and you can't write them because you can't test through the API.

When we skin and wrap an API, we have the chance to get all of our code under test except for a thin layer of delegation from the wrapper to the real API classes.

Responsibility-Based Extraction is good in these circumstances:

- The API is more complicated.
- You have a tool that provides a safe extract method support, or you feel confident that you can do the extractions safely by hand.

Balancing the advantages and disadvantages of these techniques is kind of tricky. *Skin and Wrap the API* is more work, but it can be very useful when we want to isolate ourselves from third-party libraries, and that need comes up often. See Chapter 14, *Dependencies on Libraries Are Killing Me*, for details. When we use *Responsibility-Based Extraction*, we might end up extracting some of our own logic with the API code just so that we can extract a method with a higher-level name. If we do, our code can depend on higher-level interfaces rather than low-level API calls, but we might not be able to get the code we've extracted under test.

Many teams use both techniques: a thin wrapper for testing and a higher-level wrapper to present a better interface to their application.

Chapter 16

I Don't Understand the Code Well Enough to Change It

Stepping into unfamiliar code, especially legacy code, can be scary. Over time, some people become relatively immune to the fear. They develop confidence from confronting and slaying monsters in code over and over again, but it is tough not to be afraid. Everyone runs into demons that they can't slay from time to time. If you dwell on it before you start to look at the code, that makes it worse. You never know whether a change is going to be simple or a weeklong hair-pulling exercise that leaves you cursing the system, your situation, and nearly everything around you. If we understood everything we need to know to make our changes, things would go smoother. How can we get that understanding?

Here's a typical situation. You find out about a feature that you need to add to a system. You sit down and you start to browse the code. Sometimes you can find out everything you need to know quickly, but in legacy code, it can take some time. All the while, you are making a mental list of the things you have to do, trading off one approach against another. At some point, you might feel like you are making progress and you feel confident enough to start. In other cases, you might start to get dizzy from all of the things that you are trying to assimilate. Your code reading doesn't seem to be helping, and you just start working on what you know how to do, hoping for the best.

There are other ways of gaining understanding, but many people don't use them because they are so caught up in trying to understand the code in the most immediate way that they can. After all, spending time trying to understand something looks and feels suspiciously like not working. If we can get through the understanding bit very fast, we can really start to earn our pay. Does that sound silly? It does to me, too, but often people do act that way—and it's unfortunate because we can do some simple, low-tech things to start work on a more solid footing.

Notes/Sketching

When reading through code gets confusing, it pays to start drawing pictures and making notes. Write down the name of the last important thing that you saw, and then write down the name of the next one. If you see a relationship between them, draw a line. These sketches don't have to be full-blown UML diagrams or function call graphs using some special notation—although, if things get more confusing, you might want to get more formal or neater to organize your thoughts. Sketching things out often helps us see things in a different way. It's also a great way of maintaining our mental state when we are trying to understand something particularly complex.

Figure 16.1 is a re-creation of a sketch that I drew with another programmer the other day as we were browsing code. We drew it on the back of a memo (the names in the sketch have been changed to protect the innocent).

The sketch is not very intelligible now, but it was fine for our conversation. We learned a bit and established an approach for our work.

Doesn't everyone do this? Well, yes and no. Few people do it frequently. I suspect that the reason is because there really isn't any guidance for this sort of thing, and it's tempting to think that every time we put pen to paper, we should be writing a snippet of code or using UML syntax. UML is fine, but so are blobs and lines and shapes that would be indecipherable to anyone who wasn't there when we drew them. The precision doesn't have to be on paper. The paper is just a tool to make conversation go easier and help us remember the concepts we're discussing and learning.

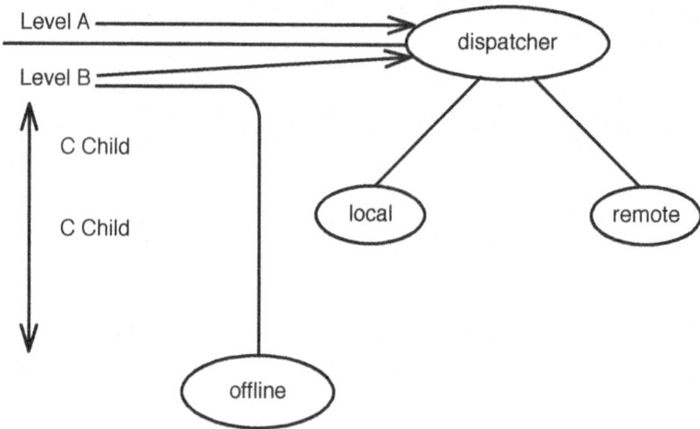

Figure 16.1 *Sketch.*

The really great thing about sketching parts of a design as you are trying to understand them is that it is informal and infectious. If you find this technique useful, you don't have to push for your team to make it part of its process. All you have to do is this: Wait until you are working with someone trying to understand some code, and then make a little sketch of what you are looking at as you try to explain it. If your partner is really engaged in learning that part of the system too, he or she will look at the sketch and go back and forth with you as you figure out the code.

When you start to do local sketches of a system, often you are tempted to take some time to understand the big picture. Take a look at Chapter 17, *My Application Has No Structure*, for a set of techniques that make it easier to understand and tend a large code base.

Listing Markup

Sketching isn't the only thing that aids understanding. Another technique that I often use is *listing markup*. It is particularly useful with very long methods. The idea is simple and nearly everyone has done it at some time or another, but, frankly, I think it is underused.

The way to mark up a listing depends on what you want to understand. The first step is to print the code that you want to work with. After you have, you can use *listing markup* as you try to do any of the following activities.

Separating Responsibilities

If you want to separate responsibilities, use a marker to group things. If several things belong together, put a special symbol next to each of them so that you can identify them. Use several colors, if you can.

Understanding Method Structure

If you want to understand a large method, line up blocks. Often indentation in long methods can make them impossible to read. You can line them up by drawing lines from the beginnings of blocks to the ends, or by commenting the ends of blocks with the text of the loop or condition that started them.

The easiest way to line up blocks is inside out. For instance, when you are working in one of the languages in the C family, just start reading from the top of the listing past each opening brace until you get to the first closing brace. Mark that one and then go back and mark the one that matches it. Keep reading until you get to the next closing brace, and do the same thing. Look backward until you get to the opening brace that matches it.

Extract Methods

If you want to break up a large method, circle code that you'd like to extract. Annotate it with its coupling count (see Chapter 22, *I Need to Change a Monster Method and I Can't Write Tests for It*).

Understand the Effects of a Change

If you want to understand the effect of some change you are going to make, instead of making an *effect sketch (155)*, put a mark next to the code lines that you are going to change. Then put a mark next to each variable whose value can change as a result of that change and every method call that could be affected. Next, put marks next to the variables and methods that are affected by the things you just marked. Do this as many times as you need to, to see how effects propagate from the change. When you do that, you'll have a better sense of what you have to test.

Scratch Refactoring

One of the best techniques for learning about code is refactoring. Just get in there and start moving things around and making the code clearer. The only problem is, if you don't have tests, this can be pretty hazardous business. How do you know that you aren't breaking anything when you do all of this refactoring to understand the code? The fact is, you can work in a way in which you don't need to care—and it's pretty easy to do. Check out the code from your version-control system. Forget about writing tests. Extract methods, move variables, refactor it whatever way you want to get a better understanding of it—just don't check it in again. Throw that code away. This is called *Scratch refactoring*.

The first time I mentioned this to someone I was working with, he thought it was wasteful, but we learned an incredible amount about the code that we were working on in that half hour of moving things around. After that, he was sold on the idea.

Scratch refactoring is great way of getting down to the essentials and really learning how a piece of code works, but there are a couple of risks. The first risk is that we make some gross mistake when we refactor that leads us to think that the system is doing something that it isn't. When that happens, we have a false view of the system, and that can cause some anxiety later when we start to really refactor. The second risk is related. We could get so attached to the way that the code turns out that we start to think about it in those terms all the time. It doesn't sound like that should be so bad, but it can be. There are many reasons why we might not end up with the same structure when we do get around to really refactoring. We might see a better way of structuring the code later. Our code could change between now and then, and we might have different insights. If we are too attached to the end point of a *Scratch refactoring*, we'll miss out on those insights.

Scratch refactoring is a good way to convince yourself that you understand the most important things about the code, and that, in itself, can make the work go easier. You feel reasonably confident that there isn't something scary behind every corner—or, if there is, you'll at least have some notice before you get there.

Delete Unused Code

If the code you are looking at is confusing and you can determine that some of it isn't used, delete it. It isn't doing anything for you except getting in your way.

Sometimes people feel that deleting code is wasteful. After all, someone spent time writing that code—maybe it can be used in the future. Well, that is what version-control systems are for. That code will be in earlier versions. You can always look for if you ever decide that you need it.

Chapter 17

My Application Has No Structure

Long-lived applications tend to sprawl. They might have started out with a well-thought-out architecture, but over the years, under schedule pressure, they can get to the point where nobody really understands their complete structure. People can work for years on a project and not have any idea where new features are intended to go; they just know the hacks that have been placed in the system recently. When they add new features, they go to the "hack points" because those are the areas that they know best.

There is no easy remedy for this sort of thing, and the urgency of the situation varies widely. In some cases, programmers run up against a wall. It's difficult to add new features, and that brings the entire organization into crisis mode. People are charged with the task of figuring out whether it would be better to re-engineer or rewrite the system. In other organizations, the system limps along for years. Yes, it takes longer than it should to add new features, but that is just considered the price of doing business. Nobody knows how much better it could be or how much money is being lost because of poor structure.

When teams aren't aware of their architecture, it tends to degrade. What gets in the way of this awareness?

- The system can be so complex that it takes a long time to get the big picture.
- The system can be so complex that there is no big picture.
- The team is in a very reactive mode, dealing with emergency after emergency so much that they lose sight of the big picture.

Traditionally, many organizations have used the role of architect to solve these problems. Architects are usually charged with the task of working out the big picture and making decisions that preserve the big picture for the team. That can work, but there is one strong caveat. An architect has to be out in the team, working with the members day to day, or else the code diverges from the big picture. There are two ways this can happen: Someone could be doing something inappropriate in the code or the big picture itself could need to be modified. In some of the worst situations I've encountered with teams, the architect of a group has a completely different view of the system than the programmers. Often this happens because the architect has other responsibilities and can't get into the code or can't communicate with the rest of the team often enough to really know what is there. As a result, communication breaks down across the organization.

The brutal truth is that architecture is too important to be left exclusively to a few people. It's fine to have an architect, but the key way to keep an architecture intact is to make sure that everyone on the team knows what it is and has a stake in it. Every person who is touching the code should know the architecture, and everyone else who touches the code should be able to benefit from what that person has learned. When everyone is working off of the same set of ideas, the overall system intelligence of the team is amplified. If you have, say, a team of 20 and only 3 people know the architecture in detail, either those 3 have to do a lot to keep the other 17 people on track or the other 17 people just make mistakes caused by unfamiliarity with the big picture.

Telling the Story of the System

How can we get a big picture of a large system? There are many ways to do this. The book *Object-Oriented Reengineering Patterns*, by Serge Demeyer, Stephane Ducasse, and Oscar M. Nierstrasz (Morgan Kaufmann Publishers, 2002), contains a catalog of techniques that deal with just this issue. Here I describe several others that are rather powerful. If you practice them often on a team, they will help keep architectural concerns alive in the team—and that's perhaps the most important thing you can do to preserve architecture. It is hard to pay attention to something that you don't think about often.

Telling the Story of the System

When I work with teams, I often use a technique that I call "telling the story of the system." To do it well, you need at least two people. One person starts off by asking another, "What is the architecture of the system?" Then the other person tries to explain the architecture of the system using only a few concepts, maybe as few as two or three. If you are the person explaining, you have to pretend that the other person knows nothing about the system. In only a few sentences, you have to explain what the pieces of the design are and how they interact. After you say those few sentences, you have articulated what you feel are the most essential things about the system. Next, you pick the next most important things to say about the system. You keep going until you've said just about everything important about the core design of the system.

When you start to do this, you'll notice an odd feeling. To really convey the system architecture that briefly, you have to simplify. You might say, "The gateway gets rule sets from the active database," but as you say that, part of you might be screaming, "No! The gateway gets rule sets from the active database, but it also gets them from the current working set." When you say the simpler thing, it kind of feels like you are lying; you just aren't telling the whole story. But you are telling a simpler story that describes an easier-to-understand architecture. For instance, why does the gateway have to get rule sets from more than one place? Wouldn't it be simpler if it was unified?

Pragmatic considerations often keep things from getting simple, but there is value in articulating the simple view. At the very least, it helps everyone understand what would've been ideal and what things are there as expediencies. The other important thing about this technique is that it really forces you to think about what is important in the system, the most important things to communicate?

Teams can go only so far when the system they work on is a mystery to them. In an odd way, having a simple story of how a system works just serves as a roadmap, a way of getting your bearing as you search for the right places to add features. It can also make a system a lot less scary.

On your team, tell the story of the system often, just so that you share a view. Tell it in different ways. Trade off whether one concept is more important than another. As you consider changes to the system, you'll notice that some changes fall more in line with the story. That is, they make the briefer story feel like less of a lie. If you have to choose between two ways of doing something, the story can be a good way to see which one will lead to an easier-to-understand system.

Here is an example of this sort of story telling in action. Here's a session discussing JUnit. It does assume that you know a little bit about the architecture of JUnit. If you don't, take a little while to look at JUnit's source code. You can download it from www.junit.org.

What is the architecture of JUnit?

JUnit has two primary classes. The first is called `Test`, and the other is called `TestResult`. Users create tests and run them, passing them a `TestResult`. When a test fails, it tells the `TestResult` about it. People can then ask the `TestResult` for all of the failures that have occurred.

Let's list the simplifications:

1. There are many other classes in JUnit. I'm saying that `Test` and `TestResult` are primary only because I think so. To me, their interaction is the core interaction in the system. Others might have a different, equally valid view of the architecture.

2. Users don't create test objects. Test objects are created from test case classes via reflection.

3. `Test` isn't a class; it's an interface. The tests that run in JUnit are usually written in subclasses of a class named `TestCase`, which implements `Test`.

4. People generally don't ask `TestResults` for failures. `TestResults` register listeners, which are notified whenever a `TestResult` receives information from a test.

5. Tests report more than failures: They report the number of tests run and the number of errors. (Errors are problems that occur in the test that aren't explicitly checked for. Failures are failed checks.)

Telling the Story of the System

Do these simplifications give us any insight into how JUnit could be simpler? A little. Some simpler xUnit testing frameworks make `Test` a class and drop `TestCase` entirely. Other frameworks merge errors and failures so that they are reported the same way.

Back to our story.
Is that all?

> No. Tests can be grouped into objects called suites. We can run a suite with a test result just like a single test. All of the tests inside it run and tell the test result when they fail.

What simplifications do we have here?

1. `TestSuites` do more than just hold and run a set of tests. They also create instances of `TestCase`-derived classes via reflection.

2. There is another simplification, sort of a left over from the first one. Tests don't actually run themselves. They pass themselves to the `TestResult` class, which, in turn, calls the test-execution method back on the test itself. This back and forth happens at a rather low level. Thinking about it the simple way is kind of convenient. It is a bit of a lie, but it is actually the way JUnit used to be when it was a little simpler.

Is that all?

> No. Actually, Test is an interface. There is a class called TestCase that implements Test. Users subclass TestCase and then write their tests as public void methods that start with the word test in their subclass. The TestSuite class uses reflection to build up a group of tests that can be run in a single call to TestSuite's run method.

We can go further, but what I've shown so far gives a sense of the technique. We start out by making a brief description. When we simplify and rip away detail to describe a system, we are really abstracting. Often when we force ourselves to communicate a very simple view of a system, we can find new abstractions.

If a system isn't as simple as the simplest story we can tell about it, does that mean that it's bad? No. Invariably, as systems grow, they get more complicated. The story gives us guidance.

Suppose that we were going to add a new feature to JUnit. We want to generate a report of all the tests that don't call any assertions when we run them. What options do we have given what was described in JUnit?

One option is to add a method to the TestCase class called buildUsageReport that runs each method and then builds up a report of all of the methods that don't call an assert method. Would that be a good way of adding this feature? What would it do to our story? Well, it would add another little "lie of omission" from our briefest description of the system:

> JUnit has two primary classes. The first is called Test, and the other is called TestResult. Users create tests and run them, passing along a TestResult. When a test fails, it tells the TestResult about it. People can then ask the TestResult for all of the failures that have occurred.

It seems that Tests now have this completely different responsibility: generating reports, which we never mention.

What if we went about adding the feature in a different way? We could alter the interaction between TestCase and TestResult so that TestResult gets a count of the number of assertions run whenever a test runs. Then we can make a report-building class and register it with TestResult as a listener. How does that impact the story of the system? It could be a good reason to generalize it a little. Tests don't just tell TestResults about the number of failures; they also tell them about the number of errors, the number of tests run, and the number of assertions run. We could change our brief story to this:

> JUnit has two primary classes. The first is called `Test`, and the other is called `TestResult`. Users create tests and run them, passing them a `TestResult`. When a test runs, it passes information about the test run to the `TestResult`. People can then ask the `TestResult` for information about all of the test runs.

Is that better? Frankly, I like the original, the version that described recording failures. To me, it is one of the core behaviors of JUnit. If we change the code so that `TestResults` record the number of assertions run, we'd still be lying a bit, but we're already glossing over the other information that we send from tests to test results. The alternative, putting the responsibility for running a bunch of cases and building a report from them on `TestCase`, would be a bolder lie: We aren't talking about this additional responsibility of `TestCase` at all. We're better off having tests report the number of assertions run as they execute. Our first story is generalized a little bit more but at least it is still substantially true. That means that our changes are falling more in line with the architecture of the system.

Naked CRC

Naked CRC

In the early days of object orientation, many people struggled with the issue of design. It's hard to get used to object orientation when most of your programming experience is in the use of procedural languages. Simply put, the way that you think about your code is different. I remember the first time someone tried to show me an object-oriented design on a piece of paper. I looked at all the shapes and lines and heard the description, but the question that I kept wanting to ask was "Where's `main()`? Where is the entry point for all of these new object things?" I was bewildered for a little while, but then it started to click. The problem wasn't just mine, though. It seemed like most of the industry was struggling with the same issues at roughly the same time. Frankly, every day people new to the industry confront these issues when they encounter object-oriented code for the first time. It's still happening.

In the 1980s, Ward Cunningham and Kent Beck were dealing with this issue. They were trying to help people start to think about design in terms of objects. At the time, Ward was using a tool named Hypercard, which allows you to create cards on a computer display and form links among them. Suddenly, the insight was there. Why not use real index cards to represent classes? It would make them tangible and easy to discuss. Should we talk about the `Transaction` class? Sure, here is its card—on it we have its responsibilities and collaborators.

CRC stands for Class, Responsibility, and Collaborations. You mark up each card with a class name, its responsibilities, and a list of its collaborators (other classes that this class communicates with). If you think that a responsibility doesn't belong on a particular class, cross it out and write it on another class card, or create another class card altogether.

Although CRC became rather popular for a while, eventually there was a large push toward diagrams. Nearly everyone teaching OO on the planet had their own notation for classes and relationships. Eventually, there was a large multiyear effort to consolidate notations. UML was the result, and many people thought that ended any talk of how to design systems. People started to think that the notation was a method, that UML was a way of developing systems: Draw plenty of diagrams, and then write code afterward. It took a while for people to realize that although UML is a good notation for documenting systems, it's not the only way of working with the ideas that we use to build systems. At this point, I know that there is a much better way of communicating about design on a team. It's a technique that some testing friends of mine dubbed Naked CRC because it is just like CRC, except that you don't write on the cards. Unfortunately, it isn't all that easy to describe in a book. Here's my best attempt.

Naked CRC

Several years ago, I met Ron Jeffries at a conference. He'd promised me that he would show me how he could explain an architecture using cards in a way that made the interactions rather vivid and memorable. Sure enough, he did. This is the way that it works. The person describing the system uses a set of blank index cards and lays them down on a table one by one. He or she can move the cards, point at them, or do whatever else is needed to convey the typical objects in the system and how they interact.

Here is an example, a description of an online voting system:

"Here's how the real-time voting system works. Here is a client session" (points at card).

"Each session has two connections, an incoming connection and an outgoing connection" (lays down each card on the original one and points at each, in turn).

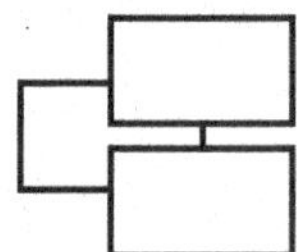

"When it starts up, a session is created on the server over here" (lays down the card on the right).

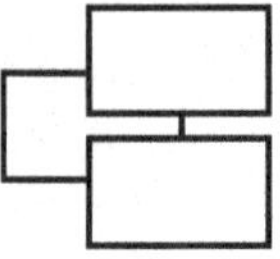

"Server sessions have two connections apiece also" (puts down the two cards representing the connections on the card on the right).

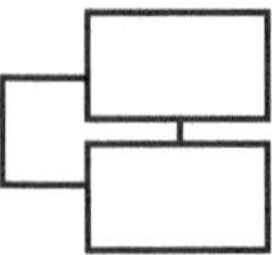

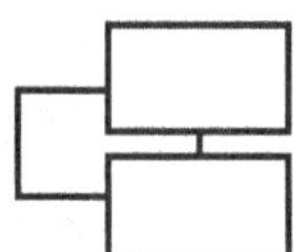

"When a server session comes up, it registers with the vote manager (lays down the card for the vote manager above the server session).

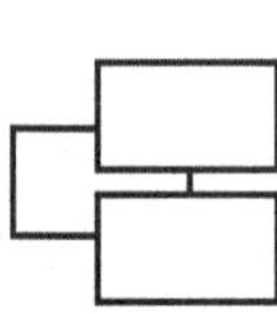

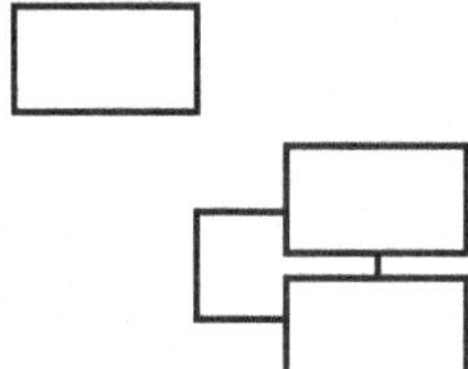

"We can have many sessions on the server side" (puts down another set of cards for a new server session and its connections).

"When a client votes, the vote is sent to the session on the server side" (motions with hands from one of the connections on the client-side session to a connection on a server-side session).

"The server session replies with an acknowledgment and then records the vote with the vote manager" (points from the server session back to the client session, and then points from that server session to the vote manager).

"Afterward, the vote manager tells each server session to tell its client session what the new vote count is" (points from the vote manager card to each server session, in turn).

I'm sure that this description is lacking something because I'm not able to move the cards around on the table or point at them the way I would if we were sitting at a table together. Still, this technique is pretty powerful. It makes pieces of a system into tangible things. You don't have to use cards; anything that is handy is fine. The key is that you are able to use motion and position to show how parts of the system interact. Often those two things can make involved scenarios easier to grasp. For some reason, these carding sessions make designs more memorable also.

There are just two guidelines in Naked CRC:

1. Cards represent instances, not classes.
2. Overlap cards to show a collection of them.

Conversation Scrutiny

In legacy code, it's tempting to avoid creating abstractions. When I'm looking at four or five classes that have about a thousand lines of code apiece, I'm not thinking about adding new classes as much as I'm trying to figure out what has to change.

Because we are so distracted when we're trying to figure out these things, often we miss things that can give us additional ideas. Here's an example. I was working with several members of a team once, and they were going through the exercise of making a large chunk of code executable from several threads. The code was rather complicated and there were several opportunities for deadlock. We realized that if we could guarantee that resources were locked in and unlocked in a particular order, we could avoid deadlock in the code. We started to look at how we could modify the code to enable this. All the while, we were talking about this new locking policy and figuring out how to maintain counts in arrays to enable it. When one of the other programmers started to write the policy code inline, I said, "Wait, we're talking about a locking policy, right? Why don't we create a class called `LockingPolicy` and maintain the counts in there? We can use method names that really describe what we are trying to do, and that will be clearer than code that bumps counts in an array."

Conversation Scrutiny

The terrible thing is that the team wasn't inexperienced. There were some other very good-looking areas of the code base, but there is something mesmerizing about large chunks of procedural code: They seem to beg for more.

Listen to conversations about your design. Are the concepts you're using in conversation the same as the concepts in the code? I wouldn't expect them all to be. Software has to satisfy stronger constraints than just being easy to talk about, but if there isn't a strong overlap between conversation and code, it's important to ask why. The answer is usually a mixture of two things: The code hasn't been allowed to adapt to the team's understanding, or the team needs to understand it differently. In any case, being very tuned to the concepts people naturally use to describe the design is powerful. When people talk about design, they are trying to make other people understand them. Put some of that understanding in the code.

In this chapter, I've described a couple of techniques for uncovering and communicating the architecture of large existing systems. Many of the techniques are also perfectly good ways of working out the design of new systems. Design is design, regardless of when it happens in the development cycle. One of the worst mistakes a team can make is it to feel that design is over at some point in development. If design is "over" and people are still making changes, chances are good that new code will appear in poor places, and classes will bloat because no one feels comfortable introducing new abstractions. There is no surer way to make a legacy system worse.

Chapter 18

My Test Code Is in the Way

When you first start writing unit tests, it might feel unnatural. One thing that people commonly encounter is a sense that their tests are just in the way. They browse around their project and sometimes forget whether they are looking at test code or production code. The fact that you start to end up with a lot of test code doesn't help. Unless you start to establish some conventions, you can end up swamped.

Class Naming Conventions

One of the first things to establish is a class naming convention. Generally, you'll have at least one unit test class for each class that you work on, so it makes sense to make the unit test class name a variation of the class name. A couple of conventions are used. The most common ones use the word *Test* as a prefix or a suffix of the class name. So, if we have a class named `DBEngine`, we could call our test class `TestDBEngine` or `DBEngineTest`. Does it matter? Not really. Personally, I like the *Test* suffix convention. If you have an IDE that lists classes alphabetically, each class lines up next to its test class, and that makes it easier to navigate among them.

What other classes come up in testing? Often it's useful to fake classes for some of the collaborators of the classes in a package or directory. The convention I use for those is to use the prefix *Fake*. This groups all of them together alphabetically in a browser but somewhat away from the main classes in the package. This is convenient because often the fake classes are subclasses of classes in other directories.

One other kind of class, the *testing subclass*, is often used in testing. A *testing subclass* is a class that you write when you want to test a class, but it has some dependencies that you want to separate out. It's the subclass that you write when you use *Subclass and Override Method (401)*. The naming convention that I use for testing subclasses is the name of the class prefixed by the word

word *Testing*. If classes in a package or directory are listed alphabetically, all of the testing subclasses are grouped together.

Here is an example listing of a directory for a small accounting package:

- `CheckingAccount`
- `CheckingAccountTest`
- `FakeAccountOwner`
- `FakeTransaction`
- `SavingsAccount`
- `SavingsAccountTest`
- `TestingCheckingAccount`
- `TestingSavingsAccount`

Notice that each production class is next to its test class. The fakes group together and the testing subclasses group together.

Test Location

I'm not dogmatic about this arrangement. It works in many cases, but there are lots of variations and reasons to vary it. The key thing to remember is that ergonomics is important. It's important to consider how easy it will be to navigate back and forth between your classes and your tests.

Test Location

So far in this chapter, I've been making the assumption that you'll place your testing code and your production code in the same directories. Generally, this is the easiest way to structure a project, but there are definitely some things that you have to consider when you decide whether to do this.

The main thing to consider is whether there are size constraints on your application's deployment. An application that runs on a server that you control might not have many constraints. If you can stand taking up essentially twice the amount of space in the deployment (the binaries for the production code and its tests), it is easy enough to keep the code and the tests in the same directories and to deploy all of the binaries.

On the other hand, if the software is a commercial product and runs on someone else's computer, the size of the deployment could be a problem. You can attempt to keep all of the testing code separate from the production source, but consider whether this affects how you navigate your code.

Sometimes it doesn't make any difference, as this example shows. In Java, a package can span two different directories:

```
source
    com
        orderprocessing
            dailyorders
test
    com
        orderprocessing
            dailyorders
```

We can put the production classes in the dailyorders directory under `source`, and test classes in the dailyorders directory under `test`, and they can be seen as being in the same package. Some IDEs actually show you classes in those two directories in the same view so that you don't have to care where they are physically located.

In many other languages and environments, location does make a difference. If you have to navigate up and down directory structures to go back and forth between your code and its tests, it is like paying a tax as you work. People will just stop writing tests, and the work will go slower.

An alternative is to keep the production code and the test code in the same location but to use scripts or build settings to remove the test code from the deployment. If you use good naming conventions for your classes, this can work out fine.

Above all, if you choose to separate test and production code, make sure it is for a good reason. Quite often teams separate the code for aesthetic reasons: They just can't stand the idea of putting their production code and tests together. Later that navigation in the project is painful. You can get used to having tests right next to your production source. After a period of time working that way, it just feels normal.

Chapter 19

My Project Is Not Object Oriented. How Do I Make Safe Changes?

The title of this chapter is a bit provocative. We can make safe changes in any language, but some languages make change easier than others. Even though object orientation has pretty much pervaded the industry, there are many other languages and ways of programming. There are rule-based languages, functional programming languages, constraint-based programming languages—the list goes on. But of all of these, none are as widespread as the plain old procedural languages, such as C, COBOL, FORTRAN, Pascal, and BASIC.

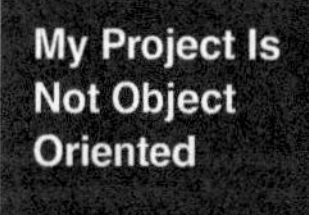

Procedural languages are especially challenging in a legacy environment. It's important to get code under test before modifying it, but the number of things you can do to introduce unit tests in procedural languages is pretty small. Often the easiest thing to do is think really hard, patch the system, and hope that your changes were right.

This testing dilemma is pandemic in procedural legacy code. Procedural languages often just don't have the seams that OO (and many functional) programming languages do. Savvy developers can work past this by managing their dependencies carefully (there is a lot of great code written in C, for instance), but it is also easy to end up with a real snarl that is hard to change incrementally and verifiably.

Because breaking dependencies in procedural code is so hard, often the best strategy is to try to get a large chunk of the code under test before doing anything else and then use those tests to get some feedback while developing. The techniques in Chapter 12, *I Need to Make Many Changes in One Area. Do I Have to Break Dependencies for All the Classes Involved?* can help. They apply to procedural code as well as object-oriented code. In short, it pays to look for a *pinch point (180)* and then use the *link seam (36)* to break dependencies well enough to get the code in a test harness. If your language has a macro preprocessor, you can use the *preprocessing seam (33)* as well.

That's the standard course of action, but it isn't the only one. In the rest of this chapter, we look at ways to break dependencies locally in procedural programs, how to make verifiable changes more easily, and ways of moving forward when we're using a language that has a migration path to OO.

An Easy Case

Procedural code isn't always a problem. Here's an example, a C function from the Linux operating system. Would it be hard to write tests for this function if we had to make some changes to it?

```
void set_writetime(struct buffer_head * buf, int flag)
{
    int newtime;

    if (buffer_dirty(buf)) {
        /* Move buffer to dirty list if jiffies is clear */
        newtime = jiffies + (flag ? bdf_prm.b_un.age_super :
            bdf_prm.b_un.age_buffer);
        if(!buf->b_flushtime || buf->b_flushtime > newtime)
            buf->b_flushtime = newtime;
    } else {
        buf->b_flushtime = 0;
    }
}
```

A Hard Case

To test this function, we can set the value of the `jiffies` variable, create a `buffer_head`, pass it into the function, and then check its values after the call. In many functions, we're not so lucky. Sometimes a function calls a function that calls another function. Then it calls something hard to deal with: a function that actually does I/O someplace or comes from some vendor's library. We want to test what the code does, but too often the answer is "It does something cool, but only something outside the program will know about it, not you."

A Hard Case

Here is a C function that we want to change. It would be nice if we could put it under test before we do:

```
#include "ksrlib.h"

int scan_packets(struct rnode_packet *packet, int flag)
{
    struct rnode_packet *current = packet;
    int scan_result, err = 0;

    while(current) {
        scan_result = loc_scan(current->body, flag);
        if(scan_result & INVALID_PORT) {
            ksr_notify(scan_result, current);
        }
        ...
        current = current->next;
    }
    return err;
}
```

This code calls a function named `ksr_notify` that has a bad side effect. It writes out a notification to a third party system, and we'd rather that it didn't do that while we're testing.

One way to handle this is to use a *link seam (36)*. If we want to test without calling the functions in that library, we can make a library that contains fakes: functions that have the same names as the original functions but that don't really do what they are intended to do. In this case, we can write a body for `ksr_notify` that looks like this:

```
void ksr_notify(int scan_code, struct rnode_packet *packet)
{
}
```


We can build it in a library and link to it. The `scan_packets` function will behave exactly the same, except for one thing: It won't send the notification. But that's fine if we want to pin down other behavior in the function before changing it.

Is that the strategy we should use? It depends. If there are a lot of functions in the ksr library and we consider their calls to be sort of peripheral to the main logic of the system, then, yes, it would make sense to create a library of fakes and link to it during test. On the other hand, if we want to sense through those functions or we want to vary some of the values that they return, using *link seams (36)* isn't as nice; it's actually pretty tedious. Because the substitution happens at link time, we can provide only one function definition for each executable that we build. If we want a fake `ksr_notify` function to behave one way in one test and another way in another test, we have to put code in the body and set up conditions in the test that will force it to act a certain way. All in all, it is kind of messy. Unfortunately, many procedural languages don't leave us with any other options.

In C, there is another alternative. C has a macro preprocessor that we can use to make it easier to write tests against the scan_packets function. Here is the file that contains scan_packets after we've added testing code:

```
#include "ksrlib.h"

#ifdef TESTING
#define ksr_notify(code,packet)
#endif

int scan_packets(struct rnode_packet *packet, int flag)
{
    struct rnode_packet *current = packet;
    int scan_result, err = 0;

    while(current) {
        scan_result = loc_scan(current->body, flag);
        if(scan_result & INVALID_PORT) {
            ksr_notify(scan_result, current);
        }
        ...
        current = current->next;
    }
    return err;
}

#ifdef TESTING
#include <assert.h>
int main () {
    struct rnode_packet packet;
    packet.body = ...
    ...
    int err = scan_packets(&packet, DUP_SCAN);
    assert(err & INVALID_PORT);
    ...
    return 0;
}
#endif
```


In this code, we have a preprocessing define, TESTING, that defines the call to ksr_notify out of existence when we are testing. It also provides a little stub that contains tests.

Mixing tests and source into a file like this isn't really the clearest thing we can do. Often it makes code harder to navigate. An alternative is to use file inclusion so that the tests and production code are in different files:

```
#include "ksrlib.h"

#include "scannertestdefs.h"

int scan_packets(struct rnode_packet *packet, int flag)
{
    struct rnode_packet *current = packet;
    int scan_result, err = 0;

    while(current) {
        scan_result = loc_scan(current->body, flag);
        if(scan_result & INVALID_PORT) {
            ksr_notify(scan_result, current);
        }
        ...
        current = current->next;
    }
    return err;
}

#include "testscanner.tst"
```

With this change, the code looks reasonably close to what it would look like without the testing infrastructure. The only difference is that we have an `#include` statement at the end of the file. If we forward declare the functions we are testing, we can move everything in the bottom include file into the top one.

To run the tests, we just have to define `TESTING` and build this file by itself. When `TESTING` is defined, the `main( )` function in `testscanner.tst` will be compiled and linked into an executable that will run the tests. The `main( )` function we have in that file runs only tests for the scanning routines. We can set up things to run groups of tests at the same time by defining separate testing functions for each of our tests.


```
#ifdef TESTING
#include <assert.h>
void test_port_invalid() {
    struct rnode_packet packet;
    packet.body = ...
    ...
    int err = scan_packets(&packet, DUP_SCAN);
    assert(err & INVALID_PORT);
}

void test_body_not_corrupt() {
    ...
}

void test_header() {
    ...
```

```
}
#endif
```

In another file, we can call them from `main`:

```
int main() {
    test_port_invalid();
    test_body_not_corrupt();
    test_header();

    return 0;
}
```

We can go even further by adding registration functions that make test grouping easier. See the various C unit-testing frameworks available at www.xprogramming.com for details.

Although macro preprocessors are easily misused, they are actually very useful in this context. File inclusion and macro replacement can help us get past dependencies in the thorniest code. As long as we restrict rampant usage of macros to code that runs under test, we don't have to be too concerned that we'll misuse macros in ways that will affect the production code.

C is one of the few mainstream languages that have a macro preprocessor. In general, to break dependencies in other procedural languages, we have to use the *link seam (36)* and attempt to get larger areas of code under test.

Adding New Behavior

In procedural legacy code, it pays to bias toward introducing new functions rather than adding code to old ones. At the very least, we can write tests for the new functions that we write.

How do we avoid introducing dependency traps in procedural code? One way (outlined in Chapter 8, *How Do I Add a Feature?*) is to use *test-driven development (88)* (TDD). TDD works in both object-oriented and procedural code. Often the work of trying to formulate a test for each piece of code that we're thinking of writing leads us to alter its design in good ways. We concentrate on writing functions that do some piece of computational work and then integrate them into the rest of the application.

Often we have to think about what we are going to write in a different way to do this. Here's an example. We need to write a function called `send_command`. The `send_command` function is going to send an ID, a name, and a command string to another system through a function called `mart_key_send`. The code for the function won't be too bad. We can imagine that it will look something like this:

```
void send_command(int id, char *name, char *command_string) {
    char *message, *header, *footer;
    if (id == KEY_TRUM) {
        message = ralloc(sizeof(int) + HEADER_LEN + ...
        ...
    } else {
        ...
    }
    sprintf(message, "%s%s%s", header, command_string, footer);
    mart_key_send(message);

    free(message);
}
```

But how would we write a test for a function like that? Especially because the only way to find out what happens is to be right where the call to `mart_key_send` is? What if we took a slightly different approach?

We could test all of that logic before the `mart_key_send` call if it was in another function. We might write our first test like this:

```
char *command = form_command(1,
                             "Mike Ratledge",
                             "56:78:cusp-:78");
assert(!strcmp("<-rsp-Mike Ratledge><56:78:cusp-:78><-rspr>",
               command));
```

Then we can write a `form_command` function, which returns a command:

```
char *form_command(int id, char *name, char *command_string)
{
    char *message, *header;
    if (id == KEY_TRUM) {
        message = ralloc(sizeof(int) + HEADER_LEN + ...
        ...
    } else {
        ...
    }
    sprintf(message, "%s%s%s", header, command_string, footer);

    return message;
}
```

When we have that, we can write the simple `send_command` function that we need:

```
void send_command(int id, char *name, char *command_string) {
    char *command = form_command(id, name, command_string);
    mart_key_send(command);

    free(message);
}
```

In many cases, this sort of a reformulation is exactly what we need to move forward. We put all of the pure logic into one set of functions so we can keep them free of problematic dependencies. When we do this, we end up with little wrapper functions such as send_command, which bind our logic and our dependencies. It's not perfect, but it's workable when the dependencies aren't too pervasive.

In other cases, we need to write functions that will be littered with external calls. There isn't much computation in these functions, but the sequencing of the calls that they make is very important. For example, if we are trying to write a function that calculates interest on a loan, the straightforward way of doing it might look something like this:

```
void calculate_loan_interest(struct temper_loan *loan, int calc_type)
{
    ...
    db_retrieve(loan->id);
    ...
    db_retrieve(loan->lender_id);
    ...
    db_update(loan->id, loan->record);
    ...
    loan->interest = ...
}
```


What do we do in a case like this? In many procedural languages, the best choice is to just skip writing the test first and write the function as best we can. Maybe we can test that it does the right thing at a higher level. But in C, we have another option. C supports function pointers, and we can use them to get another seam in place. Here's how:

We can create a struct that contains pointers to functions:

```
struct database
{
    void (*retrieve)(struct record_id id);
    void (*update)(struct record_id id, struct record_set *record);
    ...
};
```

We can initialize those pointers to the addresses of the database-access functions. We can pass that struct to any new functions we write that need to access the database. In production code, the functions can point to the real database-access functions. We can have them point at fakes when we are testing.

With earlier compilers, we might have to use the old-style function pointer syntax:

```
extern struct database db;
(*db.update)(load->id, loan->record);
```

But with others, we can call these functions in a very natural object-oriented style:

```
extern struct database db;
db.update(load->id, loan->record);
```

This technique isn't C specific. It can be used in most languages that support function pointers, delegates or similar mechanisms.

Taking Advantage of Object Orientation

In object-oriented languages, we have *object seams (40)*. They have some nice properties:

- They are easy to notice in code.
- They can be used to break code down into smaller, more understandable pieces.
- They provide more flexibility. Seams that you introduce for testing might be useful when you have to extend your software.

Unfortunately, not all software can be easily migrated to objects, but, in some cases, it is far easier than others. Many procedural languages have evolved into object-oriented languages. Microsoft's Visual Basic language only recently became fully object oriented, there are OO extensions to COBOL and Fortran, and most C compilers give you capability to compile C++, too.

When your language gives you the option to move toward object orientation, you have more options. The first step is usually to use *Encapsulate Global References (339)* to get the pieces you are changing under test. We can use it to get out of the bad dependency situation we had in the scan_packets function earlier in the chapter. Remember that the problem we had was with the ksr_notify function: We didn't want it to really notify whenever we ran our tests.

```
int scan_packets(struct rnode_packet *packet, int flag)
{
    struct rnode_packet *current = packet;
    int scan_result, err = 0;

    while(current) {
        scan_result = loc_scan(current->body, flag);
        if(scan_result & INVALID_PORT) {
            ksr_notify(scan_result, current);
        }
        ...
        current = current->next;
```

```
    }
    return err;
}
```

The first step is to compile under C++ rather than under C. This can be either a small or a large change, depending on how we handle it. We can bite the bullet and attempt to recompile the entire project in C++, or we can do it piece by piece, but it does take some time.

When we have the code compiling under C++, we can start by finding the declaration of the ksr_notify function and wrapping it in a class:

```
class ResultNotifier
{
public:
    virtual void ksr_notify(int scan_result,
                            struct rnode_packet *packet);
};
```

We can also introduce a new source file for the class and put a default implementation there:

```
extern "C" void ksr_notify(int scan_result,
                           struct rnode_packet *packet);

void ResultNotifier::ksr_notify(int scan_result,
                                struct rnode_packet *packet)
{
    ::ksr_notify(scan_result, packet);
}
```


Notice that we're not changing the name of the function or its signature. We're using *Preserve Signatures (312)* so that we minimize any chance of errors.

Next, we declare a global instance of ResultNotifier and put it into a source file:

```
ResultNotifier globalResultNotifier;
```

Now we can recompile and let the errors tell us where we have to change things. Because we've put the declaration of ksr_notify in a class, the compiler doesn't see a declaration of it at global scope any longer.

Here's the original function:

```
#include "ksrlib.h"

int scan_packets(struct rnode_packet *packet, int flag)
{
    struct rnode_packet *current = packet;
    int scan_result, err = 0;
```

```
    while(current) {
        scan_result = loc_scan(current->body, flag);
        if(scan_result & INVALID_PORT) {
            ksr_notify(scan_result, current);
        }
        ...
        current = current->next;
    }
    return err;
}
```

To make it compile now, we can use an extern declaration to make the globalResultNotifier object visible and preface ksr_notify with the name of the object:

```
#include "ksrlib.h"

extern ResultNotifier globalResultNotifier;

int scan_packets(struct rnode_packet *packet, int flag)
{
    struct rnode_packet *current = packet;
    int scan_result, err = 0;

    while(current) {
        scan_result = loc_scan(current->body, flag);
        if(scan_result & INVALID_PORT) {
             globalResultNotifier.ksr_notify(scan_result, current);
        }
        ...
        current = current->next;
    }
    return err;
}
```


At this point, the code works the same way as it has. The ksr_notify method on ResultNotifier delegates to the ksr_notify function. How does that do us any good? Well, it doesn't—yet. The next step is to find some way of setting things up so that we can use this ResultNotifier object in production and use another one when we are testing. There are many ways of doing this, but one that carries us further in this direction is to *Encapsulate Global References (339)* again and put scan_packets in another class that we can call Scanner.

```
class Scanner
{
public:
    int scan_packets(struct rnode_packet *packet, int flag);
};
```

Now we can apply *Parameterize Constructor (379)* and change the class so that it uses a ResultNotifier that we supply:

```
class Scanner
{
private:
    ResultNotifier& notifier;
public:
        Scanner();
        Scanner(ResultNotifier&  notifier);

    int scan_packets(struct rnode_packet *packet, int flag);
};


// in the source file

Scanner::Scanner()
: notifier(globalResultNotifier)
{}

Scanner::Scanner(ResultNotifier&  notifier)
: notifier(notifier)
{}
```

It's All Object Oriented

When we make this change, we can find the places where scan_packets is being used, create an instance of Scanner, and call it fromthe instance.

These changes are pretty safe and pretty mechanical. They aren't great examples of object-oriented design, but they are good enough to use as a wedge to break dependencies and allow us to test as we move forward.

It's All Object Oriented

Some procedural programmers like to beat up on object orientation; they consider it unnecessary or think that its complexity doesn't buy anything. But when you really think about it, you begin to realize that all procedural programs are object oriented; it's just a shame that many contain only one object. To see this, imagine a program with about 100 functions. Here are their declarations:

```
...
int db_find(char *id, unsigned int mnemonic_id,
         struct db_rec **rec);
...
...
void process_run(struct gfh_task **tasks, int task_count);
...
```

Now imagine that we can put all of the declarations in one file and surround them with a class declaration:

```
class program
{
public:
    ...
    int db_find(char *id, unsigned int mnemonic_id,
             struct db_rec **rec);
    ...
    ...
    void process_run(struct gfh_task **tasks, int task_count);
    ...
};
```

Now we can find each function definition (here's one):

```
int db_find(char              *id,
         unsigned int      mnemonic_id,
         struct db_rec     **rec);
{
    ...
}
```


And prefix its name with the name of the class:

```
int program::db_find(char              *id,
                  unsigned int      mnemonic_id,
                  struct db_rec     **rec)
{
    ...
}
```

Now we have to write a new `main( )`function for the program:

```
int main(int ac, char **av)
{
    program the_program;

    return the_program.main(ac, av);
}
```

Does that change the behavior of the system? Not really. That change was just a mechanical process, and it kept the meaning and behavior of the program exactly the same. The old C system was, in reality, just one big object. When we start using *Encapsulate Global References (339)* we're making new objects, and subdividing the system in ways which make it easier to work with.

When procedural languages have object-oriented extensions, they allow us to move in this direction. This isn't deep object-orientation; it's just using objects enough to break up the program for testing.

What can we do besides extracting dependencies when our language supports OO? For one thing, we can incrementally move it toward a better object design. In general, this means that you have to group related functions in classes and extract plenty of methods so that you can break apart tangled responsibilities. For more advice on this, see Chapter 20, *This Class Is Too Big and I Don't Want It to Get Any Bigger.*

Procedural code doesn't present us with as many options as object-oriented code does, but we can make headway in procedural legacy code. The particular seams that a procedural language presents critically affect the ease of the work. If the procedural language you are using has an object-oriented successor, I recommend moving toward it. *Object seams (40)* are good for far more than getting tests in place. Link and preprocessing seams are great for getting code under test, but they really don't do much to improve design beyond that.

Chapter 20

This Class Is Too Big and I Don't Want It to Get Any Bigger

Many of the features that people add to systems are little tweaks. They require the addition of a little code and maybe a few more methods. It's tempting to just make these changes to an existing class. Chances are, the code that you need to add must use data from some existing class, and the easiest thing is to just add code to it. Unfortunately, this easy way of making changes can lead to some serious trouble. When we keep adding code to existing classes, we end up with long methods and large classes. Our software turns into a swamp, and it takes more time to understand how to add new features or even just understand how old features work.

I visited a team once that had what looked like a nice architecture on paper. They told me what the primary classes were and how they communicated with each other in the normal cases. Then, they showed me a couple of nice UML diagrams that showed the structure. I was surprised when I started to look at the code. Each of their classes could really be broken out into about 10 or so, and doing that would help them get past their most pressing problems.

What are the problems with big classes? The first is confusion. When you have 50 or 60 methods on a class, it's often hard to get a sense of what you have to change and whether it is going to affect anything else. In the worst cases, big classes have an incredible number of instance variables, and it is hard to know what the effects are of changing a variable. Another problem is task scheduling. When a class has 20 or so responsibilities, chances are, you'll have an incredible number of reasons to change it. In the same iteration, you might have several programmers who have to do different things to the class. If they are working concurrently, this can lead to some serious thrashing, particularly because of the third problem: Big classes are a pain to test. Encapsulation is a good thing, right? Well, don't ask testers about that; they are liable to bite your head off. Classes that are too big often hide too much. Encapsulation is great when it helps us reason about about code. It helps us know that certain things can be changed only under certain circumstances. However, when we encapsulate too much, the stuff inside rots and festers. There isn't any easy way to sense the effects of change, so people fall back on *Edit and Pray (9)* programming. At that point, either changes take far too long or the bug count increases. You have to pay for the lack of clarity somehow.

The first issue to confront when we have big classes is this: How can we work without making things worse? The key tactics we can use here are *Sprout Class (63)* and *Sprout Method (59)*. When we have to make changes, we should consider putting the code into a new class or a new method. *Sprout Class (63)* really keeps things from getting much worse. When you put new code into a new class, sure, you might have to delegate from the original class, but at least you aren't making it much bigger. *Sprout Method (59)* helps also, but in a more subtle way. If you add code in a new method, yes, you will have an additional method, but at the very least, you are identifying and naming another thing that the class does; often the names of methods can give you hints about how to break down a class into smaller pieces.

The key remedy for big classes is refactoring. It helps to break down classes into sets of smaller classes. But the biggest issue is figuring out what the smaller classes should look like. Fortunately, we have some guidance.

Single-Responsibility Principle (SRP)

Every class should have a single responsibility: It should have a single purpose in the system, and there should be only one reason to change it.

The single-responsibility principle is kind of hard to describe because the idea of a responsibility is kind of nebulous. If we look at it in a very naïve way, we might say, "Oh, that means that every class should have only a single method, right?" Well, methods can be seen as responsibilities. A `Task` is responsible for running using its `run` method, for telling us how many subtasks it has with `taskCount` method, and so on. But what we mean by a responsibility really comes into focus when we talk about *main purpose*. Figure 20.1 shows an example.

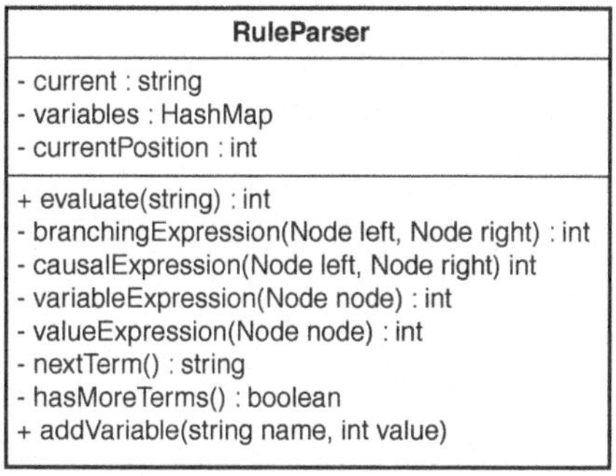

```
RuleParser
- current : string
- variables : HashMap
- currentPosition : int
+ evaluate(string) : int
- branchingExpression(Node left, Node right) : int
- causalExpression(Node left, Node right) int
- variableExpression(Node node) : int
- valueExpression(Node node) : int
- nextTerm() : string
- hasMoreTerms() : boolean
+ addVariable(string name, int value)
```

Figure 20.1 *Rule parser.*

We have a little class here that evaluates strings containing rule expressions in some obscure language. What responsibilities does it have? We can look at the name of the class to find one responsibility: It parses. But is that its main purpose? Parsing doesn't seem to be it. It seems that it evaluates also.

What else does it do? It holds on to a current string, the string that it is parsing. It also holds on to a field that indicates the current position while it is parsing. Both of those mini-responsibilities seem to fit under the category of parsing.

Let's take a look at the other variable, the `variables` field. It holds onto a set of variables that the parser uses so that it can evaluate arithmetic expressions such as `a + 3`. If someone calls the method `addVariable` with the arguments `a` and `1`, the expression `a + 3` will evaluate to `4`. So, it seems that there is this other responsibility, variable management, in this class.

Are there more responsibilities? Another way to find them is to look at method names. Is there a natural way to group the names of the methods? It seems that the methods kind of fall into these groups:

evaluate	branchingExpression	nextTerm	addVariable
	causalExpression	hasMoreTerms	
	variableExpression		
	valueExpression		

The `evaluate` method is an entry point of the class. It is one of only two public methods, and it denotes a key responsibility of the class: evaluation. All of the methods that end with the *Expression* suffix are kind of the same. Not only are they named similarly, but they all accept `Nodes` as arguments and return an int that indicates the value of a subexpression. The `nextTerm` and `hasMoreTerms` methods are similar, too. They seem to be about some special form of tokenization for terms. As we said earlier, the `addVariable` method is concerned with variable management.

To summarize, it seems that `RuleParser` has the following responsibilities:

- Parsing
- Expression evaluation
- Term tokenization
- Variable management

If we had to come up with a design from scratch that separated all of these responsibilities, it might look something like Figure 20.2.

Is this overkill? It could be. Often people who write little language interpreters merge parsing and expression evaluation; they just evaluate as they parse. But although that can be convenient, often it doesn't scale well as a language grows. Another responsibility that is kind of meager is that of `SymbolTable`. If the only responsibility of `SymbolTable` is to map variable names to integers, the class isn't giving us much advantage over just using a hash table or a list. Nice design, but guess what? It is pretty hypothetical. Unless we are choosing to rewrite this part of the system, our little multiclass design is a castle in the sky.

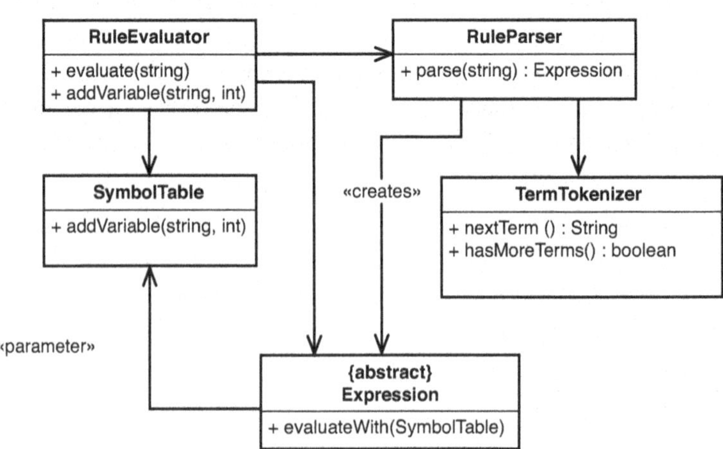

Figure 20.2 *Rule classes with responsibilities separated.*

In real-world cases of big classes, the key is to identify the different responsibilities and then figure out a way to incrementally move toward more focused responsibilities.

Seeing Responsibilities

In the `RuleParser` example in the last section, I showed a particular decomposition of a class into smaller classes. When I did that breakdown, I did it pretty much by rote. I listed all of the methods and started to think about what their purposes were. The key questions I asked were "Why is this method here?" and "What is it doing for the class?" Then I grouped them into lists, putting together methods that had a similar reason for being there.

I call this way of seeing responsibilities method grouping. It's only one of many ways of seeing responsibilities in existing code.

Learning to see responsibilities is a key design skill, and it takes practice. It might seem odd to talk about a design skill in this context of working with legacy code, but there really is little difference between discovering responsibilities in existing code and formulating them for code that you haven't written yet. The key thing is to be able to see responsibilities and learn how to separate them well. If anything, legacy code offers far more possibilities for the application of design skill than new features do. It is easier to talk about design tradeoffs when you can see the code that will be affected, and it is also easier to see whether structure is appropriate in a given context because the context is real and right in front of us.

This section describes a set of heuristics that we can use to see responsibilities in existing code. Note that we are not inventing responsibilities; we're just discovering what is there. Regardless of what structure legacy code has, its pieces do identifiable things. Sometimes they are hard to see, but these techniques can help. Try to apply them even with code that you don't have to change immediately. The more you start noticing the responsibilities inherent in code, the more you learn about it.

Heuristic #1: Group Methods

Look for similar method names. Write down all of the methods on a class, along with their access types (public, private, and so on), and try to find ones that seem to go together.

This technique, method grouping, is a pretty good start, particularly with very large classes. The important thing is to recognize that you don't have to categorize all of the names into new classes. Just see if you can find some that look like they are part of a common responsibility. If you can identify some of these responsibilities that are a bit off to the side of the main responsibility of the class, you have a direction in which you can take the code over time. Wait until you have to modify one of the methods you've categorized, and then decide whether you want to extract a class at that point.

Method grouping is a great team exercise also. Put up poster boards in your team room with lists of the method names for each of your major classes. Team members can mark up the posters over time, showing different groupings of methods. The whole team go over the groupings and decide which ones to target over time.

Heuristic #2: Look at Hidden Methods

Pay attention to private and protected methods. If a class has many of them, it often indicates that there is another class in the class dying to get out.

Big classes can hide too much. This question comes up over and over again from people new to unit testing: "How do I test private methods?" Many people spend a lot of time trying to figure out how to get around this problem, but, as I mentioned in an earlier chapter, the real answer is that if you have the urge to test a private method, the method shouldn't be private; if making the method public bothers you, chances are, it is because it is part of a separate responsibility: it should be on another class.

The `RuleParser` class earlier in this section is a quintessential example of this. It has two public methods: `evaluate` and `addVariable`. Everything else is private. What would the `RuleParser` class be like if we made `nextTerm` and `hasMoreTerms` public? Well, it would seem pretty odd. Users of the parser might get the idea that they have to use those two methods along with `evaluate` to parse and evaluate expressions. It would be odd to have those methods public on the `RuleParser` class, but it is far less odd—and, actually, perfectly fine—to make them public methods on a `TermTokenizer` class. This doesn't make `RuleParser` any less encapsulated. Even though `nextTerm` and `hasMoreTerms` are public on `TermTokenizer`, they are accessed privately in a `parser`. This is shown in Figure 20.3.

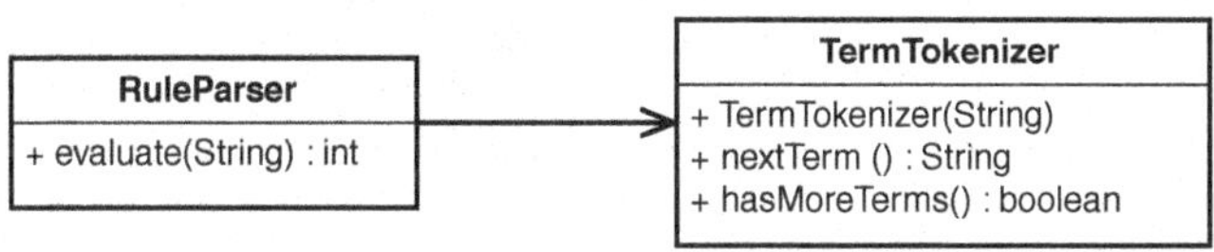

Figure 20.3 `RuleParser` *and* `TermTokenizer`.

Heuristic #3: Look for Decisions That Can Change

Look for decisions—not decisions that you are making in the code, but decisions that you've already made. Is there some way of doing something (talking to a database, talking to another set of objects, and so on) that seems hard-coded? Can you imagine it changing?

When you are trying to break up a big class, it's tempting to pay a lot of attention to the names of the methods. After all, they are one of the most noticeable things about a class. But the names of methods don't tell the whole story. Often big classes house methods that do many things at many different levels of abstraction. For instance, a method named `updateScreen()`might generate text for a display, format it, and send it to several different GUI objects. Looking at the method name alone, you'd have no idea how much work is going on and how many responsibilities are nestled in that code.

For this reason, it pays to do a little extract method refactoring before really settling on classes to extract. What methods should you extract? I handle this by looking for decisions. How many things are assumed in the code? Is the code calling methods from a particular API? Is it assuming that it will always be accessing the same database? If the code is doing these things, it's a good idea to extract methods that reflect what you intend at a high level. If you are getting particular information from a database, extract a method named after the information you are getting. When you do these extractions, you have many more methods, but you also might find that method grouping is easier. Better than that, you might find that you completely encapsulated some resource behind a set of methods. When you extract a class for them, you'll have broken some dependencies on low-level details.

Heuristic #4: Look for Internal Relationships

Look for relationships between instance variables and methods. Are certain instance variables used by some methods and not others?

It's really hard to find classes in which all the methods use all of the instance variables. Usually there is some sort of "lumping" in a class. Two or three methods might be the only ones that use a set of three variables. Often the names help you see this. For instance, in the `RulerParser` class, there is a collection named variables and a method named `addVariable`. That shows us that there is an obvious relationship between that method and that variable. It doesn't tell us that there aren't other methods that access that variable, but at least we have a place to start looking.

Another technique we can use to find these "lumps" is to make a little sketch of the relationships inside a class. These are called *feature sketches*. They show which methods and instance variables each method in a class uses, and they are pretty easy to make. Here is an example:

```
class Reservation
{
    private int duration;
    private int dailyRate;
    private Date date;
    private Customer customer;
    private List fees = new ArrayList();

    public Reservation(Customer customer, int duration,
            int dailyRate, Date date) {
        this.customer = customer;
        this.duration = duration;
        this.dailyRate = dailyRate;
        this.date = date;
    }

    public void extend(int additionalDays) {
        duration += additionalDays;
    }

    public void extendForWeek() {
        int weekRemainder = RentalCalendar.weekRemainderFor(date);
        final int DAYS_PER_WEEK = 7;
        extend(weekRemainder);
        dailyRate = RateCalculator.computeWeekly(
                                    customer.getRateCode())
                        / DAYS_PER_WEEK;
    }

    public void addFee(FeeRider rider) {
        fees.add(rider);
    }

    int getAdditionalFees() {
        int total = 0;
```

```
        for(Iterator it = fees.iterator(); it.hasNext(); ) {
            total += ((FeeRider)(it.next())).getAmount();
        }
        return total;
    }

    int getPrincipalFee() {
        return dailyRate
                * RateCalculator.rateBase(customer)
                * duration;
    }

    public int getTotalFee() {
        return getPrincipalFee() + getAdditionalFees();
    }
}
```

The firststep is to draw circles for each of the variables, as shown in Figure 20.4.

Next, we look at each method and put down a circle for it. Then we draw a line from each method circle to the circles for any instance variables and methods that it accesses or modifies. It's usually okay to skip the constructors. Generally, they modify each instance variable.

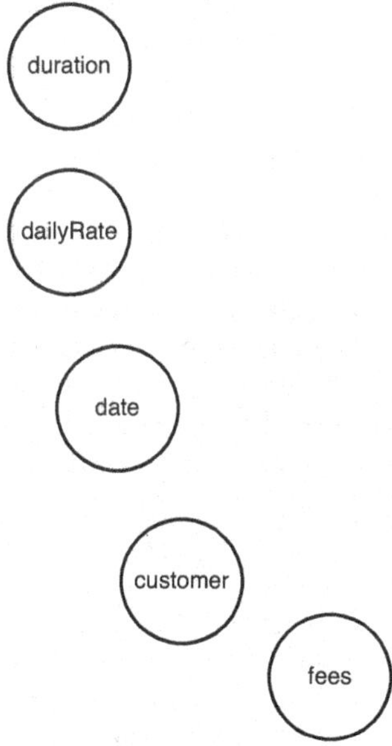

Figure 20.4 Variables in the Reservation *class.*

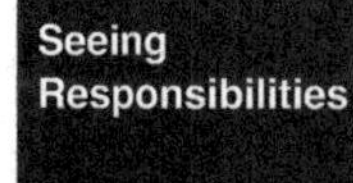

Figure 20.5 shows the diagram after we've added a circle for the `extend` method:

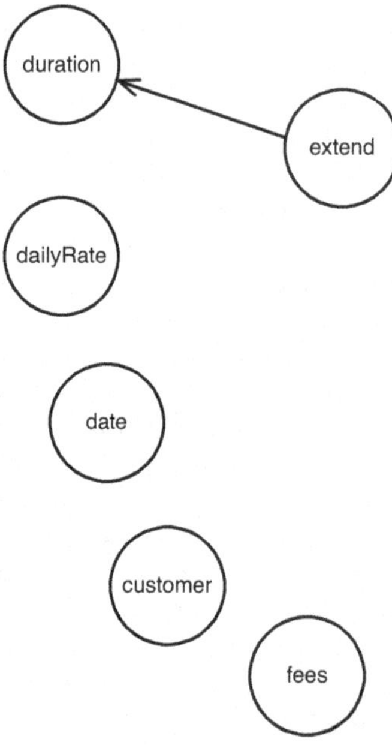

Figure 20.5 `extend` *uses duration.*

Seeing Responsibilities

If you've already read the chapters that describe effect sketching, you might notice that these *feature sketches* look a lot like *effect sketches (155)*. Essentially, they are pretty close. The main difference is that the arrows are reversed. In *feature sketches*, arrows point in the direction of a method or variable that is used by another method or variable. In *effect sketches*, the arrow points toward methods or variables that are impacted by other methods and variables.

These are two different, completely legitimate ways of looking at interactions in a system. *Feature sketches* are great for mapping the internal structure of classes. *Effect sketches (155)* are great for reasoning forward from a point of change.

Is it confusing that they look somewhat the same? Not really. These sketches are disposable tools. They are the sort of thing that you sit down and draw up with a partner for about 10 minutes before you make your changes. Afterward you throw them away. There is little value in keeping them around, so there is little likelihood that they will be confused with each other.

Figure 20.6 shows the sketch after we've added circles for each feature and lines for all of the features they use:

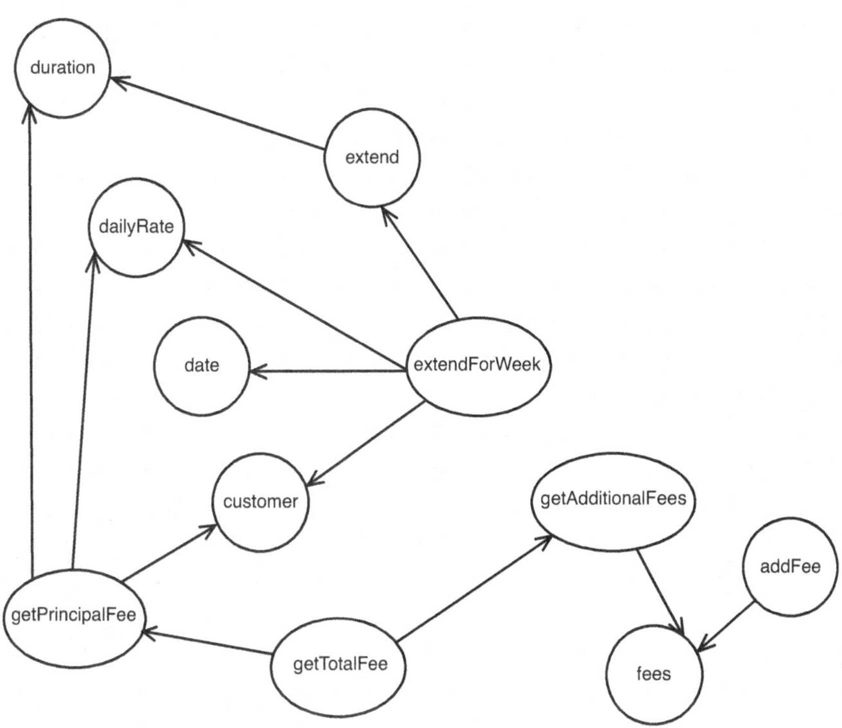

Figure 20.6 *Feature sketch for* `Reservation`.

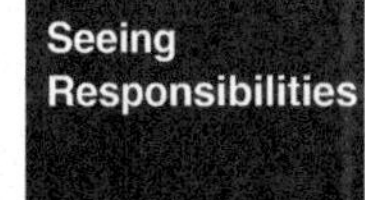

What can we learn from this sketch? One obvious thing is that there is a little bit of clustering in this class. The `duration`, `dailyRate`, `date`, and `customer` variables are used primarily by `getPrincipalFee`, `extend`, and `extendForWeek`. Are any of these methods public? Yes, `extend` and `extendForWeek` are, but `getPrincipalFee` isn't. What would our system be like if we made this cluster into its own class (see Figure 20.7)?

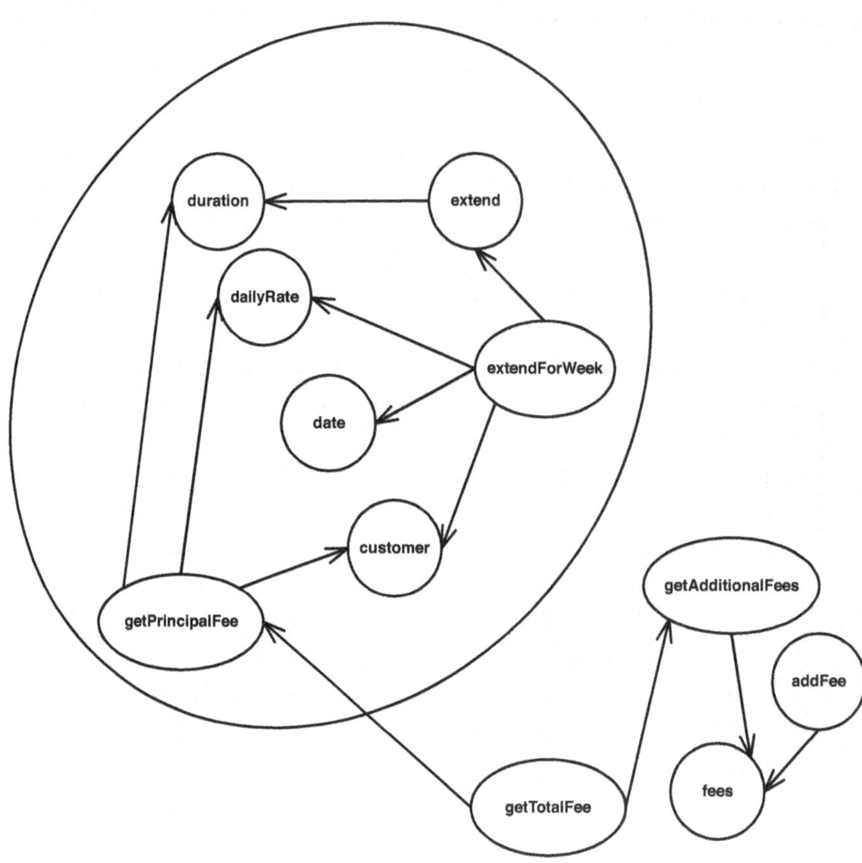

Figure 20.7 *A cluster in* Reservation.

The big bubble in the diagram could be a new class. It would need to have extend, extendForWeek, and getPrincipalFee as public methods, but all of the other methods could be private. We could keep fees, addFee, getAdditionalFees, and getTotalFee in the Reservation class and delegate to the new class (see Figure 20.8).

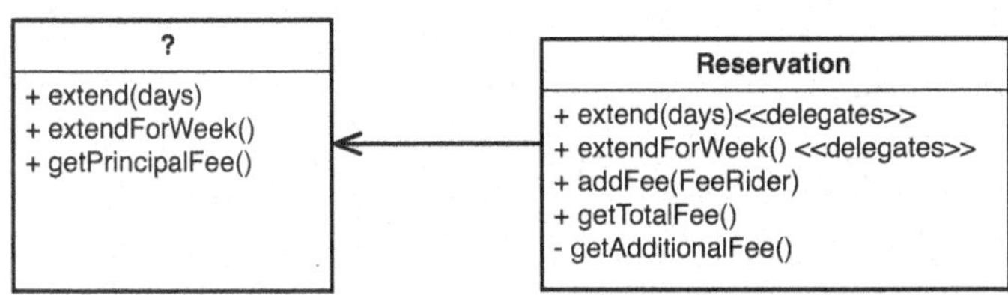

Figure 20.8 `Reservation` *using a new class.*

The key thing to figure out before attempting this is whether this new class has a good, distinct responsibility. Can we come up with a name for it? It seems to do two things: extend a reservation and calculate its principal fee. It seems that `Reservation` is a good name, but we are already using it for the original class.

Here's another possibility. We could flip things around. Instead of extracting all of the code in the big circle, we can extract the other code, as in Figure 20.9.

We can call the class that we extract `FeeCalculator`. That could work, but the `getTotalFee` method needs to call `getPrincipalFee` on `Reservation`—or does it?

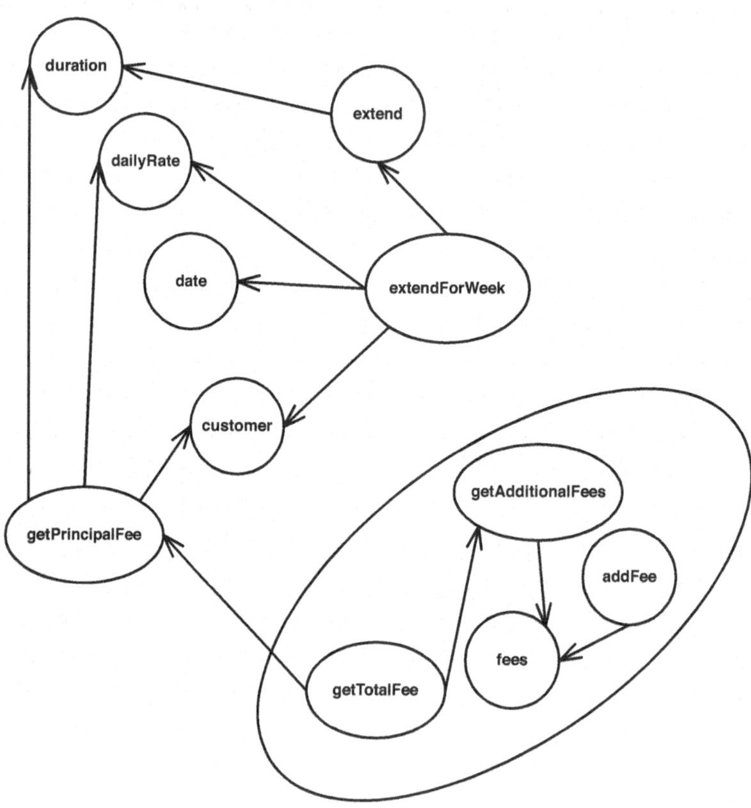

Figure 20.9 *Seeing* `Reservation` *in another way.*

Seeing Responsibilities

What if we call `getPrincipalFee` in `Reservation` and then pass that value to the `FeeCalculator`? Here is a sketch of the code:

```
public class Reservation
{
    ...
    private FeeCalculator calculator = new FeeCalculator();

    private int getPrincipalFee() {
        ...
    }

    public Reservation(Customer customer, int duration,
            int dailyRate, Date date) {
        this.customer = customer;
        this.duration = duration;
        this.dailyRate = dailyRate;
        this.date = date;
    }

    ...

    public void addFee(FeeRider fee) {
        calculator.addFee(fee);
    }

    public getTotalFee() {
        int baseFee = getPrincipalFee();
        return calculator.getTotalFee(baseFee);
    }

}
```

Our structure ends up looking like Figure 20.10.

We can even consider moving getPrincipalFee over to FeeCalculator to make the responsibilities align with the class names better, but considering that getPrincipalFee depends on a number of variables in Reservation, it might be better to keep it where it is.

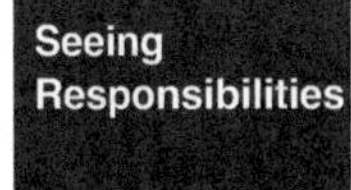

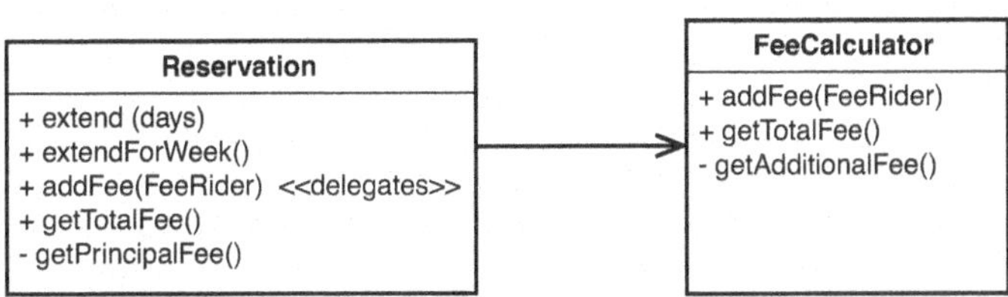

Figure 20.10 *Reservation using* FeeCalculator.

Feature sketches are a great tool for finding separate responsibilities in classes. We can try to group the features and figure out what classes we can extract based upon the names. But in addition to helping us find responsibilities, feature sketches allow us to see the dependency structure inside classes, and that can often be just as important as responsibility when we are deciding what to extract. In this example, there were two strong clusters of variables and methods. The only connection between them is the call of `getPrincipalFee` inside `getTotalFee`. In feature sketches, we often see these connections as a small set of lines connecting larger clusters. I call this a *pinch point (180)*, and I talk about them more in Chapter 12, *I Need to Make Many Changes in One Area. Do I Have to Break Dependencies for All the Classes Involved?*

Sometimes when you draw a sketch, you don't find any pinch points. They aren't always there. But at the very least, seeing the names and the dependencies among the features can help.

When you have the sketch, you can play around with different ways of breaking up the class. To do this, circle groups of features. When you circle features, the lines that you cross can define the interface of a new class. As you circle, try to come up with a class name for each group. Frankly, aside from anything that you choose to do or not do when you extract classes, this is a great way of increasing your naming skill. It's also a good way of exploring design alternatives.

Heuristic #5: Look for the Primary Responsibility

Try to describe the responsibility of the class in a single sentence.

Seeing Responsibilities

The *Single Responsibility Principle* tells us that classes should have a single responsibility. If that's the case, it should be easy to write it down in a single sentence. Try it with one of the big classes in your system. As you think of what the clients need and expect from the class, add clauses to the sentence. The class does this, and this, and this, and that. Is there any one thing that seems more important than anything else? If there is, you might have found the key responsibility of the class. The other responsibilities should probably be factored out into other classes.

There are two ways to violate the *Single Responsibility Principle*. It can be violated at the interface level and at the implementation level. SRP is violated at the interface level when a class presents an interface that makes it appear that it is responsible for a very large number of things. For instance, the interface to this class (see Figure 20.11) looks like it can be broken into three or four classes.

```
ScheduledJob
----------------------------------
+ addPredecessor(ScheduledJob)
+ addSuccessor(ScheduledJob)
+ getDuration() : int
+ show();
+ refesh()
+ run()
+ postMessage() : void
+ isVisible() : boolean
+ isModified() : boolean
+ persist()
+ acquireResources()
+ releaseResources()
+ isRunning()
+ getElapsedTime()
+ pause()
+ resume()
+ getActivities()
...
```

Figure 20.11 *The* `ScheduledJob` *class.*

The SRP violation that we care most about is violation at the implementation level. Plainly put, we care whether the class really does all of that stuff or whether it just delegates to a couple of other classes. If it delegates, we don't have a large monolithic class; we just have a class that is a facade, a front end for a bunch of little classes and that can be easier to manage.

Figure 20.12 shows the `ScheduledJob` class with responsibilities delegated to a few other classes.

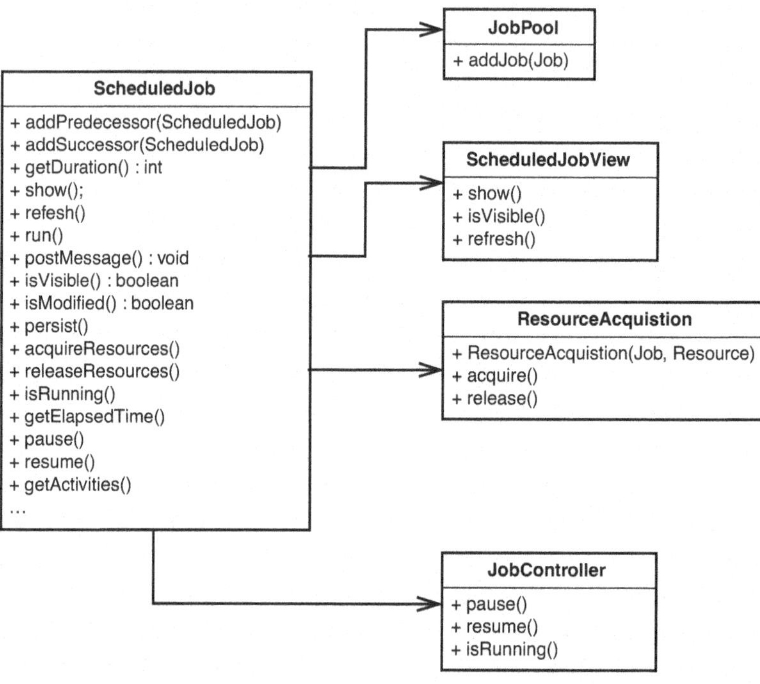

Figure 20.12 `ScheduledJob` *with extracted classes.*

Seeing Responsibilities

The *Single Responsibility Principle* is still violated at the interface level, but at the implementation level things are a bit better.

How would we solve the problem at the interface level? That's a bit harder. The general approach is to see if some of the classes we delegate to can actually be used directly by clients. For instance, if only some clients are interested in running `ScheduledJob`s, we could refactor toward something like this:

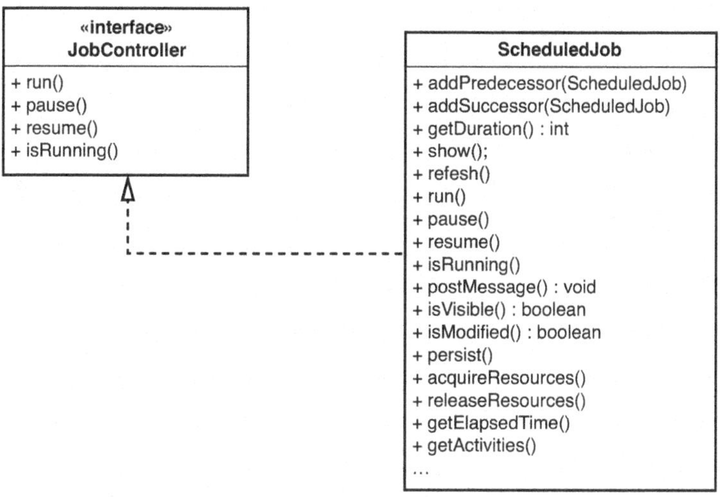

Figure 20.13 *A client-specific interface for* `ScheduledJob`.

Now clients that are concerned only with controlling jobs can accept `ScheduledJobs` as `JobControllers`. This technique of making an interface for a particular set of clients keeps the design in line with the *Interface Segregation Principle.*

Interface Segregation Principle (ISP)

When a class is large, rarely do all of its clients use all of its methods. Often we can see different groupings of methods that particular clients use. If we create an interface for each of these groupings and have the large class implement those interfaces, each client can see the big class through that particular interface. This helps us hide information and also decreases dependency in the system. The clients no longer have to recompile whenever the large class does.

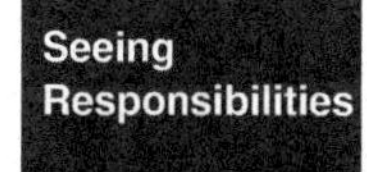

When we have interfaces for particular sets of clients, we can often start to move code from the big class to a new class that uses the original class, as you can see in Figure 20.14.

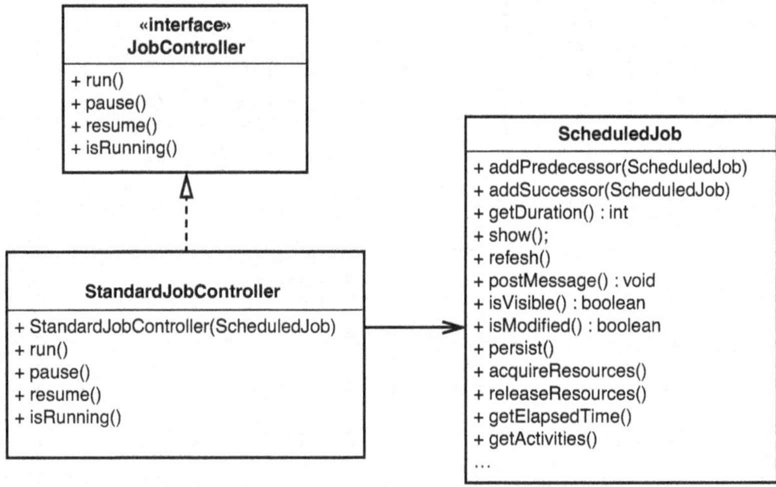

Figure 20.14 *Segregating the interface of* `ScheduledJob`.

Instead of having `ScheduledJob` delegate to a `JobController`, we've made a `JobController` delegate to `ScheduledJob`. Now whenever a client wants to run a `ScheduledJob`, it creates a `JobController`, passing it a `ScheduledJob`, and uses the `JobController` to handle its execution.

Seeing Responsibilities

This sort of refactoring is nearly always tougher than it sounds. Often to do it, you have to expose more methods in the public interface of the original class (`ScheduledJob`) so that the new front (`StandardJobController`) has access to everything it needs to do its work. Often it takes quite a bit of work to make a change like this. Client code now has to be changed to use the new class rather than the old one; to do that safely, you need to have tests around those clients. The nice thing about this refactoring, though, is that it does allow you to whittle away at the interface of a big class. Notice that `ScheduledJob` no longer has the methods that are on `JobController`.

Heuristic #6: When All Else Fails, Do Some Scratch Refactoring

If you are having a lot of trouble seeing responsibilities in a class, do some scratch refactoring.

Scratch refactoring (212) is a powerful tool. Just remember that it is an artificial exercise. The things you see when you "scratch" are not necessarily the things you'll end up with when you refactor.

Heuristic #7: Focus on the Current Work

Pay attention to what you have to do right now. If you are providing a different way of doing anything, you might have identified a responsibility that you should extract and then allow substitution for.

It is easy to become overwhelmed by the number of distinct responsibilities you can identify in a class. Remember that the changes you currently are making are telling you about some particular way that the software can change. Often just recognizing that way of changing is enough to see the new code you write as a separate responsibility.

Other Techniques

The heuristics for identifying responsibilities can really help you dig in and find new abstractions in old classes, but they are just tricks. The way to really get better at identification is to read more. Read books about design patterns. More important, read other people's code. Look at open-source projects, and just take some time to browse and see how other people do things. Pay attention to how classes are named and the correspondence between class names and the names of methods. Over time, you'll get better at identifying hidden responsibilities, and you'll just start to see them when you browse unfamiliar code.

Moving Forward

When you've identified a bunch of different responsibilities in a large class, there are only two other issues to deal with: strategy and tactics. Let's talk about strategy first.

Strategy

What should we do when we've identified all of these separate responsibilities? Should we take a week and start to whack at the big classes in the system? Should we break them all down into little bits? If you have time to do that, it's great, but it's rare. It can also be risky. In nearly every case that I've seen, when teams go on a large refactoring binge, system stability breaks down for a little while, even if they are being careful and writing tests as they go. If you are early in your release cycle, are willing to accept the risk, and have time, a refactoring binge can be fine. Just don't let the bugs dissuade you from other refactoring.

The best approach to breaking down big classes is to identify the responsibilities, make sure that everyone else on the team understands them, and then break down the class on an as-needed basis. When you do that, you spread out the risk of the changes and can get other work done as you go.

Tactics

In most legacy systems, the most that you can hope for in the beginning is to start to apply the SRP at the implementation level: Essentially, extract classes from your big class and delegate to them. Introducing SRP at the interface level requires more work. The clients of your class have to change, and you need tests for them. Nicely, introducing SRP at the implementation level makes it easier to introduce it at the interface level later. Let's look at the implementation case first.

The techniques that you use to extract classes depend upon a number of factors. One is how easily you can get tests around the methods that could be affected. It pays to take a look at the class and list all of the instance variables and methods that you'll have to move. From this, you should get a good idea of what methods you should write tests for. In the case of the `RuleParser` class that we looked at previously, if we were considering breaking out a `TermTokenizer` class, we'd want to move the string field named `current` and the `currentPosition` field, as well as `hasMoreTerms` and `nextTerm`. The fact that `hasMoreTerms` and `nextTerm` are private means that we can't really write tests directly for them. We could make them public (after all, we are going to move them anyway), but it might be just as easy to create a `RuleParser` in a test harness and give it a set of strings to evaluate. If we do that, we'll have tests that cover `hasMoreTerms` and `nextTerm`, indirectly, and we'll be able to move them to a new class safely.

Unfortunately, many big classes are hard to instantiate in test harnesses. See Chapter 9, *I Can't Get This Class into a Test Harness*, for a set of tips that you can use to move forward. If you are able to get the class instantiated, you might have to use the tips in Chapter 10, *I Can't Run This Method in a Test Harness*, to get tests in place also.

If you are able to get tests in place, you can start to extract a class in a very straightforward way, using the *Extract Class* refactoring described in Martin Fowler's book *Refactoring: Improving the Design of Existing Code* (Addison-

Wesley, 1999). However, if you aren't able to get tests in place, you can still move forward, albeit in a slightly riskier way. This is a very conservative approach, and it works regardless of whether you have a refactoring tool. Here are the steps:

1. Identify a responsibility that you want to separate into another class.
2. Figure out whether any instance variables will have to move to the new class. If so, move them to a separate part of the class declaration, away from the other instance variables.
3. If you have whole methods that you want to move to the new class, extract the bodies of each of them to new methods. The name of each new method should be the same as its old name, but with a unique common prefix in front of the name, something like `MOVING`, all in capital letters. If you are not using a refactoring tool, remember to *Preserve Signatures (312)* when you extract the methods. As you extract each method, put it in that separate part of the class declaration, next to the variables you are moving.
4. If parts of methods should go to the other class, extract them from the original methods. Use that prefix `MOVING` again for their names, and put them in the separate section.
5. At this point, you should have a section of your class that has instance variables that you need to move, along with a bunch of methods that you want to move also. Do a text search of the current class and all of its subclasses, to make sure that none of the variables that you are going to move is used outside of the methods you are going to move. It is important not to *Lean on the Compiler (315)* in this step. In many OO languages, a derived class can declare variables with the same name as variables in a base class. Often this is called *shadowing*. If your class shadows any variables and other uses of the variables are hanging around, you could change the behavior of your code when you move the variables. Likewise, if you *Lean on the Compiler (315)* to find uses of a variable that is shadowing another, you won't find all of the places it is being used. Commenting out the declaration of a shadowed variable just makes the one that it shadows visible.
6. At this point, you can move all of the instance variables and methods you've separated directly to the new class. Create an instance of the new class in the old class, and *Lean on the Compiler (315)* to find places where the moved methods have to be called on the instance rather than on the old class.

7. After you've done the move and the code compiles, you can start to remove the `MOVING` prefix on all of the moved methods. *Lean on the Compiler (315)* to navigate to the places where you need to change the names.

The steps for this refactoring are rather involved, but if you are in a very complex piece of code, they are necessary if you want to extract classes safely without tests.

There are a couple of things that can go wrong when you extract classes without tests. The most subtle bugs that we can inject are bugs related to inheritance. Moving a method from one class to another is pretty safe. You can *Lean on the Compiler (315)* to aid your work, but in most languages all bets are off if you attempt to move a method that overrides another method. If you do, callers of the method on the original class will now call a method with the same name from a base class. A similar situation can occur with variables. A variable in a subclass can hide a variable with the same name in a superclass. Moving it just makes the one that was hidden visible.

To get past these problems, we don't move the original methods at all. We create new methods by extracting the bodies of the old ones. The prefix is just a mechanical way of generating a new name and making sure that it doesn't clash with other names before the move. Instance variables are a little trickier: We have that manual step of searching for uses of variables before we use them. It is possible to make mistakes with this. Be very careful, and do it with a partner.

After Extract Class

Extracting classes from a big class is often a good first step. In practice, the biggest danger for teams doing this is getting overambitious. You might have done a *Scratch refactoring (212)* or developed some other view of what the system *should* look like. But remember, the structure you have in your application works. It supports the functionality; it just might not be tuned toward moving forward. Sometimes the best thing that you can do is formulate a view of how a large class is going to look after refactoring and then just forget about it. You did it to discover what is possible. To move forward, you have to be sensitive to what is there and move that not necessarily toward the ideal design, but at least in a better direction.

Chapter 21

I'm Changing the Same Code All Over the Place

This can be one of the most frustrating things in legacy systems. You need to make a change, and you think, "Oh, that's all." Then you discover that you have to make the same change over and over again because there are about a dozen places with similar code in your system. You might get the sense that if you reengineered or restructured your system, you might not have this problem, but who has time for that? So you are left with another sore point in the system, something that adds up to general yuckiness.

If you know about refactoring, you're in a better position. You know that removing duplication doesn't have to be a grand effort such as in reengineering or re-architecting. It's something that you can do in small chunks as you do your work. Over time, the system will get better as long as people aren't introducing duplication behind your back. If they are, you can take steps with them short of physical violence, but that is another issue. The key question is, is it worth it? What do we get when we zealously squeeze duplication out of an area of code? The results are surprising. Let's take a look at an example.

We have a little Java-based networking system, and we have to send commands to a server. The two commands that we have are called `AddEmployeeCmd` and `LogonCommand`. When we need to issue a command, we instantiate it a command object and pass an output stream to its `write` method.

Here are the listings for both command classes. Do you see any duplication here?


```
import java.io.OutputStream;

public class AddEmployeeCmd {
    String name;
    String address;
    String city;
    String state;
    String yearlySalary;
```

```
    private static final byte[] header = {(byte)0xde, (byte)0xad};
    private static final byte[] commandChar = {0x02};
    private static final byte[] footer = {(byte)0xbe, (byte)0xef};
    private static final int SIZE_LENGTH = 1;
    private static final int CMD_BYTE_LENGTH = 1;

    private int getSize() {
        return header.length +
                SIZE_LENGTH +
                CMD_BYTE_LENGTH +
                footer.length +
                name.getBytes().length + 1 +
                address.getBytes().length + 1 +
                city.getBytes().length + 1 +
                state.getBytes().length + 1 +
                yearlySalary.getBytes().length + 1;
    }

    public AddEmployeeCmd(String name, String address,
                          String city, String state,
                          int yearlySalary) {
        this.name = name;
        this.address = address;
        this.city = city;
        this.state = state;
        this.yearlySalary = Integer.toString(yearlySalary);
    }

    public void write(OutputStream outputStream)
                throws Exception {
        outputStream.write(header);
        outputStream.write(getSize());
        outputStream.write(commandChar);
        outputStream.write(name.getBytes());
        outputStream.write(0x00);
        outputStream.write(address.getBytes());
        outputStream.write(0x00);
        outputStream.write(city.getBytes());
        outputStream.write(0x00);
        outputStream.write(state.getBytes());
        outputStream.write(0x00);
        outputStream.write(yearlySalary.getBytes());
        outputStream.write(0x00);
        outputStream.write(footer);
    }
}
```

```
import java.io.OutputStream;

public class LoginCommand {
    private String userName;
    private String passwd;
    private static final byte[] header
              = {(byte)0xde, (byte)0xad};
    private static final byte[] commandChar = {0x01};
    private static final byte[] footer
              = {(byte)0xbe, (byte)0xef};
    private static final int SIZE_LENGTH = 1;
    private static final int CMD_BYTE_LENGTH = 1;

    public LoginCommand(String userName, String passwd) {
        this.userName = userName;
        this.passwd = passwd;
    }

    private int getSize() {
        return header.length +  SIZE_LENGTH +  CMD_BYTE_LENGTH +
              footer.length + userName.getBytes().length + 1 +
              passwd.getBytes().length + 1;
    }

    public void write(OutputStream outputStream)
              throws Exception {
        outputStream.write(header);
        outputStream.write(getSize());
        outputStream.write(commandChar);
        outputStream.write(userName.getBytes());
        outputStream.write(0x00);
        outputStream.write(passwd.getBytes());
        outputStream.write(0x00);
        outputStream.write(footer);
    }
}
```

Figure 21.1 shows the classes in UML.

AddEmployeeCmd
name : String
address : String
city : String
stat : String
yearlySalary : String
- header : byte []
- commandChar : byte []
- footer : byte []
- SIZE_LENGTH : int
- CMD_BYTE_LENGTH : int
- getSize() : int
+ AddEmployeeCmd(...)
+ write(OutputStream)

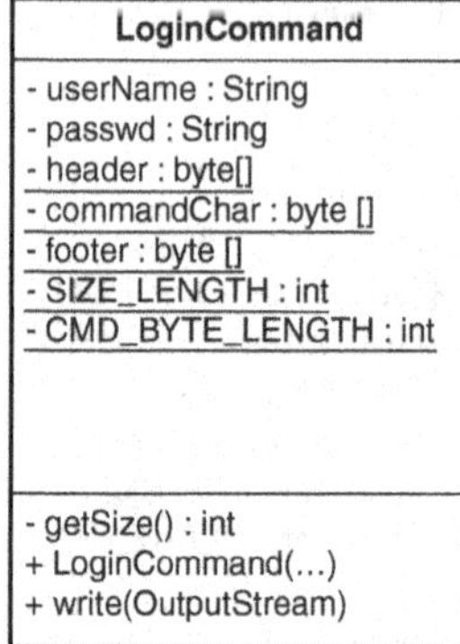

Figure 21.1 `AddEmployeeCmd` *and* `LoginCommand`.

It looks like there is a lot of duplication, but so what? The amount of code is pretty small. We could refactor it, cutting out duplication, and make it smaller, but is that going to make our lives easier? Maybe yes, maybe no; it's hard to tell just by looking at it.

Let's try to identify pieces of duplication and remove it, and see where we end up. Then we can decide whether the duplication removal was really helpful.

The first thing that we need is a set of tests that we'll run after each refactoring. Fortunately, we have them. We'll cut them out of the description here for brevity, but remember that they are there.

First Steps

My first reaction when I am confronted by duplication is to step back and get a sense of the full scope of it. When I do that, I start thinking about what kind of classes I'll end up with and what the extracted bits of duplication will look like. Then I realize that I'm really over-thinking it. Removing small pieces of duplication helps, and it makes it easier to see larger areas of duplication later. For instance, in the `write` method of `LoginCommand`, we have this code:

```
outputStream.write(userName.getBytes());
outputStream.write(0x00);
outputStream.write(passwd.getBytes());
outputStream.write(0x00);
```

When we write out a string, we also write a terminating null character (`0x00`). We can extract the duplication like this. Create a method named `writeField` that accepts a string and an output stream. The method then writes the string to the stream and finishes up by writing a null.

```
void writeField(OutputStream outputStream, String field) {
    outputStream.write(field.getBytes());
    outputStream.write(0x00);

}
```

Deciding Where to Start

When we go through a series of refactorings to remove duplication, we can end up with different structures, depending on where we start. For instance, imagine that we have a method like this:

```
void c() { a(); a(); b(); a(); b(); b(); }
```

It can be broken down like this:

```
void c() { aa(); b(); a(); bb(); }
```

or like this:

```
void c() { a(); ab(); ab(); b(); }
```

So, which should we choose? The truth is, it doesn't make much difference structurally. Both groupings are better than what we had, and we can refactor them into the other grouping, if we need to. These aren't final decisions. I decide by paying attention to the names that I would use. If I can find a name for two repeated calls to a(), that makes more sense, in context, than a name for a call to a() followed by a call to b(), then I'll use it.

Another heuristic that I use is to start small. If I can remove tiny pieces of duplication, I do those first because often it makes the big picture clearer.

When we have that method, we can replace each pair of string/null writes, running our tests periodically to make sure we haven't broken anything. Here is the write method of LoginCommand after the change:


```
public void write(OutputStream outputStream)
          throws Exception {
  outputStream.write(header);
  outputStream.write(getSize());
  outputStream.write(commandChar);
  writeField(outputstream, username);
  writeField(outputStream, passwd);
  outputStream.write(footer);
}
```

That takes care of the problem for the LoginCommand class, but it doesn't do a thing for us in the AddEmployeeCmd class. AddEmployeeCmd has similar repeating sequences of string/null writes in its `write` method also. Because both classes are commands, we can introduce a superclass for them called `Command`. When we have it, we can pull `writeField` up into the superclass so that it can be used in both commands (see Figure 21.2).

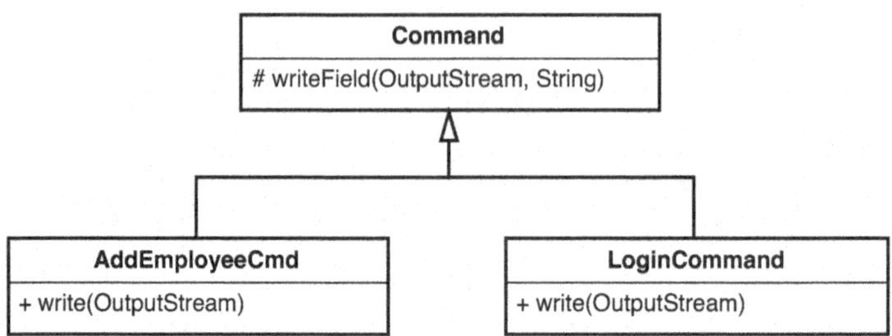

Figure 21.2 *Command hierarchy.*

We can go back over to `AddEmployeeCmd` now and replace its string/null writes with calls to `writeField`. When we're done, the `write` method for `AddEmployeeCmd` looks like this:

```
public void write(OutputStream outputStream)
          throws Exception {
   outputStream.write(header);
   outputStream.write(getSize());
   outputStream.write(commandChar);
   writeField(outputStream, name);
   writeField(outputStream, address);
   writeField(outputStream, city);
   writeField(outputStream, state);
   writeField(outputStream, yearlySalary);
   outputStream.write(footer);
}
```

First Steps

The `write` for `LoginCommand` looks like this:

```
public void write(OutputStream outputStream)
          throws Exception {
   outputStream.write(header);
   outputStream.write(getSize());
   outputStream.write(commandChar);
   writeField(outputstream, userName);
   writeField(outputStream, passwd);
   outputStream.write(footer);
}
```

The code is a little cleaner, but we're not done yet. The write methods for AddEmployeeCmd and LoginCommand have the same form: write the header, the size, and the command char; then write a bunch of fields; and, finally, write the footer. If we can extract the difference, writing the fields, we end up with a LoginCommand write method that looks like this:

```
public void write(OutputStream outputStream)
          throws Exception {
   outputStream.write(header);
   outputStream.write(getSize());
   outputStream.write(commandChar);
   writeBody(outputstream);
   outputStream.write(footer);
}
```

Here is the extracted writeBody:

```
private void writeBody(OutputStream outputStream)
          throws Exception {
   writeField(outputstream, userName);
   writeField(outputStream, passwd);
}
```

The write method for AddEmployeeCmd looks exactly the same, but its writeBody looks like this:

```
private void writeBody(OutputStream outputStream) throws Exception {
   writeField(outputStream, name);
   writeField(outputStream, address);
   writeField(outputStream, city);
   writeField(outputStream, state);
   writeField(outputStream, yearlySalary);
}
```

> When two methods look roughly the same, extract the differences to other methods. When you do that, you can often make them exactly the same and get rid of one.

The write methods for both classes look exactly the same. Can we move the write method up into the Command class? Not yet. Even though both writes look the same, they use data from their classes: header, footer, and commandChar. If we are going to try to make a single write method, it would have to call methods from the subclasses to get that data. Let's take a look at the variables in AddEmployeeCmd and LoginCommand:

```
public class AddEmployeeCmd extends Command {
    String name;
    String address;
    String city;
    String state;
    String yearlySalary;
```

```
    private static final byte[] header
            = {(byte)0xde, (byte)0xad};
    private static final byte[] commandChar = {0x02};
    private static final byte[] footer
            = {(byte)0xbe, (byte)0xef};
    private static final int SIZE_LENGTH = 1;
    private static final int CMD_BYTE_LENGTH = 1;
    ...
}

public class LoginCommand extends Command {
    private String userName;
    private String passwd;

    private static final byte[] header
            = {(byte)0xde, (byte)0xad};
    private static final byte[] commandChar = {0x01};
    private static final byte[] footer
            = {(byte)0xbe, (byte)0xef};
    private static final int SIZE_LENGTH = 1;
    private static final int CMD_BYTE_LENGTH = 1;
    ...
}
```

Both classes have a lot of common data. We can pull header, footer, SIZE_LENGTH, and CMD_BYTE_LENGTH up to the Command class because they all have the same values. I'm going to make them protected temporarily so that we can recompile and test:

```
public class Command {
    protected static final byte[] header
            = {(byte)0xde, (byte)0xad};
    protected static final byte[] footer
            = {(byte)0xbe, (byte)0xef};
    protected static final int SIZE_LENGTH = 1;
    protected static final int CMD_BYTE_LENGTH = 1;
    ...
}
```

First Steps

Now we're left with the commandChar variable in both subclasses. It has a different value for each of them. One simple way of handling this is to introduce an abstract getter on the Command class:

```
public class Command {
    protected static final byte[] header
            = {(byte)0xde, (byte)0xad};
    protected static final byte[] footer
            = {(byte)0xbe, (byte)0xef};
    protected static final int SIZE_LENGTH = 1;
    protected static final int CMD_BYTE_LENGTH = 1;
```

```
    protected abstract char [] getCommandChar();
    ...
}
```

Now we can replace the commandChar variables on each subclass with a getCommandChar override:

```
public class AddEmployeeCmd extends Command {
    protected char [] getCommandChar() {
        return new char [] { 0x02};
    }
    ...
}

public class LoginCommand extends Command {
    protected char [] getCommandChar() {
        return new char [] { 0x01};
    }
    ...
}
```

Okay, now, it is safe to pull up the write method. Once we do, we end up with a Command class that looks like this:

```
public class Command {
    protected static final byte[] header
            = {(byte)0xde, (byte)0xad};
    protected static final byte[] footer
            = {(byte)0xbe, (byte)0xef};
    protected static final int SIZE_LENGTH = 1;
    protected static final int CMD_BYTE_LENGTH = 1;

    protected abstract char [] getCommandChar();

    protected abstract void writeBody(OutputStream outputStream);

    protected void writeField(OutputStream outputStream,
                              String field) {
        outputStream.write(field.getBytes());
        outputStream.write(0x00);
    }

    public void write(OutputStream outputStream)
            throws Exception {
        outputStream.write(header);
        outputStream.write(getSize());
        outputStream.write(commandChar);
        writeBody(outputstream);
        outputStream.write(footer);
    }
}
```

Notice that we had to introduce an abstract method for writeBody and put it up in Command also (see Figure 21.3).

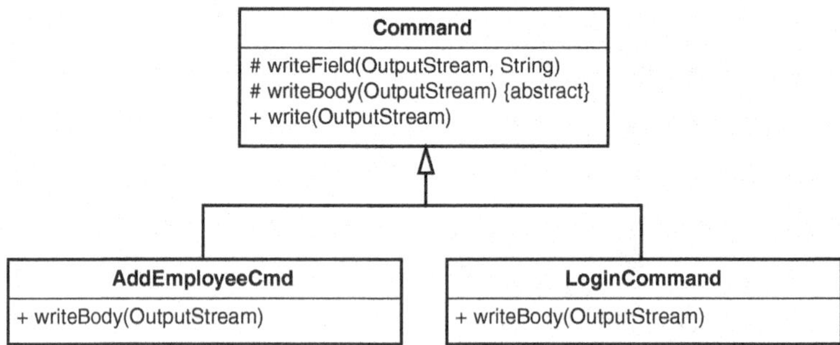

Figure 21.3 *Pulling up* writeField, writeBody, *and* write.

After we've moved up the write method, the only things that remain in each of the subclasses are the getSize methods, the getCommandChar method, and the constructors. Here's the LoginCommand class again:

```
public class LoginCommand extends Command {
    private String userName;
    private String passwd;

    public LoginCommand(String userName, String passwd) {
        this.userName = userName;
        this.passwd = passwd;
    }

    protected char [] getCommandChar() {
        return new char [] { 0x01};
    }

    protected int getSize() {
        return header.length +  SIZE_LENGTH +  CMD_BYTE_LENGTH +
               footer.length + userName.getBytes().length + 1 +
                passwd.getBytes().length + 1;
    }
}
```

That is a pretty slim class. AddEmployeeCmd looks pretty similar. It has a getSize method and a getCommandChar method, and not much else. Let's look at the getSize methods a little more closely:

Here is the one for LoginCommand:

```
protected int getSize() {
   return header.length +  SIZE_LENGTH +
           CMD_BYTE_LENGTH + footer.length +
           userName.getBytes().length + 1 +
           passwd.getBytes().length + 1;
}
```

And here is the one for AddEmployeeCmd:

```
private int getSize() {
   return header.length +  SIZE_LENGTH +
           CMD_BYTE_LENGTH + footer.length +
           name.getBytes().length + 1 +
           address.getBytes().length + 1 +
           city.getBytes().length + 1 +
           state.getBytes().length + 1 +
           yearlySalary.getBytes().length + 1;
}
```

What is the same and what is different? It looks like they both add the header, the size length, the command byte length, and the footer length. Then they add the sizes of each of their fields. What if we extract what is computed differently: the size of the fields? We call the resulting method getBodySize().

```
private int getSize() {
   return header.length +  SIZE_LENGTH
      + CMD_BYTE_LENGTH + footer.length + getBodySize();
}
```

If we do that, we end up with the same code in each method. We add up the size of all of the bookkeeping data, and then we add the size of the body, which is the total of the sizes of all of the fields. After we do this, we can move getSize up into the Command class and have different implementations for getBodySize in each subclass (see Figure 21.4).

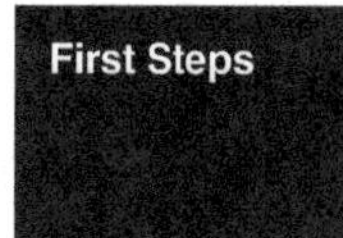

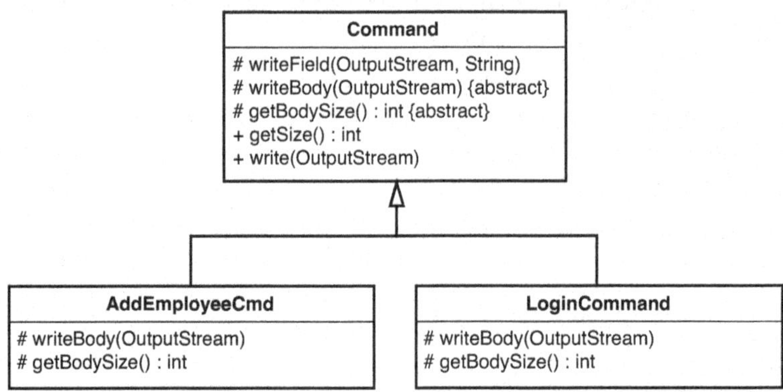

Figure 21.4 *Pulling up* getSize.

Let's look at where we are now. We have this implementation of getBody in AddEmployeeCmd:

```
protected int getBodySize() {
   return name.getBytes().length + 1 +
         address.getBytes().length + 1 +
         city.getBytes().length + 1 +
         state.getBytes().length + 1 +
         yearlySalary.getBytes().length + 1;
}
```

We've ignored some rather blatant duplication here. It is kind of small, but let's be zealous and remove it completely:

```
protected int getFieldSize(String field) {
   return field.getBytes().length + 1;
}

protected int getBodySize() {
   return getFieldSize(name) +
         getFieldSize(address) +
         getFieldSize(city) +
         getFieldSize(state) +
         getFieldSize(yearlySalary);
}
```

First Steps

If we move the getFieldSize method up to the Command class, we can use it in the getBodySize method of LoginCommand also:

```
protected int getBodySize() {
   return getFieldSize(name) + getFieldSize(password);
}
```

Is there more duplication here at all? Actually, there is, but just a little. Both LoginCommand and AddEmployeeCmd accept a list of parameters, get their sizes, and write them out. Except for the commandChar variable, that accounts for all of the remaining differences between the two classes? What if we remove the duplication by generalizing it a little? If we declare a list in the base class, we can add to it in each subclass constructor like this:

```
class LoginCommand extends Command
{
    ...
    public LoginCommand(String name, String password) {
        fields.add(name);
        fields.add(password);
    }
    ...
}
```

When we add to the fields list in each subclass, we can use the same code to calculate the body size:

```
int getBodySize() {
     int result = 0;
     for(Iterator it = fields.iterator(); it.hasNext(); ) {
        String field = (String)it.next();
        result += getFieldSize(field);
     }
     return result;
}
```

Likewise, the writeBody method can look like this:

```
void writeBody(Outputstream outputstream) {
   for(Iterator it = fields.iterator(); it.hasNext(); ) {
      String field = (String)it.next();
      writeField(outputStream, field);
   }
}
```


We can pull up those methods to the superclass. When we've done that, we've truly removed all of the duplication. Here is what the Command class looks like. To make things more sensible, we've made all the methods that are no longer accessed in subclasses private:

```
public class Command {
   private static final byte[] header
            = {(byte)0xde, (byte)0xad};
   private static final byte[] footer
            = {(byte)0xbe, (byte)0xef};
   private static final int SIZE_LENGTH = 1;
   private static final int CMD_BYTE_LENGTH = 1;
```

```
    protected List fields = new ArrayList();
    protected abstract char [] getCommandChar();

    private void writeBody(Outputstream outputstream) {
        for(Iterator it = fields.iterator(); it.hasNext(); ) {
            String field = (String)it.next();
            writeField(outputStream, field);
        }
    }

    private int getFieldSize(String field) {
        return field.getBytes().length + 1;
    }

    private int getBodySize() {
        int result = 0;
        for(Iterator it = fields.iterator(); it.hasNext(); ) {
            String field = (String)it.next();
            result += getFieldSize(field);
        }
        return result;
    }

    private int getSize() {
        return header.length +  SIZE_LENGTH
            + CMD_BYTE_LENGTH + footer.length
            + getBodySize();
    }

    private void writeField(OutputStream outputStream,
                            String field) {
        outputStream.write(field.getBytes());
        outputStream.write(0x00);
    }

    public void write(OutputStream outputStream)
            throws Exception {
        outputStream.write(header);
        outputStream.write(getSize());
        outputStream.write(commandChar);
        writeBody(outputstream);
        outputStream.write(footer);
    }
}
```


The `LoginCommand` and `AddEmployeeCmd` classes are now incredibly thin:

```
public class LoginCommand extends Command {
    public LoginCommand(String userName, String passwd) {
        fields.add(username);
```

```
        fields.add(passwd);
    }

    protected char [] getCommandChar() {
        return new char [] { 0x01};
    }
}

public class AddEmployeeCmd extends Command {
    public AddEmployeeCmd(String name, String address,
                          String city, String state,
                          int yearlySalary) {
        fields.add(name);
        fields.add(address);
        fields.add(city);
        fields.add(state);
        fields.add(Integer.toString(yearlySalary));
    }

    protected char [] getCommandChar() {
        return new char [] { 0x02 };
    }
}
```

Figure 21.5 is a UML diagram that shows where we end up.

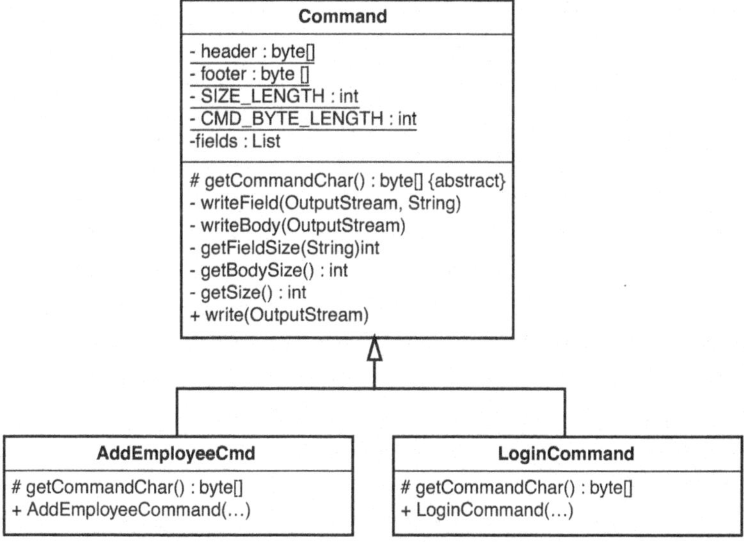

Figure 21.5 *Command hierarchy with duplication pulled up.*

Okay, so where are we now? We've removed so much duplication that we have just shells of classes. All of the functionality is in the Command class. In fact, it makes sense to wonder whether we really need separate classes for these two commands at all. What are the alternatives?

We could get rid of the subclasses and add a static method to the Command class that allows us to send a command:

```
List arguments = new ArrayList();
arguments.add("Mike");
arguments.add("asdsad");
Command.send(stream, 0x01, arguments);
```

But that would be a lot of work for clients. One thing is for sure: We do have to send two different command chars, and we don't want the user to have to keep track of them.

Instead, we could add a different static method for each command that we want to send:

```
Command.SendAddEmployee(stream,
        "Mike", "122 Elm St", "Miami", "FL", 10000);

Command.SendLogin(stream, "Mike", "asdsad");
```

But that would force all of our client code to change. Right now, there are many places in our code where we construct AddEmployeeCmd and LoginCommand objects.

Maybe we are better off leaving the classes the way that they are now. Sure, the subclasses are pretty tiny, but does that really hurt anything? Not really.

Are we done? No, there is one little thing that we need to do now, something we should've done earlier. We can rename AddEmployeeCmd to AddEmployeeCommand. That would make the names of the two subclasses consistent. We're less likely to be wrong when we use names consistently.

First Steps

Abbreviations

Abbreviations in class and method names are problematic. They can be okay when they are used consistently, but in general, I don't like to use them.

One team I worked with attempted to use the words *manager* and *management* in nearly every class name in the system. That naming convention didn't help much, but what made it worse was the fact that they abbreviated *manager* and *management* in an incredible number of different ways. For example, some classes were named XXXXMgr, and others were named XXXXMngr. When you were ready to use a class, you actually had to look it up most of the time to see if you had the name right. More than 50 percent of the time, I was wrong when I attempted to guess which suffix was used for a particular class.

So, we've removed all of the duplication. Has it made things better or worse? Let's play out a couple of scenarios. What happens when we need to add a new command? Well, we can just subclass Command and create it. Let's compare that to what we would have to do in the original design. We could create a new command and then cut/copy and paste code from another command, changing all of the variables. But if we do that, we are introducing more duplication and making things worse. Beyond that, it is error prone. We could mess up the use of the variables and get it wrong. No, it would definitely take a little longer to do it before we removed duplication.

Do we lose any flexibility because of what we've done? What if we had to send commands that are made of something other than strings? We've already solved that problem, in a way. The AddEmployeeCommand class already accepts an integer, and we convert it to a string to send it as a command. We can do the same thing with any other type. We have to convert it to a string somehow to send it. We can do it in the constructor of any new subclass.

What if we have a command with a different format? Suppose that we need a new command type that can nest other commands in its body. We can do that easily by subclassing Command and overriding its writeBody method:

```
public class AggregateCommand extends Command
{
    private List commands = new ArrayList();
    protected char [] getCommandChar() {
        return new char [] { 0x03 };
    }

    public void appendCommand(Command newCommand) {
        commands.add(newCommand);
    }

    protected void writeBody(OutputStream out) {
        out.write(commands.getSize());
        for(Iterator it = commands.iterator(); it.hasNext(); ) {
            Command  innerCommand = (Command)it.next();
            innerCommand.write(out);
        }
    }
}
```


Everything else just works.

Imagine doing this if we hadn't removed the duplication.

This last example highlights something very important. When you remove duplication across classes, you end up with very small focused methods. Each of them does something that no other method does, and that gives us an incredible advantage: orthogonality.

Orthogonality is a fancy word for independence. If you want to change existing behavior in your code and there is exactly one place you have to go to make that change, you've got orthogonality. It is as if your application is a big box with knobs surrounding the outside. If there is only one knob per behavior for your system, changes are easy to make. When you have rampant duplication, you have more than one knob for each behavior. Think about writing fields. In the original design, if we had to use a `0x01` terminator for fields rather than a `0x00` terminator, we would have had to go through the code and make that change in many places. Imagine if someone asked us to write out two `0x00` terminators for each field. That would be pretty bad, too: no single-purpose knobs. But in the code we've refactored, we can edit or override `writeField` if we want to change how fields are written, and we can override `writeBody` when we need to handle special cases such as command aggregation. When behavior is localized in single methods, it's easy to replace it or add to it.

In this example, we've been doing many things—moving methods and variables from class to class, breaking down methods—but most of it has been mechanical. We've just paid attention to duplication and removed it. The only creative thing that we've really done is come up with names for the new methods. The original code didn't mention fields or a command bodies, but in a way, the concepts were there in the code. For instance, some variables were being treated differently, and we called them fields. At the end of the process, we ended up with a much neater orthogonal design, but it didn't feel like we were designing. It was more like we were noticing what was there and moving the code closer to its essence, closer to what it really was.

One of the startling things that you discover when you start removing duplication zealously is that designs emerge. You don't have to plan most of the knobs in your application; they just happen. It isn't perfect. For instance, it would be nice if this method on `Command`:

First Steps

```
public void write(OutputStream outputStream)
        throws Exception {
    outputStream.write(header);
    outputStream.write(getSize());
    outputStream.write(commandChar);
    writeBody(outputstream);
    outputStream.write(footer);
}
```

Looked like this:

```
public void write(OutputStream outputStream)
          throws Exception {
    writeHeader(outputStream);
    writeBody(outputstream);
    writeFooter(outputStream);
}
```

Now we have a knob for writing headers and another for writing footers. We can add knobs as we need to, but it's nice when they happen naturally.

Duplication removal is a powerful way of distilling a design. It not only makes a design more flexible, but it also makes change faster and easier.

Open/Closed Principle

The Open/Closed Principle is a principle that was first articulated by Bertrand Meyer. The idea behind it is that code should be open for extension but closed to modification. What does that mean? It means that when we have good design, we just don't have to change code much to add new features.

Does the code that we ended up with in this chapter exhibit these properties? Yes. We just looked at a number of change scenarios. In many of them, very few methods had to change. In some cases, we were able to add the feature just by subclassing. Of course, after subclassing, it is important to remove duplication (see *Programming by Difference (101)* for more information about how to add features by subclassing and integrate them by refactoring).

When we remove duplication, our code often naturally starts to fall in line with the *Open/Closed Principle.*

Chapter 22

I Need to Change a Monster Method and I Can't Write Tests for It

One of the hardest things about working in legacy code is dealing with large methods. In many cases, you can avoid refactoring long methods by using the *Sprout Method (59)* and *Sprout Class (63)* techniques. Even when you are able to avoid it, though, it's just a shame that you have to. Long methods are quagmires in a code base. Whenever you have to change them, you have to go back and attempt to understand them again, and then you have to make your changes. Often that takes longer than it would if the code was cleaner.

Long methods are a pain, but monster methods are worse. A monster method is a method that is so long and so complex that you really don't feel comfortable touching it. Monster methods can be hundreds or thousands of lines long, with enough scattered indentation to make navigation nearly impossible. When you have monster methods you're tempted to print them on a couple of yards of continuous-feed paper and lay them out in a hallway so that you and your coworkers can figure them out.

I was once on the road at a meeting, and as we were walking back to our hotel rooms, a friend of mine said, "Hey, you've got to see this." He went into his room and pulled out his laptop and showed me a method that went on for more than a thousand lines. My friend knew that I'd been studying refactoring and said, "How in the world would you refactor this?" We started thinking it through. We knew that testing was key, but where do you even begin with such a big method?

This chapter outlines what I've learned since then.

Varieties of Monsters

Monster methods come in a couple of varieties. These aren't necessarily distinct types. Methods out in the field are kind of like platypuses—they look like mixtures of several types.

Bulleted Methods

A bulleted method is a method with nearly no indentation. It is just a sequence of code chunks that reminds you of a bulleted list. Some of the code in the chunks might be indented, but the method itself isn't dominated by indentation. When you look at a bulleted method and squint your eyes, you see something like Figure 22.1.

This is the general form of a bulleted method. If you are lucky, someone will have put extra lines between the sections or comments to show you that they do somewhat distinct things. In an ideal world, you'd be able to just extract a method for each of the sections, but often the methods don't refactor easily that way. The space between the sections is a little bit deceptive because often temporary variables are declared in one section and used in the next. Breaking down the method often isn't as easy as just copying and pasting out code. Despite this, bulleted methods are a little less intimidating than the other varieties, mainly because that lack of wild indentation allows us to keep our bearings.

```
void Reservation::extend(int additionalDays)
{
    int status = RIXInterface::checkAvailable(type, location, startingDate);

    int identCookie = -1;
    switch(status) {
        case NOT_AVAILABLE_UPGRADE_LUXURY:
            identCookie = RIXInterface::holdReservation(Luxury,location,startingDate,
                additionalDays +additionalDays);
            break;
        case NOT_AVAILABLE_UPGRADE_SUV:
        {
            int theDays = additionalDays + additionalDays;
            if (RIXInterface::getOpCode(customerID) != 0)
                theDays++;
            identCookie = RIXInterface::holdReservation(SUV,location,startingDate, theDays);
        }
        break;
        case NOT_AVAILABLE_UPGRADE_VAN:
            identCookie = RIXInterface::holdReservation(Van,
                location,startingDate, additionalDays + additionalDays);
          break;
        case AVAILABLE:
        default:
            RIXInterface::holdReservation(type,location,startingDate);
            break;
    }

    if (identCookie != -1 && state == Initial) {
        RIXInterface::waitlistReservation(type,location,startingDate);
    }

    Customer c = res_db.getCustomer(customerID);

    if (c.vipProgramStatus == VIP_DIAMOND) {
        upgradeQuery = true;
    }

    if (!upgradeQuery)
        RIXInterface::extend(lastCookie, days + additionalDays);
    else {
        RIXInterface::waitlistReservation(type,location,startingDate);
        RIXInterface::extend(lastCookie, days + additionalDays +1);
    }
        ...
}
```

Figure 22.1 *Bulleted method.*

Varieties of Monsters

Snarled Methods

A snarled method is a method dominated by a single large, indented section. The simplest case is a method that has one large conditional statement, as in Figure 22.2.

```
Reservation::Reservation(VehicleType type, int customerID, long startingDate, int days, XLocation l)
: type(type), customerID(customerID), startingDate(startingDate), days(days), lastCookie(-1),
state(Initial), tempTotal(0)
{
        location = l;
        upgradeQuery = false;

        if (!RIXInterface::available()) {
                RIXInterface::doEvents(100);
                PostLogMessage(0, 0, "delay on reservation creation");
                int holdCookie = -1;
                switch(status) {
                        case NOT_AVAILABLE_UPGRADE_LUXURY:
                                holdCookie = RIXInterface::holdReservation(Luxury,l,startingDate);
                                if (holdCookie != -1) {
                                    holdCookie |= 9;
                                }
                                break;
                        case NOT_AVAILABLE_UPGRADE_SUV:
                                holdCookie = RIXInterface::holdReservation(SUV,l,startingDate);
                                break;
                        case NOT_AVAILABLE_UPGRADE_VAN:
                                holdCookie = RIXInterface::holdReservation(Van,l,startingDate);
                                break;
                        case AVAILABLE:
                        default:
                                RIXInterface::holdReservation;
                                state = Held;
                                break;
                }
        }
        ...
}
```

Figure 22.2 *Simple snarled method.*

But that sort of a snarl nearly has the same qualities as a bulleted method. The snarls that demand your full appreciation are methods with the form shown in Figure 22.3.

The best way to know whether you have a real snarl is to try to line up the blocks in a long method. If you start to feel vertigo, you've run into a snarled method.

```
Reservation::Reservation(VehicleType type, int customerID, long startingDate, int days, XLocation l)
: type(type), customerID(customerID), startingDate(startingDate), days(days), lastCookie(-1),
state(Initial), tempTotal(0)
{
    location = l;
    upgradeQuery = false;

    while(!RIXInterface::available()) {
        RIXInterface::doEvents(100);
        PostLogMessage(0, 0, "delay on reservation creation");
        int holdCookie = -1;
        switch(status) {
            case NOT_AVAILABLE_UPGRADE_LUXURY:
                holdCookie =
                RIXInterface::holdReservation(Luxury,l,startingDate);
                if (holdCookie != -1) {
                    if (l == GIG && customerID == 45) {
                        // Special #1222
                        while (RIXInterface::notBusy()) {
                            int code =
                            RIXInterface::getOpCode(customerID);
                            if (code == 1 || customerID > 0)) {
                                PostLogMessage(1, 0, "QEX PID");
                                for (int n = 0; n < 12; n++) {
                                    int total = 2000;
                                    if (state == Initial || state == Held)
                                    {
                                        total += getTotalByLocation(location);
                                        tempTotal = total;
                                        if (location == GIG && days > 2)
                                        {
                                            if (state == Held)
                                                total += 30;
                                        }
                                    }
                                    RIXInterface::serveIDCode(n, total);
                                }
                            } else {
                                RIXInterface::serveCode(customerID);
                            }
                        }
                    }
                }
                break;
            case NOT_AVAILABLE_UPGRADE_SUV:
                holdCookie =
                RIXInterface::holdReservation(SUV,l,startingDate);
                break;
            case NOT_AVAILABLE_UPGRADE_VAN:
                holdCookie =
                RIXInterface::holdReservation(Van,l,startingDate);
                break;
            case AVAILABLE:
            default:
                RIXInterface::holdReservation(type,l,startingDate);
                state = Held;
                break;
        }
    }
    ...
}
```

Figure 22.3 *Very snarled method.*

Most methods are not purely bulleted or snarled, but something in between. Many snarls have long bulleted sections hidden deep in their nesting, but because they are nested it is hard to write tests that pin down their behavior. Snarls present unique challenges.

When you are refactoring long methods, the presence or absence of a refactoring tool makes a big difference. Nearly every refactoring tool supports the *extract method* refactoring because there is an incredible amount of leverage in that support. If a tool can extract methods for you safely, you don't need tests to verify your extractions. The tool does the analysis for you, and all that is left is learning how to use extractions to put a method into decent shape for further work.

When you don't have extract method support, cleaning up monster methods is more challenging. You often have to be more conservative because your work is bounded by the tests you can get in place.

Tackling Monsters with Automated Refactoring Support

When you have a tool that extracts methods for you, you have to be clear about what it can and can't do for you. Most refactoring tools today do simple method extractions and a variety of other refactorings, but they don't handle all the auxiliary refactoring that people often want to do when they break up large methods. For instance, often we're tempted to reorder statements to group them for extraction. No current tool does the analysis needed to see whether reordering can be done safely. That's a shame because it can be a source of bugs.

To use refactoring tools effectively with large methods, it pays to make a series of changes solely with the tool and to avoid all other edits to the source. This might feel like refactoring with one hand behind your back, but it gives you a clean separation between changes that are known to be safe and changes that aren't. When you refactor like this, you should avoid even simple things, such as reordering statements and breaking apart expressions. If your tool supports variable renaming, that's great, but if it doesn't, put that off until later.

> When doing automated refactoring without tests, use the tool exclusively. After a series of automated refactorings, you can often get tests in place that you can use to verify any manual edits that you make.

Tackling Monsters with Automated Refactoring Support

When you do your extractions, these should be your key goals:

1. To separate logic from awkward dependencies
2. To introduce seams that make it easier to get tests in place for more refactoring

Here is an example:

```
class CommoditySelectionPanel
{
    ...
    public void update() {
        if (commodities.size() > 0
                && commodities.GetSource().equals("local")) {
            listbox.clear();
            for (Iterator it = commodities.iterator();
                    it.hasNext(); ) {
                Commodity commodity = (Commodity)it.next();
                if (commodity.isTwilight()
                        && !commodity.match(broker))
                    listbox.add(commodity.getView());
            }
        }
        ...
    }
    ...
}
```

In this method, a lot of things could be cleaned up. One of the odd things is that this sort of filtering work is happening on a panel class, something that should ideally just be responsible for display. Untangling this code is bound to be difficult. If we want to start writing tests against the method as it stands now, we could write them against the list box state, but that wouldn't move us too far along toward making the design better.

With tool-based refactoring support, we can start to name high-level pieces of the method and break dependencies at the same time. This is what the code would look like after a series of extractions.

```
class CommoditySelectionPanel
{
    ...
    public void update() {
        if (commoditiesAreReadyForUpdate()) {
            clearDisplay();
            updateCommodities();
        }
        ...
    }

    private boolean commoditiesAreReadyForUpdate() {
        return commodities.size() > 0
                && commodities.GetSource().equals("local");
    }
```

```
    private void clearDisplay() {
        listbox.clear();
    }

    private void updateCommodities() {
        for (Iterator it = commodities.iterator(); it.hasNext(); ) {
            Commodity commodity = (Commodity)it.next();
            if (singleBrokerCommodity(commodity)) {
                displayCommodity(commodity.getView());
            }
        }
    }

    private boolean singleBrokerCommodity(Commodity commodity) {
        return commodity.isTwilight() && !commodity.match(broker);
    }

    private void displayCommodity(CommodityView view) {
        listbox.add(view);
    }

    ...
}
```

Frankly, the code in `update` doesn't look that different structurally; it is still just an if-statement with some work inside of it. But the work has been delegated to methods now. The `update` method looks like a skeleton of the code that it came from. And what about those names? They seem a little hokey, don't they? But they are a good starting point. At the very least, they allow the code to communicate at a higher level, and they introduce seams that allow us to break dependencies. We can *Subclass and Override Method (401)* to sense through `displayCommodity` and `clearDisplay`. After we've done that, we can look at the possibility of making a display class and moving those methods over it, using those tests as leverage. In this case, however, it would be more appropriate to see if we can move `update` and `updateCommodities` to another class and leave `clearDisplay` and `displayCommodity` here so that we can take advantage of the fact that this class is a panel, a display. We can rename methods later as they settle into place. After additional refactoring, our design can end up looking something like Figure 22.4.

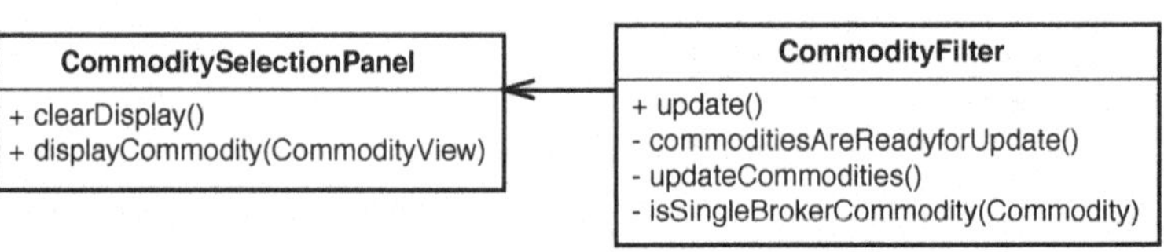

Figure 22.4 *Logic class extracted from* `CommoditySelectionPanel`.

The key thing to remember when you use an automated tool to extract methods is that you can do a lot of coarse work safely and handle the details after you get other tests in place. Don't be too concerned about methods that seem like they don't fit the class. Often they point toward the need to extract a new class later. See Chapter 20, *This Class Is Too Big and I Don't Want It to Get Any Bigger*, for more ideas on how to do this.

The Manual Refactoring Challenge

When you have automated refactoring support, you don't have to do anything special to start breaking down large methods. Good refactoring tools check each refactoring that you attempt and disallow ones that they can't perform safely. But when you don't have a refactoring tool, correctness is something that you have to work to maintain, and tests are the strongest tool around.

Monster methods make testing, refactoring, and feature addition very difficult. If you are able to create instances of the class housing the method in a test harness, you can attempt to devise some set of test cases that will give you confidence as you break down the method. If the logic in the method is particularly complex, this can be a nightmare. Fortunately, in those cases, we can use a couple of techniques. Before we look at them, though, let's look at what can go wrong when we extract methods.

Here is a little list. It doesn't contain every possible error, but it has the most common ones:

1. We can forget to pass a variable into the extracted method. Often the compiler tells us about the missing variable (unless it has the same name as an instance variable), but we could just think that it needs to be a local variable and declare it in the new method.
2. We could give the extracted method a name that hides or overrides a method with the same name in a base class.
3. We could make a mistake when we pass in parameters or assign return values. We could do something really silly, such as return the wrong value. More subtly, we could return or accept the wrong types in the new method.

Quite a few things can go wrong. The techniques in this section can help make extraction less risky when we don't have tests in place.

Introduce Sensing Variable

We might not want to add features to production code when we're refactoring it, but that doesn't mean that we can't add any code. Sometimes it helps to add a variable to a class and use it to sense conditions in the method that we want to refactor. When we've done the refactoring that we need to do, we can get rid of that variable, and our code will be in a clean state. This is called *Introduce Sensing Variable*. Here is an example. We start with a method on a Java class named DOMBuilder. We want to clean it up, but, unfortunately, we don't have a refactoring tool:

```
public class DOMBuilder
{
    ...
    void processNode(XDOMNSnippet root, List childNodes)
    {
        if (root != null) {
            if (childNodes != null)
                root.addNode(new XDOMNSnippet(childNodes));
            root.addChild(XDOMNSnippet.NullSnippet);
        }
        List paraList = new ArrayList();
        XDOMNSnippet snippet = new XDOMNReSnippet();
        snippet.setSource(m_state);
        for (Iterator it = childNodes.iterator();
                it.hasNext();) {
            XDOMNNode node = (XDOMNNode)it.next();
            if (node.type() == TF_G || node.type() == TF_H ||
                    (node.type() == TF_GLOT && node.isChild())) {
                paraList.addNode(node);
            }
            ...
        }
        ...
    }
    ...
}
```

In this example, it seems like a lot of the work in the method happens to an XDOMNSnippet. That means that we should be able to write whatever tests we need by passing different values as arguments to this method. But, in actuality, a lot of work happens tangentially, things that can be sensed in only a very indirect way. In a situation like this, we can introduce sensing variables to aid our work; for instance, we could introduce an instance variable to see that a node is added to the paraList when it has the proper node type.

The Manual Refactoring Challenge

```
public class DOMBuilder
{
```

```
    public boolean nodeAdded = false;
    ...
    void processNode(XDOMNSnippet root, List childNodes)
    {
        if (root != null) {
            if (childNodes != null)
                root.addNode(new XDOMNSnippet(childNodes));
            root.addChild(XDOMNSnippet.NullSnippet);
        }
        List paraList = new ArrayList();
        XDOMNSnippet snippet = new XDOMNReSnippet();
        snippet.setSource(m_state);
        for (Iterator it = childNodes.iterator();
                    it.hasNext(); ) {
            XDOMNNode node = (XDOMNNode)it.next();
            if (node.type() == TF_G || node.type() == TF_H ||
                    (node.type() == TF_GLOT && node.isChild())) {
                paraList.add(node);
                nodeAdded = true;
            }
            ...
        }
        ...
    }
    ...
}
```

With that variable in place, we still have to engineer the input to produce a case that covers that condition. When we do, we can extract that piece of logic, and our tests should still pass.

Here is a test that shows us that we add a node when the node type is TF_G:

```
void testAddNodeOnBasicChild()
{
    DOMBuilder builder = new DomBuilder();
    List children = new ArrayList();
    children.add(new XDOMNNode(XDOMNNode.TF_G));
    builder.processNode(new XDOMNSnippet(), children);

    assertTrue(builder.nodeAdded);
}
```

Here is a test that shows that we don't add a node when we have the wrong node type:


```
void testNoAddNodeOnNonBasicChild()
{
    DOMBuilder builder = new DomBuilder();
    List children = new ArrayList();
    children.add(new XDOMNNode(XDOMNNode.TF_A));
    builder.processNode(new XDOMNSnippet(), children);
```

```
    assertTrue(!builder.nodeAdded);
}
```

With these tests in place, we should feel better about extracting the body of the condition that determines whether nodes are added. We can copy the entire condition. The test we just wrote shows that the node was added when the condition was exercised.

```
public class DOMBuilder
{
    void processNode(XDOMNSnippet root, List childNodes)
    {
        if (root != null) {
            if (childNodes != null)
                root.addNode(new XDOMNSnippet(childNodes));
            root.addChild(XDOMNSnippet.NullSnippet);
        }
        List paraList = new ArrayList();
        XDOMNSnippet snippet = new XDOMNReSnippet();
        snippet.setSource(m_state);
        for (Iterator it = childNodes.iterator();
                it.hasNext();) {
            XDOMNNode node = (XDOMNNode)it.next();
            if (isBasicChild(node)) {
                paraList.addNode(node);
                nodeAdded = true;
            }
            ...
        }
        ...
    }
    private boolean isBasicChild(XDOMNNode node) {
        return node.type() == TF_G
            || node.type() == TF_H
            || node.type() == TF_GLOT && node.isChild());
    }
    ...
}
```

Later, we can remove the flag and the test.

In this case, I used a boolean variable. I just wanted to see whether the node was still added after we extracted the condition. I felt pretty confident that I could extract the entire body of the condition without introducing errors, so I didn't test all of the logic of the condition. These tests just provided a quick way of checking to make sure that the condition was still part of the code path after the extraction. For more guidance on how much testing to do during method extraction see *Targeted Testing (189)* in Chapter 13, *I Need to Make a Change but I Don't Know What Tests to Write.*

When you are using *sensing variables*, it is a good idea to keep them in the class over a series of refactorings and delete them only after your refactoring session. I often do this so that I can see all of the tests that I write to do the extractions and undo them easily if I find that I want to extract in a different way. When I'm done, I end up deleting these tests or refactoring them so that they test the methods I extract rather than the original method.

Sensing variables are a key tool for teasing apart monster methods. You can use them to do some refactoring deep inside snarled methods, but you can also use them to progressively de-snarl methods. For example, if we have a method that nests most of its code deep inside a set of conditional statements, we can use sensing variables to extract top-level conditional statements or extract the bodies of those conditional statements into new methods. We can use sensing variables to work on those new methods as well until we've de-snarled the code.

Extract What You Know

Another strategy that we can use when we are working with monster methods is to start small and find little pieces of code that we can extract confidently without tests, and then add tests to cover them. Okay, I need to say this in a different way because everyone's idea of "little" is different. When I say "little," I mean two or three lines—five, at most, a chunk of code that you can easily name. The key thing to pay attention to when you do these little extractions is the *coupling count* of the extraction. The *coupling count* is the number of values that pass into and out of the method you are extracting. For example, if we extract a `max` method out of the following method, its count will be 3:

```
void process(int a, int b, int c) {
    int maximum;
    if (a > b)
        maximum = a;
    else
        maximum = b;
    ...
}
```

Here is the code after the extraction:

```
void process(int a, int b, int c) {
    int maximum = max(a,b);
    ...
}
```


The *coupling count* of the method is 3: two variables in and one variable out. It is good to favor extractions with a small count because it is not as easy to make a mistake. When you are trying to pick extractions, look for a small number of lines and start counting the variables that come in and go out. Accesses of instance variables don't count; they don't pass through the interface of the method we are extracting.

The key danger in a method extraction is a type conversion error; for instance, passing an int as a double.. We have a better chance of avoiding those if we extract only methods that have a low coupling count. When we've identified a possible extraction, we should look back and find where each variable that is passed is declared, to make sure that we get the method signature right.

If extractions with a low coupling count are safer, then extractions with a count of `0` must be the safest of all—and they are. You can make a lot of headway in a monster method by just extracting methods that don't accept any parameters and don't return any values. These methods are really commands to do something. You tell the object to do something to its state, or, more sleazily, you tell the object to do things with some global state. Regardless, when you attempt to name chunks of code like this, you often end up getting more insight into what the chunk is about and how it is supposed to affect the object. This sort of insight can cascade into more insights and cause you to see your design from different, more productive perspectives.

When you use *Extract What You Know*, make sure that you don't choose chunks that are too large. And if the coupling count is greater than `0`, often it pays to use a *sensing variable*. After you extract, write a few tests for the method you extracted.

When you use this technique with small chunks, it is hard to see progress as you whittle away at a monster method, but progress has a way of sneaking up on you. Every time that you go back and extract another little piece that you know, you clarify the method a little bit. Over time, you might get a better sense of the method's scope and what directions you'd like to take it in.

When I don't have a refactoring tool, I often start to extract `0`-count methods just to get a sense of the overall structure. Often it is a good prelude to testing and further work.

If you have a bulleted method, you might think that you'll be able to extract many `0`-count methods and that each chunk of code in the bulleted method will be a good one. Sometimes you'll find chunks that are like that, but often chunks use temporary variables declared before them. Sometimes you have to ignore the "chunk structure" of a bulleted method and look for low-count methods inside chunks and across chunks.

Gleaning Dependencies

Sometimes there is code in a monster method that is kind of secondary to the method's main purpose. It is necessary, but it isn't terribly complex, and if you accidentally break it, it will be obvious. But although all of that is true, you simply cannot take a chance on breaking the main logic of the method. In cases like these, you can use a technique called *gleaning dependencies*. You write tests for the logic that you need to preserve. Afterward, you extract things that the tests do not cover. When you do this, you can at least have confidence that you are preserving the important behavior. Here is a simple example:

```
void addEntry(Entry entry) {
    if (view != null && DISPLAY == true) {
        view.show(entry);
    }
    ...
    if (entry.category().equals("single")
            || entry.category("dual")) {
        entries.add(entry);
        view.showUpdate(entry, view.GREEN);
    }
    else {
        ...
    }
}
```

If we make a mistake with the display code, we'll see it pretty quickly. An error in the `add` logic, though, is something that might take quite a while to find. In a case like this, we can write tests for the method and verify that the `adds` happen under the right conditions. Then when we are confident that all of that behavior is covered, we can extract the display code and know that our extraction will not affect entry addition.

In some ways, *Gleaning Dependencies* feels like a cop-out. You are preserving one set of behaviors and working with another in an unprotected way. But not all behaviors are equal in an application. Some are more critical, and we can recognize that when we work.

Gleaning Dependencies is particularly powerful when critical behavior is tangled with other behavior. When you have solid tests for the critical behavior, you can do a lot of editing that technically isn't all covered by tests, but it helps you to preserve key behavior.

Break Out a Method Object

Sensing variables are a very powerful tool in our arsenal, but sometimes you notice that you already have variables that would be ideal for sensing but they are local to the method. If they were instance variables, you could sense through them after a method runs. You can turn local variables into instance variables, but, in many cases, that can be confusing. The state that you put there will be common only to the monster method and the methods that you extract from it. Although it will be reinitialized every time the monster method is called, it can be hard to understand what the variables will hold if you want to call methods that you've extracted independently.

One alternative is *Break Out Method Object (330)*. This technique was first described by Ward Cunningham, and it epitomizes the idea of an invented abstraction. When you break out a method object, you create a class whose only responsibility is to do the work of your monster method. The parameters of the method become parameters to a constructor on the new class, and the code of the monster method can go into a method named `run` or `execute` on the new class. When the code has been moved to the new class, we're in a great position to refactor. We can turn the temporary variables in the method into instance variables and sense through them as we break down the method.

Breaking out a method object is a pretty drastic move, but unlike introducing a *sensing variable*, the variables that you are using are needed for production. This allows you to build up tests that you can keep. See *Break Out Method Object (330)* for a detailed example.

Strategy

The techniques I've described in this chapter can help you break up monster methods for additional refactoring or feature addition. This section contains some guidance about how to make structural tradeoffs as you do this work.

Skeletonize Methods

When you have a conditional statement and you are looking for places to extract a method, you have two choices. You can extract the condition and the body together, or you can extract them separately. Here is an example:

```
if (marginalRate() > 2 && order.hasLimit()) {
    order.readjust(rateCalculator.rateForToday());
```

```
        order.recalculate();
    }
```

If you extract the condition and the body to two different methods, you are in a better position to reorganize the logic of the method later:

```
    if (orderNeedsRecalculation(order)) {
        recalculateOrder(order, rateCalculator);
    }
```

I call this *skeletonizing* because when you are done, all that is left in the method is a skeleton: the control structure and delegations to other methods.

Find Sequences

When you have a conditional statement and you are looking for places to extract a method, you have two choices. You can extract the condition and the body together or you can extract them separately. Here is another example:

```
    ...
    if (marginalRate() > 2 && order.hasLimit()) {
        order.readjust(rateCalculator.rateForToday());
        order.recalculate();
    }
    ...
```

If you extract the condition and the body to the same method, you are in a better position to identify a common sequence of operations:

```
    ...
    recalculateOrder(order, rateCalculator);
    ...


void recalculateOrder(Order order,
                      RateCalculator rateCalculator) {
    if (marginalRate() > 2 && order.hasLimit()) {
        order.readjust(rateCalculator.rateForToday());
        order.recalculate();
    }
}
```

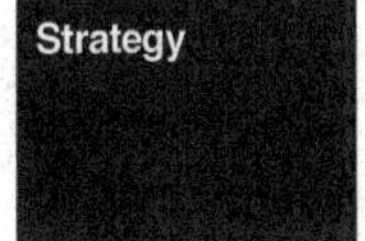

It might turn out that the rest of the method is just a sequence of operations that happen one after another, and it will be clearer if we are able to see that sequence.

Wait, did I just give completely conflicting advice? Yes, I did. The fact is, I often go back and forth between *skeletonizing methods* and *finding sequences.*

will need to be refactored after it is clarified. I attempt to find sequences when I feel that identifying an overarching sequence will make the code clearer.

Bulleted methods lean me toward finding sequences, and snarled methods lean me toward skeletonizing, but your choice of strategy really depends upon the design insights you get when you are doing your extractions.

Extract to the Current Class First

When you start to extract methods from a monster method, you'll probably notice that some of the chunks of code that you are extracting really belong in other classes. One strong indication is the name you're tempted to use. If you look at a piece of code and you are tempted to use the name of one of the variables you are using in it, chances are good that the code belongs on the class of that variable. That would be the case in this snippet:

```
if (marginalRate() > 2 && order.hasLimit()) {
   order.readjust(rateCalculator.rateForToday());
   order.recalculate();
}
```

It looks like we could call this piece of code `recalculateOrder`. That would be a decent name, but if we are using the word *order* in the method name, maybe this piece of code should move onto the `Order` class and be called `recalculate`. Yes, there is a method named `recalculate` already, so we might want to think about what makes this recalculation different and use that information in the name, or rename the `recalculate` method that is already there. Regardless, it looks like this piece of code belongs on that class.

Although it is tempting to extract directly to another class, don't do it. Use the awkward name first. The name `recalculateOrder` is awkward, but it lets us do some easily undoable extractions and explore whether we've extracted the right chunk of code to move forward. We can always move the method to another class later when the best direction for our changes presents itself. In the meantime, extracting to the current class moves us forward and it is less error prone.

Extract Small Pieces

Strategy

I mentioned this earlier, but I want to underscore it: Extract small pieces first. Before you extract this small piece of a monster method, it looks like it won't make any difference at all. After you extract more pieces, you'll probably see the original method in a different way. You might see a sequence that was obscured before or see a better way for the method to be organized. When you see those directions, you can move toward them. This is a far better strategy than trying to break up a method into large chunks from the beginning. Too often that isn't as easy as it looks; it isn't as safe. It's easier to miss the details, and the details are what make the code work.

Be Prepared to Redo Extractions

There are many ways to slice a pie and many ways to break down a monster method. After you make some extractions, you'll usually find better ways to accommodate new features more easily. Sometimes the best way to move forward is to undo an extraction or two and re-extract. When you do this, it doesn't mean that the first extractions were wasted effort. They gave you something very important: insight into old design and into a better way of moving forward.

Chapter 23

How Do I Know That I'm Not Breaking Anything?

Code is a strange sort of building material. Most materials that you can make things from, such as metal, wood, and plastic, fatigue. They break when you use them over time. Code is different. If you leave it alone, it never breaks. Short of the stray cosmic ray flipping a bit on your storage media, the only way it gets a fault is for someone to edit it. Run a machine made of metal over and over again, and it will eventually break. Run the same code over and over again, and, well, it will just run over and over again.

This puts a large burden on us as developers. Not only are we the primary agents that introduce faults in software, but it's also pretty easy to do so. How easy is it to change code? Mechanically, it is pretty simple. Anyone can open a text editor and spew the most arcane nonsense into it. Type in a poem. Some of them compile (go to www.ioccc.org and see the Obfuscated C code contest for details). Humor aside, it really is amazing how easy it is to break software. Have you ever tracked down a mysterious bug only to discover that it was some stray character that you accidentally typed? Some character that was entered when the cover of a book dropped down as you passed it to someone over your keyboard? Code is pretty fragile material.

In this chapter, we discuss a variety of ways to reduce risk when we edit. Some of them are mechanical and some are psychological (ouch!), but focusing on them is important, especially as we break dependencies in legacy code to get tests in place.

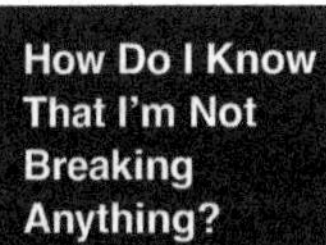

Hyperaware Editing

What do we do when we edit code, really? What are we trying to accomplish? We usually have large goals. We want to add a feature or fix a bug. It's great to know what those goals are, but how do we translate them into action?

When we sit down at a keyboard, we can classify every keystroke that we make into one of two categories. The keystroke either changes the behavior of the software or it doesn't. Typing text in a comment? That doesn't change behavior. Typing text in a string literal? That does, most of the time. If the string literal is in code that is never called, behavior won't change. The keystroke that you do later to finish a method call that uses that string literal, well, that one changes behavior. So technically, holding down the spacebar when you are formatting your code is refactoring in a very micro sense. Sometimes typing code is refactoring also. Changing a numeric literal in an expression that is used in your code isn't refactoring; it's a *functional change,* and it's important to know that when you are typing.

This is the meat of programming, knowing exactly what each of our keystrokes does. This doesn't mean that we have to be omniscient, but anything that helps us know—really know—how we are affecting software when we type can help us reduce bugs. *Test-driven development (88)* is very powerful in this way. When you can get your code into a test harness and run tests against it in less than a second, you can run the tests whenever you need to incredibly fast and really know what the effects of a change are.

> If it isn't out by the time this book is released, I suspect that someone will soon develop an IDE that allows you to specify a set of tests that will run at every keystroke. It would be an incredible way of closing the feedback loop.
>
> It has to happen. It just seems inevitable. There are already IDEs that check syntax on each keystroke and change the color of code when there are errors. Edit-triggered testing is the next step.

Tests foster hyperaware editing. Pair programming does also. Does hyperaware-editing sound exhausting? Well, too much of anything is exhausting. The key thing is that it isn't frustrating. Hyperaware editing is a flow state, a state in which you can just shut out the world and work sensitively with the code. It can actually be very refreshing. Personally, I get far more tired when I'm not getting any feedback. At that point, I get scared that I'm breaking the code without knowing it. I'm struggling to maintain all of this state in my head, remembering what I've changed and what I haven't, and thinking about how I'll be able to convince myself later that I've really done what I set out to do.

Hyperaware Editing

Single-Goal Editing

I don't expect that everyone's first impressions of the computer industry are the same, but when I first thought about becoming a programmer, I was really captivated by stories about super-smart programmers, those guys and gals who could keep the state of an entire system in their heads, write correct code on the fly, and know immediately whether some change was right or wrong. It's true that people vary widely in their ability to hold on to large amounts of arcane detail in their heads. I can do that, to some degree. I used to know many of the obscure parts of the C++ programming language, and, at one point, I had decent recall of the details of the UML metamodel before I realized that being a programmer and knowing that much about the details of UML was really pointless and somewhat sad.

The truth is, there are many different kinds of "smart." Holding on to a lot of state mentally can be useful, but it doesn't really make us better at decision-making. At this point in my career, I think I'm a much better programmer than I used to be, even though I know less about the details of each language I work in. Judgment is a key programming skill, and we can get into trouble when we try to act like super-smart programmers.

Has this ever happened to you? You start to work on one thing, and then you think, "Hmm, maybe I should clean this up." So you stop to refactor a bit, but you start to think about what the code should really look like, and then you pause. That feature you were working on still needs to be done, so you go back to the original place where you were editing code. You decide that you need to call a method, and then you hop over to where the method is, but you discover that the method is going to need to do something else, so you start to change it while the original change was pending and (catching breath) your pair partner is next to you yelling "Yeah, yeah, yeah! Fix that and then we'll do this." You feel like a racehorse running down the track, and your partner isn't really helping. He's riding you like a jockey or, worse, a gambler in the stands.

Well, that's how it goes on some teams. A pair has an exciting programming episode, but the last three quarters of it involve fixing all of the code they broke in the previous quarter. Sounds horrible, right? But, no, sometimes it's fun. You and your partner get to saunter away from the machine like heroes. You met the beast in its lair and killed it. You're top dog.

Is it worth it? Let's look at another way of doing this.

You need to make a change to a method. You already have the class in a test harness, and you start to make the change. But then you think, "Hey, I'll need to change this other method over here," so you stop and you navigate to it. It looks messy, so you start to reformat a line or two to see what is going on. Your partner looks at you and says, "What are you doing?" You say, "Oh, I was checking to see if we'll have to change method X." Your partner says, "Hey let's do one thing at a time." Your partner writes down the name of method X on a piece of paper next to the computer, and you go back and finish the edit. You run your tests and notice that all of them pass. Then you go over and look at the other method. Sure enough, you have to change it. You start to write another test. After a bit more programming, you run your tests and start to integrate. You and your partner look over to the other side of the table. There you see two other programmers. One is yelling "Yeah, yeah, yeah! Fix that and then we'll do this." They've been working on that task for hours, and they look pretty exhausted. If history is any guide, they'll fail integration and spend a few more hours working together.

I have this little mantra that I repeat to myself when I'm working: "Programming is the art of doing one thing at a time." When I'm pairing, I always ask my partner to challenge me on that, to ask me "What are you doing?" If I answer more than one thing, we pick one. I do the same for my partner. Frankly, it's just faster. When you are programming, it is pretty easy to pick off too big of a chunk at a time. If you do, you end up thrashing and just trying things out to make things work rather than working very deliberately and really knowing what your code does.

Preserve Signatures

When we edit code there are many ways we can make mistakes. We can misspell things, we can use the wrong data type, we can type one variable and mean another—the list is endless. Refactoring is particularly error-prone. Often it involves very invasive editing. We copy things around and make new classes and methods; the scale is much larger than just adding in a new line of code.

In general, the way to handle the situation is to write tests. When we have tests in place, we're able to catch many of the errors that we make when we change code. Unfortunately, in many systems, we have to refactor a bit just to make the system testable enough to refactor more. These initial refactorings (the dependency-breaking techniques in the catalog in Chapter 25) are meant to be done without tests, and they have to be particularly conservative.

When I first started using these techniques, it was tempting to do too much. When I needed to extract the entire body of a method, rather than just copying and pasting the arguments when I declared a method, I did other cleanup work

as well. For example, when I had to extract the body of a method and make it static (*Expose Static Method (345)*), like this:

```
public void process(List orders,
                    int dailyTarget,
                    double interestRate,
                    int compensationPercent) {
    ...
    // complicated code here
    ...
}
```

I extracted it like this, creating a couple of helper classes along the way.

```
public void process(List orders,
                    int dailyTarget,
                    double interestRate,
                    int compensationPercent) {
    processOrders(new OrderBatch(orders),
                  new CompensationTarget(dailyTarget,
                    interestRate * 100,
                    compensationPercent));
}
```

I had good intentions. I wanted to make the design better as I was breaking dependencies, but it didn't work out very well. I ended up making foolish mistakes, and with no tests to catch them, often they were found far later than they needed to be.

When you are breaking dependencies for test, you have to apply extra care. One thing that I do is *Preserve Signatures* whenever I can. When you cut/copy and paste entire method signatures from place to place you minimize any chance of errors.

In the previous example, I would end up with code like this:

```
public void process(List orders,
                    int dailyTarget,
                    double interestRate,
                    int compensationPercent) {
        processOrders(orders, dailyTarget, interestRate,
                          compensationPercent);
}

private static void processOrders(List orders,
                          int dailyTarget,
                          double interestRate,
                          int compensationPercent) {
    ...
}
```

The argument editing that I had to perform to do this was very easy. Essentially, only a couple of steps were involved:

1. I copied the entire argument list into my cut/copy paste buffer:

```
List orders,
int dailyTarget,
double interestRate,
int compensationPercent
```

2. Then I typed the new method declaration:

```
private void processOrders() {
}
```

3. I pasted the buffer into the new method declaration:

```
private void processOrders(List orders,
                           int dailyTarget,
                           double interestRate,
                           int compensationPercent) {
}
```

4. I then typed the call for the new method:

```
processOrders();
```

5. I pasted the buffer into the call:

```
processOrders(List orders,
              int dailyTarget,
              double interestRate,
              int compensationPercent);
```

6. Finally, I deleted the types, leaving the names of the arguments:

```
processOrders(orders,
              dailyTarget,
              interestRate,
              compensationPercent);
```

When you do these moves over and over again, they become automatic and you can feel more confidence in your changes. You can concentrate on some of the other lingering issues that can cause errors when you break dependencies. For instance, is your new method hiding a method with the same name signature in a base class?

Preserve Signatures

A couple of different scenarios exist for *Preserve Signatures.* You can use the technique to make new method declarations. You can also use it to create a set of instance methods for all of the arguments to a method when you are doing the *Break out Method Object* refactoring. See *Break out Method Object (330)* for details.

Lean on the Compiler

The primary purpose of a compiler is to translate source code into some other form, but in statically typed languages, you can do much more with a compiler. You can take advantage of its type checking and use it to identify changes you need to make. I call this practice *leaning on the compiler.* Here is an example of how to do it.

In a C++ program, I have a couple of global variables.

```
double domestic_exchange_rate;
double foreign_exchange_rate;
```

A set of methods in the same file uses the variables, but I want to find some way to change them under test so I use the *Encapsulate Global References (339)* technique from the catalog.

To do this, I write a class around the declarations and declare a variable of that class.

```
class Exchange
{
public:
    double domestic_exchange_rate;
    double foreign_exchange_rate;
};

Exchange exchange;
```

Now I compile to find all of the places where the compiler can't find `domestic_exchange_rate` and `foreign_exchange_rate`, and I change them so that they are accessed off the exchange object. Here are before and after shots of one of those changes:

```
total = domestic_exchange_rate * instrument_shares;
```

becomes:

```
total = exchange.domestic_exchange_rate * instrument_shares;
```

The key thing about this technique is that you are letting the compiler guide you toward the changes you need to make. This doesn't mean that you stop thinking about what you need to change; it just means that you can let the compiler do the legwork for you, in some cases. It's just very important to know what the compiler is going to find and what it isn't so that we aren't lulled into false confidence.

Lean on the Compiler involves two steps:

1. Altering a declaration to cause compile errors
2. Navigating to those errors and making changes.

You can lean on the compiler to make structural changes to your program, as we did in the *Encapsulate Global References (339)* example. You can also use it to initiate type changes. One common case is changing the type of a variable declaration from a class to an interface, and using the errors to determine which methods need to be on the interface.

Leaning on the compiler isn't always practical. If your builds take a long time, it might be more practical to search for the places where you need to make changes. See Chapter 7, *It Takes Forever to Make a Change*, for ways of getting past that problem. But when you can do it, *Lean on the Compiler* is a useful practice. But be careful; you can introduce subtle bugs if you do it blindly.

The language feature that gives us the most possibility for error when we lean is inheritance. Here's an example:

We have a class method named getX() in a Java class:

```
public int getX() {
    return x;
}
```

We want to find all occurrences of it so that we comment it out:

```
/*
public int getX() {
    return x;
} */
```

Now we recompile.

Guess what? We didn't get any errors. Does this mean that getX() is an unused method? Not necessarily. If getX() is declared as a concrete method in a superclass, commenting out getX in our current class will just cause the one in the superclass to be used. A similar situation can occur with variables and inheritance.

Lean on the Compiler is a powerful technique, but you have to know what its limits are; if you don't, you can end up making some serious mistakes.

Pair Programming

Chances are, you've already heard of *Pair Programming*. If you are using Extreme Programming (XP) as your process you are probably doing it. Good. It is a remarkably good way to increase quality and spread knowledge around a team.

If you aren't pair programming right now, I suggest that you try it. In particular, I insist that you pair when you use the dependency-breaking techniques I've described in this book.

It's easy to make a mistake and have no idea that you've broken the software. A second set of eyes definitely helps. Let's face it, working in legacy code is surgery, and doctors never operate alone.

For more information about pair programming, see *Pair Programming Illuminated* by Laurie Williams and Robert Kessler (Addison-Wesley 2002) and visit www.pairprogramming.com.

Chapter 24

We Feel Overwhelmed. It Isn't Going to Get Any Better

Working in legacy code is difficult. There is no denying it. Although every situation is different, one thing is going to make the job worth it to you as a programmer or not: figuring out what is in it for you. For some people, it is a paycheck, and there isn't anything wrong with that—we all have to make a living. But there really ought to be some other reason why you are programming.

If you were lucky, you started out in this business writing code because you thought it was fun. You sat down with your first computer ecstatic with all of the possibilities, all of the cool things you could do by programming a computer. It was something to learn and something to master, and you thought, "Wow, this is fun. I can make a great career if I get very good at this."

Not everyone comes to programming this way, but even for people who didn't, it is still possible to connect with what is fun about programming. If you can—and some of your coworkers can, too—it really doesn't matter what kind of system you are working on. You can do neat things with it. The alternative is just dejection. It isn't any fun, and frankly, we all deserve better than that.

Often people who spend time working on legacy systems wish they could work on green-field systems. It's fun to build systems from scratch, but frankly, green-field systems have their own set of problems. Over and over again, I've seen the following scenario play out: An existing system becomes murky and hard to change over time. People in the organization get frustrated with how long it takes to make changes in it. They move their best people (and sometimes their trouble-makers!) onto a new team that is charged with the task of "creating the replacement system with a better architecture." In the beginning, everything is fine. They know what the problems were with the old architecture, and they spend some time coming up with a new design. In the meantime, the rest of the developers are working on the old system. The system is in service, so they receive requests for bug fixes and occasionally new features. The business looks soberly at each new feature and decides whether it needs to be in the old system or whether the client can wait for the new system. In many cases, the client can't wait, so the change goes in both. The green-field team has to do double-duty, trying to replace a system that is constantly changing. As the months go by it becomes clearer that they are not going to be able to replace the old system, the system you're maintaining. The pressure increases. They work days, nights, and weekends. In many cases, the rest of the organization discovers that the work that you are doing is critical and that you are tending the investment that everyone will have to rely on in the future.

The grass isn't really much greener in green-field development.

The key to thriving in legacy code is finding what motivates you. Although many of us programmers are solitary creatures, there really isn't much that can replace working in a good environment with people you respect who know how to have fun at work. I've made some of my best friends at work and, to this day, they are the people I talk to when I've learned something new or fun while programming.

Another thing that helps is to connect with the larger community. These days, getting in touch with other programmers to learn and share more about the craft is easier than it ever was. You can subscribe to mailing lists on the Internet, attend conferences, and use all these resources to network, share strategies and techniques, and generally stay on top of software development.

Even when you have a bunch of people on a project who care about the work and care about making things better, another form of dejection can set in. Sometimes people are dejected because their code base is so large that they and their teammates could work on it for 10 years but still not have made it more than 10 percent better. Isn't that a good reason to be dejected? Well, I've visited teams with millions of lines of legacy code who looked at each day as a challenge and as a chance to make things better and have fun. I've also seen teams with far better code bases who are dejected. The attitude we bring to the work is important.

TDD some code outside of work. Program for fun a little bit. Start to feel the difference between the little projects you make and the big project at work. Chances are, your project at work can have the same feel if you can get the pieces you work with to run into a fast test harness.

If morale is low on your team, and it's low because of code quality, here's something that you can try: Pick the ugliest most obnoxious set of classes in the project, and get them under test. When you've tackled the worst problem as a team, you'll feel in control of your situation. I've seen it again and again.

As you start to take control of your code base, you'll start to develop oases of good code. Work can really be enjoyable in them.

Part III

Dependency-Breaking Techniques

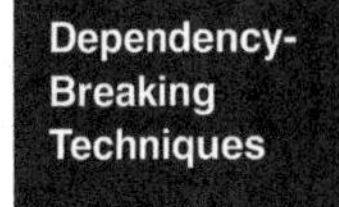

Chapter 25

Dependency-Breaking Techniques

In this chapter, I've written up a set of dependency-breaking techniques. This list is not exhaustive; these are just some techniques that I've used with teams to decouple classes well enough to get them under test. Technically, these techniques are refactorings—each of them preserves behavior. But unlike most refactorings written up in the industry so far, these refactorings are intended to be done without tests, to get tests in place. In most cases, if you follow the steps carefully, the chance of mistakes is small. This doesn't mean that they are completely safe. It is still possible to make mistakes when you perform them, so you should exercise care when you use them. Before you use these refactorings, see Chapter 23, *How Do I Know That I'm Not Breaking Anything?*

The tips in that chapter can help you use these techniques safely so that you can get tests in place. When you do, you'll be able to make more invasive changes with more confidence that you aren't breaking anything.

These techniques do not immediately make your design better. In fact, if you have good design sense, some of these techniques will make you flinch. These techniques can help you get methods, classes, and clusters of classes under test, and your system will be more maintainable because of it. At that point, you can use test-supported refactorings to make the design cleaner.

A few of the refactorings in this chapter were described by Martin Fowler in his book *Refactoring: Improving the Design of Existing Code* (Addison-Wesley, 1999). I've included them here with different steps. They've been tailored so that they can be used safely without tests.

Adapt Parameter

Adapt Parameter

When I make changes to methods, I often run into dependency headaches caused by method parameters. Sometimes I find it hard to create the parameter I need; at other times, I need to test the effect of the method on the parameter. In many cases, the class of the parameter doesn't make it easy. If the class is one that I can modify, I can use *Extract Interface (362)* to break the dependency. *Extract Interface* is often the best choice when it comes to breaking parameter dependencies.

In general, we want to do something simple to break dependencies that prevent testing, something that doesn't have possibilities for errors. However, in some cases, *Extract Interface (362)* doesn't work very well. If the parameter's type is pretty low level, or specific to some implementation technology, extracting an interface could be counterproductive or impossible.

> Use *Adapt Parameter* when you can't use *Extract Interface (362)* on a parameter's class or when a parameter is difficult to fake.

Here is an example:

```
public class ARMDispatcher
{
    public void populate(HttpServletRequest request) {
        String [] values
            = request.getParameterValues(pageStateName);
        if (values != null && values.length  > 0)
        {
            marketBindings.put(pageStateName + getDateStamp(),
                               values[0]);
        }
        ...
    }
    ...
}
```

In this class, the `populate` method accepts an `HttpServletRequest` as a parameter. `HttpServletRequest` is an interface that is part of Sun's J2EE standard for Java. If we were going to test `populate` the way it looks now, we'd have to create a class that implements `HttpServletRequest` and provide some way to fill it with the parameter values it needs to return under test. The current Java SDK documentation shows that there are about 23 method declarations on `HttpServletRequest`, and that doesn't count the declarations from its superinterface that we'd have to implement. It would be great to use *Extract Interface (362)* to make a narrower interface that supplies only the methods we need, but we can't extract an interface from another interface. In Java, we would need to have HttpServletRequest extend the one we are extracting, and we can't modify a standard interface that way. Fortunately, we do have other options.

Several mock object libraries are available for J2EE. If we download one of them, we can use a mock for HttpServletRequest and do the testing we need to do. This can be a real time saver; if we go this route, we won't have to spend time making a fake servlet request by hand. So, it looks like we have a solution—or do we?

When I'm breaking dependencies, I always try to look ahead and see what the result will look like. Then I can decide whether I can live with the aftermath. In this case, our production code will look pretty much the same, and we will have done a lot of work to keep HttpServletRequest, an API interface, in place. Is there a way to make the code look better and make the dependency breaking easier? Actually, there is. We can wrap the parameter that is coming in and break our dependency on the API interface entirely. When we've done that, the code will look like this:

```
public class ARMDispatcher
    public void populate(ParameterSource source) {
        String values = source.getParameterForName(pageStateName);
        if (value != null) {
            marketBindings.put(pageStateName + getDateStamp(),
                               value);
        }
        ...
    }
}
```

What have we done here? We've introduced a new interface named ParameterSource. At this point, the only method that it has is one named getParameterForName. Unlike the HttpServletRequest getParmeterValue method, the getParameterForName returns only the first. We wrote the method that way because we care about only the first parameter in this context.

Move toward interfaces that communicate responsibilities rather than implementation details. This makes code easier to read and easier to maintain.

Here is a fake class that implements ParameterSource. We can use it in our test:

```
class FakeParameterSource implements ParameterSource
{
    public String value;

    public String getParameterForName(String name) {
        return value;
    }
}
```

Adapt Parameter

And the production parameter source looks like this:

```
class ServletParameterSource implements ParameterSource
{
    private HttpServletRequest request;

    public ServletParameterSource(HttpServletRequest request) {
        this.request = request;
    }

    String getParameterValue(String name) {
        String [] values = request.getParameterValues(name);
        if (values == null || values.length < 1)
            return null;
        return values[0];
    }
}
```

Superficially, this might look like we're making things pretty for pretty's sake, but one pervasive problem in legacy code bases is that there often aren't any layers of abstraction; the most important code in the system often sits intermingled with low-level API calls. We've already seen how this can make testing difficult, but the problems go beyond testing. Code is harder to understand when it is littered with wide interfaces containing dozens of unused methods. When you create narrow abstractions targeted toward what you need, your code communicates better and you are left with a better seam.

If we move toward using ParameterSource in the example, we end up decoupling the population logic from particular sources. We won't be tied to specific J2EE interfaces any longer.

> *Adapt Parameter* is one case in which we don't *Preserve Signatures (312)*. Use extra care.

Adapt Parameter can be risky if the simplified interface that you are creating for the parameter class is too different from the parameter's current interface. If we are not careful when we make those changes, we could end up introducing subtle bugs. As always, remember that the goal is to break dependencies well enough to get tests in place. Your bias should be toward making changes that you feel more confident in rather than changes that give you the best structure. Those can come after your tests. For instance, in this case we may want to alter ParameterSource so that clients of it don't have to check for null when they call its methods (see *Null Object Pattern (112)* for details).

> Safety first. Once you have tests in place, you can make invasive changes much more confidently.

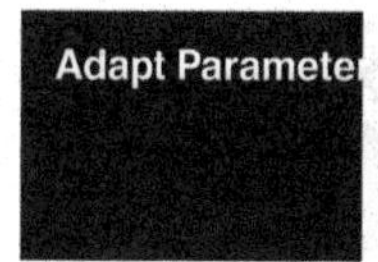

Steps

To use *Adapt Parameter*, perform the following steps:

1. Create the new interface that you will use in the method. Make it as simple and communicative as possible, but try not to create an interface that will require more than trivial changes in the method.
2. Create a production implementer for the new interface.
3. Create a fake implementer for the interface.
4. Write a simple test case, passing the fake to the method.
5. Make the changes you need to in the method to use the new parameter.
6. Run your test to verify that you are able to test the method using the fake.

Break Out Method Object

Long methods are very tough to work with in many applications. Often if you can instantiate the class that contains them and get them into a test harness, you can start to write tests. In some cases, the work that it takes to make a class separately instantiable is large. It may even be overkill for the changes you need to make. If the method that you need to work with is small and doesn't use instance data, use *Expose Static Method (345)* to get your changes under test. On the other hand, if your method is large or does use instance data and methods, consider using *Break Out Method Object*. In a nutshell, the idea behind this refactoring is to move a long method to a new class. Objects that you create using that new class are called method objects because they embody the code of a single method. After you've used *Break Out Method Object*, you can often write tests for the new class easier than you could for the old method. Local variables in the old method can become instance variables in the new class. Often that makes it easier to break dependencies and move the code to a better state.

Here is an example in C++ (large chunks of the class and method have been removed to preserve trees):

```
class GDIBrush
{
public:
    void draw(vector<point>& renderingRoots,
              ColorMatrix& colors,
              vector<point>& selection);
    ...

private:
    void drawPoint(int x, int y, COLOR color);
    ...

};

void GDIBrush::draw(vector<point>& renderingRoots,
                    ColorMatrix& colors,
                    vector<point>& selection)
{
    for(vector<points>::iterator it = renderingRoots.begin();
            it != renderingRoots.end();
            ++it) {
        point p = *it;
        ...

        drawPoint(p.x, p.y, colors[n]);
    }
    ...

}
```

The GDIBrush class has a long method named draw. We can't easily write tests for it, and it is going to be very difficult to create an instance of GDIBrush in a test harness. Let's use *Break Out Method Object* to move draw to a new class.

The first step is to create a new class that will do the drawing work. We can call it Renderer. After we've created it, we give it a public constructor. The arguments of the constructor should be a reference to the original class, and the arguments to the original method. We need to *Preserve Signatures (312)* on the latter.


```
class Renderer
{
public:
    Renderer(GBIBrush *brush,
             vector<point>& renderingRoots,
             ColorMatrix &colors,
             vector<point>& selection);
    ...

};
```

After we've created the constructor, we add instance variables for each of the constructor arguments and initialize them. We do this as a set of cut/copy/paste moves, too, to *Preserve Signatures (312)*.

```
class Renderer
{
private:
    GDIBrush *brush;
    vector<point>& renderingRoots;
    ColorMatrix& colors;
    vector<point>& selection;

public:
    Renderer(GDIBrush *brush,
             vector<point>& renderingRoots,
             ColorMatrix& colors,
             vector<point>& selection)
        : brush(brush), renderingRoots(renderingRoots),
          colors(colors), selection(selection)
        {}

};
```

You might be looking at this and saying, "Hmmm, it looks like we are going to be in the same position. We are accepting a reference to a GDIBrush, and we can't instantiate one of those in our test harness. What good does this do us?" Wait, we are going to end up in a different place.

After we've made the constructor, we can add another method to the class, a method that will do the work that was done in the draw() method. We can call it draw() also.


```
class Renderer
{
private:
    GDIBrush *brush;
    vector<point>& renderingRoots;
    ColorMatrix& colors;
    vector<point>& selection;

public:
    Renderer(GDIBrush *brush,
             vector<point>& renderingRoots,
             ColorMatrix& colors,
             vector<point>& selection)
        : brush(brush), renderingRoots(renderingRoots),
          colors(colors), selection(selection)
        {}

    void draw();
};
```

Now we add the body of the draw() method to Renderer. We copy the body of the old draw() method into the new one and *Lean on the Compiler (315)*.

```
void Renderer::draw()
{
    for(vector<points>::iterator it = renderingRoots.begin();
            it != renderingRoots.end();
            ++it) {
        point p = *it;
        ...
        drawPoint(p.x, p.y, colors[n]);
    }
    ...

}
```

If the draw() on Renderer has any references to instance variables or methods from GDIBrush, our compile will fail. To make it succeed, we can make getters for the variables and make the methods that it depends on public. In this case, there is only one dependency, a private method named drawPoint. After we make it public on GDIBrush, we can access it from a reference to the Renderer class and the code compiles.

Now we can make GDIBrush's draw method delegate to the new Renderer.

```
void GDIBrush::draw(vector<point>& renderingRoots,
                    ColorMatrix &colors,
                    vector<point>& selection)
{
    Renderer renderer(this, renderingRoots,
                      colors, selection);
    renderer.draw();
}
```

Now back to the GDIBrush dependency. If we can't instantiate GDIBrush in a test harness, we can use *Extract Interface* to break the dependency on GDIBrush completely. The section on *Extract Interface (362)* has the details, but briefly, we create an empty interface class and make the GDIBrush implement it. In this case, we can call it PointRenderer because drawPoint is the method on GDIBrush that we really need access to in the Renderer. Then we change the reference that the Renderer holds from GDIBrush to PointRenderer, compile, and let the compiler tell us what methods have to be on the interface. Here is what the code looks like at the end:

```
class PointRenderer
{
    public:
        virtual void drawPoint(int x, int y, COLOR color) = 0;
};


class GDIBrush : public PointRenderer
{
public:
    void drawPoint(int x, int y, COLOR color);
    ...
};


class Renderer
{
private:
    PointRender *pointRenderer;
    vector<point>& renderingRoots;
    ColorMatrix& colors;
    vector<point>& selection;

public:
    Renderer(PointRenderer *renderer,
             vector<point>& renderingRoots,
             ColorMatrix& colors,
             vector<point>& selection)
        : pointRenderer(pointRenderer),
          renderingRoots(renderingRoots),
```

```
        colors(colors), selection(selection)
    {}

    void draw();
};

void Renderer::draw()
{
    for(vector<points>::iterator it = renderingRoots.begin();
            it != renderingRoots.end();
            ++it) {
        point p = *it;
        ...
        pointRenderer->drawPoint(p.x,p.y,colors[n]);
    }
    ...

}
```

Figure 25.1 shows what it looks like in UML.

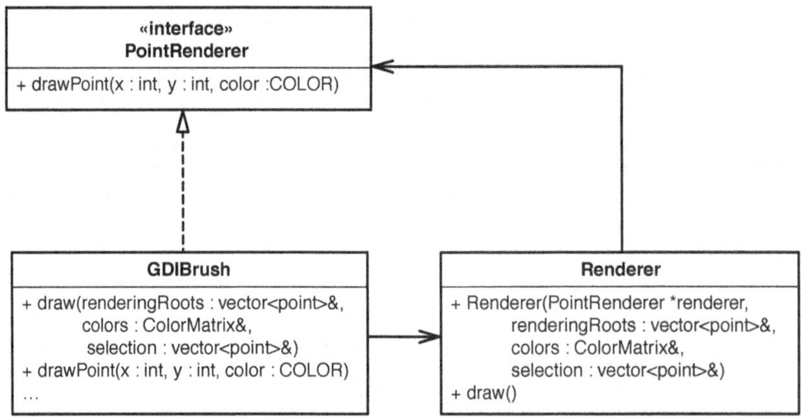

Figure 25.1 `GDIBrush` *after Break Out Method Object.*

Our ending point is a little odd. We have a class (`GDIBrush`) that implements a new interface (`PointRenderer`), and the only use of that interface is by an object (a `Renderer`) that is created by the class. You might have a sick feeling in the pit of your stomach because we've made details that were private in the original class public so that we could use this technique. Now the `drawPoint` method that was private in `GDIBrush` is exposed to the world. The important thing to notice is that this isn't really the end.

Over time, you'll grow disgusted with the fact that you can't instantiate the original class in a test harness, and you will break dependencies so that you can. Then you'll look at other options. For instance, does `PointRenderer` need to be an interface? Can it be a class that holds a `GDIBrush`? If it can, maybe you can start to move to a design based on this new concept of `Renderers`.

That is only one of the simple refactorings we may be able to do when we get the class under test. The resulting structure might invite many more.

Break Out Method Object has several variations. In the simplest case, the original method doesn't use any instance variables or methods from the original class. We don't need to pass it a reference to the original class. In other cases, the method only uses data from the original class. At times, it makes sense to put this data into a new data-holding class and pass it as an argument to the method object.

The case that I show in this section is the worst case; we need to use methods on the original class, so we use *Extract Interface (362)* and start to build up some abstraction between the method object and the original class.

Steps

You can use these steps to do *Break out Method Object* safely without tests:

1. Create a class that will house the method code.

2. Create a constructor for the class and *Preserve Signatures (312)* to give it an exact copy of the arguments used by the method. If the method uses an instance data or methods from the original class, add a reference to the original class as the first argument to the constructor.

3. For each argument in the constructor, declare an instance variable and give it exactly the same type as the variable. *Preserve Signatures (312)* by copying all the arguments directly into the class and formatting them as instance variable declarations. Assign all of the arguments to the instance variables in the constructor.

4. Create an empty execution method on the new class. Often this method is called `run()`. We used the name `draw` in the example.

5. Copy the body of the old method into the execution method and compile to *Lean on the Compiler (315)*.

6. The error messages from the compiler should indicate where the method is still using methods or variables from the old class. In each of these

cases, do what it takes to get the method to compile. In some cases, this is as simple as changing a call to use the reference to the original class. In other cases, you might have to make methods public on the original class or introduce getters so that you don't have to make instance variables public.

7. After the new class compiles, go back to the original method and change it so that it creates an instance of the new class and delegates its work to it.
8. If needed, use *Extract Interface (362)* to break the dependency on the original class.

Definition Completion

In some languages, we can declare a type in one place and define it in another. The languages in which this capability is most apparent are C and C++. In both of them, we can declare a function or method in one place and define it someplace else, usually in an implementation file. When we have this capability, we can use it to break dependencies.

Here is an example:

```
class CLateBindingDispatchDriver : public CDispatchDriver
{
public:
                CLateBindingDispatchDriver ();
    virtual    ~CLateBindingDispatchDriver ();

    ROOTID      GetROOTID (int id) const;

    void        BindName (int id,
                          OLECHAR FAR *name);
    ...

private:
    CArray<ROOTID, ROOTID& > rootids;

};
```

This is the declaration of a little class in a C++ application. Users create `CLateBindingDispatchDrivers` and then use the `BindName` method to associate names with IDs. We want to provide a different way of binding names when we use this class in a test. In C++, we can do this using *Definition Completion.* The `BindName` method was declared in the class header file. How can we give it a different definition under test? We can include the header containing this class declaration in the test file and provide alternate definitions for the methods before our tests.

```
#include "LateBindingDispatchDriver.h"

CLateBindingDispatchDriver::CLateBindingDispatchDriver() {}

CLateBindingDispatchDriver::~CLateBindingDispatchDriver() {}

ROOTID GetROOTID (int id) const { return ROOTID(-1); }

void BindName(int id, OLECHAR FAR *name) {}


TEST(AddOrder,BOMTreeCtrl)
{
```

```
    CLateBindingDispatchDriver driver;
    CBOMTreeCtrl  ctrl(&driver);

    ctrl.AddOrder(COrderFactory::makeDefault());
    LONGS_EQUAL(1, ctrl.OrderCount());
}
```


When we define these methods directly in the test file, we are providing the definitions that will be used in the test. We can provide null bodies for methods that we don't care about or put in sensing methods that can be used across all of our tests.

When we use *Definition Completion* in C or C++, we are pretty much obligated to create a separate executable for the tests that use the completed definitions. If we don't, they will clash with the real definitions at link time. One other downside is that we now have two different sets of definitions for the methods of a class, one in a test source file and another in a production source file. This can be a big maintenance burden. It can also confuse debuggers if we don't set up the environment correctly. For these reasons, I don't recommend using *Definition Completion* except in the worst dependency situations. Even then, I recommend doing it just to break initial dependencies. Afterwards, you should bring the class under test quickly so that the duplicate definitions can be removed.

Steps

To use *Definition Completion* in C++, follow these steps:

1. Identify a class with definitions you'd like to replace.
2. Verify that the method definitions are in a source file, not a header. If they are in a header, move then into the source file..
3. Include the header in the test source file of the class you are testing.
4. Verify that the source files for the class are not part of the build.
5. Build to find missing methods.
6. Add method definitions to the test source file until you have a complete build.

Encapsulate Global References

When you are trying to test code that has problematic dependencies on globals, you essentially have three choices. You can try to make the globals act differently under test, you can link to different globals, or you can encapsulate the globals so that you can decouple things further. The last option is called *Encapsulate Global References*. Here is an example in C++:

```
bool AGG230_activeframe[AGG230_SIZE];
bool AGG230_suspendedframe[AGG230_SIZE];

void AGGController::suspend_frame()
{
    frame_copy(AGG230_suspendedframe,
               AGG230_activeframe);
    clear(AGG230_activeframe);
    flush_frame_buffers();
}

void AGGController::flush_frame_buffers()
{
    for (int n = 0; n < AGG230_SIZE; ++n) {
        AGG230_activeframe[n] = false;
        AGG230_suspendedframe[n] = false;
    }
}
```

In this example, we have some code that does work with a few global arrays. The `suspend_frame` method needs to access the active and suspended frames. At first glance, it looks like we can make the frames members of the `AGGController` class, but some other classes (not shown) use the frames. What can we do?

One immediate thought is that we can pass them as parameters to the `suspend_frame` method using *Parameterize Method (383)*, but after we do that, we'll have to pass them as parameters to any methods that `suspend_frame` calls that need them. In this case, `flush_frame_buffer` is an offender.

The next option is to pass both frames as constructor arguments to `AGGController`. We could do that, but it is worth taking a look at other places where they are used. If it seems that whenever we use one we are also using the other, we could bundle them together.

> If several globals are always used or are modified near each other, they belong in the same class.

The best way to handle this situation is to look at the data, the active and suspended frames, and think about whether we can come up with a good name for a new class that would hold both of them. Sometimes this is a little tricky. We have to think about what that data means in the design and then consider why it is there. If we create a new class, eventually we'll move methods onto it, and, chances are, the code for those methods already exists someplace else where the data is used.

> When naming a class, think about the methods that will eventually reside on it. The name should be good, but it doesn't have to be perfect. Remember that you can always rename the class later.

In the previous example, I'd expect that, over time, the `frame_copy` and `clear` methods might move to the new class that we are going to create. Is there work that is common to the suspended frame and the active frame? It looks like there is, in this case. The `suspend_frame` function on `AGGController` could probably move to a new class as long as it contains both the `suspended_frame` array and the `active_frame` array. What could we call this new class? We could just call it `Frame` and say that each frame has an active buffer and a suspended buffer. This requires us to change our concepts and rename variables a bit, but what we will get in exchange is a smarter class that hides more detail.

> The class name that you find might already be in use. If so, consider whether you can rename whatever is using that name.

Here's how we do it, step by step.

First, we create a class that looks like this:

```
class Frame
{
public:
    // declare AGG230_SIZE as a constant
    enum { AGG230_SIZE = 256 };

    bool AGG230_activeframe[AGG230_SIZE];
    bool AGG230_suspendedframe[AGG230_SIZE];

};
```

We've left the names of the data the same intentionally, just to make the next step easier. Next, we declare a global instance of the `Frame` class:

```
Frame  frameForAGG230;
```

Next, we comment out the original declarations of the data and attempt to build:

```
// bool AGG230_activeframe[AGG230_SIZE];
// bool AGG230_suspendedframe[AGG230_SIZE];
```

At this point, we get all sorts of compile errors telling us that AGG_activeframe and AGG230_suspendedframe don't exist, threatening us with terrible consequences. If the build system is sufficiently petulant, it rounds things off with an attempt at linking, leaving us with about 10 pages of unresolved link errors. We could get upset, but we expected all of that to happen, didn't we?

To get past all of those errors, we can stop at each one and place frameForAGG230. in front of each reference that is causing trouble.

```
void AGGController::suspend_frame()
{
    frame_copy(frameForAGG230.AGG230_suspendedframe,
               frameForAGG230.AGG230_activeframe);
    clear(frameForAGG20.AGG230_activeframe);
    flush_frame_buffer();
}
```

When we are done doing that, we have uglier code, but it will all compile and work correctly, so it is a behavior-preserving transformation. Now that we've finished it, we can pass a Frame object through the constructor of the AGGController class and get the separation we need to move forward.

> Referencing a member of a class rather than a simple global is only the first step. Afterward, consider whether you should use *Introduce Static Setter (372)*, or parameterize the code using *Parameterize Constructor (379)* or *Parameterize Method (383)*.

So, we've introduced a new class by adding global variables to a new class and making them public. Why did we do it this way? After all, we spent some time thinking about what to call the new class and what sorts of methods to place on it. We could have started by creating a fake Frame object that we could delegate to in AGG_Controller, and we could have moved all of the logic that uses those variables onto a real Frame class. We could have done that, but it is a lot to attempt all at once. Worse, when we don't have tests in place and we are trying to do the minimal work we need to get tests in place, it is best to leave logic alone as much as possible. We should avoid moving it and try to get separation by putting in seams that allow us to call one method instead of another or access one piece of data rather than another. Later, when we have more tests in place, we can move behavior from one class to another with impunity.

When we've passed the frame into the AGGController, we can do a little renaming to make things a little clearer. Here is our ending state for this refactoring:

```
class Frame
{
public:
    enum { BUFFER_SIZE = 256 };
    bool activebuffer[BUFFER_SIZE];
```

```
    bool suspendedbuffer[BUFFER_SIZE];
};

Frame  frameForAGG230;

void AGGController::suspend_frame()
{
    frame_copy(frame.suspendedbuffer,
               frame.activebuffer);
    clear(frame.activeframe);
    flush_frame_buffer();
}
```

It might not seem like much of an improvement, but it is an extremely valuable first step. After we've moved the data to a class, we have separation and are poised to make the code much better over time. We might even want to have a `FrameBuffer` class at some point.

> When you use *Encapsulate Global References*, start with data or small methods. More substantial methods can be moved to the new class when more tests are in place.

In the previous example, I showed how to do *Encapsulate Global References* with global data. You can do the same thing with non-member functions in C++ programs. Often when you are working with some C API, you have calls to global functions scattered throughout an area of code that you want to work with. The only seam that you have is the linkage of calls to their respective functions. You can use *Link Substitution (377)* to get separation, but you can end up with better structured code if you use *Encapsulate Global References* to build another seam. Here is an example.

In a piece of code that we want to put under test, there are calls to two functions: `GetOption(const string optionName)` and `setOption(string name, Option option)`. They are just free functions, functions not attached to any class, but they are used prolifically in code like this:

```
void ColumnModel::update()
{
    alignRows();
    Option resizeWidth = ::GetOption("ResizeWidth");
    if (resizeWidth.isTrue()) {
        resize();
    }   else {
        resizeToDefault();
    }
}
```

In a case such as this, we could look at some old standbys, techniques such as *Parameterize Method (383)* and *Extract and Override Getter(352)*, but if the

calls are across multiple methods and multiple classes, it would be cleaner to use *Encapsulate Global References*. To do this, create a new class like this:

```
class OptionSource
{
public:
    virtual         ~OptionSource() = 0;
    virtual Option  GetOption(const string& optionName) = 0;
    virtual void    SetOption(const string& optionName,
                              const Option& newOption) = 0;
};
```

The class contains abstract methods for each of the free functions that we need. Next, subclass to make a fake for the class. In this case, we could have a map or a vector in the fake that allows us to hold on to a set of options that will be used during tests. We could provide an add method to the fake or just a constructor that accepts a map—whatever is convenient for the tests. When we have the fake, we can create the real option source:

```
class  ProductionOptionSource : public OptionSource
{
public:
    Option GetOption(const string& optionName);
    void SetOption(const string& optionName,
                   const Option& newOption) ;
};

Option ProductionOptionSource::GetOption(
        const string& optionName)
{
    ::GetOption(optionName);
}

void ProductionOptionSource::SetOption(
        const string& optionName,
        const Option& newOption)
{
    ::SetOption(optionName, newOption);
}
```

To encapsulate references to free functions, make an interface class with fake and production subclasses. Each of the functions in the production code should do nothing more than delegate to a global function.

This refactoring turned out well. We introduced a seam and ended up doing a simple delegation to the API function. Now that we've done that, we can parameterize the class to accept an OptionSource object so that we can use a fake one under test and the real one in production.

Encapsulate Global References

In the previous example, we put the functions in a class and made them virtual. Could we have done it some other way? Yes, we could have made free functions that delegate to other free functions or added them to a new class as static functions, but neither of those approaches would have given us good seams. We would have had to use the *link seam (36)* or the *preprocessing seam (33)* to substitute one implementation for another. When we use the class and virtual function approach and parameterize the class, the seams that we have are explicit and easy to manage.

Steps

To *Encapsulate Global References*, follow these steps:

1. Identify the globals that you want to encapsulate.
2. Create a class that you want to reference them from.
3. Copy the globals into the class. If some of them are variables, handle their initialization in the class.
4. Comment out the original declarations of the globals.
5. Declare a global instance of the new class.
6. *Lean on the Compiler (315)* to find all the unresolved references to the old globals.
7. Precede each unresolved reference with the name of the global instance of the new class.
8. In places where you want to use fakes, use *Introduce Static Setter (372)*, *Parameterize Constructor (379)*, *Parameterize Method (383)* or *Replace Global Reference with Getter (399)*.

Expose Static Method

Working with classes that can't be instantiated in a test harness is pretty tricky. Here is a technique that I use in some cases. If you have a method that doesn't use instance data or methods, you can turn it into a static method. When it is static, you can get it under test without having to instantiate the class. Here's an example in Java.

We have a class with a `validate` method, and we need to add a new validation condition. Unfortunately, the class it is on would be very hard to instantiate. I'll spare you the trauma of looking at the whole class, but here is the method we need to change:

```
class RSCWorkflow
{
    ...
    public void validate(Packet packet)
            throws InvalidFlowException {
        if (packet.getOriginator().equals( "MIA")
                || packet.getLength() > MAX_LENGTH
                || !packet.hasValidCheckSum()) {
            throw new InvalidFlowException();
        }
        ...
    }
    ...
}
```

What can we do to get this method under test? When we look closely at it, we see that the method uses a lot of methods on the `Packet` class. In fact, it would really make sense to move `validate` onto the `Packet` class, but moving the method isn't the least risky thing we can do right now; we definitely won't be able to *Preserve Signatures (312)*. If you don't have automated support to move methods, often it is better to get some tests in place first. *Expose Static Method* can help you do that. With tests in place, you can make the change you need to make and have much more confidence moving the method afterward.

> When you are breaking dependencies without tests, *Preserve Signatures (312)* of methods whenever possible. If you cut/copy and paste whole method signatures, you have less of a chance of introducing errors.

The code here doesn't depend on any instance variables or methods. What would it look like if the `validate` method was public static? Anyone anyplace in the code could write this statement and validate a packet:

```
RSCWorkflow.validate(packet);
```

Expose Static Method

Chances are, whoever created the class never would've imagined that someone would make that method static someday, much less public. So, is it a bad thing to do? No, not really. Encapsulation is a great thing for classes, but the static area of a class isn't really part of the class. In fact, in some languages, it is part of another class, sometimes known as the metaclass of the class.

When a method is static, you know that it doesn't access any of the private data of the class; it is just a utility method. If you make the method public, you can write tests for it. Those tests will support you if you choose to move the method to another class later.

> Static methods and data really do act as if they are part of a different class. Static data lives for the life of a program, not the life of an instance, and statics are accessible without an instance.
>
> The static portions of a class can be seen as a "staging area" for things that don't quite belong to the class. If you see a method that doesn't use any instance data, it is a good idea to make it static to make it noticeable until you figure out what class it really belongs on.

Here is the `RSCWorkflow` class after we've extracted a static method for `validate`.

```
public class RSCWorkflow {
    public void validate(Packet packet)
            throws InvalidFlowException {
        validatePacket(packet);
    }

    public static void validatePacket(Packet packet)
            throws InvalidFlowException {
        if (packet.getOriginator() == "MIA"
                || packet.getLength() <= MAX_LENGTH
                || packet.hasValidCheckSum()) {
            throw new InvalidFlowException();
        }
        ...
    }
    ...
}
```

In some languages there is a simpler way of doing *Expose Static Method.* Instead of extracting a static method from your original method you can just make the original method static. If the method is being used by other classes, it can still be accessed off an instance of its class. Here is an example:

```
RSCWorkflow workflow = new RCSWorkflow();
...
// static call that looks like a non-static call
workflow.validatePacket(packet);
```

However, in some languages, you get a compilation warning for doing this. It's best to try to get code into a state in which there are no compile warnings.

If you are concerned that someone might start to use the static in a way that would cause dependency problems later, you can expose the static method using some non-public access mode. In languages such as Java and C#, which have package or internal visibility, you can restrict access to the static or make it protected and access it through a *testing subclass*. In C++, you have the same options: You can make the static method protected or use a namespace.

Steps

To *Expose Static Method*, follow these steps:

1. Write a test that accesses the method that you want to expose as a public static method of the class.
2. Extract the body of the method to a static method. Remember to *Preserve Signatures (312)*. You'll have to use a different name for the method. Often you can use the names of parameters to help you come up with a new method name. For example, if a method named `validate` accepts a `Packet`, you can extract its body as a static method named `validatePacket`.
3. Compile.
4. If there are errors related to accessing instance data or methods, take a look at those features and see if they can be made static also. If they can, make them static so that the system will compile.

Extract and Override Call

Extract and Override Call

At times, the dependencies that get in the way during testing are rather localized. We might have a single method call that we need to replace. If we can break the dependency on a method call, we can prevent odd side effects in our testing or sense values that are passed to the call.

Let's look at an example:

```
public class PageLayout
{
    private int id = 0;
    private List styles;
    private StyleTemplate template;
    ...
    protected void rebindStyles() {
        styles = StyleMaster.formStyles(template, id);
        ...
    }
    ...
}
```

PageLayout makes a call to a static function named formStyles on a class named StyleMaster. It assigns the return value to an instance variable: styles. What can we do if we want to sense through formStyles or separate our dependency on StyleMaster? One option is to extract the call to a new method and override it in a *testing subclass*. This is known as *Extract and Override Call*.

Here is the code after the extraction:

```
public class PageLayout
{
    private int id = 0;
    private List styles;
    private StyleTemplate template;
    ...
    protected void rebindStyles() {
        styles = formStyles(template, id);
        ...
    }


    protected List formStyles(StyleTemplate template,
                              int id) {
        return StyleMaster.formStyles(template, id);
    }
    ...
}
```

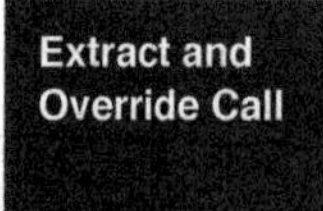

Now that we have our own local formStyles method, we can override it to break the dependency. "In this example, we don't need styles for the things that we are testing right now, so we can just return an empty list.

```
public class TestingPageLayout extends PageLayout {
    protected List formStyles(StyleTemplate template,
                              int id) {
        return new ArrayList();
    }
    ...
}
```

As we develop tests that need various styles, we can alter this method so that we can configure what will be returned.

Extract and Override Call is a very useful refactoring; I use it very often. It is an ideal way to break dependencies on global variables and static methods. In general, I tend to use it unless there are many different calls against the same global. If there are, I often use *Replace Global Reference with Getter (399)* or *Parameterize Constructor (379)* instead.

If you have an automated refactoring tool, *Extract and Override Call* is trivial. You can do it using the *Extract Method (415)* refactoring. However, if you don't, use the following steps. They allow you to extract any call safely, even if you don't have tests in place.

Steps

To *Extract and Override Call*, follow these steps:

1. Identify the call that you want to extract. Find the declaration of its method. Copy its method signature so that you can *Preserve Signatures (312)*.

2. Create a new method on the current class. Give it the signature you've copied.

3. Copy the call to the new method and replace the call with a call to the new method.

4. Introduce a testing subclass and override the new method.

Extract and Override Factory Method

Extract and Override Factory Method

Object creation in constructors can be vexing when you want to get a class under test. Sometimes the work that is happening in those objects shouldn't happen in a test harness. At other times, you just want to get a sensing object in place, but you can't because that object's creation is hard-coded in a constructor.

> Hard-coded initialization work in constructors can be very hard to work around in testing.

Let's look at an example:

```
public class WorkflowEngine
{
    public WorkflowEngine () {
        Reader reader
            = new ModelReader(
                AppConfig.getDryConfiguration());

        Persister persister
            = new XMLStore(
                AppConfiguration.getDryConfiguration());

        this.tm = new TransactionManager(reader, persister);
        ...
    }
    ...
}
```

WorkflowEngine creates a TransactionManager in its constructor. If the creation was someplace else, we could introduce some separation more easily. One of the options we have is to use *Extract and Override Factory Method.*

> *Extract and Override Factory Method* is pretty powerful, but it does have some language-specific issues. For instance, you can't do it in C++. C++ does not allow virtual function calls to resolve to functions in derived classes. Java and many other languages do allow this. In C++, *Supersede Instance Variable* and *Extract and Override Getter (352)* are good alternatives. See the example in *Supersede Instance Variable (404)* for a discussion of this problem.

```
public class WorkflowEngine
{
    public WorkflowEngine () {
        this.tm = makeTransactionManager();
        ...
    }
```

```
    protected TransactionManager makeTransactionManager() {
        Reader reader
            = new ModelReader(
                AppConfiguration.getDryConfiguration());

        Persister persister
            = new XMLStore(
                AppConfiguration.getDryConfiguration());

        return new TransactionManager(reader, persister);
    }
    ...
}
```


When we have that factory method, we can subclass and override it so that we can return a new transaction manager whenever we need one:

```
public class TestWorkflowEngine extends WorkflowEngine
{
    protected TransactionManager makeTransactionManager() {
        return new FakeTransactionManager();
    }
}
```

Steps

To *Extract and Override Factory Method*, follow these steps:

1. Identify an object creation in a constructor.
2. Extract all of the work involved in the creation into a factory method.
3. Create a *testing subclass* and override the factory method in it to avoid dependencies on problematic types under test.

Extract and Override Getter

Extract and Override Factory Method (350) is a powerful way of separating dependencies on types, but it doesn't work in all cases. The big "hole" in its applicability is C++. In C++, you can't call a virtual function in a derived class from a base class's constructor. Fortunately, there is a workaround for the case in which you are only creating the object in a constructor, not doing any additional work with it.

The gist of this refactoring is to introduce a getter for the instance variable that you want to replace with a fake object. You then refactor to use the getter every place in the class. You can then subclass and override the getter to provide alternate objects under test.

In this example, we create a transaction manager in a constructor. We want to set things up so that the class can use this transaction manager in production and a sensing one under test.

Here is what we start with:

```
// WorkflowEngine.h
class WorkflowEngine
{
private:
    TransactionManager    *tm;
public:
    WorkflowEngine ();
    ...
}

// WorkflowEngine.cpp
WorkflowEngine::WorkflowEngine()
{
    Reader *reader
        = new ModelReader(
            AppConfig.getDryConfiguration());

    Persister *persister
        = new XMLStore(
            AppConfiguration.getDryConfiguration());

    tm = new TransactionManager(reader, persister);
    ...
}
```

And here is what we end up with:

```
// WorkflowEngine.h
class WorkflowEngine
```

```
{
private:
    TransactionManager    *tm;

protected:
        TransactionManager *getTransactionManager() const;

public:
                        WorkflowEngine ();
    ...
}


// WorkflowEngine.cpp
WorkflowEngine::WorkflowEngine()
:tm (0)
{
    ...
}

TransactionManager *WorkflowEngine::getTransactionManager() const
{
    if (tm == 0) {
        Reader *reader
            = new ModelReader(
                AppConfig.getDryConfiguration());

        Persister *persister
            = new XMLStore(
                AppConfiguration.getDryConfiguration());

        tm = new TransactionManager(reader,persister);
    }
    return tm;
}
...
```

The first thing we do is introduce a *lazy getter*, a function which creates the transaction manager on first call. Then we replace all uses of the variable with calls to the getter.

A *lazy getter* is a method that looks like a normal getter to all of its callers. The key difference is that lazy getters create the object they are supposed to return the first time they are called. To do this, they usually contain logic that looks like this. Notice how the instance variable `thing` is being initialized

```
Thing getThing() {
    if (thing == null) {
        thing = new Thing();
    }
    return thing;
}
```

Lazy getters are also used in the *Singleton Design Pattern (372)*.

When we have that getter, we can subclass and override to plug in another object:

```
class TestWorkflowEngine : public WorkflowEngine
{
public:
    TransactionManager  *getTransactionManager()
                          { return &transactionManager; }

    FakeTransactionManager  transactionManager;
};
```

When you use *Extract and Override Getter*, you have to be very conscious of object lifetime issues, particularly in a non-garbage-collected language such as C++. Make sure that you delete the testing instance in a way that is consistent with how the code deletes the production instance.

In a test, we can easily access the fake transaction manager if we need to:

```
TEST(transactionCount, WorkflowEngine)
{
    auto_ptr<TestWorkflowEngine>  engine(new TestWorkflowEngine);
    engine.>run();
    LONGS_EQUAL(0,
        engine.>transactionManager.getTransactionCount());
}
```

One downside of *Extract and Override Getter* is that there is a chance that someone will use the variable before it is initialized. For this reason, it's good to make sure that all of the code in the class is using the getter.

Extract and Override Getter is not a technique that I use very often. When there is just a single method on an object that is problematic, it is far easier to use *Extract and Override Call (348)*. But, *Extract and Override Getter* is a better choice when there are many problematic methods on the same object. If you can get rid of all of those problems by extracting a getter and overriding it, it is a clear win.

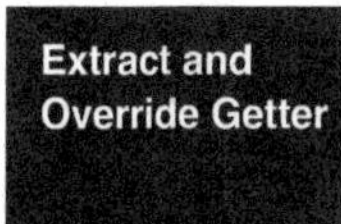

Steps

To *Extract and Override Getter*, follow these steps:

1. Identify the object you need a getter for.
2. Extract all of the logic needed to create the object into a getter.
3. Replace all uses of the object with calls to the getter, and initialize the reference that holds the object to null in all constructors.
4. Add the first-time logic to the getter so that the object is constructed and assigned to the reference whenever the reference is null.
5. Subclass the class and override the getter to provide an alternative object for testing.

Extract Implementer

Extract Implementer

Extract Interface (362) is a handy technique, but one part of it is hard: naming. I often run into cases where I want to extract an interface but the name I want to use is already the name of the class. If I am working in an IDE that has support for renaming classes and *Extract Interface*, this is easy to take care of. When I don't, I have a few choices:

- I can make up a foolish name.
- I can look at the methods I need and see if they are a subset of the public methods on the class. If they are, they might suggest another name for the new interface.

One thing that I usually stop short of is putting an "I" prefix on the name of the class to make a name for the new interface, unless it is already the convention in the code base. There is nothing worse than working in an unfamiliar area of code in which half the type names start with *I* and half don't. Half of the time that you type the name of a type, you'll be wrong. You'll either have missed the needed *I* or not.

> Naming is a key part of design. If you choose good names, you reinforce understanding in a system and make it easier to work with. If you choose poor names, you undermine understanding and make life hellish for the programmers who follow you.

When the name of a class is perfect for the name of an interface and I don't have automated refactoring tools, I use *Extract Implementer* to get the separation I need. To extract an implementer of a class, we turn the class into an interface by subclassing it and pushing all of its concrete methods down into that subclass. Here is an example in C++:

```
// ModelNode.h
class ModelNode
{
private:
    list<ModelNode *>    m_interiorNodes;
    list<ModelNode *>    m_exteriorNodes;
    double               m_weight;
    void                 createSpanningLinks();

public:
    void addExteriorNode(ModelNode *newNode);
    void addInternalNode(ModelNode *newNode);
    void colorize();
    ...

};
```

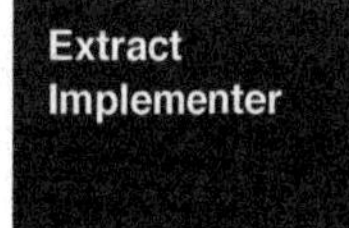

The first step is to copy the declaration of the `ModelNode` class completely over into another header file and change the name of the copy to `ProductionModelNode`. Here is a portion of the declaration for the copied class:

```
// ProductionModelNode.h
class ProductionModeNode
{
private:
    list<ModelNode *>    m_interiorNodes;
    list<ModelNode *>    m_exteriorNodes;
    double               m_weight;
    void                 createSpanningLinks();
public:
    void addExteriorNode(ModelNode *newNode);
    void addInternalNode(ModelNode *newNode);
    void colorize();
    ...
};
```

The next step is to go back to the `ModelNode` header and strip out all non-public variable declarations and method declarations. Next, we make all of the remaining public methods pure virtual (abstract):

```
// ModelNode.h
class ModelNode
{
public:
    virtual void addExteriorNode(ModelNode *newNode) = 0;
    virtual void addInternalNode(ModelNode *newNode) = 0;
    virtual void colorize() = 0;
    ...
};
```

At this point, `ModelNode` is a pure interface. It contains only abstract methods. We are working in C++, so we should also declare a pure virtual destructor and define it an implementation file:

```
// ModelNode.h
class ModelNode
{
public:
    virtual         ~ModelNode () = 0;
    virtual void     addExteriorNode(ModelNode *newNode) = 0;
    virtual void     addInternalNode(ModelNode *newNode) = 0;
    virtual void     colorize() = 0;
    ...
};

// ModelNode.cpp
ModelNode::~ModelNode()
```

```
{}
```

Now we go back to the ProductionModelNode class and make it inherit the new interface class:


```
#include "ModelNode.h"
class ProductionModelNode : public ModelNode
{
private:
    list<ModelNode *>    m_interiorNodes;
    list<ModelNode *>    m_exteriorNodes;

    double               m_weight;
    void                 createSpanningLinks();

public:
    void addExteriorNode(ModelNode *newNode);
    void addInternalNode(ModelNode *newNode);
    void colorize();
    ...

};
```

At this point, ProductionModelNode should compile cleanly. If you build the rest of the system, you'll find the places where the people attempt to instantiate ModelNodes. You can change them so that ProductionModelNodes are created instead. In this refactoring, we're replacing the creation of objects of one concrete class with objects of another, so we aren't really making our overall dependency situation better. However, it's good to take a look at those areas of object creation and try to figure out whether a factory can be used to reduce dependencies further.

Steps

To *Extract Implementer*, follow these steps:

1. Make a copy of the source class's declaration. Give it a different name. It's useful to have a naming convention for classes you've extracted. I often use the prefix Production to indicate that the new class is the production code implementer of an interface.

2. Turn the source class into an interface by deleting all non-public methods and all variables.

3. Make all of the remaining public methods abstract. If you are working in C++, make sure that none of the methods that you make abstract are overridden by non-virtual methods.

4. Examine all imports or file inclusions in the interface file, and see if they are necessary. Often you can remove many of them. You can *Lean on the Compiler (315)* to detect these. Just delete each in turn, and recompile to see if it is needed.

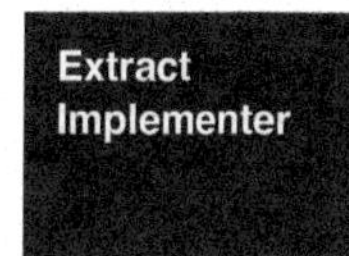

5. Make your production class implement the new interface.
6. Compile the production class to make sure that all method signatures in the interface are implemented.
7. Compile the rest of the system to find all of the places where instances of the source class were created. Replace these with creations of the new production class.
8. Recompile and test.

A More Complex Example

Extract Implementer is relatively simple when the source class doesn't have any parent or child classes in its inheritance hierarchy. When it does, we have to be a little cleverer. Figure 25.2 shows `ModelNode` again, but in Java with a superclass and a subclass:

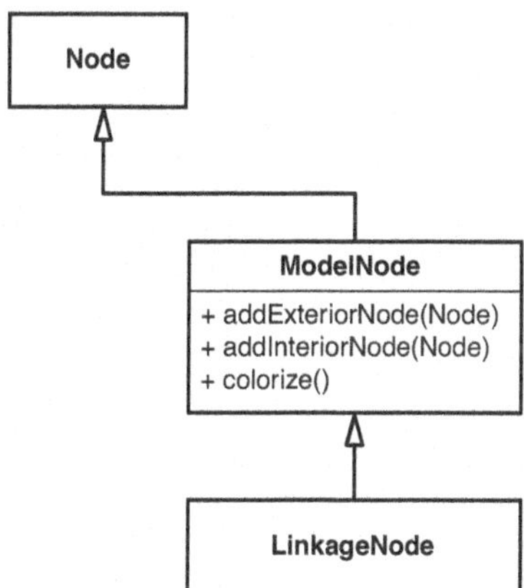

Figure 25.2 `ModelNode` *with superclass and subclass.*

In this design, `Node`, `ModelNode`, and `LinkageNode` are all concrete classes. `ModelNode` uses protected methods from `Node`. It also supplies methods that are used by its subclass, `LinkageNode`. *Extract Implementer* requires a concrete class that can be converted into an interface. Afterward, you have an interface and a concrete class.

Here's what we can do in this situation. We can perform *Extract Implementer* on the Node class, placing the ProductionNode class below Node in the inheritance hierarchy. We also change the inheritance relationship so that ModelNode inherits ProductionNode rather than Node. Figure 25.3 shows what the design looks like afterward.

Extract Implementer

Next, we do *Extract Implementer* on ModelNode. Because ModelNode already has a subclass, we introduce a ProductionModelNode into the hierarchy between ModelNode and LinkageNode. When we've done that, we can make the ModelNode interface extend Node as shown in Figure 25.4.

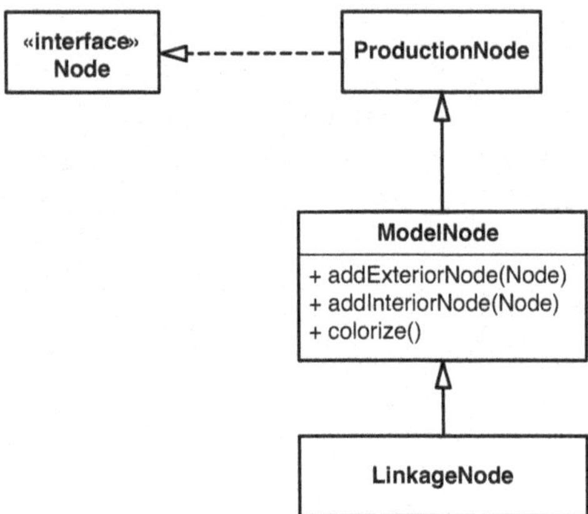

Figure 25.3 *After Extract Implementer on* Node.

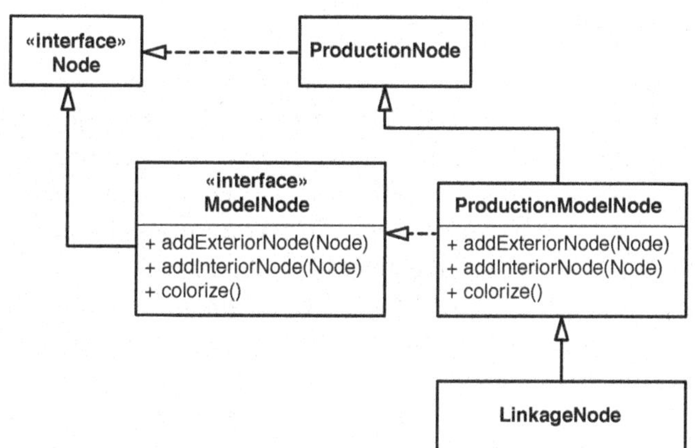

Figure 25.4 *Extract Implementer on* `ModelNode`.

When you have a class embedded in a hierarchy like this, you really have to consider whether you are better off using *Extract Interface (362)* and picking different names for your interfaces. It is a far more direct refactoring.

Extract Interface

Extract Interface

In many languages, *Extract Interface* is a one of the safest dependency-breaking techniques. If you get a step wrong, the compiler tells you immediately, so there is very little chance of introducing a bug. The gist of it is that you create an interface for a class with declarations for all of the methods that you want to use in some context. When you've done that, you can implement the interface to sense or separate, passing a fake object into the class you want to test.

There are at least three ways of doing *Extract Interface* and a couple of little "gotchas" to pay attention to. The first way is to use automated refactoring support if you are lucky enough to have it. Tools that support this usually provide some way of selecting methods on a class and typing in the name of the new interface. Really good ones ask you if you want to have them search through the code and find places where they can change references to use the new interface. Tools like that can save you a lot of work.

If you don't have automated support for interface extraction, you can use the second way of extracting a method: You can extract it incrementally using the steps I outline in this section.

The third way of extracting an interface is to cut/copy and paste several methods from a class at once and place their declarations in an interface. It isn't as safe as the first two methods, but it still is pretty safe, and often it is the only practical way of extracting an interface when you don't have automated support and your builds take a very long time.

Let's extract an interface using the second method. Along the way, we'll discuss some of the things to watch out for.

We need to extract an interface to bring a `PaydayTransaction` class under test. Figure 25.5 shows `PaydayTransaction` and one of its dependencies, a class named `TransactionLog`.

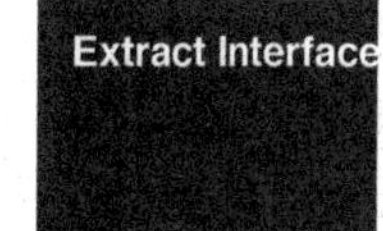

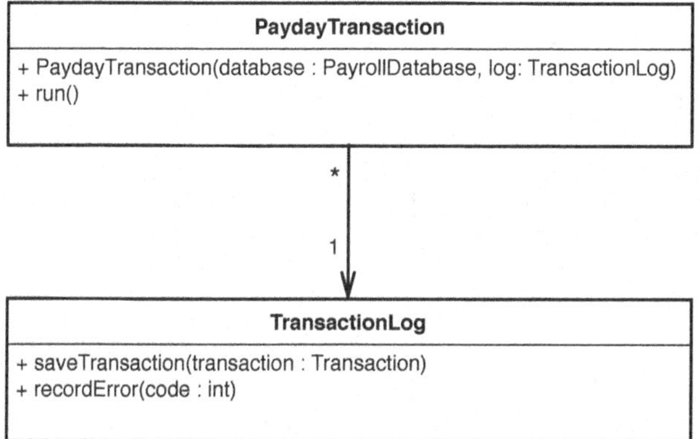

Figure 25.5 `PaydayTransaction` *depending on* `TransactionLog`.

Here's our first attempt at a test case:

```
void testPayday()
{
    Transaction t = new PaydayTransaction(getTestingDatabase());
    t.run();

    assertEquals(getSampleCheck(12),
              getTestingDatabase().findCheck(12));
}
```

But we have to pass in some sort of a `TransactionLog` to make it compile. Let's create a call to a class that doesn't exist yet, `FakeTransactionLog`.

```
void testPayday()
{
    FakeTransactionLog aLog = new FakeTransactionLog();
    Transaction t = new PaydayTransaction(
                        getTestingDatabase(),
                        aLog);
    t.run();

    assertEquals(getSampleCheck(12),
              getTestingDatabase().findCheck(12));
}
```

To make this code compile, we have to extract an interface for the `TransactionLog` class, make a class named `FakeTransactionLog` implement the interface, and then make it possible for `PaydayTransaction` to accept a `FakeTransactionLog`.

First things first: We extract the interface. We create a new empty class called TransactionRecorder. If you are wondering where that name came from, take a look at the following note.

Extract Interface

Interface Naming

Interfaces are relatively new as programming constructs. Java and many .NET languages have them. In C++, you have to mimic them by creating a class that contains nothing but pure virtual functions.

When interfaces were first introduced in languages, some people started naming interfaces by placing an *I* before the name of the class they were gleaned from. For instance, if you had an Account class and you wanted an interface, you could give it the name IAccount. The advantage to this sort of naming is that you don't really have to think about the name when you do the extraction. Naming is as simple as adding a prefix. The disadvantage is that you end up with a lot of code that has to know whether it is dealing with an interface. Ideally, it shouldn't care one way or another. You also end up with a code base in which some names have *I* prefixes and some don't. Removing the *I* if you want to go back to a regular class ends up being a pervasive change. If you don't make the change, the name stays in the code as a subtle lie.

When you are developing new classes, the easiest thing to do is create simple class names, even for big abstractions. For instance, if we are writing an accounting package, we can start with a class that is just called Account. Then we can start to write tests to add new functionality. At some point, you might want Account to be an interface. If you do, you can create a subclass underneath it, push down all of the data and methods, and make Account an interface. When you do that, you don't have to go through your code renaming the type of every reference to Account.

In cases such as the PaydayTransaction example, in which we already have a nice name for an interface (TransactionLog), we can do the same thing. The downside is that pushing down data and methods to a new subclass takes a lot of steps. But when the risk is small enough, I use it sometimes. This technique is called *Extract Implementer (356)*.

If I don't have many tests and I want to extract an interface to get more in place, I often try to come up with a new name for the interface. Sometimes it takes a little while to think of one. If you don't have tools that will rename classes for you, it pays to try to solidify the name that you want to use before the number of places that use it grows too large.

```
interface TransactionRecorder
{
}
```

Now we move back and make TransactionLog implement the new interface.

```
public class TransactionLog implements TransactionRecorder
{
    ...
}
```

Next we create FakeTransactionLog as an empty class.

```
public class FakeTransactionLog implements TransactionRecorder
{
}
```


Everything should compile fine because all we've done is introduce a few new classes and change a class so that it implements an empty interface.

At this point, we launch into the refactoring full force. We change the type of each reference in the places where we want to use the interface. PaydayTransaction uses a TransactionLog; we need to change it so that it uses a TransactionRecorder. When we've done that, when we compile, we find a bunch of cases in which methods are being called from a TransactionRecorder, and we can get rid of the errors one by one by adding method declarations to the TransactionRecorder interface and empty method definitions to the FakeTransactionLog.

Here's an example:

```
public class PaydayTransaction extends Transaction
{
    public PaydayTransaction(PayrollDatabase db,
                             TransactionRecorder log) {
        super(db, log);
    }

    public void run() {
        for(Iterator it = db.getEmployees(); it.hasNext(); ) {
            Employee e = (Employee)it.next();
            if (e.isPayday(date)) {
                e.pay();
            }
        }
        log.saveTransaction(this);
    }
    ...
}
```

In this case, the only method that we are calling on TransactionRecorder is saveTransaction. Because TransactionRecorder doesn't have a saveTransaction method yet, we get a compile error. We can make our test compile just by adding that method to TransactionRecorder and FakeTransactionLog.

```
interface TransactionRecorder
{
    void saveTransaction(Transaction transaction);
}

public class FakeTransactionLog implements TransactionRecorder
{
```

```
    void saveTransaction(Transaction transaction) {
    }
}
```


And we are done. We don't have to create a real TransactionLog in our tests.

You might look at this and say, "Well, it isn't really done; we haven't added the recordError method to the interface and the fake." True, the recordError method is there on TransactionLog. If we needed to extract the whole interface, would have added a signature for that method also, but the fact is, we didn't need it for the test. Although it's nice to have an interface that covers all of the public methods of a class, if we march down that road, we could end up doing much more work than we need to bring a piece of the application under test. If you have your sights on a design in which certain key abstractions have interfaces that completely cover a set of public methods on their classes, remember that you can get there incrementally. At times, it is better to hold off until you can get more test coverage before making a pervasive change.

> When you extract an interface, you don't have to extract all of the public methods on the class you are extracting from. *Lean on the Compiler (315)* to find the ones that are being used.

In most cases, interface extraction is easy. It only becomes difficult when you are dealing with non-virtual methods. In Java, these could be static methods. Languages such as C# and C++ also allow non-virtual instance methods. For more details about dealing with these, see the accompanying sidebar.

Steps

To *Extract Interface* without automated support, follow these steps:

1. Create a new interface with the name you'd like to use. Don't add any methods to it yet.
2. Make the class that you are extracting from implement the interface. This can't break anything because the interface doesn't have any methods. But it is good to compile and run your test just to verify that.
3. Change the place where you want to use the object so that it uses the interface rather than the original class.
4. Compile the system and introduce a new method declaration on the interface for each method use that the compiler reports as an error.

Extract Interface and Non-Virtual Functions

If you have a call like this in your code: `bondRegistry.newFixedYield(client)` in many languages, it is hard to tell by looking at it whether the method is a static method or a virtual or non-virtual instance method. In languages that allow non-virtual instance methods, you can get into some trouble if you extract an interface and add the signature of one of the classes non-virtual methods to it. In general, if your class has no subclasses, you can make the method virtual and then extract the interface. Everything will be fine. But if your class has subclasses, pulling the method signature up into an interface can break the code. Here is an example in C++. We have a class with a non-virtual method:

```
class BondRegistry
{
public:
    Bond *newFixedYield(Client *client) { ... }
};
```

And we have a subclass that has a method with the same name and signature:

```
class PremiumRegistry : public BondRegistry
{
public:
    Bond *newFixedYield(Client *client) { ... }
};
```

If we extract an interface from `BondRegistry`:

```
class BondProvider
{
public:
    virtual Bond *newFixedYield(Client *client) = 0;
};
```

and have `BondRegistry` implement it:

```
class BondRegistry : public BondProvider { … };
```

(continues)

Extract Interface

we could break code that looks like this by passing in a PremiumRegistry:

```
void disperse(BondRegistry *registry) {
    ...
    Bond *bond = registry->newFixedYield(existingClient);
    ...
}
```

Before we extracted the interface, BondRegistry's newFixedYield method was called because the compile-time type of the registry variable is BondRegistry. If we make newFixedYield virtual in the process of extracting the interface, we change the behavior. The method on PremiumBondRegistry is called. In C++, when we make a method virtual in a base class, methods that override it in subclasses become virtual. Note that we don't have this problem in Java or C#. In Java, all instance methods are virtual. In C#, things are a little safer because adding an interface does not affect existing calls to non-virtual methods.

In general, creating a method in a derived class with the same signature as a non-virtual method in the base isn't good practice in C++ because it can lead to misunderstandings. If you want to have access to a non-virtual function through an interface and it isn't on a class with no subclasses, the best thing to do is add a new virtual method with a new name. That method can delegate to a non-virtual or even a static method. You just have to make sure that the method does the right thing for all of the subclasses below the one that you are extracting from.

Introduce Instance Delegator

People use static methods on classes for many reasons. One of the most common reasons is to implement the *Singleton Design Pattern (372)*. Another common reason to use static methods is to create utility classes.

Utility classes are pretty easy to find in many designs. They are classes that don't have any instance variables or instance methods. Instead, they consist of a set of static methods and constants.

People create utility classes for many reasons. Most of the time, they are created when it is hard to find a common abstraction for a set of methods. The `Math` class in the Java JDK is an example of this. It has static methods for trigonometric functions (cos, sin, tan) and many others. When languages designers build their languages from objects "all the way down," they make sure that numeric primitives know how do these things. For instance, you should be able to call the method `sin()` on the object `1` or any other numeric object and get the right result. At the time of this writing, Java does not support math methods on primitive types, so the utility class is a fair solution, but it is also a special case. In nearly all cases, you can use plain old classes with instance data and methods to do your work.

If you have static methods in your project, chances are good that you won't run into any trouble with them unless they contain something that is difficult to depend on in a test. (The technical term for this is *static cling)*. In these cases, you might wish that you could use an *object seam (40)* to substitute in some other behavior when the static methods are called. What do you do in this case?

One thing that can do is start to introduce delegating instance methods on the class. When you do this, you have to find a way to replace the static calls with method calls on an object. Here is an example:

```
public class BankingServices
{
    public static void updateAccountBalance(int userID,
                                            Money amount) {
        ...
    }
    ...
}
```

Here we've got a class that contains nothing but static methods. I've shown only one here, but you get the idea. We can add an instance method to the class like this and have it delegate to the static method:

```
public class BankingServices
{
```

Introduce Instance Delegator

```
    public static void updateAccountBalance(int userID,
                                            Money amount) {
        ...
    }

    public void updateBalance(int userID, Money amount) {
        updateAccountBalance(userID, amount);
    }
    ...
}
```

In this case, we've added an instance method named updateBalance and made it delegate to the static method updateAccountBalance.

Now in the calling code, we can replace references like this:

```
public class SomeClass
{
    public void someMethod() {
        ...
        BankingServices.updateAccountBalance(id, sum);
    }
}
```

with this:

```
public class SomeClass
{
    public void someMethod(BankingServices services) {
        ...
        services.updateBalance(id, sum)
    }
    ...
}
```

Notice that we can pull this off only if we can find some way to externally create the BankingServices object that we are using. It is an additional refactoring step, but in statically typed languages, we can *Lean on the Compiler (315)* to get the object in place.

This technique is straightforward enough with many static methods, but when you start to do it with utility classes, you might start to feel uncomfortable. A class with 5 or 10 static methods and only one or two instance methods does look weird. It looks even weirder when they are just simple methods delegating to static methods. But when you use this technique, you can get an object seam in place easily and substitute different behaviors under test. Over time, you might get to the point that every call to the utility class comes through the delegating methods. At that time, you can move the bodies of the static methods into the instance methods and delete the static methods.

Steps

To *Introduce Instance Delegator*, follow these steps:

1. Identify a static method that is problematic to use in a test.
2. Create an instance method for the method on the class. Remember to *Preserve Signatures (312)*. Make the instance method delegate to the static method.
3. Find places where the static methods are used in the class you have under test. Use *Parameterize Method (383)* or another dependency-breaking technique to supply an instance to the location where the static method call was made.
4. Replace the problematic call to the original static method with a call to the delegator on the instance introduced in step 3.

Introduce Static Setter

Maybe I am a purist, but I don't like global mutable data. When I visit teams, it is usually the most apparent hurdle to getting portions of their system into test harnesses. You want to pull out a set of classes into a test harness, but you discover that some of them need to be set up in particular states to be used at all. When you have your harness set up, you have to run down the list of globals to make sure that each one has the state you need for the condition you want to test. Quantum physicists didn't discover "spooky action at a distance"; in software, we've had it for years.

All griping about globals aside, many systems have them. In some systems, they are very direct and un-self-conscious; someone just declared a variable someplace. In others, they are dressed up as singletons with strict adherence to the *Singleton Design Pattern*. In any case, getting a fake in place for sensing is very straightforward. If the variable is an unabashed global, sitting outside a class or plainly out in the open as a public static variable, you can just replace the object. If the reference is `const` or `final`, you might have to remove that protection. Leave a comment in the code saying that you are doing it for test and that people shouldn't take advantage of the access in production code.

The Singleton Design Pattern

The *Singleton Design Pattern* is a pattern that many people use to make sure that there can only be one instance of a particular class in a program. There are three characteristics that most singletons share:

1. The constructors of a singleton class are usually made private.

2. A static member of the class holds the only instance of the class that will ever be created in the program.

3. A static method is used to provide access to the instance. Usually this method is named `instance` or `getInstance`.

Although singletons do prevent people from making more than one instance of a class in production code, they also prevent people from making more than one instance of a class in a test harness.

Replacing singletons is just a little more work. Add a static setter to the singleton to replace the instance, and then make the constructor protected. You can then subclass the singleton, create a fresh object, and pass it to the setter.

You might be left a little queasy by the idea that you are removing access protection when you use static setter, but remember that the purpose of access protection is to prevent errors. We are putting in tests to prevent errors also. It just turns out that, in this case, we need the stronger tool.

Here is an example of *Introduce Static Setter* in C++:

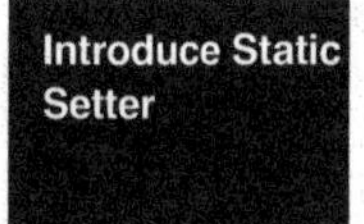


```
void MessageRouter::route(Message *message) {
    ...
    Dispatcher *dispatcher
            = ExternalRouter::instance()->getDispatcher();
    if (dispatcher != NULL)
        dispatcher->sendMessage(message);
}
```

In the `MessageRouter` class, we use singletons in a couple of places to get dispatchers. The `ExternalRouter` class is one of those singletons. It uses a static method named `instance` to provide access to the one and only instance of `ExternalRouter`. The `ExternalRouter` class has a getter for a dispatcher. We can replace the dispatcher with another one by replacing the external router that serves it.

This is what the `ExternalRouter` class looks like before we introduce the static setter:

```
class ExternalRouter
{
private:
    static ExternalRouter *_instance;
public:
    static ExternalRouter *instance();
    ...
};

ExternalRouter *ExternalRouter::_instance = 0;

ExternalRouter *ExternalRouter::instance()
{
    if (_instance == 0) {
        _instance = new ExternalRouter;
    }
    return _instance;
}
```

Notice that the router is created on the first call to the `instance` method. To substitute in another router, we have to change what `instance` returns. The first step is to introduce a new method to replace the instance.

```
void ExternalRouter::setTestingInstance(ExternalRouter *newInstance)
{
    delete _instance;
    _instance = newInstance;
}
```

Introduce Static Setter

Of course, this assumes that we are able to create a new instance. When people use the singleton pattern, they often make the constructor of the class private to prevent people from creating more than one instance. If you make the constructor protected, you can subclass the singleton to sense or separate and pass the new instance to the `setTestingInstance` method. In the previous example, we'd make a subclass of `ExternalRouter` named `TestingExternalRouter` and override the `getDispatcher` method so that it returns the dispatcher we want, a fake dispatcher.

```
class TestingExternalRouter : public ExternalRouter
{
public:
    virtual void Dispatcher *getDispatcher() const {
        return new FakeDispatcher;
    }
};
```

This might look like a rather roundabout way of substituting in a new dispatcher. We end up creating a new `ExternalRouter` just to substitute dispatchers. We can take some shortcuts, but they have different tradeoffs. Another thing that we can do is add a boolean flag to `ExternalRouter` and let it return a different dispatcher when the flag is set. In C++ or C#, we can use conditional compilation to select dispatchers also. These techniques can work well, but they are invasive and can get unwieldy if you use them throughout an application. In general, I like to keep separation between production and test code.

Using a setter method and a protected constructor on a singleton is mildly invasive, but it does help you get tests in place. Could people misuse the public constructor and make more than one singleton in the production system? Yes, but in my opinion, if it is important to have only one instance of an object in a system, the best way to handle it is to make sure everyone on the team understands that constraint.

> One alternative to decreasing constructor protection and subclassing is to use *Extract Interface (362)* on the singleton class and supply a setter that accepts an object with that interface. The downside of this is that you have to change the type of the reference you use to hold the singleton in the class and the type of the return value of the `instance` method. These changes can be quite involved, and they don't really move us to a better state. The ultimate "better state" is to reduce global references to the singleton to the point that it can just become a normal class.

In the previous example, we replaced a singleton using a static setter. The singleton was an object that served up another object, a dispatcher. Occasionally, we see a different kind of global in systems, a global factory. Rather than holding on to an instance, they serve up fresh objects every time you call one of

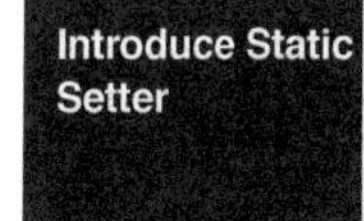

their static methods. Substituting in another object to return is kind of tricky, but often you can do it by having the factory delegate to another factory. Let's take a look at an example in Java:

```
public class RouterFactory
{
    static Router makeRouter() {
        return new EWNRouter();
    }
}
```

RouterFactory is a straightforward global factory. As it stands, it doesn't allow us to replace the routers it serves under test, but we can alter it so that it can.

```
interface RouterServer
{
    Router makeRouter();
}

public class RouterFactory
{
    static Router makeRouter() {
        return server.makeRouter();
    }

    static setServer(RouterServer server) {
        this.server = server;
    }

    static RouterServer server = new RouterServer() {
        public RouterServer makeRouter() {
            return new EWNRouter();
        }
    };
}
```

In a test, we can do this:

```
protected void setUp() {
    RouterServer.setServer(new RouterServer() {
        public RouterServer makeRouter() {
            return new FakeRouter();
        }
    });
}
```

It is important to remember that in any of these static setter patterns, you are modifying state that is available to all tests. You can use the tearDown method in xUnit testing frameworks to put things back into some known state before the rest of your tests execute. In general, I do that only when using the wrong state in the next test could be misleading. If I am substituting in a fake MailSender in all of my tests, putting in another doesn't make much sense. On the other hand, if I have global that keeps state that affects the results of the system, often I do the same thing in the setUp and tearDown methods to make sure that I've left things in a clean state:


```
protected void setUp() {
    Node.count = 0;
    ...
}

protected void tearDown() {
    Node.count = 0;
}
```

At this point, I'm imagining you with my mind's eye. You are sitting there disgusted at the carnage that I am wreaking on the system just to be able to get some tests in place. And you are right: These patterns can uglify parts of a system considerably. Surgery is never pretty, particularly at the beginning. What can you do to get the system back to a decent state?

One thing to consider is parameter passing. Take a look at the classes that need access to your global and consider whether you can give them a common superclass. If you can, you can pass the global to them upon creation and slowly move away from having globals at all. Often people are scared that every class in the system will require some global. Often you'll be surprised. I once worked on an embedded system that encapsulated memory management and error reporting as classes, passing a memory object or error reporter to whoever needed it. Over time, there was a clean separation between classes that needed those services and classes that didn't. The ones that needed them just had a common superclass. The objects that were passed throughout the system were created at the start of the program, and it was barely noticeable.

Steps

To *Introduce Static Setter*, follow these steps:

1. Decrease the protection of the constructor so that you can make a fake by subclassing the singleton.

2. Add a static setter to the singleton class. The setter should accept a reference to the singleton class. Make sure that the setter destroys the singleton instance properly before setting the new object.

3. If you need access to private or protected methods in the singleton to set it up properly for testing, consider subclassing it or extracting an interface and making the singleton hold its instance as reference whose type is the type of the interface.

Link Substitution

Object orientation gives us wonderful opportunities to substitute one object for another. If two classes implement the same interface or have the same superclass, you can substitute one for another pretty easily. Unfortunately, people working in procedural languages such as C don't have that option. When you have a function like this, there is no way to substitute one function for another at compile time, short of using the preprocessor:

```
void account_deposit(int amount);
```

Are there other alternatives? Yes, you can *Link Substitution* to replace one function with another. To do this, create a dummy library that has functions with the same signatures as the functions that you want to fake. If you are sensing, you need to set up some mechanism for saving notifications and querying them. You can use files, global variables, or anything that would be convenient under test.

Here is an example:

```
void account_deposit(int amount)
{
    struct Call *call =
        (struct Call *)calloc(1, sizeof (struct Call));
    call->type = ACC_DEPOSIT;
    call->arg0 = amount;
    append(g_calls, call);
}
```

In this case, we are interested in sensing, so we create a global list of calls to record each time that this function (or any other one we are faking) is called. In a test, we could check the list after we exercise a set of objects and see if the mocked functions were called in the appropriate order.

I've never tried to use *Link Substitution* with C++ classes, but I suppose that it is possible. I'm sure that the mangled names that C++ compilers produce would make it rather difficult; however, when making calls to C functions, it is very practical. The most useful case is when faking external libraries. The best libraries to fake are those that are mostly pure data sinks: You call functions in them, but you don't often care about the return values. For example, graphics libraries are particularly useful to fake with *Link Substitution*.

Link Substitution can also be used in Java. Create classes with the same names and methods, and change your classpath so that calls resolve to them rather than the classes with bad dependencies.

Steps

To use *Link Substitution*, follow these steps:

1. Identify the functions or classes that you want to fake.
2. Produce alternative definitions for them.
3. Adjust your build so that the alternative definitions are included rather than the production versions.

Parameterize Constructor

If you are creating an object in a constructor, often the easiest way to replace it is to externalize its creation, create the object outside the class, and make clients pass it into the constructor as a parameter. Here is an example.

We start with this:

```
public class MailChecker
{
    public MailChecker (int checkPeriodSeconds) {
        this.receiver = new MailReceiver();
        this.checkPeriodSeconds = checkPeriodSeconds;
    }
    ...
}
```

Then we introduce a new parameter like this:

```
public class MailChecker
{
    public MailChecker (MailReceiver receiver,
                        int checkPeriodSeconds) {
        this.receiver = receiver;
        this.checkPeriodSeconds = checkPeriodSeconds;
    }
    ...
}
```

One reason people don't often think of this technique is that they assume that it forces all clients to pass an additional argument. However, you can write a constructor that keeps the original signature around:

```
public class MailChecker
{
    public MailChecker (int checkPeriodSeconds) {
        this(new MailReceiver(), checkPeriodSeconds);
    }

    public MailChecker (MailReceiver receiver,
                        int checkPeriodSeconds) {
        this.receiver = receiver;
        this.checkPeriodSeconds = checkPeriodSeconds;
    }
    ...

}
```

If you do, you can supply different objects for testing, and the clients of the class don't have to know the difference.

Parameterize Constructor

Let's do it step by step. Here is our original code:

```
public class MailChecker
{
    public MailChecker (int checkPeriodSeconds) {
        this.receiver = new MailReceiver();
        this.checkPeriodSeconds = checkPeriodSeconds;
    }
    ...
}
```

We make a copy of the constructor:

```
public class MailChecker
{
    public MailChecker (int checkPeriodSeconds) {
        this.receiver = new MailReceiver();
        this.checkPeriodSeconds = checkPeriodSeconds;
    }

    public MailChecker (int checkPeriodSeconds) {
        this.receiver = new MailReceiver();
        this.checkPeriodSeconds = checkPeriodSeconds;
    }
    ...
}
```

Then we add a parameter to it for the `MailReceiver`:

```
public class MailChecker
{
    public MailChecker (int checkPeriodSeconds) {
        this.receiver = new MailReceiver();
        this.checkPeriodSeconds = checkPeriodSeconds;
    }

    public MailChecker (MailReceiver receiver,
                        int checkPeriodSeconds) {
        this.receiver = new MailReceiver();
        this.checkPeriodSeconds = checkPeriodSeconds;
    }
    ...
}
```

Next we assign that parameter to the instance variable, getting rid of the `new` expression.

```
public class MailChecker
{
    public MailChecker (int checkPeriodSeconds) {
        this.receiver = new MailReceiver();
        this.checkPeriodSeconds = checkPeriodSeconds;
```

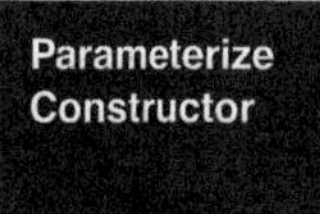


```
    }

    public MailChecker (MailReceiver receiver,
                        int checkPeriodSeconds) {
        this.receiver = receiver;
        this.checkPeriodSeconds = checkPeriodSeconds;
    }

    ...
}
```

Now, we go back to the original constructor and remove its body, replacing it with a call to the new constructor. The original constructor uses `new` to create the parameter it needs to pass.

```
public class MailChecker
{
    public MailChecker (int checkPeriodSeconds) {
        this(new MailReceiver(), checkPeriodSeconds);
    }

    public MailChecker (MailReceiver receiver,
                        int checkPeriodSeconds) {
        this.receiver = receiver;
        this.checkPeriodSeconds = checkPeriodSeconds;
    }
    ...
}
```

Are there any downsides to this technique? Actually, yes, there is one. When we add a new parameter to a constructor, we are opening the door to further dependencies on the parameter's class. Users of the class can use the new constructor in production code and increase dependencies across the system. However, in general, that is a rather small concern. *Parameterize Constructor* is a very easy refactoring and it is one that I tend to use a lot.

> In languages that allow default arguments, there is a simpler way of doing Parameterize Constructor. We can simply add a default argument to the existing constructor:

Here is a constructor that has been parameterized this way in C++:

```
class AssemblyPoint
{
public:
    AssemblyPoint(EquipmentDispatcher *dispatcher
                  = new EquipmentDispatcher);
    ...
};
```

There is only one downside when we do this in C++. The header file containing this class declaration has to include the header for `EquipmentDispatcher`. If it wasn't for the constructor call, we might have been able to use a forward declaration for `EquipmentDispatcher`. For this reason, I don't use default arguments often in C++.

Steps

To *Parameterize Constructor*, follow these steps:

1. Identify the constructor that you want to parameterize and make a copy of it.
2. Add a parameter to the constructor for the object whose creation you are going to replace. Remove the object creation and add an assignment from the parameter to the instance variable for the object.
3. If you can call a constructor from a constructor in your language, remove the body of the old constructor and replace it with a call to the old constructor. Add a new expression to the call of the new constructor in the old constructor. If you can't call a constructor from another constructor in your language, you may have to extract any duplication among the constructors to a new method.

Parameterize Method

You have a method that creates an object internally, and you want to replace the object to sense or separate. Often the easiest way to do this is to pass the object from the outside. Here is an example in C++:


```
void TestCase::run() {
    delete m_result; m_result=0;
    m_result = new TestResult;
    try {
        setUp();
        runTest(m_result);
    }
    catch (exception& e) {
        result->addFailure(e, this);
    }
    tearDown();
}
```

Here we have a method that creates a TestResult object whenever it is called. If we want to sense or separate, we can pass it as a parameter.

```
void TestCase::run(TestResult *result) {
    delete m_result;
    m_result = result;
    try {
        setUp();
        runTest(m_result);
    }
    catch (exception& e) {
        result->addFailure(e, this);
    }
    tearDown();
}
```

We can use a little forwarding method that keeps the original signature intact:

```
void TestCase::run() {
    run(new TestResult);
}
```

Parameterize Method

> In C++, Java, C#, and many other languages, you can have two methods with the same name on a class, as long as the signatures are different. In the example, we take advantage of this and use the same name for the new parameterized method and the original method. Although this saves some work, at times it can be confusing. An alternative is to use the type of the parameter in the name of the new method. For instance, in this case, we could keep `run()` as the name of the original method but call the new method `runWithTestResult(TestResult)`.

As with *Parameterize Constructor (379)*, *Parameterize Method* can allow clients to become dependent on new types that were used in the class before but were not present at the interface. If I think that this will become an issue, I consider *Extract and Override Factory Method (350)* instead.

Steps

To *Parameterize Method*, follow these steps:

1. Identify the method that you want to replace and make a copy of it.
2. Add a parameter to the method for the object whose creation you are going to replace. Remove the object creation and add an assignment from the parameter to the variable that holds the object.
3. Delete the body of the copied method and make a call to the parameterized method, using the object creation expression for the original object.

Primitivize Parameter

In general, the best way to make a change to a class is to create an instance in a test harness, write a test for the change you want to make, and then make the change to satisfy the test. But sometimes the amount of work that you have to do to get a class under test is ridiculously large. One team that I visited inherited a legacy system with domain classes that transitively depended on nearly every other class in the system. As if that wasn't bad enough, they all were tied into a persistence framework as well. Getting one of those classes into a testing framework would have been doable, but the team wouldn't have been able to make progress on features for a while if they spent all of that time fighting with the domain classes. To get some separation, we used this strategy. The following example has been changed to protect the innocent.

In a music-composition tool, a track contains several sequences of musical events. We need to find "dead time" in each sequence so that we can fill it with little recurring musical patterns. We need to write a method named `bool Sequence::hasGapFor(Sequence& pattern) const`. The method should return a value that indicates whether a pattern can be fit into a sequence.

Ideally, this method would be on a class named `Sequence`, but `Sequence` is one of those awful classes that would try to suck the world into our test harness when we tried to instantiate it. To start to write that method, we have to figure out how to write a test for it. The thing that makes it possible for us is that sequences have an internal representation that can be simplified. Every sequence consists of a vector of events. Unfortunately, events have the same problem as sequences: terrible dependencies that lead to build problems. Luckily, to do this calculation, we need only the durations of each event. We can write another method that will do the calculation on ints. When we have it, we can write `hasGapFor` and let it do its work by delegating to the other method.

Let's start writing the first method. Here is a test for it:

```
TEST(hasGapFor, Sequence)
{
    vector<unsigned int> baseSequence;
    baseSequence.push_back(1);
    baseSequence.push_back(0);
    baseSequence.push_back(0);

    vector<unsigned int> pattern;
    pattern.push_back(1);
    pattern.push_back(2);

    CHECK(SequenceHasGapFor(baseSequence, pattern));
}
```

The function SequenceHasGapFor is just a free function; it is not part of any class, but it operates on a representation built of primitives—in this case, unsigned integers. If we build up the functionality for SequenceHasGapFor in a testing harness, we can write a rather simple function on Sequence that delegates to the new functionality:


```
bool Sequence::hasGapFor(Sequence& pattern) const
{
    vector<unsigned int> baseRepresentation
            = getDurationsCopy();

    vector<unsigned int> patternRepresentation
            = pattern.getDurationsCopy();

    return SequenceHasGapFor(baseRepresentation,
                             patternRepresentation);
}
```

This function needs another function to get an array of the durations, so we write it:

```
vector<unsigned int> Sequence::getDurationsCopy() const
{
    vector<unsigned int> result;
    for (vector<Event>::iterator it = events.begin();
            it != events.end(); ++it) {
        result.push_back(it->duration);
    }
    return result;
}
```

At this point, we've been able to get the feature in, but in a very poor way. Let's make a list of all of the horrible things we've done here:

1. Exposed the internal representation of Sequence.
2. Made the implementation of Sequence a little tougher to understand by pushing some of it off into a free function.
3. Written some untested code (we couldn't really write a test for getDurationsCopy()).
4. Duplicated data in the system.
5. Prolonged the problem. We haven't started to do the hard work of breaking dependencies between our domain classes and the infrastructure. (That is the one thing that will make a large difference as we move forward, and it is still ahead of us.)

In spite of all of those downsides, we were able to add a tested feature. I don't like to do this refactoring, but I will use it if my back is against the wall. Often it is a good predecessor to *Sprout Class (63)*. To see this, imagine wrapping `SequenceHasGapFor` in a class called `GapFinder`.

Primitivize Parameter (385) leaves code in a rather poor state. Overall, it is better to add the new code to the original class or to use *Sprout Class (63)* to build up some new abstractions that can serve as a base for further work. The only time I use *Primitivize Parameter* is when I feel confident that I will take the time to bring the class under test later. At that point, the function can be folded into the class as a real method.

Steps

To *Primitivize Parameter*, follow these steps:

1. Develop a free function that does the work you would need to do on the class. In the process, develop an intermediate representation that you can use to do the work.
2. Add a function to the class that builds up the representation and delegates it to the new function.

Pull Up Feature

Sometimes you have to work with a cluster of methods on a class, and the dependencies that keep you from instantiating the class are unrelated to the cluster. By "unrelated," I mean that the methods you want to work with don't directly or indirectly reference any of the bad dependencies. You could do *Expose Static Method (345)* or *Break Out Method Object (330)* repeatedly, but that wouldn't necessarily be the most direct way to deal with the dependency.

In this situation, you can pull up the cluster of methods, the feature, into an abstract superclass. When you have that abstract superclass, you can subclass it and create instances of the subclass in your tests. Here is an example:

```
public class Scheduler
{
    private List items;

    public void updateScheduleItem(ScheduleItem item)
            throws SchedulingException {
        try {
            validate(item);
        }
        catch (ConflictException e) {
            throw new SchedulingException(e);
        }
        ...
    }

    private void validate(ScheduleItem item)
            throws ConflictException {
        // make calls to a database
        ...
    }

    public int getDeadtime() {
        int result = 0;
        for (Iterator it = items.iterator(); it.hasNext(); ) {
            ScheduleItem item = (ScheduleItem)it.next();
            if (item.getType() != ScheduleItem.TRANSIENT
                    && notShared(item)) {
                result += item.getSetupTime() + clockTime();
            }
            if (item.getType() != ScheduleItem.TRANSIENT) {
                result += item.finishingTime();
            }
            else {
                result += getStandardFinish(item);
            }
```

```
        }
        return result;
    }
}
```


Suppose that we want to make modifications to getDeadTime, but we don't care about updateScheduleItem. It would be nice not to have to deal with the dependency on the database at all. We could try to make getDeadTime static, and use *Expose Static Method (345)*, but we are using many non-static features of the Scheduler class. *Break Out Method Object (330)* is another possibility, but this is a rather small method, and those dependencies on other methods and fields of the class will make the work more involved than we want it to be just to get the method under test.

Another option is to pull up the method that we care about into a superclass. When we do that, we can leave the bad dependencies in this class, where they will be out of the way for our tests. Here is what the class looks like afterward:

```
public class Scheduler extends SchedulingServices
{
    public void updateScheduleItem(ScheduleItem item)
            throws SchedulingException {
        ...
    }

    private void validate(ScheduleItem item)
            throws ConflictException {
        // make calls to the database
        ...
    }
    ...
}
```

We've pulled getDeadtime (the feature we want to test) and all of the features it uses into an abstract class.

```
public abstract class SchedulingServices
{
    protected List items;

    protected boolean notShared(ScheduleItem item) {
        ...
    }

    protected  int getClockTime() {
        ...
    }

    protected int getStandardFinish(ScheduleItem item) {
        ...
```

Pull Up Feature

```
    }

    public int getDeadtime() {
        int result = 0;
        for (Iterator it = items.iterator(); it.hasNext(); ) {
            ScheduleItem item = (ScheduleItem)it.next();
            if (item.getType() != ScheduleItem.TRANSIENT
                    && notShared(item)) {
                result += item.getSetupTime() + clockTime();
            }
            if (item.getType() != ScheduleItem.TRANSIENT) {
                result += item.finishingTime();
            }
            else {
                result += getStandardFinish(item);
            }
        }
        return result;
    }
    ...
}
```

Now we can make a *testing subclass* that allows us to access those methods in a test harness:

```
public class TestingSchedulingServices extends SchedulingServices
{
    public TestingSchedulingServices() {
    }

    public void addItem(ScheduleItem item) {
        items.add(item);
    }
}

import junit.framework.*;

class SchedulingServicesTest extends TestCase
{
    public void testGetDeadTime() {
        TestingSchedulingServices services
            = new TestingSchedulingServices();
        services.addItem(new ScheduleItem("a",
                          10, 20, ScheduleItem.BASIC));
        assertEquals(2, services.getDeadtime());
    }
    ...
}
```

So, what we've done here is pull methods that we want to test up into an abstract superclass and create a concrete subclass that we can use to test them.

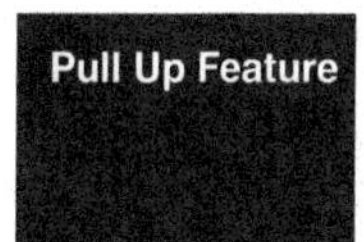

Is this a good thing? From a design point of view, it is less than ideal. We've spread a set of features across two classes just to make it easier to test. The spread can be confusing if the relationship among the features in each of the classes isn't very strong, and that is the case here. We have `Scheduler`, which is responsible for updating scheduling items, and `SchedulingServices`, which is responsible for a variety of things, including getting the default times for items and calculating the dead time. A better factoring would be to have `Scheduler` delegate to some validator object that knows how to talk to the database, but if that step looks too risky to do immediately or there are other bad dependencies, pulling up features is a good first step. If you *Preserve Signatures (312)* and *Lean on the Compiler (315)*, it is far less risky. We can move toward delegation later when more tests are in place.

Steps

To do *Pull Up Feature*, follow these steps:

1. Identify the methods that you want to pull up.
2. Create an abstract superclass for the class that contains the methods.
3. Copy the methods to the superclass and compile.
4. Copy each missing reference that the compiler alerts you about to the new superclass. Remember to *Preserve Signatures (312)* as you do this, to reduce the chance of errors.
5. When both classes compile successfully, create a subclass for the abstract class and add whatever methods you need to be able to set it up in your tests.

> You might be wondering why we make the superclass abstract. I like to make it abstract so that the code is easier to understand. It is great to be able to look at the code in an application and know that every concrete class is being used. If you search the code and find concrete classes that are not being instantiated anyplace, they could appear to be "dead code."

Push Down Dependency

Some classes have only a few problematic dependencies. If the dependencies are contained in only a few method calls, you can use *Subclass and Override Method (401)* to get them out of the way when you are writing tests. But if the dependencies are pervasive, *Subclass and Override Method* might not work. You might have to use *Extract Interface (362)* several times to remove dependencies on particular types. *Push Down Dependency* is another option. This technique helps you to separate problematic dependencies from the rest of the class, making it easier to work with in a test harness.

When you use *Push Down Dependency*, you make your current class abstract. Then you create a subclass that will be your new production class, and you push down all the problematic dependencies into that class. At that point you can subclass your original class to make its methods available for testing. Here is an example in C++:

```
class OffMarketTradeValidator : public TradeValidator
{
private:
    Trade& trade;
    bool flag;

    void showMessage() {
        int status  = AfxMessageBox(makeMessage(),
                                    MB_ABORTRETRYIGNORE);
        if (status == IDRETRY) {
            SubmitDialog dlg(this,
                    "Press okay if this is a valid trade");
            dlg.DoModal();
            if (dlg.wasSubmitted()) {
                g_dispatcher.undoLastSubmission();
                flag = true;
            }
        }
        else
        if (status == IDABORT) {
            flag = false;
        }
    }

public:
    OffMarketTradeValidator(Trade& trade)
    : trade(trade), flag(false)
    {}

    bool isValid() const {
```

```
        if (inRange(trade.getDate())
                && validDestination(trade.destination)
                && inHours(trade) {
            flag = true;
        }
        showMessage();
        return flag;
    }
    ...
};
```


If we need to make changes in our validation logic, we could be in trouble if we don't want to link UI-specific functions and classes into our test harness. *Push Down Dependency* is a good option in this case.

Here is what the code would look like after *Push Down Dependency:*

```
class OffMarketTradeValidator : public TradeValidator
{
protected:
    Trade& trade;
    bool flag;
    virtual void showMessage() = 0;

public:
    OffMarketTradeValidator(Trade& trade)
    : trade(trade), flag(false) {}

    bool isValid() const {
        if (inRange(trade.getDate())
                && validDestination(trade.destination)
                && inHours(trade) {
            flag = true;
        }
        showMessage();
        return flag;
    }
    ...
};

class WindowsOffMarketTradeValidator
        : public OffMarketTradeValidator
{
protected:
    virtual void showMessage() {
        int status  = AfxMessageBox(makeMessage(),
                            MB_ABORTRETRYIGNORE);
        if (status == IDRETRY) {
            SubmitDialog dlg(this,
                "Press okay if this is a valid trade");
            dlg.DoModal();
```

Push Down Dependency

```
            if (dlg.wasSubmitted()) {
                g_dispatcher.undoLastSubmission();
                flag = true;
            }
        }
        else
        if (status == IDABORT) {
            flag = false;
        }
    }
    ...
};
```

When we have the UI-specific work pushed down in a new subclass (`WindowsOffMarketValidator`), we can create another subclass for testing. All it has to do is null out the `showMessage` behavior:

```
class TestingOffMarketTradeValidator
        : public OffMarketTradeValidator
{
protected:
    virtual void  showMessage() {}
};
```

Now we have a class that we can test that doesn't have any dependencies on the UI. Is using inheritance in this way ideal? No, but it helps us get part of the logic of a class under test. When we have tests for `OffMarketTradeValidator`, we can start to clean up the retry logic and pull it up from the `WindowsOffMarketTradeValidator`. When only the UI calls are left, we can move toward delegating them to a new class. That new class ends up holding the only UI dependencies.

Steps

To *Push Down Dependency*, follow these steps:

1. Attempt to build the class that has dependency problems in your test harness.

2. Identify which dependencies create problems in the build.

3. Create a new subclass with a name that communicates the specific environment of those dependencies.

4. Copy the instance variables and methods that contain the bad dependencies into the new subclass, taking care to preserve signatures. Make methods protected and abstract in your original class, and make your original class abstract.

5. Create a testing subclass and change your test so that you attempt to instantiate it.

6. Build your tests to verify that you can instantiate the new class.

Replace Function with Function Pointer

Replace Function with Function Pointer

When you need to break dependencies in procedural languages, you don't have as many options as you would in object-oriented languages. You can't use *Encapsulate Global References (339)* or *Subclass and Override Method (401)*. All of those options are closed. You can use *Link Substitution (377)* or *Definition Completion (337)*, but often they are overkill for smaller bouts of dependency breaking. *Replace Function with Function Pointer* is one alternative in languages that support function pointers. The most well-known language with this support is C.

Different teams have different points of view on function pointers. On some teams, they are seen as horribly unsafe because it is possible to corrupt their contents and end up calling through some random area of memory. On other teams, they are seen as a useful tool, to be used with care. If you lean more toward the "used with care" camp, you can separate dependencies that would be difficult or impossible to otherwise.

First things first. Let's take a look at a function pointer in its natural environment. The following example shows the declaration of a few function pointers in C and a couple of calls through them:

```
struct base_operations
{
    double (*project)(double,double);
    double (*maximize)(double,double);
};

double default_projection(double first, double second) {
    return second;
}

double maximize(double first, double second) {
    return first + second;
}

void init_ops(struct base_operations *operations) {
    operations->project = default_projection;
    operations->maximize = default_maximize;
}

void run_tesselation(struct node *base,
                     struct base_operations *operations) {
    double value = operations->project(base.first, base.second);
    ...
}
```

With function pointers, you can do some very simple object-based programming, but how useful are they when breaking dependencies? Consider this scenario:

You have a networking application that stores packet information in an online database. You interact with the database through calls that look like this:


```
void db_store(
    struct receive_record *record,
    struct time_stamp receive_time);
struct receive_record * db_retrieve(time_stamp search_time);
```

We could use *Link Substitution (377)* to link to new bodies for these functions, but sometimes *Link Substitution* causes nontrivial build changes. We might have to break down libraries to separate out the functions that we want to fake. More important, the seams we get with *Link Substitution* are not the sort you'd want exploit to vary behavior in production code. If you want to get your code under test and provide flexibility to, for instance, vary the type of database that your code can talk to, *Replace Function with Function Pointer* can be useful. Let's go through the steps:

First we find the declaration of the function that we want to replace.

```
// db.h
void db_store(struct receive_record *record,
              struct time_stamp receive_time);
```

Then we declare a function pointer with the same name.

```
// db.h
void db_store(struct receive_record *record,
              struct time_stamp receive_time);

void (*db_store)(struct receive_record *record,
                 struct time_stamp receive_time);
```

Now we rename the original declaration

```
// db.h
void db_store_production(struct receive_record *record,
                         struct time_stamp receive_time);

void (*db_store)(struct receive_record *record,
                 struct time_stamp receive_time);
```

Then we initialize the pointer in a C source file:

```
// main.c
extern void db_store_production(
                struct receive_record *record,
                struct time_stamp receive_time);

void initializeEnvironment() {
```

```
    db_store = db_store_production;
    ...
}

int main(int ac, char **av) {
    initializeEnvironment();
    ...
}
```

Now we find the definition of the db_store function and rename it `db_store_production`.

```
// db.c
void db_store_production(
        struct receive_record *record,
        struct time_stamp receive_time) {
    ...
}
```

We can now compile and test.

With the function pointers in place, tests can provide alternative definitions for sensing or separation.

> *Replace Function with Function Pointer* is a good way to break dependencies. One of the nice things about it is that it happens completely at compile time, so it has minimal impact on your build system. However, if you are using this technique in C, consider upgrading to C++ so that you can take advantage of all of the other seams that C++ provides you. At the time of this writing, many C compilers offer switches to allow you to do mixed C and C++ compilation. When you use this feature, you can migrate your C project to C++ slowly, taking only the files that you care to break dependencies in first.

Steps

To use *Replace Function with Function Pointer*, do the following:

1. Find the declarations of the functions you want to replace.
2. Create function pointers with the same names before each function declaration.
3. Rename the original function declarations so that their names are not the same as the function pointers you've just declared.
4. Initialize the pointers to the addresses of the old functions in a C file.
5. Run a build to find the bodies of the old functions. Rename them to the new function names.

Replace Global Reference with Getter

Global variables can be a real pain when you want to work with pieces of code independently. That is all I will say about that here. I have a rather complete rant against globals in the introduction to *Introduce Static Setter (372)*. I'll spare you a repeat of it here.

One way to get past dependencies on globals in a class is to introduce getters for each of them in the class. When you have the getters, you can *Subclass and Override Method (401)* to have the getters return something appropriate. In some cases, you might go as far as using *Extract Interface (362)* to break dependencies on the class of the global. Here is an example in Java:

```
public class RegisterSale
{
    public void addItem(Barcode code) {
        Item newItem =
            Inventory.getInventory().itemForBarcode(code);
        items.add(newItem);
    }
    ...
}
```

In this code, the Inventory class is accessed as a global. "Wait?" I hear you say. "A global? It is just a call to a static method on a class." For our purposes, that counts as a global. In Java, the class itself is a global object, and it seems that it must reference some state to be capable of doing its work (returning item objects given barcodes). Can we get past this with *Replace Global Reference with Getter*? Let's try it.

First we write the getter. Note that we make it protected so that we can override it under test.

```
public class RegisterSale
{
    public void addItem(Barcode code) {
        Item newItem = Inventory.getInventory().itemForBarcode(code);
        items.add(newItem);
    }

    protected Inventory getInventory() {
        return Inventory.getInventory();
    }
    ...
}
```

Then we replace every access of the global with the getter.

```
public class  RegisterSale
{
    public void addItem(Barcode code) {
        Item newItem = getInventory().itemForBarcode(code);
        items.add(newItem);
    }

    protected Inventory getInventory() {
        return Inventory.getInventory();
    }
    ...
}
```

Now we can create a subclass of Inventory that we can use in the test. Because Inventory is a singleton, we have to make its constructor protected rather than private. After we've done that, we can subclass it like this and put in whatever logic we want to use to convert barcodes to items in a test.

```
public class FakeInventory extends Inventory
{
    public Item itemForBarcode(Barcode code) {
        ...
    }
    ...
}
```

Now we can write the class we'll use in the test.

```
class TestingRegisterSale extends RegisterSale
{
    Inventory inventory = new FakeInventory();

    protected Inventory getInventory() {
        return inventory;
    }
}
```

Steps

To *Replace Global Reference with Getter*, do the following:

1. Identify the global reference that you want to replace.
2. Write a getter for the global reference. Make sure that the access protection of the method is loose enough for you to be able to override the getter in a subclass.
3. Replace references to the global with calls to the getter.
4. Create a testing subclass and override the getter.

Subclass and Override Method

Subclass and Override Method is a core technique for breaking dependencies in object-oriented programs. In fact, many of the other dependency-breaking techniques in this chapter are variations on it.

The central idea of *Subclass and Override Method* is that you can use inheritance in the context of a test to nullify behavior that you don't care about or get access to behavior that you do care about.

Let's take a look at a method in a little application:

```
class MessageForwarder
{
    private Message createForwardMessage(Session session,
                                         Message message)
                throws MessagingException, IOException {
        MimeMessage forward = new MimeMessage (session);
        forward.setFrom (getFromAddress (message));
        forward.setReplyTo (
                new Address [] {
                    new InternetAddress (listAddress) });
        forward.addRecipients (Message.RecipientType.TO,
                               listAddress);
        forward.addRecipients (Message.RecipientType.BCC,
                               getMailListAddresses ());
        forward.setSubject (
                transformedSubject (message.getSubject ()));
        forward.setSentDate (message.getSentDate ());
        forward.addHeader (LOOP_HEADER, listAddress);
        buildForwardContent(message, forward);

        return forward;
    }
    ...
}
```

MessageForwarder has a quite a few methods that aren't shown here. One of the public methods calls this private method, createForwardMessage, to build up a new message. Let's suppose that we don't want to have a dependency on the MimeMessage class when we are testing. It uses a variable named session, and we will not have a real session when we are testing. If we want to separate out the dependency on MimeMessage, we can make createForwardMessage protected and override it in a new subclass that we make just for testing:

```
class TestingMessageForwarder extends MessageForwarder
{
    protected Message createForwardMessage(Session session,
                                           Message message) {
```

```
        Message forward = new FakeMessage(message);
        return forward;
    }
    ...
}
```


In this new subclass, we can do whatever we need to do to get the separation or the sensing that we need. In this case, we are essentially nulling out most of the behavior of `createForwardMessage`, but if we don't need it for the particular thing that we are testing right now, that can be fine.

In production code, we instantiate `MessageForwarders`; in tests, we instantiate `TestingMessageForwarders`. We were able to get separation with minimal modification of the production code. All we did was change the scope of a method from private to protected.

In general, the factoring that you have in a class determines how well you can use inheritance to separate out dependencies. Sometimes you have a dependency that you want to get rid of isolated in a small method. At other times, you have to override a larger method to separate out a dependency.

Subclass and Override Method is a powerful technique, but you have to be careful. In the previous example, I can return an empty message without a subject, from address, and so on, but that would make sense only if I was, say, testing the fact that I can get a message from one place in the software to another and don't care what the actual content and addressing are.

For me, programming is predominately visual. I see all sorts of pictures in my mind when I work, and they help me decide among alternatives. It is a shame that none of these pictures are really UML, but they help me nonetheless.

One image that comes to me often is what I call a *paper view*. I look at a method and start to see all of the ways that I can group statements and expressions. For just about any little snippet in a method that I can identify, I realize that if I can extract it to a method, I can replace it with something else during testing. It is as if I placed a piece of translucent paper on top of the one with the code. The new sheet can have a different piece of code for the snippet that I want to replace. The stack of paper is what I test, and the methods that I see through the top sheet are the ones that can be executed when I test. Figure 25.6 is an attempt to show this *paper view* of a class.

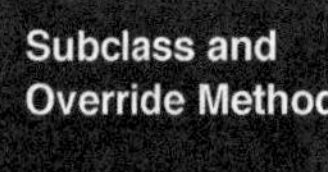


```
public class Acount
{
        public void deposit(int value) {
                balance += value:
                log.newLogMessage(date, value);
                log.flush():
        }
}
```

```
public class TestingAccount extends Account
{
        protected void newLongMessage(Date date, int value) {
        }
}
```

Figure 25.6 `TestingAccount` *superimposed on* `Account`.

The *paper view* helps me see what is possible, but when I start to use *Subclass and Override Method*, I try to override methods that already exist. After all, the goal is to get tests in place, and extracting methods without tests in place can be risky at times.

Steps

To *Subclass and Override Method*, do the following:

1. Identify the dependencies that you want to separate or the place where you want to sense. Try to find the smallest set of methods that you can override to achieve your goals.
2. Make each method overridable. The way to do this varies among programming languages. In C++, the methods have to be made virtual if they aren't already. In Java, the methods need to be made non-final. In many .NET languages, you explicitly have to make the method overridable also.
3. If your language requires it, adjust the visibility of the methods that you will override so that they can be overridden in a subclass. In Java and C#, methods must at least have protected visibility to be overridden in subclasses. In C++, methods can remain private and still be overridden in subclasses.
4. Create a subclass that overrides the methods. Verify that you are able to build it in your test harness.

Supersede Instance Variable

Object creation in constructors can be problematic, particularly when it is hard to depend upon those objects in a test. In most cases, we can use *Extract and Override Factory Method (350)* to get past this issue. However, in languages that disallow overrides of virtual function calls in constructors, we have to look at other options. One of them is *Supersede Instance Variable.*

Here's an example that shows the virtual function problem in C++:

```
class Pager
{
public:
    Pager() {
        reset();
        formConnection();
    }

    virtual void formConnection() {
        assert(state == READY);
        // nasty code that talks to hardware here
        ...
    }

    void sendMessage(const std::string& address,
                     const std::string& message) {
        formConnection();
        ...
    }
    ...
};
```

In this example, the `formConnection` method is called in the constructor. There is nothing wrong with constructors that delegate work to other functions, but there is something a little misleading about this code. The `formConnection` method is declared to be a virtual method, so it seems that we could just *Subclass and Override Method (401)*. Not so fast. Let's try it:

```
class TestingPager : public Pager
{
public:
    virtual void formConnection() {
    }
};

TEST(messaging,Pager)
{
    TestingPager pager;
```

```
    pager.sendMessage("5551212",
                      "Hey, wanna go to a party? XXXOOO");
    LONGS_EQUAL(OKAY, pager.getStatus());
}
```


When we override a virtual function in C++, we are replacing the behavior of that function in derived classes just like we'd expect, but with one exception. When a call is made to a virtual function in a constructor, the language doesn't allow the override. In the example, this means that when `sendMessage` is called, `TestingPager::formConnection` is used, and that is great: We didn't really want to send a flirty page to the information operator, but, unfortunately, we already have. When we constructed the `TestingPager`, `Page::formConnection` was called during initialization because C++ did not allow the override in the constructor.

C++ has this rule because constructor calls to overridden virtual functions can be unsafe. Imagine this scenario:

```
class A
{
public:
    A() {
        someMethod();
    }

    virtual void someMethod() {
    }
};

class B : public A
{
    C *c;
public:

    B() {
        c = new C;
    }

    virtual void someMethod() {
        c.doSomething();
    }
};
```

Here we have `B's someMethod` overriding `A`'s. But remember the order of constructor calls. When we create a `B`, `A`'s constructor is called before `B's`. So `A`'s constructor calls `someMethod`, and `someMethod` is overridden, so the one in `B` is used. It attempts to call `doSomething` on a reference of type `C`, but, guess what? It was never initialized because `B`'s constructor hasn't been run yet.

C++ prevents this from happening. Other languages are more permissive. For instance, overridden methods can be called from constructors in Java, but I don't recommend doing it in production code.

Supersede Instance Variable

In C++, this little protection mechanism prevents us from replacing behavior in constructors. Fortunately, we have a few other ways to do this. If the object that you are replacing is not used in the constructor, you can use *Extract and Override Getter (352)* to break the dependency. If you do use the object but you need to make sure that you can replace it before another method is called, you can use *Supersede Instance Variable.* Here is an example:

```
BlendingPen::BlendingPen()
{
    setName("BlendingPen");
    m_param = ParameterFactory::createParameter(
                    "cm", "Fade", "Aspect Alter");
    m_param->addChoice("blend");
    m_param->addChoice("add");
    m_param->addChoice("filter");

    setParamByName("cm", "blend");
}
```

In this case, a constructor is creating a parameter through a factory. We could use *Introduce Static Setter (372)* to get some control over the next object that the factory returns, but that is pretty invasive. If we don't mind adding an extra method to the class, we can supersede the parameter that we created in the constructor:

```
void BlendingPen::supersedeParameter(Parameter *newParameter)
{

    delete m_param;
    m_param = newParameter;

}
```

In tests, we can create pens as we need them and call `supersedeParameter` when we need to put in a sensing object.

On the surface, *Supersede Instance Variable* looks like a poor way of getting a sensing object in place, but in C++, when *Parameterize Constructor (379)* is too awkward because of tangled logic in the constructor, *Supersede Instance Variable (404)* can be the best choice. In languages that allow virtual calls in constructors, *Extract and Override Factory Method (350)* is usually a better choice.

Generally, it is poor practice to provide setters that change the base objects that an object uses. Those setters allow clients to drastically change the behavior of an object during its lifetime. When someone can make those changes, you have to know the history of that object to understand what happens when you call one of its methods. When you don't have setters, code is easier to understand.

One nice thing about using the word *supersede* as the method prefix is that it is kind of fancy and uncommon. If you ever get concerned about whether people are using the superceding methods in production code, you can do a quick search to make sure they aren't.

Steps

To *Supersede Instance Variable*, follow these steps:

1. Identify the instance variable that you want to supersede.
2. Create a method named `supersedeXXX`, where `XXX` is the name of the variable you want to supersede.
3. In the method, write whatever code you need to so that you destroy the previous instance of the variable and set it to the new value. If the variable is a reference, verify that there aren't any other references in the class to the object it points to. If there are, you might have additional work to do in the superceding method to make sure that replacing the object is safe and has the right effect.

Template Redefinition

Template Redefinition

Many of the dependency-breaking techniques in this chapter rely on core object-oriented mechanisms such as interface and implementation inheritance. Some newer language features provide additional options. For instance, if a language supplies generics and a way of aliasing types, you can break dependencies using a technique called *Template Redefinition*. Here is an example in C++:

```
// AsyncReceptionPort.h

class AsyncReceptionPort
{
private:
    CSocket m_socket;
    Packet m_packet;
    int m_segmentSize;
    ...

public:
        AsyncReceptionPort();
    void Run();
    ...
};


// AsynchReceptionPort.cpp

void AsyncReceptionPort::Run() {
    for(int n = 0; n < m_segmentSize; ++n) {
        int bufferSize = m_bufferMax;
        if (n = m_segmentSize - 1)
            bufferSize = m_remainingSize;
        m_socket.receive(m_receiveBuffer, bufferSize);
        m_packet.mark();
        m_packet.append(m_receiveBuffer,bufferSize);
        m_packet.pack();
    }
    m_packet.finalize();
}
```

If we have code like this and we want to make changes to the logic in the method, we run up against the fact that we can't run the method in a test harness without sending something across a socket. In C++, we can avoid this entirely by making `AsyncReceptionPort` a template rather than a regular class. This is what the code looks like after the change. We'll get to the steps in a second.

```
// AsynchReceptionPort.h

template<typename SOCKET> class AsyncReceptionPortImpl
{
private:
    SOCKET m_socket;
    Packet m_packet;
    int m_segmentSize;
    ...

public:
    AsyncReceptionPortImpl();
    void Run();
    ...
};

template<typename SOCKET>
void AsyncReceptionPortImpl<SOCKET>::Run() {
    for(int n = 0; n < m_segmentSize; ++n) {
        int bufferSize = m_bufferMax;
        if (n = m_segmentSize - 1)
            bufferSize = m_remainingSize;
        m_socket.receive(m_receiveBuffer, bufferSize);
        m_packet.mark();
        m_packet.append(m_receiveBuffer,bufferSize);
        m_packet.pack();
    }
    m_packet.finalize();
}

typedef AsyncReceptionPortImpl<CSocket> AsyncReceptionPort;
```

When we have this change in place, we can instantiate the template with a different type in the test file:

```
// TestAsynchReceptionPort.cpp

#include "AsyncReceptionPort.h"

class FakeSocket
{
public:
    void receive(char *, int size) { ... }
};


TEST(Run,AsyncReceptionPort)
{
    AsyncReceptionPortImpl<FakeSocket> port;
    ...
}
```

The sweetest thing about this technique is the fact that we can use a typedef to avoid having to change references all through our code base. Without it, we would have to replace every reference to `AsyncReceptionPort` with `AsyncReceptionPort<CSocket>`. It would be a lot of tedious work, but it is easier than it sounds. We can *Lean on the Compiler (315)* to make sure that we've changed all the proper references. In languages that have generics but no type-aliasing mechanism such as typedef, you will have to *Lean on the Compiler.*

In C++, you can use this technique to provide alternate definitions of methods rather than data, but it is a little messy. The rules of C++ oblige you to have a template parameter, so you can pick a variable and make its type a template parameter at random or introduce a new variable just to make the class parameterized on some type—but I would do that only as a last resort. I'd look very carefully to see if I could use the inheritance-based techniques first.

Template Redefinition in C++ has one primary disadvantage. Unless you have a C++ compiler with very good template support, code that was in implementation This can increase the dependencies in systems. Users of the template then are forced to recompile whenever the template code is changed.

In general, I bias toward using inheritance-based techniques for breaking dependencies in C++. However, *Template Redefinition* can be useful when the dependencies that you want to break are already in templatized code. Here is an example:

```
template<typename ArcContact> class CollaborationManager
{
    ...
    ContactManager<ArcContact>  m_contactManager;
    ...
};
```

If we want to break the dependency on `m_contactManager`, we can't easily use *Extract Interface (362)* on it because of the way that we are using templates here. We can, however, parameterize the template differently:

```
template<typename ArcContactManager> class CollaborationManager
{
    ...
    ArcContactManager  m_contactManager;
    ...
};
```

Steps

Here is a description of how to do *Template Redefinition* in C++. The steps might be different in other languages that support generics, but this description gives a flavor of the technique:

1. Identify the features that you want to replace in the class you need to test.
2. Turn the class into a template, parameterizing it by the variables that you need to replace and copying the method bodies up into the header.
3. Give the template another name. One mechanical way of doing this is to suffix the original name with `Impl`.
4. Add a typedef statement after the template definition, defining the template with its original arguments using the original class name.
5. In the test file, include the template definition and instantiate the template on new types that will replace the ones you need to replace for test.

Text Redefinition

Text Redefinition

Some of the newer interpreted languages give you a very nice way to break dependencies. When they are interpreted, methods can be redefined on the fly. Here is an example in the language Ruby:

```
# Account.rb
class Account
    def report_deposit(value)
        ...
    end

    def deposit(value)
        @balance += value
        report_deposit(value)
    end

    def withdraw(value)
        @balance -= value
    end
end
```

If we don't want report_deposit to run under test, we can redefine it in the test file and place tests after the redefinition:

```
# AccountTest.rb
require "runit/testcase"
require "Account"

class Account
    def report_deposit(value)
    end
end

# tests start here
class AccountTest < RUNIT::TestCase
    ...
end
```

It's important to note that we aren't redefining the entire Account class here—just the report_deposit method. The Ruby interpreter interprets all lines in a Ruby file as executable statements. The class Account statement opens the definition of the Account class so that additional definitions can be added to it. The def report_deposit(value) statement starts the process of adding a definition to the open class. The Ruby interpreter doesn't care whether there already is a definition of that method, if there is one; it just replaces it.

Text Redefinition in Ruby has one downside. The new method replaces the old one until the program ends. This can cause some trouble if you forget that a particular method has been redefined by a previous test.

We can do Text Redefinition in C and C++ also, using the preprocessor. To see an example of how to do this, look at the *Preprocessing Seam (33)* example in Chapter 4, *The Seam Model.*

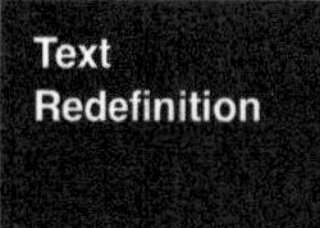

Steps

To use *Text Redefinition* in Ruby, follow these steps:

1. Identify a class with definitions that you want to replace.
2. Add a `require` clause with the name of the module that contains that class to the top of the test source file.
3. Provide alternative definitions at the top of the test source file for each method that you want to replace.

Appendix

Refactoring

Refactoring is a core technique for improving code. The canonical reference for refactoring is Martin Fowler's book *Refactoring: Improving the Design of Existing Code* (Addison-Wesley, 1999). I refer you to that book for more information about the kind of refactoring you can do when you have tests in place in code.

In this chapter, I describe one key refactoring: *Extract Method*. It should give you a flavor of the mechanics involved in refactoring with tests.

Extract Method

Of all refactorings, *Extract Method* is perhaps the most useful. The idea behind *Extract Method* is that we can systematically break up large existing methods into smaller ones. When we do this, we make our code easier to understand. In addition, we can often reuse the pieces and avoid duplicating logic in other areas of our system.

> In poorly maintained code bases, methods tend to grow larger. People add logic to existing methods, and they just continue to grow. As this happens, methods can end up doing two or three different distinct things for their callers. In pathological cases, they can end up doing tens or hundreds. *Extract Method* is the remedy in these cases.

When you want to extract a method, the first thing that you need is a set of tests. If you have tests that thoroughly exercise a method, you can extract methods from it using these steps:

1. Identify the code you want to extract, and comment it out.
2. Think of a name for the new method and create it as an empty method.
3. Place a call to the new method in the old method.
4. Copy the code that you want to extract into the new method

5. *Lean On the Compiler (315)* to find out what parameters you'll have to pass and what values you'll have to return.

6. Adjust the method declaration to accommodate the parameters and return value (if any).

7. Run your tests.

8. Delete the commented-out code.

Here is a simple example in Java:

```
public class Reservation
{
    public int calculateHandlingFee(int amount) {
        int result = 0;

        if (amount < 100) {
            result += getBaseFee(amount);
        }
        else {
            result += (amount * PREMIUM_RATE_ADJ) + SURCHARGE;
        }
        return result;
    }
    ...
}
```

The logic in the else-statement calculates the handling fee for premium reservations. We need to use that logic someplace else in our system. Instead of duplicating the code, we can extract it from here and then use it in the other place.

Here is the first step:

```
public class Reservation
{
    public int calculateHandlingFee(int amount) {
        int result = 0;

        if (amount < 100) {
            result += getBaseFee(amount);
        }
        else {
            // result += (amount * PREMIUM_RATE_ADJ) + SURCHARGE;
        }
        return result;
    }
    ...
}
```

We want to call the new method getPremiumFee, so we add the new method and its call:

```
public class Reservation
{
    public int calculateHandlingFee(int amount) {
        int result = 0;

        if (amount < 100) {
            result += getBaseFee(amount);
        }
        else {
            // result += (amount * PREMIUM_RATE_ADJ) + SURCHARGE;
            result += getPremiumFee();
        }
        return result;
    }

    int getPremiumFee() {
    }
    ...
}
```

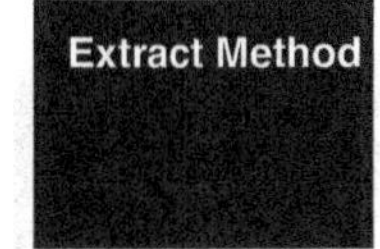

Next we copy the old code into the new method and see if it compiles:

```
public class Reservation
{
    public int calculateHandlingFee(int amount) {
        int result = 0;

        if (amount < 100) {
            result += getBaseFee(amount);
        }
        else {
            // result += (amount * PREMIUM_RATE_ADJ) + SURCHARGE;
            result += getPremiumFee();
        }
        return result;
    }

    int getPremiumFee() {
        result += (amount * PREMIUM_RATE_ADJ) + SURCHARGE;
    }
    ...
}
```

It doesn't. The code uses variables named result and amount that aren't declared. Because we are computing only a portion of the result, we can just return what we compute. We can also get hold of the amount if we make it a parameter to the method and add it to the call:

```
public class Reservation
{
    public int calculateHandlingFee(int amount) {
        int result = 0;

        if (amount < 100) {
            result += getBaseFee(amount);
        }
        else {
            // result += (amount * PREMIUM_RATE_ADJ) + SURCHARGE;
            result += getPremiumFee(amount);
        }
        return result;
    }

    int getPremiumFee(int amount) {
        return (amount * PREMIUM_RATE_ADJ) + SURCHARGE;
    }
    ...
}
```

Extract Method

Now we can run our tests and see if they still work. If they do, we can go back and get rid of the commented code:

```
public class Reservation
{
    public int calculateHandlingFee(int amount) {
        int result = 0;

        if (amount < 100) {
            result += getBaseFee(amount);
        }
        else {
            result += getPremiumFee(amount);
        }
        return result;
    }

    int getPremiumFee(int amount) {
        return (amount * PREMIUM_RATE_ADJ) + SURCHARGE;
    }
    ...
}
```

Although it isn't strictly necessary, I like to comment out code that I am going to extract; that way, if I make a mistake and a test fails, I can easily go back to what I had, get the test to pass, and then try again.

The example I've just shown is just one way of doing *Extract Method*. When you have tests, it is a relatively simple and safe operation. If you have a refactoring tool, it is even easier. All you have to do is select a portion of a method and make a menu selection. The tool checks to see if that code can be extracted as a method and prompts you for the new method's name.

Extract Method is a core technique for working with legacy code. You can use it to extract duplication, separate responsibilities, and break down long methods.

Glossary

change point A place in code where you need to make a change.

characterization test A test written to document the current behavior of a piece of software and preserve it as you change its code.

coupling count The number of values that pass in and out of a method when it is called. If there is no return value, it is the number of parameters. If there is, it is the number of parameters plus one. Coupling count can be a very useful thing to compute for small methods you'd like to extract if you have to extract without tests.

effect sketch A small hand-drawn sketch that shows what variables and method return values can be affected by a software change. Effect sketches can be useful when you are trying to decide where to write tests.

fake object An object that impersonates a collaborator of a class during testing.

feature sketch A small hand-drawn sketch that shows how methods in a class use other methods and instance variables. Feature sketches can be useful when you are trying to decide how to break apart a large class.

free function A function that is not part of any class. In C and other procedural languages, these are just called functions. In C++ they are called non-member functions. Free functions don't exist in Java and C#.

interception point A place where a test can be written to sense some condition in a piece of software.

link seam A place where you can vary behavior by linking to a library. In compiled languages, you can replace production libraries, DLLs, assemblies, or JAR files with others during testing to get rid of dependencies or sense some condition that can happen in a test.

mock object A fake object that asserts conditions internally.

object seam A place where you can vary behavior by replacing one object with another. In object-oriented languages, you usually do this by subclassing a class in your production code and overriding various methods of the class.

pinch point A narrowing in an effect sketch that indicates an ideal place to test a cluster of features.

programming by difference A way of using inheritance to add features in object-oriented systems. It can often be used as a way to get a new feature into the system quickly. The tests that you write to provoke the new feature can be used to refactor the code into a better state afterward.

seam A place where you can vary behavior in a software system without editing in that place. For instance, a call to a polymorphic function on an object is a seam because you can subclass the class of the object and have it behave differently.

test-driven development (TDD) A development process that consists of writing failing test cases and satisfying them one at a time. As you do this, you refactor to keep the code as simple as possible. Code developed using TDD has test coverage, by default.

test harness A piece of software that enables unit testing.

testing subclass A subclass made to allow access to a class for testing.

unit test A test that runs in less than 1/10th of a second and is small enough to help you localize problems when it fails.

Index

E

F

R